The History *of* Landscape Design in 100 Gardens

The History *of* Landscape Design in 100 Gardens

Linda A. Chisholm

WITH PHOTOGRAPHY BY MICHAEL D. GARBER

TIMBER PRESS • PORTLAND, OREGON

For Alan

Opposite: Roberto Burle Marx design at Copacabana Beach.

Published in 2018 by Timber Press, Inc.
The Haseltine Building
133 S.W. Second Avenue, Suite 450
Portland, Oregon 97204-3527
timberpress.com

Printed in China
Text and cover design by Adrianna Sutton

Library of Congress Cataloging-in-Publication Data
Names: Chisholm, Linda A., author. | Garber, Michael D., photographer.
Title: The history of landscape design in 100 gardens / Linda A. Chisholm; with photography by Michael D. Garber.
Description: Portland, Oregon: Timber Press, 2018. | Includes bibliographical references and index. | Identifiers: LCCN 2018001916 (print) | LCCN 2018004017 (ebook) | ISBN 9781604698671 | ISBN 9781604695298 (hardcover)
Subjects: LCSH: Landscape design—History.
Classification: LCC SB472.45 (ebook) | LCC SB472.45 .C453 2018 (print) | DDC 712/.2—dc23
LC record available at https://lccn.loc.gov/2018001916

Contents

The Bog Garden, Shute.

Preface

MANY YEARS AGO I left my Dust Bowl Oklahoma home to go to college in New York's lush and bountiful Hudson Valley. There I would take courses that in one way or another taught me that central to human experience is our relationship to our natural surroundings and that we have, from time immemorial, shaped the landscape to our ideal. As I studied the importance of rivers, I thought about the contrast between the all-but-dry Arkansas in my home city and the deep and wide Hudson on which as college students we skated in winter.

In literature, I studied Aeneas's harrowing voyage in the Mediterranean from Troy to what would become Rome, including the tricky passage between the rocky shoals of Scylla and the whirlpool of Charybdis. I considered the struggle between Captain Ahab and the great white whale Moby Dick. Courses in religion were replete with references to sea and land and to man's attempt to control through farming, fishing, and shepherding.

Then I read the great American novel *The Grapes of Wrath*, about the tragedy of my home state. There, in the nineteenth and early twentieth centuries, farmers had in ignorance cut down the forests and tall grasses that once covered the state holding the fertile topsoil in place. With the felling of the trees and poor farming practices, strong winds carried away layer upon layer of rich soil, eventually leaving the land barren. Franklin Roosevelt's Civilian Conservation Corps had planted millions of tree seedlings, but these were but saplings when I was growing up in the 1940s and 1950s. Thousands, like the Joad family in the novel, abandoned the useless farmland and migrated in their Ford pickup trucks to California where they hoped to prosper. Like the Joads, most did not. As I read this tale of man and nature, I recalled the hollow look of impoverished farmers and their ragged children that were part of my childhood.

In history courses, the theme of humankind's relationship to nature came up again and again as we studied the impact, good and bad, that we have had on the places we have settled and how we have used and re-formed the earth for our purposes.

It was Professor Joan Kennedy (later Joan Kennedy Kinnaird) who first mentioned to me the landscape designer with the unforgettable name of Capability Brown. She talked about the dramatic change in landscape design in the eighteenth century and, almost as an aside, mentioned that landscape design reflects a culture, that by studying the prevailing styles of landscape and garden design we can learn what a culture thinks and values. Of chief importance is the way people in a particular time and place experience and understand nature. I thought about how in the Oklahoma of my childhood we expressed our relationship with nature as "eking" a living out of the soil and "wrestling nature to the ground." To describe the soil we used the adjective "stubborn" so often that as a young child I thought the phrase one word. I knew that Henrik Hudson, discovering the river valley where I was studying

Lancelot Brown, 1716–1783, known to all as Capability Brown, was the most influential landscape designer in the history of the Western world. His "landscape park" design became associated with the growth of democracy, still dominates English country estates, and was exported to virtually every place the English set their flag where it is often simply called an English garden.

and that would bear his name, would not have used these words. He would have exclaimed with wonder at its endless bounty and unspeakable beauty—virgin forests harboring deer and bears, the river and streams that fed it home to fish, ducks, beavers, muskrats, otters, and turtles, and the air above rich in variety and quantity of birds.

The question of human relationships to natural surroundings followed me as I studied history in graduate school and was extended to ask what ideas, beliefs, and hopes are expressed in the designs we choose for celebrated or humble gardens. I read about the great gardens and, traveling internationally for my work, was privileged to visit many of them. My research has culminated in my teaching the history of landscape design at the New York Botanical Garden and, now, in writing this book.

In it I relate my findings through one hundred of the world's great gardens, chosen to illustrate the history and principles of landscape design and to answer the question of why a particular style became dominant at a specific time and place in history. What is the message a garden or landscape conveys and what design features illuminate the message?

I make no claim that my choices are the world's one hundred *greatest* gardens. Great gardens they are, but I selected them to illustrate important moments in the sometimes evolutionary, sometimes revolutionary history of garden and landscape design, focusing on developments from around the world that have been most influential in North America and the United Kingdom.

Some are public spaces. Many are owned and governed by a foundation including those of the National Trust in England. A number are World Heritage Sites. All of these are open to the public. In addition, photographer Michael D. Garber and I were graciously welcomed by the owners of the private estates that are not generally open.

I have written the book for those who love gardens and gardening, who love history, literature, and art, and who like to see connections. The role of horticulture and landscape design in shaping our history has been neglected until recently. I make claims about how, on occasion, plants, horticulture, and garden design changed the Western world, especially focusing on England and the United States. Fortunately, with renewed interest in healthy eating and agricultural practices, schools have added these topics to the lessons for children. We need to ensure that for adults these developments are not relegated to the sidelines for intense study by just a few because, just as landscape design was influenced by the culture of a particular time and place, so the designers and their art have influenced intellectual, political, and social history. Without such inclusion, our understanding of history is incomplete and inaccurate.

It is my hope that for those training for or practicing the profession of landscape architect or designer, knowledge of the history of landscape design will increase the array of options in their toolkit of design ideas. Landscape design, as do other arts forms, borrows freely from the past, sometimes replicating but as often adapting an old idea to suit a new purpose. To that end this book's index includes concepts, principles, design techniques, and garden features. Teachers of landscape architecture and design as well as students will, I trust, find this useful. Today's designers are, with their art, addressing age-old questions. Understanding the past is essential to understanding the present and to shaping the future.

Finally, for those who love travel the book may inspire their choice of future destinations and give them a new way of seeing and enjoying gardens. Michael Garber's photographs are extraordinary in teaching about the gardens and their history and instilling an appreciation for the artistry to be found in them.

Nyack, New York

More than Flowers

AN INTRODUCTION

THOMAS JEFFERSON WAS RIGHT about landscape design as he was about much else. It *is* an art form, a fine art form. Like other artistic expressions, a particular garden may be aesthetically satisfying or trivial, engaging or irrelevant. It can speak to a culture, affirming its predominant values or challenging them. If it is a truly great expression of art, it speaks to succeeding generations and to those of different cultures as well.

Although people today generally understand this about the other fine arts, many do not look for and therefore do not see it in garden and landscape design. They anticipate learning about nineteenth-century America when they go to a museum exhibit of paintings created in that time and place. They realize that the subject matter that caught the attention of artists, the media used, and the forms chosen express ideas, feelings, beliefs, and experiences, telling viewers about the persons and culture that produced them.

But flowers became and remain the very definition of a garden, so much so that for many who visit gardens they are the central focus. This is rather like gazing on Michelangelo's *David* and seeing only the quality of the marble. When we stand up to survey the whole, we discover the artistry of the composition. Trees, shrubs, perennials, annuals, and grasses are the brushes and oils, the musical notes and orchestral instruments, the words and their patterns, the glass, steel, concrete, wood, and stone of the landscape artist. So are rocks, water, sculpture, and garden buildings. As with other artists, the landscape designer may arrange the materials in an infinite variety of ways to express his or her ideas. When we learn about the designers, the time in which their gardens were conceived and installed, and the events and influences on their lives we understand more fully the message each seeks to convey through his or her art.

Landscape designers face greater challenges than most other artists for no other art form demands that its practitioners take into account so many variables. While they may begin with the topography, soil, water, and immovable rocks, they soon realize that landscapes are not static. They must account for the moving sun, winds, and the not-always-accurately predicted rain and snowfall. The changing seasons add complexity as do the life cycles of individual plants. Garden designers must be able to look ahead, imagining an allée of saplings at maturity. Colors change from month to month and their combinations much be taken into account. What an array of factors to consider! How very daunting!

> Of the fine arts . . . many reckon but five—Painting, sculpture, architecture, music and poetry. To these some have added oratory. . . . Others again add gardening as the 7th fine art, not horticulture, but the art of embellishing grounds by fancy.
>
> —THOMAS JEFFERSON

The entrance, Sutton Courtenay Manor.

But for the artist, landscape and garden design are rich in opportunity as well. There are innumerable materials with which to work. The canvas is large, to be treated as a whole or divided into individual garden "rooms," one different from another. Planned gardens and landscapes are ubiquitous; probably more people visit and enjoy gardens than any other art form and themselves try their hand.

Landscape design, then, is a sophisticated art. The choice and placement of shapes, the use of color, indeed the purposes to be served by the garden and the message it is to convey are made from the individual predilections of the landscape artist and from the cultural context. Renowned psychologist Erik Erikson called unions such as this the "intersection of life history and the historical moment."

The art of landscape design, like any other artistic expression, indeed reflects a culture. The biblical prophet Isaiah, living in the eighth century BC, illustrates how this is true. Speaking of his hopes for a better world, he described his ideal landscape—one that would serve as "a highway for our God"—as one in which "every valley shall be exalted, every mountain and hill made low, the crooked straight, and the rough places plain." Few in the Americas or British Isles today would wish for such a landscape or believe that it would pave the way for a better world. Who among us would want the Colorado River raised to obliterate the Grand Canyon or the Rocky Mountains shaved to sea level? Who would make straight the apple tree in grandmother's meadow, erasing the gnarls that mark the halcyon summers of childhood? Who would hope that a favorite beach be swept clean of its endlessly fascinating shells?

What would make a person—Isaiah—wish for a Nebraska-flat, ribbon-straight highway? For Isaiah life was harsh. He lived in a land of mountains and deserts. He had no car and superhighway to make his way from one place to another, only his sandaled feet. His hard life was made so by the forces of nature that surrounded him. The experience for most of us today—at least for the readers of this book—contrasts sharply with that of Isaiah. And so do our ideas of utopia that we lay out in our gardens and designed landscapes.

Understanding a work of art thus requires study of the time and place in which an artist lived and of his or her personal biography. Happily for the reader, the story of those who have shaped landscape is engaging. Some were inspired by philosophy, religion, or political conviction. Others were motivated by ambition, greed, desire for status, or simply the need to earn a living. Some sought to connect with the world, others to withdraw from it. The history of landscape design is about what and whom they loved and hated, their aspirations, achievements, and disappointments, and their relationships one with another. The history includes sultans, kings, presidents, and at least one state governor; prime ministers and members of Parliament; diplomats, military leaders, and foot soldiers; cardinals, monks, and missionaries; the titled, the landed, those in high society or seeking to be; and those who were none of the above. As well as designing gardens, one was a playwright, another a furniture designer. Others were poets, musicians, architects, or sculptors. Many painted and almost all drew. Some were professionals, some amateurs, some men, some women, some conservatives, others social reformers, and a few revolutionaries. Most were collaborative whether they wanted to be or not, for they had to work with property owners, gardeners, and, later, committees.

To fully appreciate a garden, one must look beyond the flowers, lovely as they are. Designed landscapes need a critical and interpretive eye to be fully appreciated just as do music, poetry, architecture, and painting. Knowing about the period in which a garden was conceived and the designer's personal story allows the garden visitor to better understand the way available materials were organized in space, the purpose they were meant to serve, and the message the designer wanted to convey. A contemporary designer, Roberto Burle Marx, put it this way: "A garden is the result of an arrangement of natural materials according to aesthetic laws; interwoven throughout are the artist's outlook on life, his past experiences, his affections, his attempts, his mistakes, and his successes."

But the study of landscape design should not be confined to the past alone. Great works of art are open to many meanings, generating new ways of seeing the world in future decades and centuries. This is the power that comes from studying the history of the "7th fine art."

1 Piety *and* Protection

Walled off from the forests and inspired by Muslim and Christian prayer, medieval gardens envisioned paradise.

NINTH TO FIFTEENTH CENTURIES

ONCE UPON A TIME, a thousand years ago and more, dark forests blanketed Europe. Mountains, hills, valleys, and plains were covered with evergreen fir, pine, spruce, and yew along with deciduous beech, chestnut, elm, hazel, linden, and oak. Settlements were carved from these forests and their inhabitants used the wood liberally for firewood, lumber, charcoal, resin, and potash and the forest itself for beekeeping, feeding pigs, and even grazing large animals.

But these great forests also spelled danger. Of the many perils harbored in the dense thickets none was dreaded more than wolves. Their doleful cry at night presaged a pack raid, killing poultry, pigs, and anyone foolish enough to be out-of-doors. Even more worrying was the possibility of the lone wolf appearing silently on the path ahead when the villager was fetching wood. For help, the pious turned to Saint Columbanus. But not even he had a cure for the bite from a rabid wolf. Death came quickly, but not quickly enough for those suffering the intense pain.

Wolves were not the only danger. The dense forests were also home to bears, wild boars, and brigands—the antithesis of Robin Hood—who lay in wait for the traveler. Extremely severe winters took their toll. Protein was in short supply. Disease, especially the periodic plagues, exacted a terrible price. Life in the Middle Ages was hard, nasty, brutish, and, for most, short.

For religious Christians, comfort and protection against these ills could be found only in prayer and spiritual contemplation of the heaven that the faith promised lay ahead. For believers, heaven was real and so was hell. Forgiveness was possible but only for the truly repentant who atoned for their sins with prayer and good works. People looked everywhere for signs and symbols of redemption and resurrection. Astrology and alchemy were studied intensely with the hope of finding the organizing principle of the universe. Everything was invested with cosmic meaning.

> No one knows
> Through what wild centuries
> Roves back the rose.
>
> —WALTER DE LA MARE

What features of garden design served to protect from danger and reinforce piety? Whatever their purpose, all medieval gardens had two features in common. First, they were enclosed. Dangers without called for a separation between the space within and the world beyond. Walls, fences, ditches, hedges, and moats controlled access from the hostile outside.

The Cloisters, New York City.

A source of water was the second feature common to all medieval gardens. The location of castles, monasteries, hunting parks, and towns was chosen for the availability of water. Sometimes a natural spring arising from the ground or accessible in a well was at the very center of a garden. In other places, underground piping leading from a nearby stream or river conveyed water inside the enclosure. Essential not only for human consumption and irrigating plants, water was a primary symbol of spiritual gifts. As water cleansed the body, so the water of baptism, a sacrament of the church, cleansed the soul.

Beyond these two features, each type of medieval garden had its own purpose and its own refinements. Following the breakup of the Roman Empire, society in Europe was decentralized. Towns were small, the population rarely exceeding a few thousand. They were walled and within were one or more garden areas, shared communally. Townspeople laid out beds, together planting, tending, and harvesting the herbs and vegetables.

Another kind of medieval garden was the hunting park. Developed first from necessity and later for sport, the hunting park was part of most feudal estates. There the lord set aside an area of the forest that had a source of water for animals, judiciously thinned the trees, enclosed the whole with a wall, fence, ditch, or bramble hedge, eliminated the predators, built a hunting lodge, and stocked the park with deer and wild game. Local peasants resented the rules that strictly forbade their entry. Poaching—hunting illegally on the lord's land—made for a constant game of cat and mouse. Other medieval gardens have disappeared but there remain throughout Europe ancient hunting parks and lodges, although today only a few have deer herds or serve for sport.

The castle garden had quite a different purpose. Here the master of the castle and his wife, whether king and queen or knight and lady, and their family found refreshment. Medieval manuscripts picture the lady seated in the garden, reading prayers at the canonical hours from an illuminated "book of hours." There she might also contemplate the flowers and shrubs surrounding her for most had religious meaning. Also shown in paintings is the lady in her garden with her embroidery, perhaps depicting on silk or wool the holly with its thorns and red berries reminding her of the Passion of Christ or the white lily extolling the purity of the Virgin. Or joined by her husband, she might be entertained by a musician playing the lute or by a demonstration of falconry or archery. Such *pleasaunces* or pleasure gardens were the setting for the expression of romantic love, a new concept in the Middle Ages. Here a suitor might meet the object of his passion to sing, recite poems, and declare his love, theoretically at least under the watchful eye of her chaperone.

Of prime importance in the Middle Ages was the monastery garden. Men and women created communities to observe together a rule of life that included prayer, study, and the practice of Christian virtues. Chief among them was that of welcoming strangers, Christian hospitality as it was called by Saint Benedict. Travelers knew monasteries as places of protection. They planned their journeys to move from monastery to monastery, knowing that their needs would be met. So enshrined did this custom become that the idea of sanctuary arose, guaranteeing that a person harbored within the walls of monastery or church would be safe.

LEFT A fifteenth-century French illuminated manuscript pictures a peasant knocking acorns from the forest trees to feed his pigs.

RIGHT Medieval villagers prepare the gardens in this sixteenth-century manuscript from Bruges.

Many travelers arrived at the monastery injured or ill from the hard passage through the forest. In response, monks developed the skills needed to heal, becoming the physicians of the Middle Ages and establishing in the monastery what came to be known as a hospital. Having assumed this vocation, the monks planted gardens of primarily medicinal herbs and became experts in making potions to cure a wide variety of ills.

Throughout the medieval period there was slow progress in taming the forests. As the growing population made life crowded within the walls, land was cleared adjacent to the castle, town, or monastery, and vegetable and herb gardens were moved outside, becoming more farm than garden.

Amidst the harsh and brutal reality of life in medieval Europe, there was an exception. In the years after the prophet Muhammad in the seventh century, Arab Muslims migrated west across the Mediterranean into North Africa, southern Italy, and southern Spain, there assuming power over the remnants of the Roman Empire. Called Moors,

Any violation of sanctuary was shocking beyond all imagining as when, in AD 1170, Archbishop Thomas Becket was murdered in his own cathedral. He was immediately recognized as a saint with miraculous powers. Chaucer wove tales told by pilgrims who flocked to Canterbury "from every shire's end, the holy blissful martyr there to seek, him to help them when that they were sick." The safety guaranteed by sanctuary is the reason the hunchback chose to live in the Paris cathedral of Notre-Dame.

RIGHT *Christian and Muslim Playing Chess*, from a thirteenth-century book of games.

OPPOSITE The hunting park depicted by Gaston Phoebus in *Le Livre de la chasse*.

they established a kingdom in Granada in AD 711. Under the leadership of the Caliphate of Córdoba, Islamic Spain became a model of civilization. Trade flourished with Mediterranean areas, northern Spain, and France; scholarship, the arts, architecture, science, and engineering blossomed; and the policy of religious tolerance encouraged searching dialogue among Muslims, Christians, and Jews. And the Moors built gardens attached to the palaces and mosques whose patterns and features would be replicated and adapted from the Middle Ages to the present day.

Alhambra sits high above the valley confluence
of the Darro and Genil Rivers.

Alhambra

Granada, Spain

We can only speculate as to why Queen Isabella of Spain specified in her will that she be buried at Alhambra, the palaces in Granada that, in 1492, her army wrested from Moorish control. But we can say that her burial there assured that the great treasure of Islamic art and garden design would survive.

Alhambra was begun in the ninth century as a fort, but the thirteenth- and fourteenth-century additions under the Nasrid dynasty made it famous. Then, just as Christian Spain was strengthened by the marriage of King Ferdinand of Aragon and Queen Isabella of Castile, Moorish leadership was weakened by internal feuds. As Columbus was sailing toward what would later be named America, Emir Boabdil surrendered to Isabella's army and Granada came under the rule of Christian Spain. A zealous Catholic, Isabella approved the Inquisition through which Moors and Jews were forcibly converted or persecuted and driven out of Spain. In the reconquest, mosques were destroyed or rebuilt as churches. Alhambra would undoubtedly have suffered the same fate had the Spanish not protected the final resting place of their beloved queen.

The design principles of contrast and variety are harmoniously woven at Alhambra, a visual symbol of the golden age of Moor-ruled Spain before the Inquisition. Alhambra comprises a series of residential and administrative buildings, palaces, barracks, mosques, pavilions, baths, schools, stables, cemeteries, and glorious gardens, all enclosed by a wall over a mile long that was once punctuated by thirty towers. Alhambra, "the red one," is named for its pink cast that comes from a thin layer of oxidized paleosol or fossil soil. On the terrace above are the buildings of the Palacio de Generalife, "the garden of the architect," a summer palace that the Nasrid emirs added in the fourteenth century.

There is no symmetry among buildings and no uniting axis, yet Alhambra is a pleasing whole. Water in a variety of forms provides the binding thread. Roman aqueducts that lay in ruin when the Moors assumed control of the Al-Andalus region were rebuilt and extended to bring water to the mountain palaces. Experts in hydraulics, the Moors moved water from the streams in the mountains above to Alhambra. Pools, small and large and of many different geometric shapes, together with quiet or rushing rills and soothing fountains, gave welcome relief in the hot and dry climate and provided means for the ritual washing required before worship. The sound of water dripping, bubbling, and rushing is always present.

While there is no geographic center of Alhambra, the Court of the Lions is its symbolic heart. Surrounded by halls for political and diplomatic affairs and private dwellings for the sultans and the harem, the courtyard contains a forest of slender pillars supporting a roof whose shade contrasts sharply with the sun brightening its center. The pillars themselves are a study in contrast, simple at the base and upward through the center, then ornate at the top.

ABOVE Two of the lions spew water into the rill that carries it symbolically to the four corners of the earth.

OPPOSITE, TOP The Court of the Lions is a study of *sol* and *sombra*, sun and shade.

OPPOSITE, BOTTOM Myrtle (*Myrtus communis*), a plant native to the Mediterranean region, was used abundantly to perfume the gardens of Al-Andalus. Here its dark green offers a soothing contrast to the white marble in the Court of the Myrtles.

The focal point of the Court of the Lions is the paradise garden form which was originally used in Persia. Radiating at right angles from a central pool, four rills symbolize the four rivers flowing out of the Garden of Eden to the north, south, east, and west, a narrative in the book of Genesis and in the Quran. *Pairidaēza*, or paradise, is the place where God meets man. At Alhambra a circular fountain made of marble lies at the intersection of the four rills, which are narrow and shallow channels that give a sense of coolness without using much water. The ninth-century lions surrounding the alabaster basin once told time, each of the twelve in turn spewing water to mark the hour. They stand in a circle surrounded by a rill that flows into the four radiating "rivers." At Alhambra the basic paradise form is made more interesting by the addition of smaller circular pools, perhaps representing heavenly bodies, along the course of the rills.

The Court of the Myrtles is one of simple elegance. Adjacent to the Hall of the Ambassadors where important diplomatic negotiations were conducted, it was a place of respite from official business. Here the Muslim designer demonstrated his skill in using water for reflection. Success depends on siting the reflecting pool correctly in relation to sun and shadow and positioning it at the right distance from the object to be reflected. At the Court of the Myrtles the white marble floors slope, allowing the water in the pool to come to the very bottom of the columns and thereby making the building appear to float on water. With this design the reflection of the palace is total. Three centuries later, the Taj Mahal, India's famous landmark also of Muslim tradition, would be reflected in a wide canal, one of the four rivers of Eden, emanating from a central rectangular water tank.

The art of designing and controlling a view is found not only in the reflecting pools at Alhambra but also in the design of windows through which one looks at the gardens beyond. The miradors or picture frames at Alhambra may be a simple keyhole design with little decoration or they may be ornate, just as paintings in a gallery are framed differently to complement the subject and composition. The windows extend almost to the floor as seating was on cushions, not chairs. The Mirador of Lindaraja is delicate and refined. Overhead are inscribed the words "All the arts have enriched me with their special beauty and given me their splendor and perfection. . . . Surely I am in this garden an eye filled with joy."

Built in the early 1300s, the Partal is the name given to the open portico of the Tower of the Ladies, itself a kind of mirador looking out over the Andalusian countryside into the Darro River Valley, up to the orchards of the Generalife, and immediately below to the gardens and pools. The gardens in the Generalife were lush, some with fruits, grapes, and vegetables, others with trees and shrubs such as cypress, myrtle, oriental plane tree, and sempervirens. Flowers included yellow and red Gallic roses, Madonna lilies, and crown imperials, all native to the Middle East. The tiled terraces at different levels, each surrounded by gardens, form a kind of hanging garden that may evoke an image of the legendary Hanging Gardens of Babylon, one of the Seven Wonders of the Ancient World.

As in the Christian world of the Middle Ages, piety was also a hallmark of Islamic Spain. Important in many religions is the performance of ritual washing before entering a place of worship, cleansing the body and, symbolically, the soul. The water staircase in the

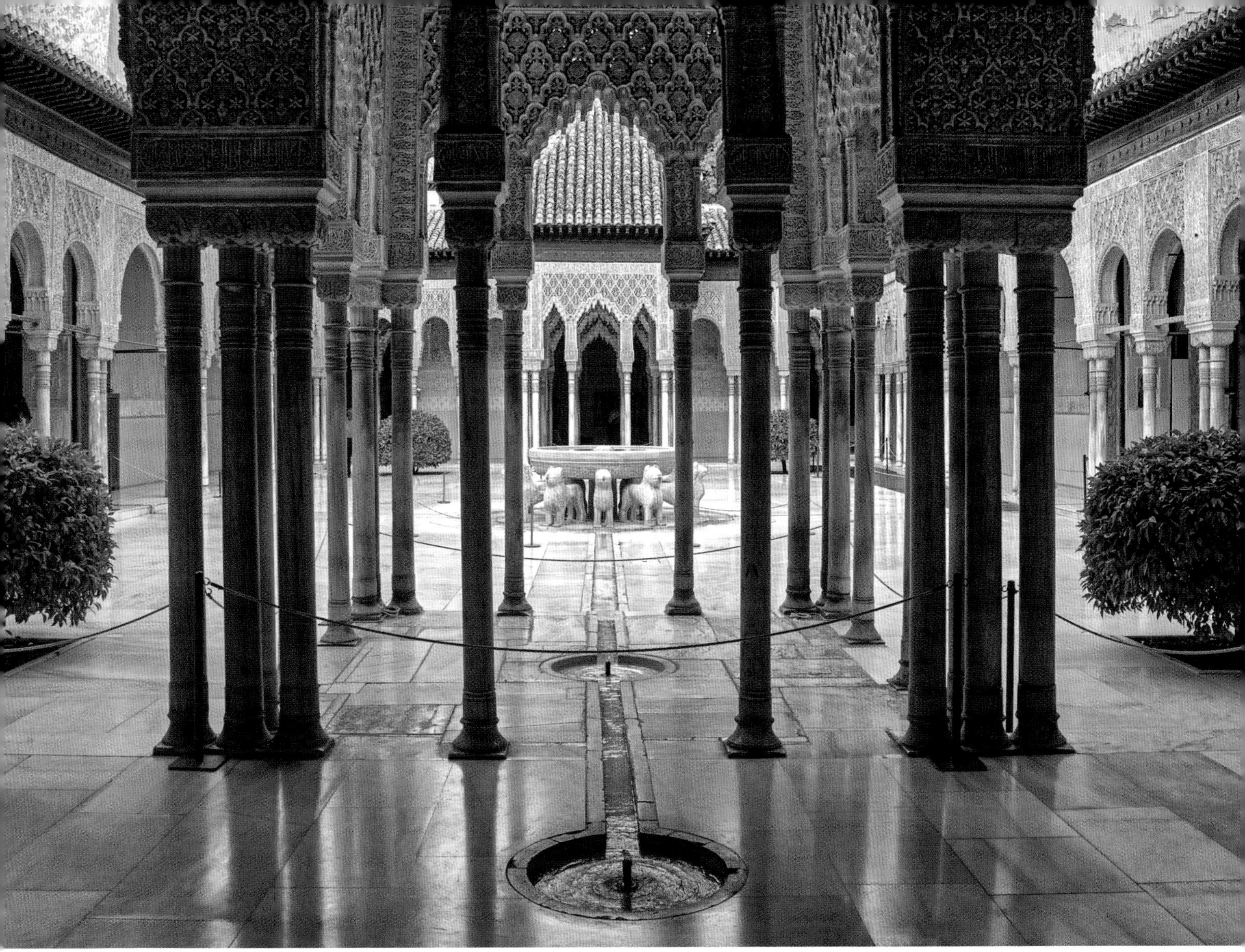

CLOCKWISE, FROM TOP LEFT

Following the Moorish practice, the laurel trees in the Partal are planted in a pit several feet below the surface, conserving water and shading roots.

The garden outside is the focus of the Mirador of Lindaraja.

Surrounded by bay trees, the mosaics of the water staircase are made of white and black stones from the rivers in the valleys below Alhambra.

Generalife was both beautiful and functional. Incorporating water in the handrail made it possible for the devout to perform their ablutions while climbing or descending the stairs. Russell Page, a renowned twentieth-century landscape architect, called the series of descending landings of the water staircase at Alhambra "the best thing in gardening that I know anywhere in the world." It might be said of all of Alhambra.

Queen Eleanor's Garden
Winchester, England

Most marriages of the Middle Ages, especially those of kings and queens, were arranged for political and economic reasons. That was true of Eleanor of Castile's marriage to King Edward I of England. But it proved also to be one of the great love relationships of medieval Europe. Perhaps one reason Eleanor was happy in Winchester was that she felt at home in the garden tended by gardeners from her father's Spanish region of Aragon.

The Great Hall is all that today remains of the castle that along with the gothic cathedral dominated the town of Winchester in the Middle Ages. But its buttressed south wall and the later Christopher Wren buildings almost adjacent provide protection for the re-creation of the garden that once lay within the walls. In the 1980s historian Sylvia Landsberg designed and supervised the installation of the current garden in the triangle only ten by thirty yards in size. To enter is to go back in time to the thirteenth century.

The garden is named for not one but two Queens Eleanor who lived at Winchester. The first, of Provence, was the wife of Henry III. Their son Edward I may have expressed love for *his* Eleanor in the original castle garden. Here he may have told her of the coming crusade on which she chose to accompany him. Perhaps here he grieved her death in Scotland and planned the Eleanor crosses he would erect at each place the funeral cortege rested on its way to Westminster Abbey.

The fountain, the garden's heart, sits in an octagonal pool from which a rill carries water to other parts of the garden. Eleanor of Castile must have remembered this Moorish garden feature from her childhood in Spain. Here a falconer might have shown his sport to amuse king and queen. The popular medieval diversion is honored in the fountain at Winchester. Patterned after a fountain in Westminster dated AD 1275, the placement of the bird of prey recognizes that he must dip his wings in water before beginning a hunting flight.

As a young woman, Eleanor might have waited on the turf bench hidden behind a wall of vines, enabling her to glimpse her suitor before he saw her. These benches or *bankes*, usually without backs, were cut into an existing hillock or made with a stone base, its hollow center filled with planting soil. The top was grass or, as often, chamomile which gave a pleasing scent when crushed. Behind the bench were often roses that also perfumed the air. At Queen Eleanor's Garden the roses are red and white, presaging the symbols of the devastating dynastic Wars of the Roses between the houses of York and Lancaster in the fifteenth century.

A fair complexion was prized in the Middle Ages. The Queens Eleanor and their ladies found shade in the arbor, an oft-used feature of medieval garden design. Some were flat-topped, but others were basket vaults made of pliable hickory or willow to support roses, grapes, or other vines. The sides were free of plantings or, as at Winchester, enclosed to provide greater protection from the sun.

At eye level, the bird stares straight ahead, for eye contact between falconer and falcon is necessary for success.

In addition to sight and scent, medieval gardens featured sound and movement. Rustling leaves, falling petals, gurgling fountains, and the rippling water of the rill were complemented by bird song and flight. Doves, used for food and fertilizer, cooed soothingly. A dovecote or columbarium provided a nesting place. These dovecotes were sometimes separate towers housing hundreds of birds, or they might be attached to a building on a wall or a roof.

Plantings at Queen Eleanor's Garden reflect medieval taste. The turf includes *Bellis perennis*, a tiny daisy. There is a prized fig tree. Hedges are made of holly and hawthorn

ABOVE The common wool clothes and fine silks worn in medieval Europe were washed only infrequently so the aroma of the low-growing herbs on the *banke* was welcomed.

RIGHT At Queen Eleanor's re-created garden, limited space allowed only a small dovecote.

Roses, honeysuckle, ivy, and gourds were used for arbor coverings at Winchester Castle.

and border plants include basil, columbines, fennel, hyssop, irises, lilies, rue, sage, violets, winter savory, and wormwood. Possibly introduced by Eleanor of Castile's gardeners are Mediterranean plants including hollyhock, lavender, and pot marigold. Ferns grace the shady corners.

Imagining the delight the original garden gave to the kings and queens, knights and ladies of the thirteenth century at Winchester Castle is not difficult in this well-researched and documented re-creation of a medieval *pleasaunce*.

The courtyard of the tenth-century monastery of San Pietro, now paved, would have been divided by paths emanating from the central well, creating four quadrants planted with turf or medicinal herbs.

San Pietro Abbey
Perugia, Italy

Most European gardens labeled as medieval are re-creations, only a few as carefully planned and researched as Queen Eleanor's Garden in Winchester. Gardens reconstructed from plans, descriptions, paintings, or the findings of archaeology are rare. The monastery garden at San Pietro in Perugia, Italy, is one such garden where medieval plans in the library were confirmed by the work of archeologists from the University of Perugia which now owns the property.

From the late tenth century, Benedictine monks occupied the basilica and surrounding buildings, built as were antique Roman houses with rooms around a central open atrium. Four paths emanating from a central water well divide the garden into quadrants, a paradise form in which paths are substituted for Persian and later Islamic rills. Here the monks might have taken their daily charge from the book of Genesis which contains creation narratives shared by Judaism, Christianity, and Islam describing the Garden of

In the Middle Ages, the tower beyond the zodiac garden at San Pietro housed the alchemist's laboratory.

Eden: "A river flowed out of Eden to water the garden, and there it divided and became four rivers. . . . The Lord God took the man and put him in the Garden of Eden to till it and keep it." The Garden of Eden was understood as the symbolic place where God speaks directly to man, bestowing blessings, giving directions, challenging excuses, and chastising for disobedience.

In the lower center, the remains of a Roman marble basin, perhaps found on site by the tenth-century monks, kept fish until cooking.

INSET The four sides of the spring recognized the four sustaining liquids, this one labeled *Fons lactis* representing milk.

A first-century Greek born in Turkey, physician Dioscorides traveled with the Roman armies. He collected plants and everywhere the army camped made notes of local remedies. He eventually produced the five-volume *De Materia Medica*, a compendium of some six hundred plants and one thousand remedies. Circulated in Latin, Greek, and Arabic during the Middle Ages, it was the standard reference work for pharmacology through the Renaissance and even beyond.

Medieval monks and nuns similarly hoped that in the monastery garden their prayers would be heard. So common did the paradise design become over many centuries that although today we may not always be aware of its original meaning, it remains an iconic form to this day.

At San Pietro, as in other monasteries, a covered walkway surrounded the interior garden and water source. A common pattern was to have a chapel at one side of the square, open from the interior cloister to the monks and with an external door for visitors. A second side served as chapter room where the monks met to conduct their business and, adjacent, the library of manuscripts. The monks' individual bedrooms, called cells, were located on a third side. Completing the square or rectangle, the fourth side accommodated the refectory, visitors' rooms, and the all-important hospital.

The paradise garden form in the cloister is only one of many symbolic designs at San Pietro. The zodiac garden was found by university archaeologists. At its center a tree grows from a spring that flows outward in four directions, representing the four liquids essential to life: milk, water, wine, and honey. In the zodiac garden the "heavens" are bounded by stones and low hedging, the beginnings of the parterre or ornamental garden with paths between the beds, a feature that was to become more elaborate with time.

Behind the cloister are raised beds for vegetables and herbs, as was the medieval custom. The pergola may have supported grapevines, climbing vegetables, or flowers. A large Roman marble basin or servatorium, perhaps once in the center of a Roman atrium, was used to keep fish fresh until it was cooked. Herbs used to dye cloth, to lay among clothes and on floors for fragrance, and to enhance the flavors of food are among the plants that would have been in the medieval garden and that are in the garden of San Pietro today. Even poison had its place, especially the black hellebore, said to be effective in killing the dreaded wolves. Above all, the physician-monks grew medicinal herbs, knowing what to plant and how to use them from the books of Dioscorides.

The sundial was another medieval garden feature, helping gardening monks know when to set work aside and gather in the church for the daily offices. These prayers were offered eight times daily according to the rule of Saint Benedict who adapted for the monastery at Monte Cassino the Jewish practice of prayer at set intervals of the day. Benedictines in Perugia and monks and nuns elsewhere continue the practice today.

Prieuré Notre-Dame d'Orsan

Maisonnais, France

Brothers of the Priory of Our Lady of Orsan in central France would have gathered each August to celebrate Saint Fiacre's Day. The man who became the patron saint of gardeners was a seventh-century Irish monk whose healing powers drew so many to his door that he beseeched the bishop of Meaux to give him a new home with greater solitude for contemplation and prayer. Legend has it that the bishop offered him whatever forestland he could

Saint Fiacre, patron saint of gardeners, with his Bible and spade.

surround with a furrow in one day. Strong from gardening, Fiacre was able to uproot trees and bramble bushes to encompass a nine-acre plot. On the land he built a solitary hermitage for himself, planted a medicinal herb garden, and established a hospice for travelers. After his death in AD 670, he was canonized.

From the tenth to the fifteenth centuries the monks of Prieuré Notre-Dame d'Orsan in central France were, like Fiacre, skilled gardeners. The growing of vegetables, fruit, medicinal and culinary herbs, and flowers, especially roses, was their vocation second only to prayer.

As in other medieval gardens, water was located at the garden's heart. At Prieuré Notre-Dame it emanates from a square fountain at the center of a paradise form, convenient for irrigating the surrounding herb, vegetable, and flower beds, the orchards, and vineyards. Radiating paths are formed by turf, highly prized in the medieval garden. Twelfth-century French cleric Hugh of Fouilloy expressed the popular belief that the color green, a symbol of rebirth and everlasting life, "nourishes the eyes and preserves the vision."

As they watered, the monks surely meditated upon the religious truth symbolized by water, expressed in this fourteenth-century poem by Guillaume de Machaut which likens the fountain to the Trinity:

> Three parts make up a fountain flow
> The Stream, the Spout, the Bowl.
> Although these are three, these three are one
> Essence the same. Even so the Waters of Salvation run.

Wood was readily available from the nearby forest and used for every possible purpose. Arbors supported grapes and roses. Low boards contained the raised beds. Palisade fencing formed by closely planted saplings that grew together as a solid and living fence protected the whole from rooting pigs and digging dogs. Wattle fencing, fashioned by driving stakes into the ground at intervals and weaving through them flexible apple shoots or young hickory, hazel, or willow branches, made the garden rabbit-proof. Slender poles gathered at the top like teepees provided support for beans and other climbing vegetables and vines. To prevent rotting, vegetables were lifted from the ground with low wattle domes.

Where town, castle, and monastery gardens were enclosed, the space for growing plants was limited. Gardeners developed a variety of techniques for making the most of the space they had. Trees and shrubs were pruned as pillars, cones, globes, pyramids, and

Wooden structures at Prieuré Notre-Dame d'Orsan were devised to fill every garden need.

obelisks so as not to block the sunlight. Topiary, the garden technique of pruning shrubs into unnatural forms, has been employed since the time of the Romans. Planting beds were edged with low-cut boxwood, germander, hyssop, lavender, rosemary, or santolina, creating rudimentary parterres.

Wooden frames on which fruit was trained assumed various shapes and sizes. Fruit trees were planted on either side of a path, then bent and lashed together, or pleached, at the top so that they grew together. Forming an arch, the pleached trees did double duty by producing fruit and providing a shaded walk. Another space-saving technique was to espalier fruit and berries, pruning the branches or canes to make flat patterns against a warm wall or as a fence, a practice that has stood the test of time.

Orchards were all-important in the medieval garden as fruit was available only if locally grown. Orchard trees were often planted in a quincunx pattern with four at the corners of a square and a fifth tree in the center. The pattern is repeated in such a way

Pear trees at the Prieuré Notre-Dame d'Orsan are pruned and trained to hug the earth, taking little space but producing a bumper crop.

that all adjacent trees in the orchard are equidistant one from another. Quincunx, used extensively for mosaics and pebble floors and on coins in ancient Rome, was invested with religious and astrological meaning in the Middle Ages. Another essential to any medieval orchard was the apiary for bees. Gardeners understood the role of bees in pollinating fruit and so bee-keeping was an important part of every gardener's job.

Quincunx was not the only pattern for planting. Mazes with their maddening dead ends were planned for amusement and games; the labyrinth, not hard to follow and leading always to the center, became the means for a spiritual journey. At Prieuré Notre-Dame high concentric hedges define the paths beside which pears, quince, grapes, and herbs fill the beds. Rhubarb grows tall within cylindrical wattle frames.

Of all the metaphysical symbols in the medieval garden, none was richer in meaning than flowers. In enclosed gardens a particular kind of flower was planted singly or

ABOVE A wattle bench surrounds an old tree in the orchard planted in a quincunx pattern at the Orsan Priory.

LEFT Bees were kept in baskets called skeps, these at the botanical garden of the University of Leiden in the Netherlands.

The Orsan Priory labyrinth brings pilgrims to the center where they finds a wattle bench surrounding a shady tree.

at least sparsely, never massed. These flowers were often pictured in medieval paintings and tapestries, perhaps most famously in the Unicorn Tapestry in which flowers encircle the mythical beast. All one hundred plants that have been identified were woven with remarkable detail and accuracy.

Medieval literature and paintings depict time and again the flowery mead, or meadow, where a mixture of wildflowers abound. The mead at Notre-Dame d'Orsan is a riot of color, but all with delicate textures and shapes. Of all the flowers, the rose was the most loved and honored. In Greco-Roman culture the rose had represented the season of spring and of love. But the piety of the Middle Ages acknowledged the virginity of Mary by giving her the title *hortus conclusus* (enclosed garden), and the rose became her symbol.

Visitors to the flowery mead at Prieuré Notre-Dame d'Orsan expect to see Mary herself with her Babe on her lap, just as she is pictured in countless medieval paintings.

The beautiful brickwork of the Old Palace at Hatfield House is complemented by the topiary and rectangular parterres.

Old Palace at Hatfield House
Hertfordshire, England

They said that she was reading the Bible under an oak in the park at Hatfield when news came that her sister was dead. *She* was now queen of England. Soon she would leave the place of her childhood to begin a reign that would be one of history's longest, most notable, and most successful.

The world Elizabeth I would rule was no longer that of her father, Henry VIII. The very topography of England had changed when she ascended the throne in 1558. The great forests had been steadily reduced for farms and then to build the great wooden sailing ships for the voyages of discovery. Society had changed as well. People were traveling to Italy to study the achievements of classical Rome and of the Italian Renaissance. The Protestant Reformation had given them new ideas about their abilities and rights. Archbishop Cranmer's Book of Common Prayer was, in his words, "in a language understanded of the people," and all parish churches were ordered to chain an English Bible to the lectern and to keep the doors of the church always open. Now everyone had access to the scriptures at any time. The faith was no longer in the hands of but a few. While retaining much that was medieval, England embraced ideas of Renaissance humanism as it did those of the Reformation. Hatfield House and its gardens embody both worlds, with features that characterized medieval gardening while embracing new Renaissance elements.

The simplicity of early medieval garden design had, by Elizabeth's reign, evolved to become elaborate. The four planting beds or turf separated by gravel paths of the simple paradise form had multiplied in number and were of intricate patterns, so much so that they became known as parterres *de broderie*, that is "of embroidery." The accompanying topiary assumed new, more complicated shapes.

The garden at Hatfield's Old Palace is sunken, enclosed on one side by the palace and on three sides by banks planted as a flowery mead with local grasses and flowers including cowslips, fritillaries, and primroses. Walls and hedges surround the whole but were not the barriers they once had been. Gardens were beginning to incorporate a larger view of the land beyond their immediate boundaries. Topiary remained popular in Tudor England as did parterres filled with flowering plants. A maze dominates the arrangement of parterres. A variation of the medieval arbor, a high-domed bench, shaded by willows trained on a coppiced frame, protected delicate skin from the sun's rays.

The basic pattern of the Hatfield garden is the paradise form, now assuming a variation that was then and is today widely used. To accommodate a round central fountain, the hedge-bordered beds were cut at the corners nearest the fountain to follow the curve of the path encircling it.

While the gardens of the Old Palace at Hatfield House exemplify features of the Tudor world that are medieval, the fountain itself with gilded stone cherub blowing his horn is based on an Italian Renaissance design dated 1490. And the gardens are intended to be viewed

"Spring," from the 1614 *Hortus Floridus* of Crispin van de Pass, boasts a jigsaw puzzle pattern of parterres, the pieces separated by gravel paths.

from above as are Italian hillside gardens. The balustrade, another Italian feature, allows viewing from the ground floor. Second-story windows show the gardens' intricate pattern from above.

The young queen loved gardens, and as her interest became known, gardens throughout England were redesigned, upgraded, renovated, and extended when a royal visit was imminent. Some were of late medieval design; others displayed the newer ideas.

The garden of the Old Palace at Hatfield House, incorporating both medieval Tudor and Italian Renaissance traditions, accurately reflects the changing culture of sixteenth-century England. After the devastating plagues of earlier centuries, health and vigor had returned to Europe. The great medieval forests had been reduced as were the dangers harbored within them. The introduction of gunpowder and its use in cannons in the fourteenth century rendered obsolete the protective wall and moat. Gardens could now

ABOVE A Renaissance cherub blows his horn from atop the fountain.

RIGHT, TOP Behind the shaded bench, a high hedge is pruned with windows for viewing the countryside beyond.

RIGHT, BOTTOM The veranda and balustrade provide one view of the garden, the second-story windows of the Old Palace another.

be more open. Travel and trade by land and sea increased. “Might makes right” which had governed much of life in the Middle Ages was superseded, at least to some degree, by law and administration. Above all, the printing press had made information readily available and more people learned to read. With these changes came a subtle shift in thinking about the world. The Age of Faith had become the Age of Man.

The Rometta, Villa d’Este.

2 The Measure *of* Mankind Is Man

Sacred groves, hillside villas, secret gardens, classical learning, and water magic in the Italian Renaissance

FIFTEENTH AND SIXTEENTH CENTURIES

TODAY, WE DESCRIBE ONE accomplished in many fields as a Renaissance person because men of the fourteenth, fifteenth, and sixteenth centuries in Italy were astonishing in the breadth of their achievements—the arts, scholarship, science, technology, literature, music, and philosophy. We wonder at the works of Leonardo da Vinci, Michelangelo, and many others of the period. Their lives were characterized by enormous energy and enormous confidence. They believed there was nothing they could not do and therefore there was nothing they would not try. They were convinced that the power of the human intellect could bring about improvement. Many believed that a Golden Age was dawning and so they set sure-footed and with boundless hope on the road to the future. Scholars have described the Renaissance as the age in which mankind discovered itself.

Along with this confidence came the conviction of many that fame, glory, praise, power, and affluence were good, to be sought, and when achieved, exhibited. The great families of the city-states—the Sforza of Milan, the Medici of Florence, the Borgia of Naples and Rome, and the elected Doge of the Republic of Venice were constantly vying to take and keep control. Patronage was the accepted practice for furthering family interests. Princes of the Catholic Church ingratiated themselves in order to be named cardinal and conspired in the papal elections, many offering or taking bribes—or worse. Positions were bought and sold. Machiavellian negotiation, manipulation, and connivance equaled the sword as the means to power. These leaders of Renaissance Italy displayed their wealth and position in magnificent villas. The accompanying gardens were extravagant and their raw materials—stone, water, evergreen shrubs, trees, and a few flowers—were not meant to celebrate nature but rather to serve as furniture in the outdoor salon, providing a setting for conversation and bargaining.

> What a piece of work is a man, how noble in reason, how infinite in faculties, in form and moving how express and admirable, in action how like an angel, in apprehension how like a god.
>
> —WILLIAM SHAKESPEARE

But the Renaissance was also the age that discovered nature. The world beyond the castle was no longer as hostile as it once had been and walls were no defense against the newly introduced gunpowder. Petrarch, an early Renaissance philosopher and scholar, is remembered as the first to ascend a mountain just for the view. Gardens that were settings for political machinations also looked out over the glorious Italian hills and countryside.

How did such a change from the God-focused piety and mysticism of the Middle Ages come about? Beginning about the middle of the fourteenth century, trade in the Mediterranean increased between the Middle East and the city-states of what is now Italy. Among the goods brought into Italy were Greek, Hebrew, and Arabic manuscripts. The defeat of the Byzantine Empire by the Ottoman Turks in the 1453 Siege of Constantinople increased the availability of such documents as scholars of Greek fled Islam-dominated areas. Italian scholars and eventually those of northern Europe studied these newly available sources, leading them to entertain new ideas and develop new skills.

From the Arabs they discovered the advantage of Arabic numerals which included zero, not part of the Roman numeral system, paving the way for previously impossible engineering feats. The great design challenge for Italian architects and garden designers was that of establishing a firm base for their villas and gardens on the steep Italian hillsides. As well as making possible new sites, Arabic mathematics allowed new architectural features. The supreme example is Filippo Brunelleschi's great dome atop the cathedral in Florence which today remains the largest unsupported brick dome in the world. Engineering also advanced in the field of hydraulics, the movement and management of water, creating a wholly new approach to water in the garden.

From a translation of the work of tenth-century Persian Alhacen, Renaissance artists learned about perspective drawing. Lorenzo Ghiberti publicized the ideas and Brunelleschi showed how to establish a vanishing point by a geometrical method used today by landscape designers and architects. Painting the outline of Florentine buildings on a mirror, Brunelleschi showed that all lines converge on the horizon when the building's lines are extended. Later Leon Battista Alberti's *Della Pittura* of 1435–36 became a guide for would-be artists, teaching them how to represent on a flat surface the way objects appear to the eye.

In literature and philosophy, scholars compared Hebrew, Latin, and Greek editions of the Bible. They pored over the classical writers including Cicero, Ovid, Pliny, Horace, and Virgil. Above all, it was Plato who intrigued and guided their thought, rivaling the former preeminence of Aristotle, and Christian humanists worked to reconcile platonic thought with Christian doctrine. A central thesis of the Renaissance was that all learning, whether sacred or profane, could not corrupt; it could only purify. Seeing no contradiction, the leaders of the church set about study of the classical writers as well as Christian theology and commissioned artists who used classical figures side by side with Christ, Mary, and the saints in their painting, sculpture, and garden design.

With this new approach came the belief that education is the road to intellectual, spiritual, and material success and power, a belief that has characterized Western civilization ever since. With the introduction of the printing press and invention of moveable type in the mid-fifteenth century, thousands of copies could be printed in a single day. The otherwise sophisticated Erasmus predicted that even the plowboy would learn to read and then would whistle the psalms as he plowed his furrow. But the hopes of the Renaissance humanists would be dashed by wars first of religion and then of nationalism. And the plowboy? He proved more likely to read the

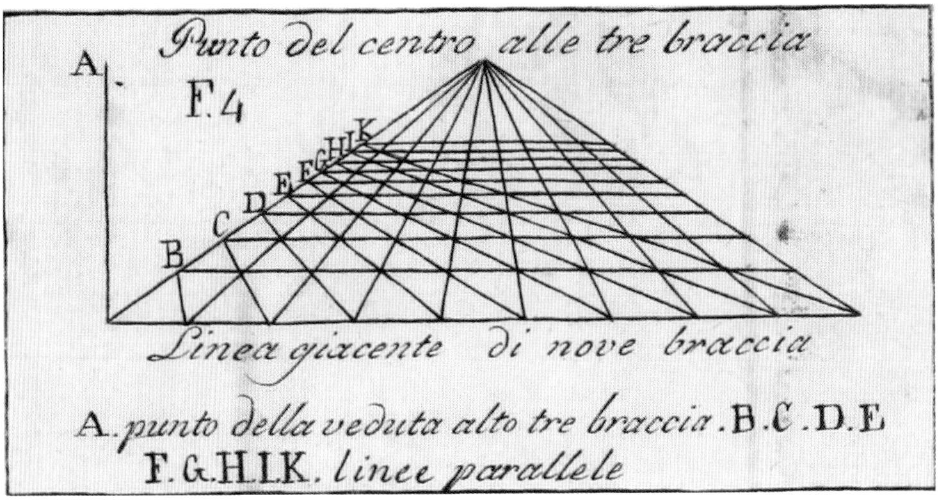

Alberti's *Della Pittura* is the first modern treatise on the art of painting, this page showing perspective drawing and the convergence of lines on the vanishing point.

tabloids than the Bible or the classics.

As Renaissance art including garden design was in the making, there were rumblings of discontent that would be played out violently across Europe and England. Protesters railed against the extravagances of the Catholic Church in Rome and their costs imposed throughout Europe. Savonarola and his books were burned in the central square of Florence; Jan Hus met the same fate in Prague. Martin Luther nailed his *Ninety-five Theses* on the Wittenberg Castle Church door and called the pope "antichrist." Reformer John Calvin held sway in nearby Geneva and his followers, French Huguenots, gained in number. Henry VIII, following the example of German electors who determined whether the people of their territory would be Catholic or Protestant, declared himself head of the Church of England.

Knowing the history of the Reformation, we must acknowledge that the Italian Renaissance gardens, both those owned by princes of the Catholic Church and by the great families—which have been visited, written about, extolled, beloved, and replicated by subsequent generations—were symbols of the church's greed and extravagance, contributing by the image they projected to the breakup of European Christendom.

Villa Medici

Fiesole, Italy

When Cosimo de' Medici, the richest and most powerful man in Florence, decided to support Marsilio Ficino in establishing a Platonic Academy, he arranged for it to be located at Villa Careggi on the hill overlooking the city and near to his own villa in Fiesole. There the work of translating all of Plato could go on and the scholar-philosophers including Giovanni Pico della Mirandola could meet at either villa, and so they did. Cosimo's Platonic Academy was a new venture and one that would intellectually and artistically greatly influence the course of the Renaissance, inspiring Ficino confidently to declare, "If we are to call any age golden . . . such is true of this, our age."

The Villa Medici was also new in concept, for unlike other Italian villas, it had been neither a fortification nor a farm. Rather, Cosimo and his chosen architect, Michelozzo Michelozzi, followed the advice of Leon Battista Alberti in *De re aedificatoria* (On the Art of Building) who in turn had borrowed from classical Latin authors Vitruvius and Pliny

ABOVE High above Florence, the villa is placed just as Alberti advised to catch the sun in winter and cooling breezes in summer.

OPPOSITE The garden at the Villa Medici Fiesole has a traditional medieval design but without the high enclosing walls.

regarding the hillside as healthy. Cosimo's Villa Medici was an ideal retreat from unsanitary and plague-ridden Florence and a model for countless other Italian villas.

It was no mean feat to secure the villa and adjacent gardens on three levels of the steep hillside. The villa's lower floor houses stables, kitchen, and storage. The upper floors for living quarters are on an axis with the top terrace gardens. As was traditional, the garden itself is geometric and enclosed with low walls framing the terraces.

But the distinguishing feature of the Villa Medici, is the view—ah, the view!—down into the valley, dominated by Il Duomo di Firenze which had been completed only ten years before the construction of Villa Medici began. Banker Cosimo must have also relished the sight of the winding Arno River and, on a clear day, a glimpse of the Ponte Vecchio on which the goldsmiths of Florence had sold their wares since medieval times. Then, looking to left and right, there was the Tuscan countryside with stands of cypresses punctuating the views.

Another feature of Villa Medici that would become part of later Italian gardens and one adopted by later generations of gardeners in Europe and North America is the *giardino segreto*, the secret garden. Located on the west side of the Medici villa in Fiesole and apart from the larger and more public garden on the east, it is small and formal, just the place to steal away from other guests for a private discussion.

Behind the entrance opening at Villa Medici in Fiesole the secret garden is adorned with boxwood hedges, climbing roses, a simple circular fountain, shade trees, stone benches, and low walls allowing views outward.

Villa d'Este
Tivoli, Italy

Designing the expansion of Villa d'Este and its gardens was the ideal commission for Pirro Ligorio, one he must have coveted dearly. He was, after all, the author of *An Attempt to Restore Ancient Rome* and *The Restoration of Hadrian's Villa*. The property of Cardinal Ippolito d'Este, formerly a monastery in Tivoli, is sited atop the mountain above what once had been Roman Emperor Hadrian's eight-square-mile villa. Ligorio knew Hadrian's villa would provide an endless source of materials, especially classical sculpture. And he could just help himself.

The cardinal, son of the infamous Lucrezia Borgia and Alfonso d'Este, was enormously rich, powerful, and ruthless, having rigged at least one papal election. He would spare no expense in enlarging and improving the villa and gardens to equal and perhaps even surpass that of the great Hadrian.

Ligorio began work on Villa d'Este in 1550, continuing until almost the end of his long life in 1583. He chose as the garden's theme the twelve labors of Hercules, hoping that the pope would see in the allusion the cardinal's labors for him. The mythic figure of the strong, skilled, and cunning Hercules would take his place in other great gardens as well. Sadly, at Villa d'Este later changes including the selling of sculpture by Este heirs destroyed the iconography.

Villa d'Este would become famous in Ligorio's generation and loved by future visitors for its innovative use of water in hundreds of pools and fountains and the clever tricks they played, demonstrating superbly the newly developed knowledge of hydraulics. For this the cardinal hired Orazio Olivieri, a brilliant engineer. His first task was to divert the River Aniene upward through a tunnel of more than three thousand feet. Then he and Ligorio put gravity to full use on the steep hillside of Tivoli in service of the water features that would define Villa d'Este, including twenty-three major fountains as well as other pools, grottoes, and countless water jets. Most innovative was the cascade, a feature that would become synonymous with Italian gardens.

The first cascade supplies the Fountain of Tivoli from behind. Also called the Ovato or Oval Fountain, it is the villa's largest, receiving water directly from the River Aniene and acting as the distribution point for the rest of the garden. The huge cascade was to serve as model for cascades at Villas Lante and Aldobrandini and many other Renaissance gardens.

The sculpture above the Oval Fountain is that of the Tiburtine Sibyl with her son, Melicertes. She is remembered as founder of Tivoli and was said to have predicted in the first century that a future emperor named Constans would make Christianity the supreme religion. Now overgrown with ferns and other water-loving plants, in the sixteenth century the niches and sculpture were pristine, quintessential examples of the glory of man's artistic achievement.

The most beloved, frequented, and photographed of the water features is the Hundred Fountains, a bold and breathtaking way of dealing with the almost vertical rise of the land. Over three hundred feet long, it is made up of three narrow terraces of gushing fountains topped with stone eagles, lilies, obelisks, and boats, all emblems of the Este family. The

The tiled Ovato is the central source of water at Villa d'Este.

middle level has long since been covered with maidenhair ferns, preventing visitors from seeing the ninety-one bas-relief scenes from Ovid's *Metamorphoses*, a widely read book during the Renaissance. In the lowest row, lion heads spew water. Complementing the villa and fountains are pebblework mosaics, an ancient Roman and Renaissance garden feature.

Visitors make the vertical descent by way of straight and curved staircases and, at the steepest points, by ramps parallel to the hillside, each easing the gradient. Crossing at oblique angles, the ramps also serve cleverly to disguise the fact that the villa is not perfectly perpendicular to the axis of the garden. The staircase embracing the Dragon Fountain has handrails with flowing water, as does the water staircase at Alhambra. At the bottom four dragons roar as they spout water, a contrast to the quiet of the circular pool from which they appear to be emerging.

Other Villa d'Este fountains were a visual delight and, wonder of wonders, made various sounds by the ingenious mixing of water and air. The Owl Fountain had a flock of metal birds that chirped prettily but who flew away when frightened by a mechanical hooting owl.

CLOCKWISE, FROM TOP LEFT

Although called the Hundred Fountains, in fact the three rows contain many more.

Looking down or up is equally enticing at the Dragon Fountain.

The Organ and Neptune Fountains are reflected in a large fish pond that recalls the rectangular pool at Hadrian's villa in the valley below.

Who could fail to be captivated by these charming stone beasts who in the Renaissance roared fiercely?

The Rometta depicts nearby Rome.

The lowest level has large reflecting pools, a grotto, and small fountains. But most impressive is the Organ Fountain which once played music. Built according to descriptions by first-century engineers Vitruvius and Hero of Alexandria, it operated by water entering a cavity, thus mixing air and water before forcing air out of the pipes. It was so finely tuned that the sound could be controlled to play specific musical notes. The water-driven keys played four-part madrigals, quickly making the organ a major tourist attraction. It lies atop the Neptune Fountain which rises forty feet above the large reflecting pools at the base.

The Rometta is another feature of Villa d'Este that attracts visitors. A miniature model of ancient Rome, it is set in a semicircle backed by a suggestion of the Seven Hills of Rome with three small cascades joining to represent the Tiber River. Originally there were replicas of the Pantheon, Colosseum, Capitol Hill, and the Arch of Titus. On top of the wall behind the stone replica of an ancient Roman boat forever-moored in the Tiber remain the statues of Victorious Rome designed by Ligorio himself, the she-wolf nursing twins Romulus and Remus, and a horse in mortal combat with a lion, all references to the founding of Rome.

The Villa d'Este is one of the world's most visited gardens. When the garden was still in the making Pope Gregory XIII had to see to believe that the music was automated and not played by a hidden organist. Other contemporary visitors included Ariosto, Cellini, Palestrina, Tasso, Titian, and Muret whose poems about the villa decode the garden's symbolism. These famous visitors were followed in turn by Corot, Robert Adam, and Franz Liszt who remained as a guest for several years.

Most visitors, both the famous and the unidentified, adore the Villa d'Este, but there have been detractors as well. French Renaissance writer Michel de Montaigne declared in 1581 that the Organ Fountain played but one note. While American novelist Henry James described d'Este as "brave indissoluble unions of the planted and the builded symmetry," his friend Edith Wharton called the Rometta "puerile," unworthy of the "august" Roman countryside, and "pitiably tawdry" in comparison to the Villa Lante.

It is no accident that many amusement parks of the nineteenth century, most notably that in Copenhagen, are named Tivoli Gardens for they sought to be as successful as Villa d'Este in attracting, impressing, and entertaining visitors. Today we would call Villa d'Este a kind of theme park, albeit with unusual grace, charm, and artistry.

Sacro Bosco (Bomarzo)

Viterbo, Italy

In every time and place there are patrons and artists who seek to express values that run counter to those prevailing in the culture. When educated, sophisticated, traveled, and experienced Pier Francesco Orsini, Duke of Bomarzo, known as Vicino, named his garden Sacro Bosco, "sacred wood," he was suggesting that his was not to be a pleasure garden. Rather he was drawing on an ancient religious belief that trees were gods or that gods dwell in trees. That there was tree worship in pagan Europe comes as no surprise, knowing the extent, dangers, and mysteries of ancient and medieval forests.

The image of the sacred grove of olive trees outside Athens, the site of the Academy of Plato, remains so enduring that we say "the groves of academe" to refer to the academic world. Sophocles named the sacred grove of Colonus near Athens as the final resting place of Oedipus. Diana—Artemis, in Greek—goddess of woods and hunt, was the one whose favor was most sought in ancient Greece and Rome. In the *Metamorphoses*, Ovid included the story of young Actaeon coming upon Diana while bathing, a story with countless appearances and a thousand interpretations in art and literature. The site of the ancient Roman sacred grove of Diana was located at Lake Nemi, not far from Vicino's castle.

It was natural that Vicino should choose the designer of Villa d'Este, because of the proximity of the two villas. Pirro Ligorio had created at Villa d'Este an exaggerated and lighthearted display of man's ingenuity. At Sacro Bosco, Vicino asked that he create the extreme opposite, a temple of dark emotions, madness, and irrationality.

OPPOSITE Whomever the first sculpture seen at Bomarzo represents, it is a violent image.

Vicino's Sacro Bosco was dedicated to his wife, Giulia Farnese, who died in 1546. But his was to be no gentle or sentimental memorial. Sacro Bosco shared one feature with other famous gardens, that of oversized, rough-cut sculpture. But with this, similarity ends. Here conventions of garden design were rejected. There are no allées, parterres, geometry, flowers, nor amusing hydraulics. Rather it is a park of fantastic tufa sculpture once brightly painted and with enigmatic inscriptions. Set in deep woods and laid out asymmetrically, it is clearly meant to evoke images that arise from the deepest and most turbulent human experiences.

Some say that the first sculpture the visitor encounters is Hercules who, barehanded, slayed the evil Cacus. Or the sculpture may refer to the ancient custom that required a challenger to kill the priest who guarded the sacred grove. Along the path are massive primordial and imaginary animals including monsters, dragons, and a giant turtle struggling out of the earth. At the garden's center is Cerberus, the three-headed dog who, seeing in all directions, guards the entrance to Hades to prevent the tormented from escaping.

Stories and speculation abound as to the purpose and message of Bomarzo which stands in such stark contrast to other Renaissance villa gardens. Over the most famous piece, the ocr (or ogre), are written the words, "Abandon thought, all ye who enter here." It is a reference to Dante's *Inferno*, in which the inscription over the Gate of Hell reads "Abandon hope, all ye who enter here." Visitors were clearly being told not to expect to find at Bomarzo the logic, reasoning, and classical study characteristic of the Renaissance. Vicino himself gave but one clue to the garden's meaning. He described himself as "dry straw before the flames of lust." The garden is filled with violent sexual images. Local rumor had it that a terrible crime, sexual in nature, occurred there, and even today some local residents will not visit the park.

After Vicino's death in 1588 the park was allowed to fall into ruin, and the family abandoned it. Only in 1949 did surrealist artist Salvador Dali and novelist Jean Cocteau seek out the legendary Bomarzo and write about it. Sacro Bosco was purchased by the Bettini family, restored, and opened to the public as the Park of Monsters—but not until it had been exorcised.

ABOVE J. R. R. Tolkien in *Lord of the Rings* gave the ancient name "orc" to his evil monsters.

RIGHT Salvador Dali painted distorted sexual experiences. This one, *Metamorphosis of Narcissus*, shows why he was fascinated with Sacro Bosco, Bomarzo.

OPPOSITE A half-clothed woman lies helpless.

Villa Lante
Bagnaia, Italy

> I want to speak about bodies changed into new forms. . . . from the world's first origins to my own time.
>
> —OVID, *METAMORPHOSES*

No garden in the Western world has been praised more than has Villa Lante. It was recognized even before it was completed as a treasure of the fine art of garden design. Visitors flocked to see the villa, including Montaigne who in 1581 reported that it is the "finest place of the sort in the world." More than three hundred years later, Edith Wharton wrote, "So perfect is it, so far does it surpass, in beauty, in preservation, and in the quality of garden-magic, all the other great pleasure-houses of Italy, that the student of garden-craft may always find fresh inspiration in its study." In addition, no garden illustrates the values and ideals of the Renaissance more successfully than does Villa Lante. What are the features that make it the pinnacle of fine landscape design and a visual summary of Renaissance values?

The measure of mankind is here clearly and comfortably man. The scale of the garden allows visitors to feel that they belong in the setting, neither cramped and awkward in the space, nor small and insignificant. The villa itself is not one building but two symmetrical squares on a scale that does not dominate but rather complements. Cardinal Gianfrancesco Gambara, owner and conceiver, was a friend, not rival, of Cardinal d'Este and his garden and villa were not intended to compete with the wonders of Villa d'Este. He chose, with felicitous result, Giacomo Barozzi da Vignola as his designer, a man who understood his vision. The cardinal had a deep affinity for nature, and Villa Lante brings together nature and design in an intimate way. The surrounding woods are not merely adjacent to but incorporated within the garden, an innovation in Renaissance design. The garden combines straight and curved lines in a pleasing relationship. Formal plantings join informal ones. The fountains and pools elucidate, not astonish.

As does every good landscape design, the cardinal's design began with a concept. Villa Lante tells the story of mankind's creation, disobedience, punishment, and redemption. Recounting the rise from primordial beginnings to civilization, Vignola used as a framework the *Metamorphoses* of Ovid. The most popular of Latin poets, Ovid was read during the Middle Ages, and then in the fifteenth and sixteenth centuries his *Metamorphoses* became the most widely read and quoted of all the books of antiquity then known. In it Ovid recounts 250 myths about the interaction among the Greek gods and the gods with humans, each tale describing a transformation. In most, water serves prominently as the agent of change. Twentieth-century landscape architect Geoffrey Jellicoe declared that "Vignola lifted landscape design into the sublime at the Villa Lante, subordinating architecture to an ancient and universal idea of cosmology."

At the Villa Lante, the stage is set at the entrance to the garden. Squared and tapered stone pillars topped with a bust, called herms, stand tall, representing the nine muses, daughters of the goddess Memory, in a circular pool backed by a wall. The winged horse Pegasus prances in the water. The viewer recalls the instant on Mount Helicon, home of

Pegasus prances in the pool at the entrance to Villa Lante, suggesting the story to come and introducing the binding thread, water.

the muses, in which a spring of water burst forth where Pegasus struck his hoof. The source of life is given. The drama laid out in the garden ahead will recall the human past through poetic and harmonic experiences, each scene united to the ones before and after by water.

From the entrance, visitors proceeding through the *boschetto* of oaks and plane trees climb the hill, recalling the Golden Age that, as Ovid wrote in Book I:

> without coercion, without laws, spontaneously nurtured the good and the true . . . . No pine tree felled in the mountains had yet reached the flowing waves to travel to other lands. . . . [there were yet] no swords and helmets. The earth herself also, freely, without the scars of ploughs, untouched by hoes, produced everything from herself . . . rivers of milk flowed . . . and golden honey . . . trickled from the green holm oak.

At the top of the hill is the grotto in which life and humankind emerge from water. Three niches hold figures made of rocks and shells, not quite recognizable as human forms yet clearly suggesting the transfiguration to come. Water pours from above into

The great flood, a story shared by Jews, Christians, and Muslims, appears in the book of Genesis, in Greek mythology, and in the Sumerian *Epic of Gilgamesh*. Recently scientists have identified it as occurring when the waters of the Mediterranean rose, spilling water over the basin's rim into the Black Sea.

a pool, the constant stream feeding the maidenhair ferns and other water-loving plants. As Ovid recounts:

> As yet there was no animal capable of higher thought that could be ruler of the rest. Then Humankind was born. . . . While other animals look to the ground, he gave human beings an upturned aspect, commanding them to look towards the skies, and, upright, raise their face to the stars.

The Deluge continues the story. Mankind disobeyed the gods, and Jupiter "resolved on a . . . punishment, to send down rain from the whole sky and drown humanity beneath the waves." The momentous event is recounted at the Villa Lante first in the courtyard where

TOP The Dolphin Fountain rises like a mountain, recalling Ovid's image of ocean dolphins swimming in the treetops during the great flood.

BOTTOM The water chain, in the form of a crayfish, also serves to link the sea image of the Dolphin Fountain above and the river images that come at the next stage of the story.

OPPOSITE Primordial beginnings.

the creation is depicted on the back wall. Side walls conceal water jets that pour forth, drenching unwary visitors, just as in the Great Deluge people were caught off-guard. Just below, the Dolphin Fountain recalls the image described vividly by Ovid in which waters rise and, breaking their bounds, cover even the mountains:

> There are dolphins in the trees, disturbing the upper branches and stirring the oak trees as they brush against them. . . . The sea in unchecked freedom has buried the hills . . . the waters wash away most living things.

But eventually Jupiter relents and the waters recede. Ovid's Triton, blowing into "his echoing conch, . . . sounded the order for retreat. . . . It was heard by all the waters on earth and in the ocean and, hearing it, were checked. Now the sea has shorelines, the brimming rivers keep to their channels." The earth is productive again, and Deucalion and Pyrrha, the man and woman who were spared, begin its repopulation.

A great stone chain contains the water on its downward flow, visually proving that the waters now keep their appointed limits. In places waist high and other places only two or three feet from the ground, the water flows at a rate controlled by varying angles of the chain. The distinctive form of the water chain refers to Cardinal Gambara. His family symbol is the crayfish since their name is similar to *gambero*, the Italian word for crayfish. At the top of the chain is the tail, the volutes resemble the articulation of the shell, and the head and pincers lie at the fountain below.

The water from the chain falls abundantly in a semicircular pattern into a large basin below. The great river gods of the Tiber and Arno who irrigate the fields recline in the niches on either side of the fountain. Flora and Pomona, goddesses of flowers and fruit, flank the fountain. Ceres, goddess of grain and agriculture who "first turned the soil with curving plough," is painted on the ceiling inside the villa.

The water from the basin disappears briefly but, continuing the center axial line of the garden, reemerges in the Cardinal's Table, whose straight lines contrast with the curves of the water chain above. The scenes reassure that the chaos of the flood has been overcome and order has returned, hope with it. Here, at the banquet table, the church enjoys both the earth's bounty and fruits of human labor. For *al fresco* celebrations, wine and fruit were placed in the channel running down the middle of the table, to be chilled by the cool water that makes its way downhill.

Now the visitor becomes fully aware of the two buildings, called casinos, placed symmetrically on either side of the garden and making up the villa, recalling that "There Mount Parnassus lifts its twin steep summits to the stars, its peaks above the clouds." Next we are shown that mankind lives and progresses not only by his labor but by his intellect. Here the tale leaves first-century Ovid, moving on to glory in the Renaissance. The Fountain of Lights joyfully and elegantly celebrates the virtues of reason and learning.

Hedge-lined paths running obliquely to the central axis ease the steep descent from the villa level. At the foot of the hill lies the Quadrato, which occupies about one acre, one-third of the total garden area. At its center, on axis with the Deluge, Dolphin Fountain, water chain, Cardinal's Table, and Fountain of Lights, lies a circular fountain within a square. Divided in four sections, here the Moorish paradise garden pattern of water and grass or flowers is reversed. Rills of water are replaced with bridges and the turf becomes water, emphasizing the role of water in metamorphosis. Each water quadrant sports a stone boat and musketeer with horn. The fountain and ponds are surrounded by twelve square beds, with parterres in various *broderie* (embroidered) patterns. An obelisk originally stood at the center of the Quadrato, spurting water from dozens of jets. It was replaced by succeeding owners of the Villa Lante with a travertine sculpture of four Moors holding aloft the stylized mountain and star that were the Montalto family emblems.

TOP The Fountain of Lights uses water jets to create the look of candles, the light of learning.

BOTTOM The center channel of the Cardinal's Table was an idea adopted by Vignola from Pliny, reminding Renaissance guests of the legacy of ancient Rome.

Villa Lante is a monument to the ideals and accomplishments of the Renaissance, employing in the design the very concepts it celebrates. Classical literature is admired and expressed. The pattern of circles and squares, to which the laws of mathematics were applied, make an orderly but varied scene. Rich ornament together with severe lines produces elegant harmony. The natural woods surrounding Villa Lante are incorporated into the design. The scale makes the visitor at one with the story being told, and the proportions at each stage project the victory of reason and civilization over the powers of darkness.

ABOVE The civilization of the Moors, a beacon of learning, is here honored at Villa Lante in the central fountain.

RIGHT At the Villa Lante the garden takes precedence over the buildings, a landscape architect's dream.

Villa Aldobrandini

Frascati, Italy

It is said that after visiting the Villa Lante Pope Clement VIII fostered the creation of Villa Aldobrandini. Like the Villa Lante, it features a great water chain, but with the chain the comparison ends. Aldobrandini has features in common with the ancient villa of Emperor Hadrian nearby and the Villa d'Este, but at such different scale and proportion as to make Villa Aldobrandini seem a wholly new creation. Indeed, Villa Aldobrandini marks the transition from Renaissance gardens to the succeeding Baroque, but, as Edith Wharton wrote of it, "before that school had found its formula."

In ancient times the property on which Villa Aldobrandini was built had been the site of Emperor Octavian's villa. In 1598 the villa became the home of Cardinal Pietro Aldobrandini. Nephew of the pope, he had expected the villa to serve as a country retreat, one to which he would return when not on papal business. But after the death of his uncle in 1610, the new pope stripped him of power and put him under virtual house arrest. Having been accustomed to moving in the highest circles of sixteenth-century Rome, he might have felt impatient and bored were it not for the endless entertainment that his villa and its garden provided.

Aldobrandini, like other Italian Renaissance villas, is high on a hillside.

He was a generous host to the constant visitors coming to see him and his remarkable villa and garden. Regrettably, on one occasion, he seems to have been too generous because his house and garden architect, Giacomo della Porta, having feasted sumptuously on ices and melons, died on his return trip to Rome.

Villa Aldobrandini is sited on a hillside rising from the valley town of Frascati from which visitors enter the grounds. Passing through the massive iron grille gate at the bottom of the hill, they proceed up the center axial road defined by allées of ilexes with parterres typical of Renaissance gardens on either side. As the center road approaches the villa, it divides, both sides winding up to the entrance of the villa.

Passing through the villa, visitors come to the courtyard where they are met with an elaborate structure. Decorated with pebbles, mosaics, and intricate stone carving and topped with a balustrade, the water theater is designed as an exedra, a form favored by architects since antiquity. Open and colonnaded, it has niches for seating and, as at Aldobrandini, is often semicircular to foster conversation. At Aldobrandini, the exedra's niches contain figures of gods and peasants which, although made of marble, pulse with vitality.

Centered above the water theater is a cascade, channeled from Monte Algido for eight miles. It begins on the hill above where, according to legend, the virgin Diana hunted in the sacred grove. The water rises sharply at the pebble and mosaic poles heading the water chain, then spirals downward over the eight shallow terraces of the cascade and in the depressions in the handrails. It disappears briefly under the terrace above the theater, to emerge again with power in the fountains below.

The scene is further enlivened by the ingenious hydraulics created by Orazio Olivieri, engineer of the waterworks at Villa d'Este. As at Villa d'Este, water pours, gushes, spews,

The exedra form, seen here at Aldobrandini, will appear again in the Baroque, neoclassical, and Romantic gardens of the seventeenth and eighteenth centuries, notably at Het Loo Palace in the Netherlands and Stowe in England.

LEFT Blind Polyphemus, whose name means "abounding in songs and legends," plays the panpipes.

RIGHT The water cascade is a spectacular sight from the palazzo or the upper loggias of the villa. A loggia is a gallery with at least one open side.

ripples, and bubbles everywhere. At Aldobrandini, the figure of mighty Atlas takes center stage, holding up the world in the form of a giant sphere spurting water from dozens of jets. In the Renaissance on one side of the theater a copper ball was suspended indefinitely three feet in the air by wind coming from a hole beneath. Birds sang, a monster roared, and, most remarkable to the English diarist John Evelyn who visited in 1645 was "the representation of a great storm . . . most natural, with such fury of rain, wind and thunder, as one would imagine oneself in extreme tempest."

Moreover, the waterworks were designed to tease. In the summer months when Rome was seething, this feature was welcomed and amusing. Evelyn reports with delight that "one can hardly step without wetting to the skin." Visitors in 1858 described how one member of the party ran to the top of the stairway to turn on a valve to soak his companion but was deceived and soaked himself with a jet "the thickness of an arm. . . . He fled with his breeches full of water and water running out into his shoes."

Not everyone was entranced with Villa Aldobrandini. Edith Wharton wrote critically of the ornate water theater: "It suffers from . . . being out of scale with the Villa's modest elevations: there is a distinct lack of harmony between the two facades." Chiefly she objected to the proximity of the water theater to the villa, noting correctly that it violates a canon

From the courtyard visitors enter the *piano nobile*.

of design that the distance between two structures should be as great as or greater than the height of the taller one.

But at Aldobrandini there is an interesting twist to the design principle. The *piano nobile*, the "noble floor," is the location within the villa of the reception hall and ballrooms. *Bel étage* in French, it is sometimes at ground level but often not, located instead on a second floor to avoid ground-level noises and the smell of horses. In this case the lowest floor is for storage, servants' quarters, stables, or other utilitarian purposes. Elegant external staircases were used to disguise the lowest floor, bringing important guests directly into the *piano nobile*. At Aldobrandini, there are two stories above the *piano nobile*, one a *piano nobile segundo*. They look directly at the cascade and the hill above, which is raked back at an angle from the vertical plane of the water theater. The garden was meant to be viewed as much from these upper loggias as from the courtyard. From them the proximity of cascade and water theater to villa does not appear so great.

Wharton was right that Villa Aldobrandini was unconventional, breaking design rules. But many visitors have admired the inconsistencies, finding the variety and juxtaposition of styles pleasing. John Evelyn declared that Aldobrandini surpasses "the most delicious places . . . for its situation, elegance, plentiful water, groves, ascents and prospect."

3 The Brink *of* Infinity

Baroque design, monarchy, ideal proportions, and exquisite illusion

SEVENTEENTH CENTURY

HISTORIANS DESIGNATE the seventeenth century in France in two ways: the Age of Reason and the Age of Absolutism. It might also be called the Age of Brilliance, for it was glittering in every way. For the tiny number of those at the top of the social hierarchy, dress was as fancy as it was ever to be. Men sported ruffled cravats and cuffs, high-heeled shoes, and curled hair that came to the waist. For those with little or no hair, there were wigs. Women wore low-cut gowns and enormous French farthingales. Cinderella carriages of glass and gold-gilt with liveried footmen carried the titled and important to extravagant events.

But the brilliance extended beyond mere entertainment and indulgence. New intellectual developments in science and mathematics challenged age-old beliefs. The Age of Reason—the Enlightenment—superseded the Age of Faith. The new theology was deism, a rejection of authority, miracles, and revelation, holding instead that observation of the natural world was sufficient to prove the existence of God. Philosophy argued for an epistemology based on crystal-clear observation.

Geometry, not theology, was now queen of the sciences. René Descartes, whom we know as the philosopher who said, "I think, therefore I am," was foremost a mathematician and geometrician. Using a coordinate (grid) system, he connected algebra to geometry, making it possible to easily manipulate equations for planes, straight lines, squares, and triangles in not only two but three dimensions, thereby simplifying the process of calculating measurements.

Following the Renaissance rebirth of perspective drawing and advances in hydraulics, these stunning developments led to practical applications. Cartography, based on triangulation—three points and triangles laid one on another—had advanced in the previous century, making possible a precision in map-making previously unknown. Surveying became an admired skill and coveted profession, just as engineering and later information technology would be in their day.

> But in my opinion, all things in nature occur mathematically.
>
> —RENÉ DESCARTES

By the mid-seventeenth century, the skills needed to advance in the profession of gardener had drastically changed with the realization that the developments in cartography could be reversed. Just as measurements of land were taken and then put on paper, so a plan on paper could be executed on a site. The gardener with knowledge of geometry could lay out a garden

A parterre, Het Loo Palace.

The Golden Mean

Also called the golden ratio, the golden section, the divine proportion

Utilized for centuries as a major aesthetic principle in art, architecture, and design, the golden mean is the perfectly proportional relationship of a whole to its parts. When any line is divided at its golden mean, the relationship of the whole line to the longer part is the same as that of the longer part to the shorter part.

When the golden mean is used to form a rectangle, the lengths of the sides are related proportionally as well: the shorter side is equal to BC and the longer side is equal to AB. The new, smaller rectangle can be divided into another square and golden rectangle.

Countless artists, architects, and landscape designers have used the golden mean to structure their work because they have found it to be the most pleasing of all proportions. In fact, scientists have discovered the use of the golden mean in Neolithic objects crafted seven to eight thousand years ago. The pyramids of Giza, the Parthenon in Athens, the cathedral of Notre-Dame in Paris, *The Last Supper* by Leonardo da Vinci, and even the dimensions of cereal boxes and credit cards are based on the golden mean.

The golden mean is satisfying perhaps because it is a proportion found throughout nature and especially in the human body. We see it in the sunflower, pine cone, cochlea of the inner ear, and double helix of DNA, to name but a few instances.

Try this yourself. Clear a mantel, a long table, or the top of a bookcase. Take a single object such as a vase or small sculpture and place is at various points. At each point, stand back and ask if you like the position. Chances are good you will choose the golden mean as the most pleasing location.

1 About 300 BC, Greek mathematician Euclid described the golden mean as the point at which, when a line is divided into two parts, the whole line (AC) is to the longer part (AB) as the longer part is to the shorter part (BC).

2 When a golden rectangle is divided at its golden mean, the larger part is always a perfect square, and the smaller part is another golden rectangle.

3 This process of subdividing can be continued indefinitely. Connecting the corners of the squares using half circles creates the golden spiral, a self-generating pattern.

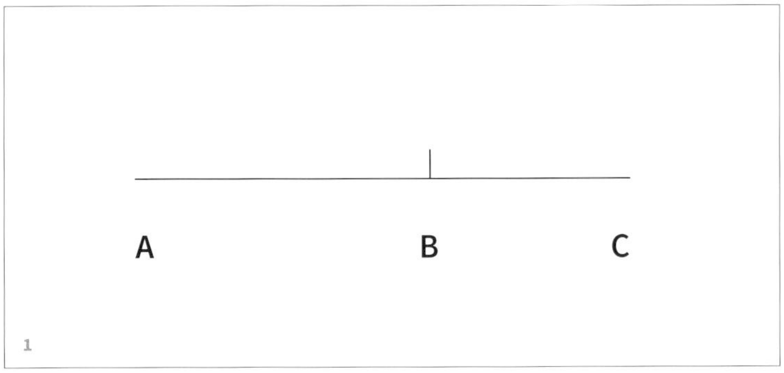

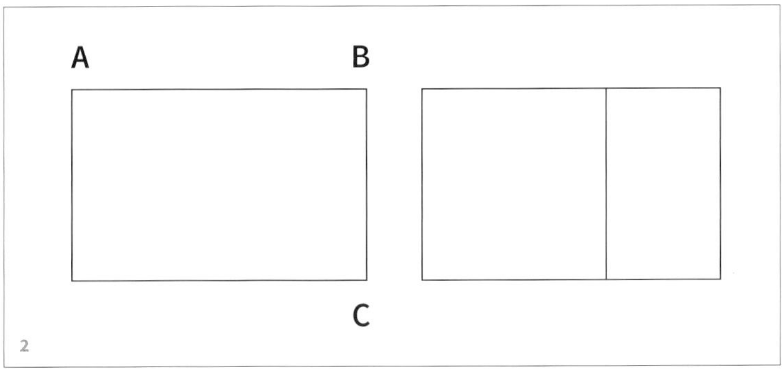

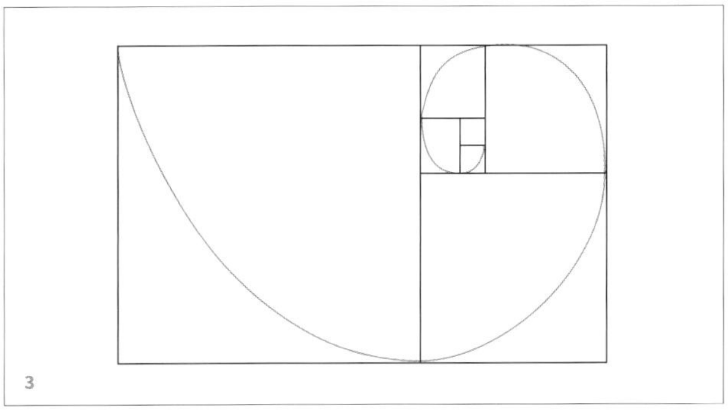

The chambered nautilus, the perfect natural spiral.

André Le Nôtre with his drawing paper, commemorated in stone at Chantilly.

with precision as never before. Nothing need be unpredictable. Lines of vantage from various positions could be designed to intersect. Moreover, even the play of light on water could be predicted precisely. The study of optics, a result of developments in geometry, provided greater knowledge of the behavior and properties of light including interaction with matter. Descartes himself made important contributions to the understanding of reflection and refraction.

Artists applied these advances in mathematics to their work. Architects decorated ceilings in châteaux, villas, palaces, and cathedrals with spirals and other geometric forms. Johann Sebastian Bach's fugues are a masterful interweaving of themes, point and counterpoint, ornamented through a series of variations, appearing in musical notation as geometric designs. Even hairdressers subjected the wig to Cartesian analytical geometry.

While there were many who learned the new skills and employed them in designing gardens, it was André Le Nôtre who rose to be head of the class, so dominating the world of garden design that he had no rivals. Born in 1613, Le Nôtre was schooled in agronomy. His father was head gardener at the Tuileries, the chief palace and residence of the French kings. He inherited two design traditions on which he was to draw liberally, the medieval gardens of the French castle and Italian Renaissance gardens.

Changed was the medieval practice of walling in the garden. By the seventeenth century the growing of vegetables and herbs had been moved outside the castle walls and the garden in the rear of a château became ornamental only. Flowers, prominent in French gardens of the Middle Ages, were used but sparingly, confined by the 1600s to the interior of parterres or planted in decorative urns. Fountains and cascades, the most prominent feature of Italian Renaissance gardens, swept into fashion in France and the Low Countries as Italian gardeners went north to work.

André Le Nôtre put his knowledge of geometry and optics to work, taking the principles a step further by using them to deceive the eye. His was the art of both precision and illusion. Like the Italian Renaissance designers of earlier centuries, Le Nôtre and other Baroque designers were confident and pleased with themselves as they manipulated the perceptions of garden visitors.

Their ideal of control was admired, not shunned, by the wider culture for the Age of Reason in France was also the Age of Absolutism. Social and political life was ordered and hierarchical. There was no such thing as the right of opposition; change in leadership was accomplished by intrigue. Judgment, whether just or unjust, was meted out summarily and punishment harsh, power supreme over right. Noble families controlled their land

and the destiny of the people who lived on it. Omnipotent kings ruled by divine right.

Garden design reflected the values and practices of the Age of Absolutism as well as those of the Age of Reason. Participatory democracy lay in the future, as did the radical change in landscape design that would reflect the new values.

The Italian villa of Isola Bella, shown here in a model, illustrates the transition from Renaissance design to that of French Baroque, combining earlier forms with the skilled use of geometry that characterizes the Baroque.

Isola Bella
Lake Maggiore, Italy

Some said that the designer of Isola Bella was inspired by the popular story *Hypnerotomachia Poliphili* (The Strife of Love in a Dream), written by Francesco Colonna a century before Isola Bella was conceived and built. Recounting an erotic dream, the romance is set on Cytherea, the mythical island near the place where Venus, goddess of love, rising from the ocean depths, was said to have made her first appearance. The hero pursues his beloved through a magical garden occupying the entire island. The story is fantastical, as are dreams, and so is Isola Bella, in the setting of Lake Maggiore, just north of Milan. "Possibly the most romantic folly in the classical world" is how distinguished twentieth-century landscape architect Sir Geoffrey Jellicoe described Isola Bella.

On one of three small islands owned by the Borromeo family, the villa and garden of Isola Bella were begun in 1632 when Count Vitalino VI hired architect Angelo Crivelli to draw plans. The concept was to take advantage of the magical setting of lake and mountains by making the island appear to be a ship plying the waters as did those of the great ocean voyages whose object was to discover the fountain of youth. The villa was to be the prow, fronted by a slim and pointed garden as bowsprit. The deck of turf was cut to appear made of boards. The stern consists of ten terraces, each hung with exotic plants. Obelisks, topped with iron Prince de Galles feather plumes, rise as the ship's masts. Dynamic figures made of stone and holding objects of iron represent Flora, goddess of Spring and fertility, together with those of Summer, Autumn, and Winter. As would passengers on the deck of a ship, they look to shore.

Moving toward the prow, on the other side of the stern are the terraces of the exuberant, three-level water theater, not unlike that at Villa Aldobrandini. Colored pebbles contrast with the white stone figures in their shell-shaped niches. But while Aldobrandini's water comes from a source above, Isola Bella's fountains are supplied by water pumped from the lake below. The helmsman of a seventeenth-century vessel held sway on the poop deck, the ship's highest point. At Isola Bella that position could be occupied by none other than Eros himself, god of erotic love, riding a unicorn, the fantastic creature that was the Borromeo family emblem.

ABOVE The Alps are a dramatic backdrop for the galleon, Isola Bella.

OPPOSITE, TOP Gardens and terraces become the ship's stern.

OPPOSITE, BOTTOM LEFT Above the water theater, Eros astride a unicorn guides the ship.

OPPOSITE, BOTTOM RIGHT The grove of Diana distracts the visitor from noticing the natural curve of the island.

The major design challenge lay in the island's natural curve near the imaginary ship's bow. To accomplish the illusion of island as ship, Crivelli would need a straight axis. He solved this geometric problem by creating a grove of Diana, a kind of open air grotto, polygonal in shape and lower by some forty steps from the deck. The descent is made by winding staircases on either side of the framing walls. The axis is resumed with a long gallery leading into the villa, but at an angle from the upper axis and following the lines of the island. The many sides of the grove successfully mislead visitors into believing that in exiting the grove toward the villa, they are following the axis above in a straight line.

Like the Italian Renaissance gardens or a modern cruise ship, Isola Bella was the site for elaborate entertaining. Just before the garden was completed in 1670 it was the scene for a brilliant party with mock naval battles and entertainment of every kind. Singers performed from boats in the water and sang from behind shrubbery. The garden itself provided a grand stage setting for any comedy, tragedy, or love story that might there be imagined or played out in reality.

The island immediately attracted visitors and has continued to do so ever since. Some have disliked the flamboyance, forgetting that the guiding concept was to transport the

visitor on a magical journey to another world, exciting and dreamlike, where prosaic reality gives way to the world of passion and imagination.

Edith Wharton, usually the voice of restraint and simplicity, defended the island:

> The landscape surrounding the Borromean Islands has precisely that quality of artificiality of exquisitely skilful arrangement and manipulation, which seems to justify, in the garden-architect, almost any excesses of the fancy. . . . The effect produced is undoubtedly one of artificiality, of a chosen exclusion of certain natural qualities, such as gloom, barrenness, and the frank ugliness into which nature sometimes lapses. There is an almost forced gaiety . . . a fixed smile of perennial loveliness. And it is as a complement to this attitude that the Borromean gardens justify themselves. . . . They are gardens anchored in a lake of dreams.

Vaux-le-Vicomte

Maincy, France

Lord High Treasurer Nicolas Fouquet aspired to succeed Cardinal Mazarin as prime minister of France, but King Louis XIV, scarcely out of boyhood, stunned the French court by assuming the position himself. Fouquet, sensing he was falling out of favor and in hopes of improving his standing in court, determined to host the most extravagant fête ever given, ostensibly to honor the young king. But unbeknownst to him, a plot against him had been laid months before by his chief rival, Minister Jean-Baptiste Colbert.

Anticipating by almost a decade the inaugural party at Isola Bella, there would be at Vaux-le-Vicomte a seven-course dinner planned by the famous chef François Vatel, French wines of the very best vintage, a poetry reading by La Fontaine, and music with Jean-Baptiste Lully directing. Molière himself would appear in his new comedy, *Les Fâcheux*, which for the first time incorporated ballet in a play. The sparkling entertainment was to be capped by a lavish fireworks display.

Everyone who was anyone wanted to be invited, to be seen in their most fashionable dress, and participate in what was bound to be scintillating conversation. Most of all, they wanted to attend in order to view for themselves the setting, Fouquet's grand new château southeast of Paris, built by architect Louis Le Vau, the interior decorated by Charles Le Brun, and the garden designed by André Le Nôtre. For three years, eighteen thousand workers had labored, leveling the ground and razing three villages, to create Vaux-le-Vicomte.

When King Louis XIV and his entourage arrived for the party that August evening in 1661, he saw before him the very essence of the Age of Reason. From the top of the grand staircase at the rear of the château, he looked down the central axis to the spot where, Fouquet explained, a dazzling gold-gilt statue of Hercules would be placed, backed by the dark woods beyond. The distance appeared longer than its actual length of two miles, but the

TOP Nicolas Fouquet's garden at Vaux-le-Vicomte. The coat of arms of the Fouquet family reads, "*Quo no ascendet?*" (What heights will he not scale?).

BOTTOM Sculpture has been acquired over the years. *Lions*, the work of Georges Gardet, was added by the ancestor of today's owners of Vaux-le-Vicomte.

apparent distance was no deterrent for the vigorous king. Although he had previously visited Vaux-le-Vicomte on more than one occasion, the king, accompanied by his cousin the Prince de Condé, La Fontaine, Fouquet, and Le Nôtre, willingly began the evening's tour.

The garden at first glance appeared symmetrical, with avenues of trees and shrubbery, pools and parterres flanking straight gravel paths. But the king would soon realize that the apparent simplicity of design is an illusion. Looking more closely, he saw that the parterres *de broderie* on the outer sides of the central axis are not mirror copies of each other, that in fact the garden is not completely symmetrical but the sides are in such perfect balance that it appears at first glance to be so.

Nature was tightly controlled, the trees and hedges pruned so often and precisely that no wind could ruffle their rigid lines. Movement and sound came from the many fountains, cascades, and pools and from the canal. Lovely sculpture and flowers in raised urns lined the paths. The garden of Vaux-le-Vicomte appeared peaceful, elegant, and very grand.

Continuing the walk, as they approached the quatrefoil reflecting pools, the king saw that they are elongated, giving the viewer the impression of greater distance. Le Nôtre may have explained how he employed *anamorphosis abscondita* or hidden distortion, the technique that enabled him to make objects appear larger or smaller, closer or farther away. Looking ahead, the king's party saw that the foreground appeared always receding. When

TOP Elongated quatrefoil pools reflect the château.

BOTTOM The canal, unseen from the château, stretches a quarter of a mile in each direction from the basin.

they turned around, the view of the château made it appear stationary, an effect produced by transverse axes of water refracting the light, consequently foreshortening the perspective.

Moreover, the design from the château terrace appeared to be an even plane conforming to the topography of the land around Paris. Le Nôtre had faced a design problem just the opposite from that of Renaissance designers who constructed terraces to deal with the almost-vertical Italian hillsides. Le Nôtre's challenge was to make his flat plane interesting. As they walked, the tour party discovered how he had incorporated many changes of level, at first hidden from view and then revealed one by one. The greatest surprise was a canal created by giving straight marble banks to the River Anqueil which flows through the property. Unseen from the château, the canal crosses the central axis at approximately the garden's golden mean.

The stairs set at a right angle to the main axis are less daunting than if in line with it. Just beyond the canal at the level seen from all parts of the garden is the grotto. A sandstone wall with seven niches supports the terrace above. In the niches are half-recumbent figures, symbolizing the river gods of the Tiber and Anqueil. Did Louis wonder why his minister had linked *his* river to that flowing through the capital of the Roman Empire?

Arriving at last at the site where one day Hercules would stand, the touring party turned to look back at the château framed in the distance. Just as Le Nôtre had planned, reverse forced perspective made it appear closer and larger, dramatizing its great size. The union of house and garden was underscored by the repetition of form, the dome on the roof of the château echoed in the dome fountain centered in a circular basin on the terrace atop the grotto.

All admired the beautiful château and remarkable garden. But the moment of pride and triumph for Nicolas Fouquet was short-lived. Colbert had convinced the king to call a special court, the *cour d'exception*, to try Fouquet, without benefit of legal counsel, for crimes against the crown including that of stealing from the royal treasury. Seized only weeks after the party, Fouquet was imprisoned for the duration of the three-year trial. Colbert urged

CLOCKWISE FROM LEFT

The dome fountain in the foreground on the terrace above the canal basin connects the eye to the form atop the château.

The river gods are reminiscent of those in Italian Renaissance gardens but now more finely wrought.

Hercules looks toward the château which appears larger and closer because of reverse forced perspective.

that he be condemned to death, but the judges recommended banishment only. All-powerful King Louis overrode their decision, sending Fouquet to the harshest of prisons where he remained until near death almost seventeen years later.

Madame Fouquet tried to hold on to Vaux-le-Vicomte, but when her son died leaving the family without issue, she sold Vaux. A succession of owners made efforts to maintain the magnificence of the château and garden, some more committed and successful than others. At last, in 1875, the estate was purchased by one who recognized that Vaux is an art treasure of such importance that it must be preserved. Hercules finally found his place. Albert Sommier's descendants today continue his work of restoration and education. Visitors now come from all over the world and like those who attended the famous party many find Vaux-le-Vicomte the most perfect garden ever built. In their book, *The Poetics of Gardens*, Charles Moore, William Mitchell, and William Turnbull Jr. identify the success of Vaux-le Vicomte: "Its finite formal geometries . . . bring us to the brink of infinity."

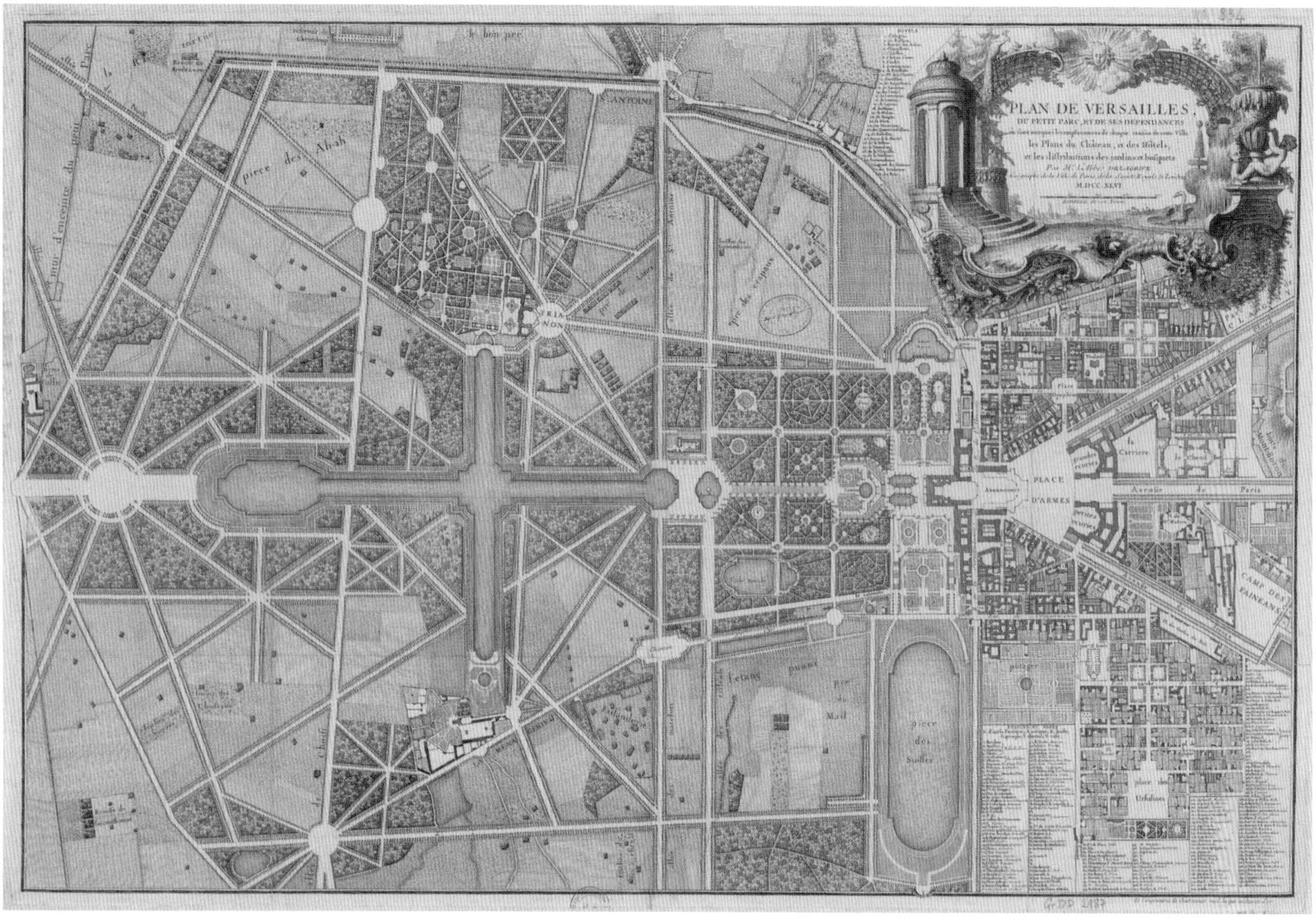

Palace of Versailles

Versailles, France

If André Le Nôtre had designed at Vaux-le-Vicomte the quintessential symbol of the Age of Reason, Versailles would be the epitome of the Age of Absolutism. Not just one central axis, but a pattern of axial thoroughfares would speak clearly: all roads lead directly to the king's bedroom, the very source of the French monarchy and its continued existence. And viewed from the great palace, these roads point to the distant horizon, suggesting the limitless extent of the king's power. Befitting a king, the design would be a tribute to the virtues of control and hierarchy, more intricate than Vaux-le-Vicomte but clearly conveying the message of centrality and omnipotence.

As a young boy, Louis had chosen Apollo as his emblem, Greek god of the sun in whose hands was the gift and control of life. Looking from the center of the palace at Versailles down the terrace, the stairs, and the long allée to the basin, the viewer is riveted by a gold-gilt

TOP The long allée and basin beyond extend as far as the eye can see, an allusion to the extent of the French monarchy's power.

BOTTOM No one seeing the Apollo sculpture could miss the reference to Louis XIV, the Sun King.

OPPOSITE The length of Versailles suggests the infinite reach of the Bourbon monarchy.

Apollo emerging from the ocean to ride his chariot through the heavens pulling the sun, daily ensuring that it rises and falls. And beyond, the long axis of basin and allées continues until no longer visible on the horizon, said by geometricians to stretch to infinity and by poets to heaven.

Not to be outdone by Minister Fouquet at Vaux-le-Vicomte, Louis XIV added insult to Fouquet's injury of imprisonment by hiring Le Nôtre, Le Vau, and Le Brun to oversee renovations and additions to the old palace and gardens at Versailles. Even before Fouquet's trial was over, thousands of items—tapestries, sculpture, furniture, and orange trees—had been confiscated from Vaux to furnish the greatly expanded Versailles. All this was necessary to realize the plan the king had formulated, a plan that was to prove one of the most brilliant administrative moves in history.

As a child, Louis and his mother had been forced to flee under cover of darkness from the palace at the Tuileries when nobles revolted against his father's rule. He would never forget the experience of being in hiding, cold, hungry, and afraid. As king, his idea was to centralize the government, bringing the disparate nobles under his control before they could plot a successful overthrow. He would create at Versailles an extravagant court and invite the nobles and their wives to live there with him, providing every diversion including food, drink, dancing, fashion, music, theater, hunting, and gardens. What duke or duchess would not prefer this life with its endless opportunities for illicit affairs and delicious gossip to the dull existence in the provinces? With potential enemies gathered in one place, the king could have his spies eavesdropping on conversations and reporting to him. He would nip in the bud the smallest hint of disloyalty.

Speaking as clearly of Absolutism as does the design is the sheer immensity of Versailles. The palace is the largest in the world; the property of more than two thousand acres includes 230 acres of formal gardens. There was never before nor has there been since such an enormous garden, all demonstrating the extent of Louis XIV's wealth and power.

But the garden also had another important function in Louis's grand design. Its purpose was to provide endless entertainment, not only for the occasional and short-term visitor but for the ten thousand who took up residence at the king's invitation either in the palace

itself or in the nearby town. If they were to remain under his watchful eye, the nobles and their wives must enjoy life at court. They would need many places on the palace grounds to explore and be amused over the months and years they remained at Versailles.

To meet this objective, Le Nôtre envisioned within the gargantuan size lighthearted joy, to be accomplished in several ways. He would satisfy the king's passion for fountains, for Louis had demanded that there be water, water everywhere. This was Le Nôtre's greatest challenge at Versailles and one in which he did not entirely succeed. Unlike other gardens he had designed, water at Versailles was scarce. Not daring to disappoint his king, Le Nôtre tried everything. His attempt to dam the Seine proved inadequate. He had a scheme for the Loire River but finally recognized the impossibility of bringing water the long distance from Orléans to Versailles. In the end he drained a nearby swamp at a huge cost in human life. An elaborate system of pipes was laid to direct the endless jets and cascades, a system still in place at Versailles. Unfortunately, the effort to obtain adequate water was unsuccessful. The fountains had to be restricted to times the king would be present and today are turned on for only a few minutes at a time.

Despite the difficulties, Versailles was awash in other ways. On the great canal Venetian gondoliers plied their boats. Outlined with lanterns for evening parties, basins in every imaginable geometric pattern reflected both the plantings around and the faces of those who gazed admiringly into them.

In addition, Le Nôtre achieved a sense of playfulness through the dozens of *bosquets* that dot the garden. High trellises made dense with vines or hedges surrounded these "little woods." Paths straight or winding lead into the center of each where the resident visitor would find a fountain, a bench, or perhaps a maze. Hide-and-go-seek with the chase ending in a kiss proved always tantalizing. Sculpture is everywhere, the statues' subjects great legends and myths. Painted lead figures from the popular fables of La Fontaine were among them, stationed in clearings in the *bosquets*, charming the stroller.

The great *orangerie* provided treats for the evening banquet. In an indoor room 450 feet long, facing south and fitted under the grand stairs, hundreds of citrus trees were kept alive during winter by fires tended day and night by young boys.

ABOVE The *orangerie* was initially supplied with citrus trees confiscated by Louis XIV from Vaux-le-Vicomte.

OPPOSITE, TOP Fountains grace every crossroads, some, as this one, dancing to Baroque music and mesmerizing the stroller.

OPPOSITE, MIDDLE Playful putti, teasing cupids, graceful muses, enticing nymphs, and fantastic animals brought delight in the seventeenth century as they do today.

OPPOSITE, BOTTOM Putti attend Diana in a pool at the crossing between *bosquets.*

André Le Nôtre, with his knowledge of geometry and optics, his eye for vantage points, and his exquisite sense of balance, had successfully unified the variety at Versailles into a harmonious whole. The king was satisfied. One day late in Le Nôtre's life when they were together at Versailles, Louis turned to him, declaring that he would appoint him to the Order of Sainte-Lazare. To the question of what he would choose as his coat of arms, Le Nôtre replied "Three snails, a head of cabbage, and my spade." Louis XIV could not but love such a humble and agreeable man who employed his genius to enhance the king's image and fulfill his grand plan, yet who never forgot his place in the hierarchical structure of society and power. Le Nôtre remained in the king's service until old age made work no longer possible.

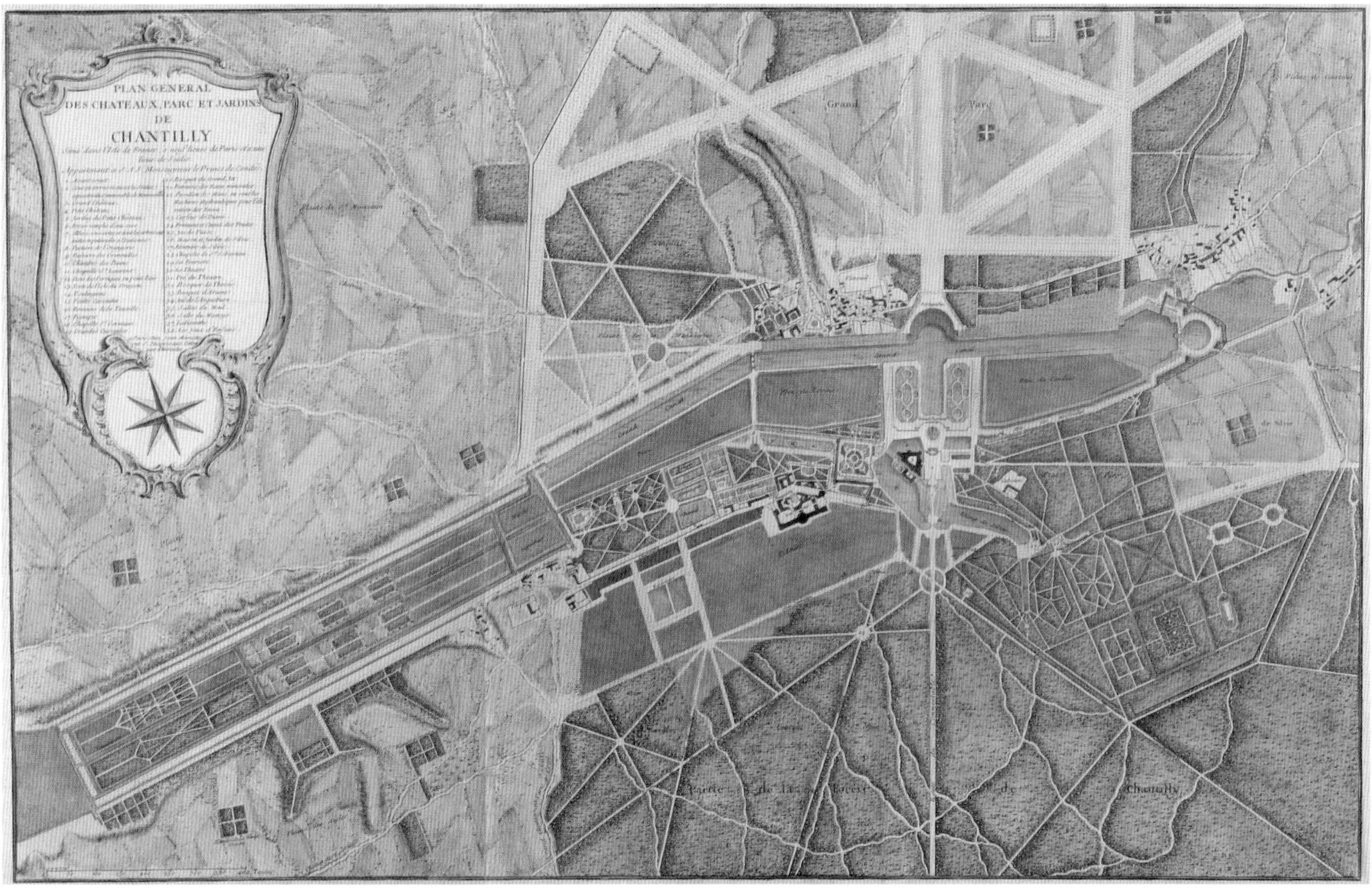

The slender épée runs vertically; the thick dagger, horizontally.

Château de Chantilly

Chantilly, France

The rebellious, difficult, and powerful Louis II de Bourbon, Prince de Condé, accompanied his cousin King Louis XIV on the fateful tour of Vaux-le-Vicomte. So impressed was the Grand Condé that, like his cousin, he hired André Le Nôtre to rebuild the garden of his château, Chantilly. The land was fertile and water plentiful, made more so by the hydraulic engineering skills of the prince himself.

It was a unique site. The castle, among the most ancient in France, is a parallelogram situated in and once protected by a large body of water with only a small wooden bridge leading to a side terrace on the east. Le Nôtre decided to abandon the accepted pattern of having the gardens emanate straight from the center of the château. Instead he used as his departure point the adjacent courtyard looking onto the meadow below. As the workmen dug and leveled, they uncovered stone boundary markers from the fifteenth century on which were incised the épée and dagger, early signs of the family escutcheon. In recognition that

TOP An easy gradient, the *grand degré* is easily managed despite its size.

BOTTOM Today the ancient boundary markers etched with the épée and dagger surround the equestrian statue of the family ancestor, Anne of Montmorency.

Chantilly was home to a long line of military heroes including his present patron, Le Nôtre used the shapes of the slim and flexible épée and sturdy dagger to outline the garden, the only known instance in which he used symbols of war in a garden design.

The épée lies on the north-south axis, terminating some ten miles from the entrance to the château. An allée of trees forms the sharp edges of the blade's shape, narrowing visually by forced perspective to create the sword's tip. The allée is laid out so that at certain times of day the sun's rays on the road between the rows of trees appear to form a ridge along the center of the blade.

As the axis continues past the castle it widens with the great water basin bounded by water parterres. These consist of a center rectangular form and four ovals, once with jet fountains surrounded by sculpture and flowers in urns. The whole is framed with an allée of rectangular hornbeams. Made from the River Nonette, the canal on the east-west axis, representing the dagger's blade, crosses the north-south axis.

At the terrace adjacent to the castle, descent to the lower level is by way of the *grand degré*, considered in Le Nôtre's time and by subsequent art historians a masterpiece of classic design. To be viewed in all its splendor, a monumental staircase must be seen in entirety from above and below, yet not appear daunting to those who must climb or descend. Le Nôtre accomplished this with generous landings and wide shallow steps. Le Nôtre–designed sculpture occupies niches on either side of the staircase.

TOP One can almost hear the horse's hooves clatter on the stones of the castle courtyard.

BOTTOM Hero indeed who can ride on water!

At the center of the terrace adjoining the castle and standing atop a twenty-five-foot pedestal is the equestrian statue of High Constable Anne of Montmorency, Huguenot ancestor of the family and famed military leader. Seen from every part of the garden, it is the anchoring focal point. Le Nôtre's use of the high terrace and the pedestal insured that horse and rider always appear backed by a clear sky, making it without reference to scale and therefore more realistic.

From the level below, visitors turn back toward the staircase and château, viewing the equestrian statue from several key vantage points. From the bottom of the *grand degré* the horse is silhouetted, galloping on the horizon as if carrying the hero home from battle, the tall plinth unseen. On the far side of the round water basin, the statue, staircase, and fountain are in view, horse and rider appearing to ride on water. Nowhere is André Le Nôtre's skill in using vantage points more dramatically demonstrated.

On the periphery of the chief garden were areas for lighthearted activities, just as at Versailles. There were tennis and croquet courts and an archery range. Painted lead figures depicting characters in La Fontaine's fables once adorned the barn and chicken house. A maze challenged the mind. Most valued was a little hamlet with winding paths, a stream, and a rustic cottage, just the right place for respite or the forbidden tryst.

At Chantilly, André Le Nôtre captured within the formal lines of seventeenth-century Baroque geometry the action and vigor of a full life, that of the Grand Condé, his family, and ancestors—and of his own. Is it any wonder that toward the end of his life he wrote to a friend, "Remember the Gardens you have seen in France, Versailles, Fontainebleau, Vaux-le-Vicomte, the Tuileries, and above all Chantilly"?

Het Loo's double parterres on either side of the central axis convey width, alluding to the inclusiveness of the Netherlands.

Het Loo Palace

Apeldoorn, Netherlands

Het Loo, the palace of William and Mary, has often been called the little Versailles, but it is not. Such a designation would have been anathema to the king and queen. Like other seventeenth-century gardens including Versailles, it has axial roads and Baroque parterres, but there the similarity ends. Het Loo is wide where the French gardens are long and narrow. It is modest in size while the French gardens seem to extend into infinity, making Het Loo's scale less pretentious and authoritarian. Het Loo boasts abundant colorful flowers from the corners of the Dutch Empire while in the French gardens stone and water predominate. At Het Loo, it is baby Hercules who takes center stage, not the great Apollo moving the sun through the heavens as at Versailles.

It is a garden that illustrates dramatically the difference—passionate, deep, and lasting—between the two kings, Louis XIV and William of Orange. In France the monarchy was inherited and absolute. In the Netherlands the history of kingship was different. The traditional title was chief stadtholder, meaning chief steward chosen by the provincial governors. By William's time the position had evolved into an inherited one but included a degree of shared leadership. Louis was devoutly Catholic, William staunchly Protestant. Louis demanded complete loyalty to the house of Bourbon and promoted uniformity of religion. Calvinism was the official religion in the Netherlands, but there was also wide tolerance of varying religions and opinions.

Further, the landscape designer chosen by William of Orange was Daniel Marot. French, he had studied with André Le Nôtre. But he was a Protestant. When in 1698 Louis XIV revoked the Edict of Nantes which had given Huguenots the right to own property, Marot feared for his life and fled, taking up residence and work in the Netherlands.

William and Mary, with advice from confidante Hans Willem Bentinck, Earl of Portland, and the skilled Daniel Marot would build a garden that stood in dramatic contrast to the palace gardens at Versailles. Het Loo would express the very essence of Dutch political theory and practice, speaking clearly of the two causes that dominated William and Mary's lives and reign: opposition to French Absolutism and defense of Protestantism.

Baby Hercules is entwined with two gold snakes that he would one day slay, perhaps suggesting absolute monarchy and Catholicism, the two powers which William and Mary thought poisonous.

When William was named chief stadtholder in 1672 he received hunting rights in Veluwe, a nearly unpopulated area to the east, rich in wildlife. Devoted as William was to the sport, he sought a lodge in the area and found it in Het Loo. He located the ideal spot for a more palatial lodge with gardens, with an abundance of streams and springs for fountains and irrigation. Work began in 1684. The center section of the palace was constructed with wings connected by colonnades to the main structure. Eventually a garden was planned.

The palace and the gardens would be a unity. When the rear door was open visitors coming to the front entrance would be able to see through the palace to the central axis of the garden. The design, as was the custom of the time, would be geometrical and essentially symmetrical. The garden near the palace follows the Dutch garden tradition. Most notably, it is smaller than the great French gardens. Unlike the grandeur of Versailles in which the visitor is dwarfed, Het Loo with its human dimensions projects welcome and belonging. Its square parterres convey width rather than length as emphasized by Le Nôtre, further underscoring the contractual nature of William's rule and suggesting an open society rather than a closed hierarchy. A brick wall encloses the garden with a sense of security and intimacy, yet without obscuring the woods or creating a sense of separation from the world

Seen from the roof of the palace are the elaborate Baroque parterres, the trees lining the canal, and the semicircular colonnade. Het Loo's width feels like all-embracing arms.

beyond. Rills line the path of the main axis, reminding the visitor of Dutch waterways.

In these late years of the seventeenth century when the palace and gardens were being built, another political development occurred, one that would alter European history and influence garden design at Het Loo. English Protestants, fearful of King James II's Catholicism, looked for a means of deposing him. They turned to Mary Stuart, married to William of Orange. She had, in their eyes, a legitimate claim to the throne as daughter of King James II. Knowing that they could count on William and Mary's defense of Protestantism, Parliament convinced William to invade England. James fled and William and Mary were named co-regents in what was called the Glorious Revolution. The garden design at Het Loo would refer to the expanded lands they now governed.

Four large urns, originally outside but now inside the palace, represent England, Scotland, Ireland, and Wales. Two globe fountains lie symmetrically on either side of the central axis. One charts the heavens, the other maps the then-known world with special note of the lands governed by William of Orange including New Amsterdam (now New York) and, through the Dutch East India Company, the islands of what is now Indonesia.

ABOVE Globe fountains are the center of a paradise garden form, with radiating paths and rills. The border parterres display flowers gathered from distant lands of the Dutch Empire.

RIGHT This elegant, throne-like structure at Het Loo, where any visitor is free to sit, is made of modest wood, a stark contrast to the gold and glitter of Versailles.

Like *berceaux*, the grotto provided a cool place in the heat of summer.

Het Loo also features superb examples of the wooden trelliswork for which Dutch gardens were known. The word *treillage* (latticework for vines) first came into use in 1698, perhaps to describe the covered colonnade at Het Loo with its curving lines and high domes. Another garden term for such a structure is *berceau* (barrel vault), which also refers to a baby's cradle. Window-like spaces are kept clear of vines so that the stroller may look out from the shaded path to the sunny gardens.

Below the *piano nobile* of the palace lies a grotto, one of Europe's most exquisite. Adorning the walls are shells, marble chips, and semiprecious stones, including a garland of pink shells on a background of blue powdered lapis lazuli. Seventeenth-century descriptions include two fountains and a large cage on the exterior that allowed birds to fly freely inside the grotto and out. A private staircase led from Queen Mary's personal apartments, giving her easy access to the grotto. Orange trees dotted the gardens then as now, symbolizing the House of Orange. They alluded to the immortality-giving golden apples of the Hesperides which Hercules snatched from the garden of Hera as his last challenge. More prosaically but of equal importance, they once provided the fruit for Queen Mary's marmalade which she made herself in the grotto.

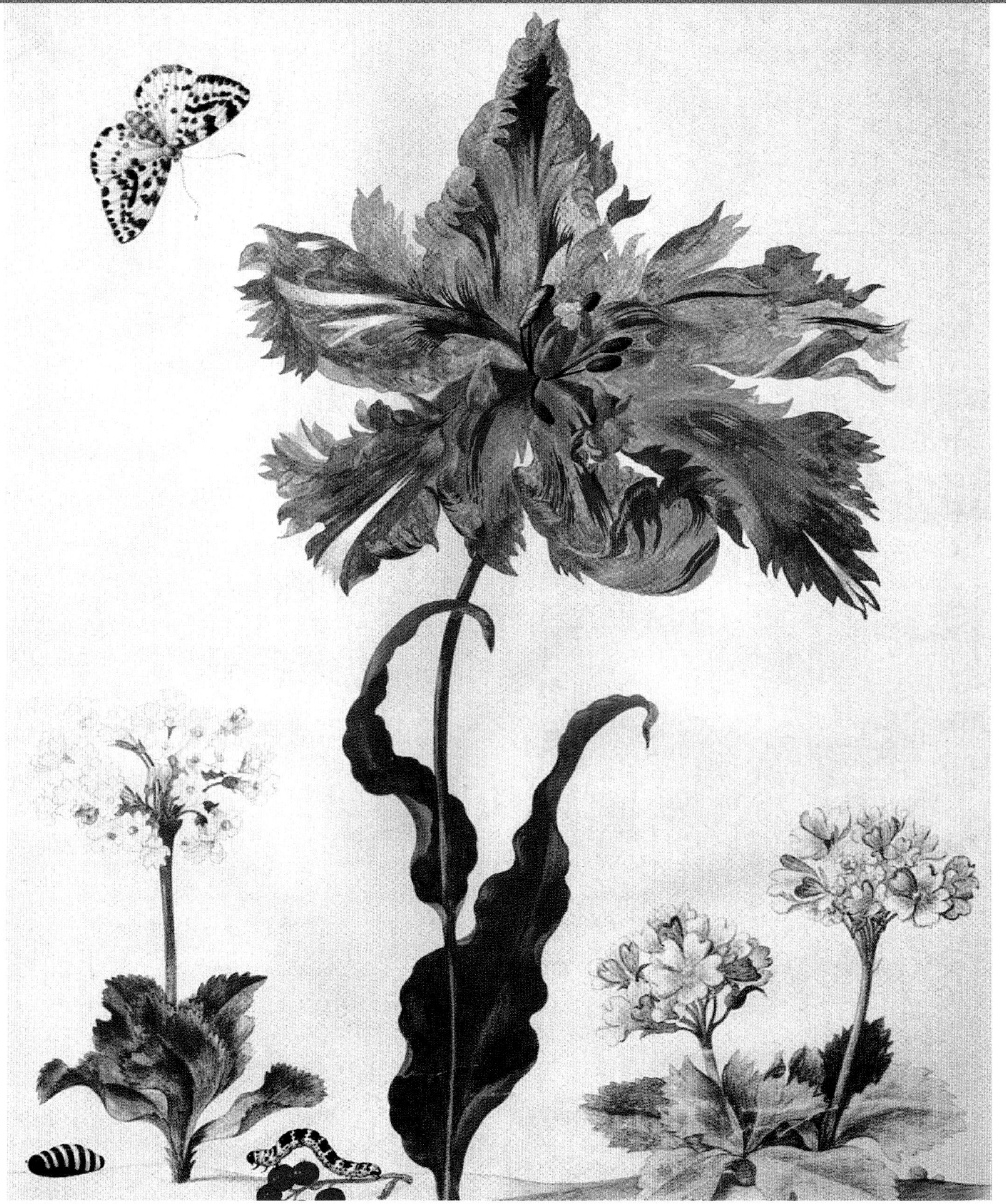

A Parrot Tulip, Auriculas, and Red Currants with a Magpie Moth, its Caterpillar and Pupa by Maria Sibylla Merian.

4 A World *of* Wonders

Sea voyages bring exotic plants in the Age of Discovery, and botanical gardens elevate science and horticulture.

SIXTEENTH THROUGH EIGHTEENTH CENTURIES

IN SCHOOL WE STUDY the English Civil War and Glorious Revolution, the American and French Revolutions. But at the same time as these momentous political events were occurring, another transformation was touching every dimension of the lives of every person great and small. The story lies in the sea voyages of the seventeenth and eighteenth centuries during the latter part of the Age of Discovery and their success in finding and returning to Europe new and productive plants.

This transformation unfolded first not on sea but on land. Silk was only one of the commodities carried along the Silk Road from China to Europe. Precious resins of myrrh and frankincense, spices including cinnamon, cumin, cardamom, and nutmeg, and countless other goods were loaded on camels, wagons, horses, and elephants to travel the four thousand miles from China to Europe beginning as early as 200 BC. But in the fifteenth century the road became very difficult and discouraging for traders. The Mongol Empire that had controlled the route was disintegrating. Local infighting of Arab tribes made the road through Persia dangerous, and when Constantinople fell in 1453 to the Ottoman Turks, trade was closed by local Arab leaders. Muslim reprisals for the reconquest of Andalusia and Alhambra by Catholic Spain further limited access to and from the West.

These events inspired adventurers to seek a sea route to China. The daring explorations of Christopher Columbus, Ferdinand Magellan, and Vasco da Gama set the stage. As seafarers rounded the capes at the southern tips of Africa and South America, the expanded world was ablaze with possibilities. The mighty oaks, chestnuts, beeches, and elms of Europe were felled by the thousands to build wooden sailing ships for these bold ventures.

At first the explorers sought gold, silver, precious metals, and spices. But by the beginning of the seventeenth century, seeds and plants were the chief object. Although the passage was long with many a voyage ending in shipwreck, the potential gain was worth the risk. Live plants would bring the most money in Europe because the difficulty of transporting them made them rare. Kept in the hold of the ship, they had to be periodically brought on deck for air and sunlight where they were also exposed to the salt spray. Most succumbed.

> Of flowers, spread athwart the garden. Aye
> Name upon name assails thy ears . . .
> Gaze on them as they grow, see how the plant
> Burgeons by stages into flower and fruit . . .
> Asleep within the seed the power lies.
>
> —JOHANN WOLFGANG VON GOETHE

The story of the explorers, botanists, naturalists, and soldiers of fortune in the Age of Discovery has made many a book. Here examples from the

Robert Cecil so treasured his head gardener, John Tradescant, that he had his portrait, complete with flowers and rake, carved as a post for the grand staircase at Hatfield House in Hertfordshire where it can be seen today.

beginning of the seventeenth century and the end of the eighteenth century are illustrative.

John Tradescant the Elder, born in 1570, worked his way up the profession of gardener and at age forty was named head gardener to Robert Cecil, first Earl of Salisbury, at Hatfield House. Cecil sent him to the Netherlands to purchase fruit trees, beginning what was to be a life of travel for Tradescant, increasing and satisfying his curiosity about the strange world beyond English shores. After Cecil's death, he became gardener for James I, traveling to Russia, the Arctic, and Algiers in search of new plants for his king. Among the plants he found were those in the genus that would one day bear his name, *Tradescantia*. On the road and from returning sailors, he also gathered oddities—shells, semiprecious stones, dried animal skins, and native masks, weapons, household tools, and vessels. He opened his collection to the curious, creating the world's first public museum which would later form the basis of the Ashmolean Museum of Oxford University.

Following in his father's profession, John Tradescant the Younger became head gardener to King Charles I who sent him to Amsterdam to purchase the coveted and dearly priced tulip bulbs newly introduced into Dutch horticulture. Then in 1628, when the English colony of Virginia was but twenty years old, John went to Jamestown. There, with the help of an Indian woman, he combed the surrounding forests, meadows, and swamps for plants yet unknown in England. When he returned home some nine years later, he brought, among other plants, phlox, asters, the bald cypress, and the tulip tree, all of which became prized by English gardeners. He is buried with his father and son at Saint Mary's Church Lambeth, now the Garden Museum.

Early in the nineteenth century the famous seaman Vice-Admiral William Bligh was buried in the same churchyard. Today he is remembered as commander of HMS *Bounty* whose crew mutinied, setting Bligh and a handful of loyal officers and men adrift in the South China Sea in a twenty-three-foot open boat with no charts. Their six weeks at sea to reach what is now East Timor is remembered as one of the greatest sea voyages of history.

What is less well known is that the *Bounty*'s mission was to bring the breadfruit plant (*Artocarpus altilis*) from Tahiti to Jamaica. Breadfruit was recognized as highly nutritious and easy to grow, fruiting for the better part of a year. Jamaican plantation owners, seeking to acquire this low-cost food for their slaves, formed a cartel. To lead the expedition they hired Bligh who had been sea master on the third and final voyage of the famous explorer Captain James Cook. Because of the mutiny the *Bounty* mission failed, but Bligh was hired again and this time succeeded in delivering six hundred plants to Saint Vincent and Jamaica.

TOP In 1796 Thomas Goose depicted Captain William Bligh directing the gathering of bread-fruit plants in Tahiti.

BOTTOM When he returned to England in 1637, John Tradescant the Younger brought *Magnolia virginiana*, one of the oldest living plants.

His tomb at the Garden Museum in London acknowledges the "celebrated navigator who first transplanted the bread-fruit tree from Otaheite to the West Indies, . . . died beloved, respected and lamented, December 7th, 1817."

In the 150 years between the Tradescants and Bligh's voyage dozens of other European botanists, naturalists, explorers, and seamen searched for seeds and plants, doubling the size of the world known to Europeans and extending by thousands the number of plants available in any one place. New fruits and vegetables made good eating and good nutrition and provided new sources of income for farmers. The inventory of plants for medicine grew exponentially as did the research in their use. These developments changed local ecologies, sometimes introducing plants that proved invasive in their new homes.

By the start of the nineteenth century, landscape and garden designers had options never known before and they sought these treasures from abroad for their clients and patrons. Plant collecting became the object of newly founded botanical gardens, the focus of scientific pursuit, the avocation of many an aristocrat or the merely curious, and, finally, the obsession of the Western world. Fortunes and empires were won and lost sometimes on the basis of a single plant as investors bet on its success. And some sought to organize the vastly expanding knowledge of plants, work that would be essential to the future of botany, agriculture, and landscape design.

L'Orto Botanico

Padua, Italy

With the influx of plants from around the world it was necessary and inevitable that there would be efforts to classify plants, both those that were native to Europe and those newly brought from overseas. Common names of plants varied from place to place and sometimes different plants were called by the same name. To correctly identify plants, long descriptions were necessary. The botanical gardens were founded to collect the new plants and to organize them in a logical system to aid in their study. Since medicinal plants were considered the most important, they became the focus of the earliest of these gardens.

With the waning of the Middle Ages, the study of medicine moved from the monasteries to the universities and their medical schools. L'Orto Botanico of Padua is the oldest botanical garden in the Western world still on its original site and adhering to its original design. Founded in 1545 by the Venetian senate only a half century after Columbus discovered America, the garden featuring natural remedies soon became a study site for the University of Padua medical faculty and students. Luigi Squalermo became the first director and here he wrote the *Semplici*, an herbal describing 1,540 plants reputed to have healing properties, which became a reference work for other botanists.

Only a few years later, more than one thousand plants were cultivated in the Padua botanical garden, coming mostly from the Mediterranean and then Asia. Included in the inundation were many that were not medicinal plants and the focus of study shifted from the healing property of plants to the plants themselves.

An herbal is a book describing plants with information about their uses in medicine, cooking, and as aromatics, often also identifying their toxic, hallucinatory, or magical powers. Herbals were produced in ancient Egypt, China, and India as well as in Europe until the late seventeenth century. Today they are having something of a revival for those seeking natural remedies for illnesses.

A garden's purpose is—or should be—the first consideration in its design. The Padua garden is surrounded by a high circular wall, needed to protect the rare plants from theft and vandalism. Within the circle is a square following the paradise garden form with four paths radiating at right angles from the center fountain. The four quadrants thus created may recall the four humors of the body as described by Hippocrates, a doctrine to which both Christian and Muslim physicians subscribed. Stone-divided beds make identification clear as each plant, separated from another, is labeled. The beds are of varying geometric shapes fitting into the quadrants of the square or together forming an inner circle adjacent to the surrounding circular wall. The medicinal plants were organized in beds by the parts of the body and diseases they were believed to heal, the exotics by the regions of the world from which they came or by characteristics they held in common. The original design served well for the study of plants over succeeding centuries, accommodating additions such as a library and laboratories.

Among the most notable of the now thousands of plants at L'Orto Botanico in Padua is *Chamaerops humilis*, known as European fan palm or Mediterranean dwarf palm. The northernmost naturally occurring palm, it grows in Italy, Malta, and coastal Spain. The Padua palm was planted in 1588 and remains one of the world's oldest living plants. Two hundred years after its planting the German poet and naturalist Johann Wolfgang von

ABOVE The central fountain is a convenient way to water plants. The tower to the right houses the Goethe palm.

BELOW High wall and stone-bordered plant beds remain today as they were at the Padua garden's origin.

Goethe visited the garden and studied the palm. Its successively differentiated leaves from bottom to top inspired his treatise *The Metamorphosis of Plants*, in which he argues that all plants come from a common plant. He looked for the archetypal plant and his observations and theories along with those of many others stimulated new thinking that transformed botanical and biological science in the nineteenth century, culminating in the work of Charles Darwin. Recognized as the birthplace of science and scientific exchange for its early plant collecting and study of botany, L'Orto Botanico of Padua remains an important botanical garden to this day.

TOP Today's botanists at Padua bring out the potted plants for a sunning.

BOTTOM At over four hundred years, the Goethe palm may be an old lady but thrives, even now producing offspring.

A view of the original Hortus Botanicus in Leiden from above.

Hortus Botanicus

Leiden, the Netherlands

Carolus Clusius had already achieved an international reputation as a botanist when, in 1593, he accepted the position as first prefect of the Hortus Botanicus in Leiden. It was the beginning of the long and distinguished history of one of the world's great botanical gardens.

> "Have you heard? Van Tol has got one. Van Tol, the plumber who lives on Oude Vest, he's got one!" "What do you mean?" "You know, that thing, the tulip—the flower with stripes. Although I don't know what he sees in it. His wife went mad: forty guilders for a small egg-shaped thing. And you can't even see it. It's in the ground. Of course, he says it will be worth eighty guilder tomorrow. That's if he can sell it. I definitely wouldn't buy it. A load of hot air if you ask me!"
>
> —STANS VAN DER VEEN, *HORTUS BOTANICUS*

In Leiden, the first city of the Netherlands to throw off the Spanish yoke and the first to establish a university in the Protestant Netherlands, the university occupied buildings once a convent but abandoned during the Protestant Reformation. The space within the cloister had served the nuns as a garden for medicinal herbs. Now it would once again be a place for growing plants but, under the direction of Clusius, not for medicine but rather for the study of botany. Clusius would reach out to his international network to gather plants from France where he had studied medicine at the University of Montpellier, from Germany where he had lived, and from Vienna where he had designed a botanical garden for Maximilian II. He would bring hundreds of plants with him for the new Hortus Botanicus at the University of Leiden.

Clusius studied the phenomenon of "breaking" in tulips in which the solid color of a tulip is broken allowing unique color variations. For centuries the phenomenon was believed to be caused by environmental conditions. Then, in 1928, mycologist Mary Cayley determined the cause to be a virus. Because the virus also often weakens the bulb, the striped tulips were taken off the market as they posed a financial threat to tulip growers. Today such tulips are almost unknown.

Among his collection were bulbs, of special interest to Clusius. While in Vienna he had met the ambassador to the Turkish court. Ambassador Ogier Ghiselin de Busbecq, having experienced the Turkish coastline, mountains, sandy soil, and the hills aglow in spring with crocuses, narcissus, fritillaries, and white Madonna lilies, obliged Clusius's passion by returning from Constantinople with bulbs as well as seeds.

Arriving in Leiden, Clusius set to the task of laying out the garden. He divided the space into four quadrants, each in turn divided into rectangular beds. A bower rather than a fountain stood at the center. Arches marked the entry to some of the paths. Wooden tuteurs supported climbing vines. Although the garden measured only 115 by 131 feet, Clusius managed to include in it more than one thousand different plants. He made a map of the garden, noting the location of each plant and showing how he had laid them out not according to their medicinal use but by common characteristics. Like any good botanist, he marked each carefully and waited through the long first winter.

When spring came, in the special corner bed that Clusius had set aside and fenced for his bulbs, dark reddish tips showed through the cold earth. A few weeks later *Tulipa* 'Semper Augustus' opened, the first tulip to bloom in the Netherlands. Enthusiasm for the new striped tulips seized the world of horticulture and gardening. King James I sent his gardener John Tradescant to buy these unusual bulbs, only one of hundreds of investors who came to Amsterdam to bid on the fascinating flowers. Costs skyrocketed, setting off unparalleled financial speculation. Finally, in 1637, the prices went too high and the tulip market crashed, bringing many to ruin. Yet the love for tulips continued unabated, and their cost became more reasonable as the number of growers increased. Holland's national industry was born. Today at the Aalsmeer Flower Auction flowers are checked and graded before being sold to bidders around the world.

The tulip was not the only exotic flower brought into the Netherlands. The Dutch East India Company established trade with and control over the South Sea Islands, now Indonesia. From Jakarta it did eight times as much business as the now more famous English East India Company until the Dutch company's collapse in 1800. With access to a wealth of unusual plants in the South Seas and ships constantly returning to Amsterdam with plants among the cargo, the study of botany flourished.

One visitor who was to add further distinction to Leiden was a young Swede, Carl Linnaeus. He had studied at universities in Lund and Uppsala and made a pioneering expedition to Lapland in search of plants. He was making a name for himself in the world of horticulture for his study of the sexual characteristics of plants and for his thinking about classification. The flood of new plants made imperative a uniform taxonomy. Linnaeus came to Leiden in 1735 where he remained to publish his *Systema Naturae* in which he described three kingdoms of nature: plants, animals, and rocks. In the years that followed he developed the system of binomial nomenclature for botanists and horticulturists. Based on the structure of Latin, it used the genus as the first identifier and the species (specific epithet) as the second, thereby ending the need for extensive descriptions and providing instead a short and accurate means of identifying a plant. There were others working on the problem of classification but Linnaeus's system eventually won the day. It remains the system used

OPPOSITE The 'Semper Augustus' tulip, shown here in a seventeenth-century watercolor, was sold for the highest price of all tulips during the craze of 1637.

ABOVE The fenced area at the left was reserved by Clusius for his precious bulbs. His carefully kept lists and plan enabled the re-creation of his garden on the original site in 2006.

RIGHT At the Aalsmeer Flower Auction, twenty million flowers change hands each day.

FAR RIGHT Linnaeus, once in residence at the university's botanical garden, is honored at Leiden for his system of classifying plants.

in botany and horticulture today, although identities are changing as a result of using DNA to determine a plant's lineage.

For the more than four hundred years since its founding, the Hortus Botanicus of the University of Leiden has continued to be at the forefront of botanical research. Plant beds laid out by botanical order were added. An orangery for exotic plants was built in the eighteenth century; a library and laboratories followed. Albert Einstein served as a special visiting professor during the 1920s. Today the collection includes over ten thousand plants. The Naturalis Biodiversity Center highlights the importance of ecological diversity and educates the public as well as the university students about issues of sustainability.

Chelsea Physic Garden

London, England

Site selection is a crucial first step in designing a garden. Teaching about medicinal plants was the chief purpose of the Chelsea Physic Garden, dictating not only its design but its location. Founded by the Worshipful Society of Apothecaries, the garden was to be the training ground for future pharmacists, a required step if they were to be properly licensed.

The site chosen for the four-acre garden is on the Thames in the Chelsea area of London. In the seventeenth century it was not roads but the river that provided the primary means of transportation and communication for the city and beyond. Its warm microclimate fostered exotic plants that farther inland would have succumbed to the cold. In addition, the society's barge, which transported those on "herborizing" expeditions to nearby sites such as Battersea or Putney Heath, could be moored there alongside those of the chandlers, vintners, goldsmiths, and others, helping to establish by proximity the legitimacy of the new profession.

It was precious land in 1673, as it is today. The Great Fire in 1666 had left huge sections of London in waste so that good land, especially on the river, was in short supply. Chelsea was a fashionable area with its grand houses and important residents, remembered then and now for once being the home of Sir Thomas More. The Chelsea Physic Garden remains on its original site, accessible to local residents and visitors from around the world. Today many garden lovers who flock to Chelsea for the most famous of annual garden shows make the short walk to visit the Physic Garden.

Over the years the land would be coveted by many for a variety of purposes, but the garden's original patron, Sir Hans Sloane, outwitted them all through clever provisions in the deed of covenant ensuring the garden's survival through good times and bad. Sloane was a wealthy doctor, having studied medicine at the French University in Orange, then at the University of Montpellier in France, and eventually at the Royal College of Physicians in London. In 1687 he traveled to Jamaica as personal physician to the governor of the island, there pursuing his interest in plants and investing in quinine as a treatment for malaria, a disease prevalent in the marshy areas of Britain.

A wood engraving shows men botanizing in the Chelsea Physic Garden near the statue of Sir Hans Sloane in 1750.

A statue of Hans Sloane stands at the center of the Chelsea Physic Garden. Today half of the surrounding planting area is dedicated to systematic order beds, the monocots on one side and dicots on the other. The medicinal beds are arranged according to use, including, for example, neurology, rheumatology, anesthesia, analgesia, and dermatology. The cardiology bed displays khella (*Ammi visnaga,* also known as toothpick-plant or bishop's weed), from which two essential drugs are now synthesized: nifedepine to treat angina and high blood pressure and amiodarone used to stabilize heart rhythm. Included is a small paradise garden whose four beds focus on plants rich in vitamins A, B, C, and E.

Sloane's involvement was of benefit to the Apothecaries' Garden, as it was originally named, in another way. He was responsible for the appointment of Philip Miller as superintendent. A Scotsman, Miller was fortuitously given the position in 1722 as he was about to be evicted from the land occupied by his large nursery. At Chelsea he called on his international connections including that with Joseph Banks in Australasia and John Bartram in North America, thereby doubling in the years from 1722 to 1771 the number of plant species in Britain.

Among the plants Miller is credited with importing and describing is *Cedrus libani* (cedar of Lebanon), a favorite of English gardeners then and now. Miller also grew *Catharanthus*

TOP Hans Sloane dominates the Chelsea Physic Garden today as he did in life. The bed in the immediate foreground now features plants used in ophthalmology.

BOTTOM Teaching remains a primary purpose of the Chelsea Physic Garden.

roseus, an important medicinal plant now cropped as vincristine, an ingredient in chemotherapy treatment for blood cancers such as leukemia and lymphoma. Conversely, *Gossypium hirsutum* (long-stapled cotton) was sent by the Chelsea Physic Garden to the English colony of Georgia in America.

As he developed the Chelsea Physic Garden, Miller compiled his *Gardeners Dictionary*, describing plants, their cultivation, and uses. Translated into Dutch, German, and French, Miller's dictionary was among the most used and influential of the many horticultural books of the eighteenth century. He used a classification system based on vegetative characteristics, rejecting until the final eighth edition of the dictionary the Linnaean system based upon sexual characteristics. *The Gardeners Dictionary* was not illustrated, but Miller encouraged botanical artists, most famously Georg Dionysius Ehret, Jacobus van Huysum, and Mary Delaney. Miller was succeeded by William Forsyth, another Scotsman, who served until 1848, continuing to increase the holdings, name plants, and teach botany.

Teaching was the original purpose of the Chelsea Physic Garden. Today the garden carries on this purpose and tradition. The signage is exceptionally good, explaining clearly and in detail the plants and their use. Added beds highlight current topics such as restoration of land damaged by pollution, over-fertilization, climate change, or natural disaster. Here the visitor sees alpine pennycress (*Thlaspi caerulescens*) which removes zinc and cadmium from soil polluted by industry; sugarbeet (*Beta vulgaris*), which removes salt from sandy soil; and the sunflower (*Helianthus annuus*), shown after the Chernobyl nuclear disaster to remove radioactive strontium. The international seed exchange established by Philip Miller in the 1700s continues. Workshops and lectures are offered to the public. Carrying on the garden's nineteenth-century practice of training young women botanists, Chelsea Physic Garden's educational programs help today's teachers learn how to plant, sustain, and teach through school gardens.

John Bartram's garden shows the simplicity of his planting beds, laid out for utilitarian, not aesthetic, purposes.

Bartram's Garden

Philadelphia, Pennsylvania

Although John Bartram and Peter Collinson never met, they formed a friendship that lasted two-thirds of the eighteenth century. Bartram was a prosperous farmer in the Quaker colony of Pennsylvania, Collinson a London nurseryman. Separated by an ocean, they were bound together by two common loyalties. Both were Quakers and both were collectors of plants. Their exchange of seeds and plants would initiate a transformation of horticulture in Europe and in what would become the United States.

Just one hundred years after John Tradescant had disembarked at Jamestown, John Bartram purchased his 102-acre farm on the west bank of the Lower Schuylkill River. Near the house he laid out the garden in simple rectangular beds which he labeled "upper kitchen," "common flowers," and "new flowers." Two allées of tall trees marked a modest descent to

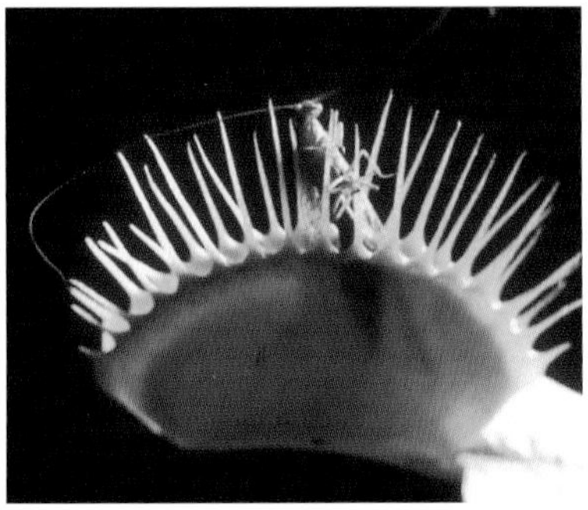

TOP The toothache tree is an example of the Doctrine of Signatures, a widely held belief that a plant's characteristics point to the part of the body it may be used to heal.

BOTTOM On his travels John Bartram discovered the carnivorous Venus flytrap, shown here with a lacewing entrapped.

the water. Here he began to indulge his passion for plants, first combing the nearby pine barrens for unusual and unknown plants, then returning with seedlings to his garden beds and to the fields surrounding his house. He was developing the first botanical garden in North America.

Soon he was traveling farther afield to Massachusetts and the Carolinas, then the New York Catskills, the Virginia Tidewater, and the Blue Ridge Mountains, directly observing and recording the natural environment of newly discovered plants. Within five years he was corresponding with Peter Collinson, sending seeds from North America in letters detailing the plants, their characteristics, and the growing conditions. As the primary supplier of plants to the great English estates, Collinson was well connected to the English gardening world. He read Bartram's letters to the influential Royal Society. Some were even published in the prestigious journal *Philosophical Transactions*. Through Collinson, John Bartram was recognized in England as a legitimate collector and scientific observer.

Bartram employed the Linnaean system of binomial nomenclature and classification that was just coming into use. But the confusion arising from common names continued. For example, *Aralia spinosa* and *Zanthoxylum americanum*, though unrelated, were both called prickly ash. Bartram distinguished the two, calling the aralia "devil's walking stick" and *Zanthoxylum americanum* "toothache tree." His insistence on clarity in identifying plants contributed to his reputation as horticulturist.

Bartram made one of his most delicious discoveries in the coastal marshes of South Carolina. He called the newly identified Venus flytrap "tipitiwitchet" and marveled at the way it lured insects with its sweet nectar, then trapped them with its miniature bear-trap, and slowly digested them. He sent this special treasure to Collinson, who in turn sent it to Linnaeus to be named and classified. Writing to thank Bartram, Collinson declared that Linnaeus would be in raptures for it seemed to be the link he sought between the plant and animal kingdoms.

Bartram's reputation grew both at home and abroad. He soon was known as one of America's intellectuals. He and Benjamin Franklin founded the highly regarded American Philosophical Society. In 1765, probably at the recommendation of Collinson, Bartram received a royal commission as king's botanist and in that capacity traveled to Florida searching for plants.

Flowering trees, rhododendrons, and mountain laurels were among the plants native to North America that he sent to Collinson in response to growing demand from the owners of the great English estates. With Collinson as middleman, Bartram also sent American native plants to Philip Miller at the Chelsea Physic Garden. Recognizing the extent of Bartram's collection, the University of Pennsylvania forwent establishing a demonstration garden of its own, instead using Bartram's garden for teaching purposes. George Washington had two boxes of plants and seeds sent to Mount Vernon from Bartram's nursery. Thomas Jefferson was a customer and advice-seeker. John Bartram and his garden established Philadelphia as the center for horticulture in the American colonies, a position it retains in the United States today.

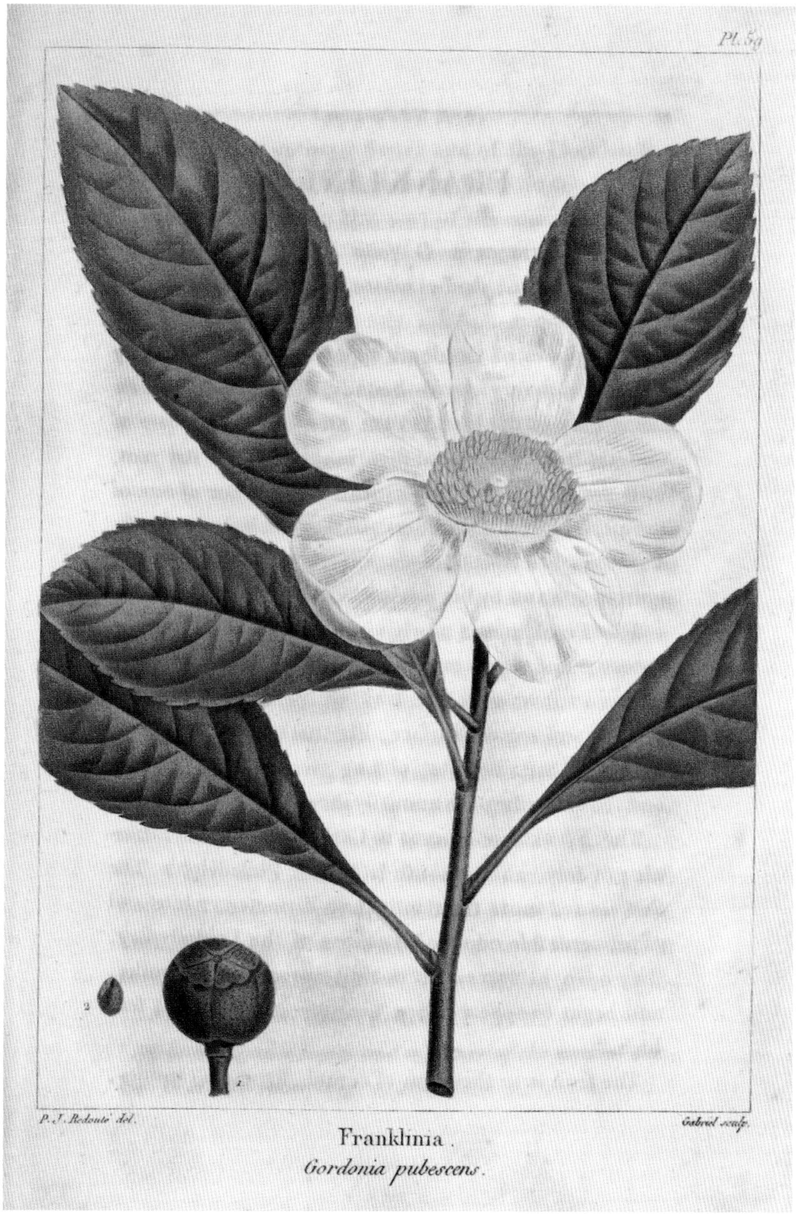

John Bartram's sons William and John found this rare and elegant tree in the colony of Georgia, naming it *Franklinia* for their father's dear friend, Benjamin Franklin. It has disappeared from the wild but grows in Bartram's garden in Philadelphia.

In 1777, when Franklin was American minister in France, he recommended that his friend send seeds to France, opening new lanes of commerce. When the first broadside appeared in 1783 listing Bartram plants for sale, it was printed in French as well as English. After John Bartram's death his sons William and John took over the collection and nursery business, receiving visitors from America and Europe, including James Madison, George Mason, and Alexander Hamilton when they were attending the Constitutional Convention in Philadelphia.

John Bartram made North America a player in the study of horticulture and botany, his scientific research standing alongside that of his counterparts in Padua, Leiden, Chelsea, and other European botanical gardens. Their collective work and the continued development of the botanical gardens changed horticulture, agriculture, medicine, and industry. Landscape design was transformed by the thousands of plants made available through the voyages of discovery and the botanical gardens that housed and studied them.

5 Augustan *and* Arcadian

Prosperity reigned, the classics were learned and used, and landscape design "lept the fence."

EARLY EIGHTEENTH CENTURY

BY 1700 PEACE had at last settled over England. The passions of the previous century gave way to reason and balance. Extreme convictions were eschewed; moderation was lauded. Although the Test Act made life miserable for those who refused to take the oath of allegiance to the Church of England, the theological base of the established church was broad enough to include most. Witch burnings were a thing of the past. The horrors of the Civil War, the beheading of King Charles I, and the harsh rule of Oliver Cromwell were, with political compromise, left behind. With the restoration of the monarchy, William and Mary now shared power with Parliament. People at all levels of society could now turn their attention to their homes, houses, gardens, and landscapes.

But within the tranquility and domesticity another kind of revolution was taking place. The new peace would transform accepted practice and enshrined convention in garden-making. By the end of the eighteenth century designed landscapes looked radically different, carrying a new message in England and Europe. The older geometric and symmetrical gardens were fewer, replaced by asymmetric designs. The enclosing walls were gone. Now incorporated were views of neighboring woods, fields, and water. Instead of gardens in which man clearly was in control, the new ideal would be "planned natural" or "designed natural," meant to seem as if nature herself were the designer.

Prosperity crowned the new peace. The empire was growing, thanks to the East India Company. The Dutch Empire was losing ground and now it was the British exploring the South Seas. India was paying handsome profits; the Americas showed potential. There was no doubt that now Britain ruled the seas. Many boldly imagined a British Empire as extensive as was that of Rome and they invested substantially in its promise.

> Prospect, animated prospect, is the theater that will always be the most frequented.
>
> —HORACE WALPOLE

The eighteenth-century English upper classes easily imagined a new Roman Empire because they were steeped in Roman history. The classics had always been central to secular education as it emerged in the sixteenth century, but now they became the mark of a new aristocratic and would-be aristocratic class. Formal and informal education focused on the Augustan Age of Latin

Temple of Fame, Studley Royal.

An Arcadian setting for the *Passage of Orpheus and Eurydice* by Nicolas Poussin.

literature. The curriculum of school, private tutor, and university demanded mastery of Latin and Greek, acquired by translating and memorizing passages from Virgil, Ovid, Cicero, Horace, Livy, and Homer among others. All who could afford to do so traveled to Italy to study the ancient sites for themselves, some staying for years.

At home, classical references were everywhere. Contemporary writers used metaphors drawn from classical stories. Frescoes painted on the walls and ceilings of the great houses told of the heroes of antiquity, especially and repeatedly the journey of Aeneas across the Mediterranean from Troy to what would be Rome. Friezes on the pediments of public buildings depicted the great battles of Roman myth and legend. Quotations from the Latin authors were incised in stone. Designed landscapes became a place to reinforce this shared body of knowledge so that the briefest reference in sculpture or garden-building called to mind whole epics and their meaning. So strong was the influence of classical history on the writers of eighteenth-century England that literature of the time was again called Augustan, evoking the analogy between the empire of ancient Rome and that of eighteenth-century Britain. All of this was to find its way into eighteenth-century gardens, a number now judged to be among England's greatest.

Artists and writers of the early eighteenth century also looked back to Greek history and to an idealistic bucolic vision. Begun in England a century or more earlier, it was called Arcadian after Arcady, the Greek province that continued a peaceful, rural existence while war raged between the great cities of Athens and Sparta. In England there was, for the most part, still concord on estates and in villages, concord that had its parallel in the accepted understanding of nature. The dangers of the countryside had disappeared with the felling of the medieval forests. Now people could look with pleasure over the tranquil hills with their clumps of majestic oak and beech, the gentle rivers, grazing sheep, placid cattle, neatly cultivated fields, sturdy farmers with ox and cart, pointed spire or square tower of parish church, and thatched or slate roofs of village houses. Obtaining a position at court was no longer the object of ambition, nor the city the place to be. It was the country that lured the powerful and wealthy.

Although as a Catholic, Poet Laureate John Dryden was unable to inherit property, in his writings he reinforced the value of country life. His translations into English not only of the *Aeneid* but also the *Eclogues* and *Georgics*, which describe and praise rural life, made these works of Virgil accessible to all. Dryden's translations inspired Alexander Pope, Horace Walpole, and many other poets and essayists of the eighteenth century to choose nature, gardening, and agriculture as their subjects. In many gardens the pastoral scene was "borrowed" and incorporated in designed landscapes.

Two greatly admired painters were Claude Lorrain and Nicolas Poussin. Both born in France at the end of the sixteenth century, they spent most of their careers in Italy where they studied classical mythology. The subjects of their paintings were Christian and classical, their settings often large pastoral landscapes with classical structures. Characterized by strong lines, their works bespeak order, logic, and clarity. Garden and landscape creators of early eighteenth-century England would use their paintings for inspiration and as models.

Literature, landscape design, and painting would be called Romantic by later critics and historians for idealizing and romanticizing nature, but the designed landscapes of early eighteenth-century Britain, reflecting as they do both classical antiquity and idyllic rural life, are best identified as Augustan and Arcadian.

Hadrian's Villa

Tivoli, Italy

As early eighteenth-century English boys and young men were studying Latin, they also were learning about Roman history, especially the century before and the two centuries after the birth of Christ. As they read their Cicero, Virgil, and Caesar's *Commentaries on the Gallic Wars*, they learned about the Roman emperors. In the reign of Hadrian, the third of the five "good" emperors, they must have seen the similarities and contrasts to their own country's history. Hadrian's reign was an era of peace that, like their own time, followed a century of violence. It was, like theirs, a time of law and at least relative justice.

But unlike eighteenth-century England where religious peace had been more or less achieved, the Roman Empire was in religious turmoil. The old Roman gods were dying. People no longer appealed to the oracles in the way they had in the past. Hundreds of cults arose, each promoting a new faith. Christianity in its early years was yet only one sect among many. Hadrian himself studied the stars and sought answers to the question of immortality in the Mysteries of Eleusis, which centered on the story of Persephone's spring return from Hades, spurring the renewal of her mother Demeter's earth. As emperor, Hadrian would himself be deified and become the object of worship for yet another cult.

Hadrian's vast villa in Tivoli (Villa Adriana in Italian) reflects his interests and his times and exhibits design features that would predominate in early eighteenth-century England as well. As the eighteenth-century English had embraced the Augustan Age of Latin literature, so landscape designers used principles and features of Roman villas.

First as military commander and then as emperor, Hadrian traveled the length and breadth of the Roman Empire. A first-rate administrator, he understood the need to stabilize and strengthen the empire and so took with him on his travels an army not only of soldiers but also of architects, engineers, and masons. They rebuilt London after a great fire and

At Villa Adriana a column with Ionic capital stands in front of a wall of bricks set in concrete.

constructed Hadrian's Wall close to what is now the border between England and Scotland to mark the northernmost extent of the Roman Empire.

Hadrian chose for his own estate the valley below Tibur, now known as Tivoli, about twenty miles from Rome. It was to serve as his retreat from the pressures of the city. Strategically placed around his eight-square-mile Arcadian landscape were temples, pavilions, a belvedere, and shrines, all located to take advantage of views of the landscape and the night skies. His architects and engineers, using concrete and bricks, made domes, arches, exedra, and colonnades with Greek columns topped by Doric, Ionic, and Corinthian capitals. The Pantheon in Rome, rebuilt in Hadrian's reign, boasts the largest unsupported concrete dome in the world. Hadrian had the form repeated at his villa in the High Baths with a large circular opening in the top to let in light, just as in the Pantheon in Rome. In the seventeenth century Nicolas Poussin and Claude Lorrain were to capture such buildings in their paintings of the Italian landscape, buildings later replicated or adapted in the great estate landscapes of early eighteenth-century England.

ABOVE The Maritime Theater in Hadrian's time may have featured a planetarium-like ceiling for the emperor to study the movement of the stars.

RIGHT Mosaics adorn later Moorish, Renaissance, and English landscape design, but none more finely wrought than those of ancient Rome, seen here at Hadrian's villa.

Today only a few columns and statues surround the Canopus.

For Hadrian's villa, the key to comfort in the hot valley was cooling water brought by aqueducts and then piped underground to the villa from the River Aniene. In addition to the baths, there were numerous *nymphaea*—grottoes, caves, fountains, pools, cascades, and other landscape features centering on water—named after the legendary Greek maidens who inhabited springs and streams.

Perhaps the most famous feature of Hadrian's villa is the Maritime Theater with a center island surrounded by a moat. Only a small wooden drawbridge provided passage to the island rooms surrounding the small courtyard. Interrupting the emperor at leisure within the walls was not to be easy. Archaeologist Salvatore Aurigemma wrote in 1962:

> The Maritime Theater is also called the Theater of the Universe, the Royal Hall for the worship of the Emperor, island of Earthly Paradise. There were plant groups so as to form a thicket, fish in the water and sparrows in the sky. There were elements of trabeation [beams and lintels] above the fluted columns with friezes adorned with sea monsters, tritons, *nereids*, and chariots driven by various birds and animals led by genii.

The crocodile fountain establishes that Hadrian's Canopus was inspired by that at the Nile.

World traveler that he was, Hadrian brought mementos from his journeys to his villa, the last encampment of his nomadic life. Sculpture from the reaches of the empire adorned his views; marbles and stones from Africa and the Orient found their way into decoration at his villa. He was sometimes criticized for his admiration of the Barbarians, but like garden designers in the eighteenth century and ever since, he insisted on incorporating his souvenirs from far-off lands into his villa buildings and landscape.

Classical sculpture placed throughout the grounds was a design feature that would characterize early eighteenth-century English landscapes. Many of the pieces at Hadrian's villa were, during the Renaissance, purloined by designer Pirro Ligorio and owner Cardinal Ippolito for the Villa d'Este built on the nearby mountain. Other pieces have found their way to museums and private collections around the world, leaving little at Hadrian's villa today.

The Canopus stirs poignancy, as it recalls the great sadness of Hadrian's life. The original is a canal at the entrance to the Nile connecting Alexandria and Abukir and renowned in antiquity for its magnificence. Emperor Hadrian had visited Egypt in AD 121 and, returning to his villa, built his Canopus surrounded by classical sculpture. Nine years later he returned to Egypt, this time accompanied by Antinous, his "beloved" youth, who drowned in the Nile. Hadrian's grief was intense. For consolation, he erected likenesses in stone of the beautiful young man, to be reflected in the waters of the Canopus as if he were Narcissus. Hadrian declared Antinous a god, and temples for his worship were erected around the Roman world. His story—the tragedy of youth, beauty, love, and death—was told and retold, eventually making its way into eighteenth-century English gardens.

Castle Howard

Yorkshire, England

Castle Howard, with elements of past and future landscape design, stands as a link between enclosed gardens and those of open spaces, and between the geometric and the new planned natural. Older formal gardens lie within a large, parklike setting, and within the asymmetrical landscape are garden buildings that act not as focal points but rather as places for viewing the property.

The designer John Vanbrugh lacked neither nerve nor imagination. In his young life he had been an employee of the East India Company stationed at the trading post in Gujarat, then soldier, spy, prisoner in the Bastille, and radical, promoting as undercover agent the armed invasion by William of Orange to depose James II. When he was in his mid-thirties, his first play was produced, launching an active career as set designer, theater manager, and author of witty and risqué plays. At first acclaimed and popular, his plays were increasingly

LEFT In a portrait attributed to Sir Godfrey Kneller, is the smug Vanbrugh writing a play or planning a garden? Jonathan Swift quipped about Vanbrugh's lack of design training, "Van's genius, without thought or lecture, Is hugely turn'd to architecture."

RIGHT The central dome of Castle Howard is reminiscent of Vaux-le-Vicomte. Fortress-like hedges make the castle look invulnerable, and despite fire and other disasters it has been home to eleven generations of Howards.

criticized by the conservative social establishment for advocating the rights of women in marriage. Then, in 1699, with no training as architect, he accepted the commission to design Castle Howard, which would become one of England's greatest estates.

As unlikely as was Vanbrugh's appointment as architect was the setting where the project was conceived. Fountain Tavern in London was the meeting place of the Kit-Cat Club, ostensibly a gathering of wits for dining, drinking, and conversation. More seriously, the club, made up of Whig politicians and intellectuals, promoted through its membership the rights of Parliament, limitations on the power of the monarchy, and Protestant succession to the English throne. Among the members were such luminaries as playwright William Congreve; essayist Joseph Addison; Sir Robert Walpole who was to become Britain's first prime minister; Charles Howard, third Earl of Carlisle; and his distant relative John Vanbrugh. By the end of a convivial evening at the club, Charles Howard had agreed that Vanbrugh should be the one to design his new castle.

Charles Howard had inherited the vast tract of land near York on which a medieval castle once stood. But by 1700 when construction of Castle Howard began, the old castle lay in ruins. Both Howard and Vanbrugh had made an extended tour of Italy including Vicenza, location of the architect Andrea Palladio, but the style they chose for the house was English Baroque. Though not trained, Vanbrugh was meticulous and he was ably assisted by architect Nicholas Hawksmoor. Breaking with tradition, Vanbrugh sited Castle Howard on a north-south axis, making every bedroom south-facing.

When Vanbrugh came to the garden design his lack of training may have served him well. He appears to have been free from conventional conceptions, just as he was in the plays

Italian Andrea Palladio, 1508–1580, is generally considered the most influential architect in English history. Popular briefly in the seventeenth century, the Palladian style returned to prominence in the eighteenth century not only in England but Prussia, other parts of Europe, and in the Americas, notably at Thomas Jefferson's home, Monticello. Based on the symmetry and proportions of Greek and Roman classical temples, the style features pediments, gables in the form of a triangle often supported by columns. It was widely used until the twentieth century for public buildings.

TOP The Pyramid Gate and walls suggest enclosure as in a medieval castle without actually encircling.

BOTTOM Wray Wood lies close to Castle Howard like forest plantations at Vaux-le-Vicomte.

OPPOSITE, TOP Architect Nicholas Hawksmoor argued for a small, Gothic structure but Vanbrugh's Roman-inspired design won the day for the family mausoleum atop a hill overlooking the Palladian bridge.

he wrote. The effect of his design is that of an oversized stage-set with scenes to enliven the imagination and create a mood, anticipating gardens to come. A former soldier himself and perhaps thinking of the medieval castle that once stood nearby, he introduced a number of military images, including massive, bastion-like, trimmed yew hedges in front of the house and the Pyramid Gate, or entrance, with crenellated walls.

ABOVE The twists and turns within the wood end in intriguing, elegant, or mysterious objects just as do the *bosquets* at Versailles.

Earlier, Lord Howard had determined to keep intact Wray Wood, a plantation of mature beech trees on the east side of the house. Straight avenues had been proposed, to be cut through the forest as at other English estates, one design calling for an enormous star of carriage roads. The earl rejected these ideas, directing instead labyrinthine gravel paths to wind and twist through the trees, each leading eventually to an urn, seat, fountain, cascade, statue, or summer house. The charm and innovation of this approach was lauded by contemporary visitors and later identified by historians as an early break with the geometric tradition of landscape design. But Vanbrugh's crenellated wall almost surrounding the wood rather like a medieval hunting park militated against the effect.

Perhaps remembering his travels in Italy, Vanbrugh designed and placed dramatic garden buildings where, as at Hadrian's villa, the visitor was meant to take in the dramatic views of

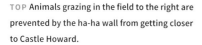

TOP Animals grazing in the field to the right are prevented by the ha-ha wall from getting closer to Castle Howard.

BOTTOM So unseen is the line of the ha-ha that today grasses are allowed to grow tall at its edge, a warning to hikers of the dangerous ditch.

the countryside. One such building, the Italianate mausoleum, moved Horace Walpole to declare that it "would tempt one to be buried alive!"

A key feature countering Vanbrugh's enclosing walls is the invisible fence that allows an unbroken view while keeping animals confined. Horace Walpole credited highly regarded landscape designer Charles Bridgeman with its invention, but it had a medieval predecessor. The French deer leap or leapy deepy encouraged deer to mount a ramp constructed in a ditch and then leap the fence that sat atop the ramp. Once inside the hunting park they were not able to jump back out. Called a ha-ha, the Bridgeman invisible fence was a new way to solve the problem of grazing animals wandering up to the house. Walls had previously kept them away. Now the open landscape provided no barrier to their joining house guests, even putting their heads in the dining room windows. The introduction of sash windows, the perfect complement to popular Palladian architecture, exacerbated the problem. Previously, casement windows left partially open acted as a deterrent.

The ha-ha proved an ingenious solution. A ditch is dug with a gentle slope on one side and a vertical retaining wall on the house side of the property. When cows or sheep come to the wall and can go no farther, they retreat to their grazing field. The land leading to

OPPOSITE Spinario, seen here at Castle Howard, was a popular subject for sculpture in eighteenth-century England, the epitome of the classical hero. The legend held that "the boy pulling the thorn" had run from Sparta to Athens with the thorn in his foot so as not to lose time warning the Athenians that the Spartan army was on the march.

the ha-ha on either side is a level plane so that from a distance the grassy sward appears unbroken. The ha-ha at Castle Howard, thought to be one of the earliest in England, points the way to the Arcadian vistas and to later landscape park design. William Kent, Capability Brown, other eighteenth-century English landscape designers, and in America, President George Washington made use of the ha-ha.

One question remains: is there an identifiable iconography at Castle Howard as there had been in many Italian Renaissance and French Baroque gardens and would be in later eighteenth-century English landscapes? In Wray Wood one can see themes of mythological rusticity—Apollo, Bacchus, Venus, Diana, a satyr ravishing a nymph, and a shepherd with his dog, all painted white. The experiences of both Charles Howard and John Vanbrugh in Italy and the constant use of classical literary allusions in eighteenth-century England suggest there might be a larger program that governed the whole layout of Castle Howard. One suggestion is that the plan bears a striking resemblance to the map of Troy, encircled by walls with fields and Grecian camp beyond, that appeared in Alexander Pope's 1716 translation of the *Iliad*. As compelling is the argument that Charles Howard simply purchased the best of what was available including pieces by renowned garden sculptors John Cheere, Andrew Carpenter, and John van Nost. In either event, Howard and Vanbrugh set the stage for other Arcadian and Augustan gardens to come.

Studley Royal

Yorkshire, England

One could accurately call Studley Royal a transition landscape but to do so would diminish its reputation as the most beautiful water garden in England. It weds design principles of the older, geometric French style with the new concept of planned natural just coming into fashion in England, creating a work of art that conveys a remarkable sense of both peacefulness and freedom.

No one needed peace and freedom more than did John Aislabie, creator of the garden at Studley Royal. He should have returned home from his political career a distinguished statesman. Instead he returned exiled, disgraced, and humiliated. Aislabie had inherited the property near York as a boy, but his demanding life in London at the beginning of the eighteenth century kept him away as he served as member of Parliament from Ripon, treasurer of the Navy, and finally chancellor of the exchequer. In the last position he promoted the South Seas Company proposal to take over the national debt through the sale of bonds, personally shepherding the bill through the House of Commons. Even when it was clear to knowledgeable insiders that the scheme was failing, Aislabie encouraged new investors.

Then, in 1720, the South Sea Bubble burst. An investigation by Parliament showed Aislabie had profited from his deception. He resigned the exchequer and was found guilty by Parliament of "the most notorious, dangerous, and infamous corruption." Expelled from the House of Commons, removed from the Privy Council, and disqualified from

ABOVE Beginning in the twelfth century, Cistercian monks and lay brothers tended sheep in the valley, made wool, and mined lead, making Fountains Abbey rich and respected.

OPPOSITE, TOP The River Skell bends sharply as it wends its way from Fountains Abbey to Aislabie's water garden.

OPPOSITE, BOTTOM LEFT On a rise at the edge of the full-moon pond, the Temple of Piety is reflected in the water, its straight lines contrasting with the graceful curves of Bacchus.

OPPOSITE, BOTTOM RIGHT In the adjacent hills Aislabie provided places for viewing the geometry of the moon ponds from above.

public office for life, he served time in the Tower of London. Upon his release he returned home ruined, all hopes dashed for his once-promising future. Licking his wounds, he pursued his interest in landscape design, pioneering a new form, finally to be remembered by history as much for creating the most elegant of gardens, now a World Heritage Site, as for his role in the Ponzi scheme.

Studley Royal lies in a unique valley. Looking in one direction one sees the majestic medieval Ripon Cathedral, in the opposite direction the remains of Fountains Abbey, once the largest monastery in England. With the dissolution of the monasteries between 1536 and 1541, the abbey was vacated and over the next three hundred years became but a romantic ruin. John Aislabie was to take full advantage of these views, his son William actually buying Fountains Abbey.

The valley is created by the little River Skell that curves dramatically not far from the abbey. On the sloping hills that rise above the river's natural channel Aislabie planted trees, not as a straight allée but to appear as if they had seeded themselves. Perhaps he had learned this from Queen Anne's gardeners, Henry Wise and George London, who used both large stretches of water and forest plantations. Aislabie included conifers, making the garden as attractive in winter as in summer. These forests form a kind of enclosure,

but different from the rigid stone walls that once enclosed Fountains Abbey, showing his imaginative adaptation of an older design concept.

The river itself straightens and then is channeled as it nears the heart of the garden at Studley Royal. Known as the moon ponds, the water garden is two crescents hugging a circular pond. They are pure geometry in the tradition of André Le Nôtre's gardens in France and Daniel Marot's at Het Loo, but unlike these gardens there is no central axis, no radiating goosefoot carriage roads, and no parterres. Again, Aislabie's achievement stands with that of other great landscape designers in transforming an older design principle into a new look, this one elegant and stately in its simplicity.

A wide ring of turf sloping slightly and gently downward to the water level forms a frame around the ponds. No plants are allowed to grow at the water's edge, a landscape feature that would be adopted in later eighteenth-century gardens. On the edge of the full-moon pond, at right angles to the river and in line with the garden's center, is the classic Temple of Piety. The finishing touch at Studley Royal is its exquisite sculpture all carefully sited so as not to be crowded, overdone, or ostentatious. All but the stone statue of Hercules and Antaeus are made of lead, recalling the work of the Fountains Abbey monks. Neptune with trident commands from the center of the circular moon pond. Bacchus graces a crescent; his counterpart, Galen, has now disappeared. Another lost sculpture is the *Dying Gladiator*, a popular subject in eighteenth-century art and one with whom Aislabie, the defeated statesman, must have felt a special affinity.

The design of Studley Royal, combining the older geometric lines of the moon ponds, the new designed natural of an Arcadian forest, classical architecture, and elegant sculpture, conveys a rare purity. We can only wonder how a man who had been deceptive in public and financial life could create such a garden. Is it because a garden is itself an illusion, a deceit? Or perhaps the act of creating the garden that would contribute to the change in landscape design was transforming for John Aislabie himself.

Rousham
Oxfordshire, England

Artists sometimes say that in the act of creation their work takes on a life of its own, and conversely those who read, listen, or look often see something not consciously put there by the creator. Because he left no extant notes, it is not possible to know just what William Kent had in mind when he designed the landscape at Rousham, but three pieces of evidence suggest his intent to present not just classical scenes but a narrative. He spent ten years in Italy studying the art of ancient Rome and of the Italian Renaissance and buying antique pieces for his patron Lord Burlington. As a painter he often used as subject scenes from classical mythology and literature. And, importantly, he set out a route so that the scenes at Rousham unfold for the visitor in a prescribed sequence as in a story.

ABOVE William Aikman's portrait of William Kent.

TOP, RIGHT The sculpture is the work of Peter Scheemakers, one of England's foremost eighteenth-century sculptors. A similar sculpture in the Rometta at the Villa d'Este also refers to the founding of Rome. Beyond on the hill, the eyecatcher beckons.

BOTTOM, RIGHT Laurels planted by Kent serve as understory to the trees, darkening the scene and deepening the sense of mystery.

Many gardens tell stories that are understood only if the visitor is familiar with the references, just as to understand stained glass in medieval churches the viewer must know the Bible stories to which the images allude. Most of today's visitors at Rousham, not being classically trained as were eighteenth-century visitors, may not appreciate fully the story being told.

But modern visitors following Kent's sequence at Rousham may be aided by a wonderful book first published in 1949: *A Hero with a Thousand Faces* by mythology scholar Joseph

Campbell. Campbell describes the monomyth, a story told and retold in cultures around the world from time immemorial to the present. While the storyline has many variations, its basic plot tells of a person who leaves the security of home to venture into the world, there to make discoveries and meet new challenges, and then to return home a changed person. It is the story of great religious leaders and the outline of countless fairy tales and legends from Virgil's *Aeneid* to *Star Wars*. Campbell says it is also every person's story because it is a metaphor for the process of growing from childhood to adulthood, from dependence to autonomy. Further, it is not a story we live but once. Rather it is repeated each time we have a new and life-changing experience if we but remember Socrates' admonition that the unexamined life is not worth living. A journey through the landscape at Rousham may serve, as does a labyrinth, as a means of personal and spiritual reflection.

At Rousham, the road to new adventures, new insights, and a changed identity begins at the house's veranda. The very design of the garden was to give the eighteenth century a new identity. Gone were the geometric lines and protective walls. As in other arenas of eighteenth-century life, a new openness and new perspectives were expressed in garden

CLOCKWISE FROM TOP LEFT

The early Roman copy of the lost Greek sculpture known as *Dying Gaul* or *Dying Gladiator* was discovered in 1623 and soon became a popular subject for garden sculpture.

Pan presides over his garden and woods.

Stone swans recall Zeus who, disguised as a swan, seduced Leda, queen of Sparta and mother of Helen of Troy. Will the seductive scene here keep the hero from pursuing his quest?

design. William Kent declared that "all nature is a garden," and garden commentator Horace Walpole wrote that Kent "lept the fence."

Stepping out onto the veranda from the house, the would-be hero views the long bowling green and commanding sculpture at its end. His eye is then drawn across the River Cherwell and up the hill beyond to the "eyecatcher." Designed and placed by Kent, it appears to be a ruined medieval building, awakening the viewer's curiosity, a herald calling him to venture forth. Striding across the bowling green, our hero comes first to the sculpture of horse and lion locked in mortal combat, a reference to the founding of Rome. It is the first suggestion that the journey will have challenges and dangers but also holds the promise of monumental consequences.

Despite any misgivings he may have, the young hero is drawn forward. Turning left as Kent directed, he at first strolls by the peaceful and pastoral scene of cattle grazing in fields adjacent to the path. He turns toward the field, only to find his passage halted by a ha-ha. Is the message that there are unattainable pleasures or that danger may be just out of sight? Should he go forward or turn back to the comfort and security of home? The house is no longer visible. He has made the separation. Hesitating but briefly, our hero turns left, entering the woods. The unknown lies ahead.

After a short walk, he emerges into a clearing. The path he has been following is high above and parallel to the River Cherwell on his right. He comes to a clearing and there finds a balustrade from which he views the river's bend below. He pauses, too, before the *Dying Gladiator* reminding him that not all heroes are successful, not all return home.

Continuing through the woods, the hero enters, as Kent directed, at the top of the astonishing Vale of Venus. He looks on the goddess from behind, to the octagonal pool below, and to the river beyond. He is glad he came on this journey, for, after all, what could be more exciting to a young man than the body of a beautiful woman? He lingers, wondering if he should make this the end of his adventure, remaining forever in this oh-so-pleasing place.

On a lower level than Venus, Pan, the god of nature, presides over his domain. As the hero descends he is suddenly aware that he is being watched. From the bordering yews opposite Pan, a faun—forest creature half man, half goat—looks the hero's way with a wickedly amused and enigmatic smile. Is he friend or foe?

Our adventurer passes behind Venus and turns down the hill toward the octagon pool, passing Venus on his right. But halfway down the slope, on his left he notices a rill, serving in the design as a small river. From time immemorial travelers have used the progress of water in streams and rivers to guide their path. Our hero turns left to follow the rill though the dark woods until he comes to the Cold Bath. Eerie, mysterious, not a little frightening, and certainly unpleasant, it brings him back to reality after the ecstasy of his fascination with Venus.

Continuing, the traveler enters a shaded arbor, with light at the end silhouetting a figure. He welcomes the idea of another person, for every hero's journey includes mentors, guides, and guardian spirits. He will seek advice about his journey and enjoy companionship. He shouts a greeting and extends his hand, only to find as he gets closer that the figure is facing away from him. He is intrigued. Who is the figure and what is he looking toward? Some

TOP, LEFT Sculpted by John van Nost and placed opposite Pan, the faun startles the visitor who, descending the vale on the far side of Venus, sees him watching from the hedge.

TOP, RIGHT William Kent set this uninviting Cold Bath in the deep woods.

RIGHT Antinous looks not backward toward the hiker but forward.

writers have called him Apollo, but more convincing is the case made by scholar Michael Symes who identifies him as the beautiful Antinous, the youth beloved by Emperor Hadrian. Like Hadrian, our hero need not travel alone.

From Antinous the path leads to the Temple of Echo where the sojourner pauses, contemplating and finally voicing his thoughts and questions as to the meaning of his odyssey.

TOP Rivers have been the symbol of a life journey in countless legends. Bridges lead to new lands and new opportunities. The Heyford Bridge is shown beautifully here.

BOTTOM Brought together here are Eros and Philia, Venus and man's best friend. Woman and dog: both may serve as guardian spirit.

His utterances echo across the valley and return recognizable but altered, reminding him that he is the same person who began his journey but also now changed. He makes his way downhill to the River Cherwell which he has seen as a barrier keeping him from his goal. Now, looking upstream, he sees Heyford Bridge which will open the larger world to him, literally and metaphorically. He crosses and climbs the hill to the eyecatcher.

Mission accomplished, the hero retraces his steps across the bridge, follows the riverside path, and, as Kent directed, turns toward home. Now he finds himself looking upward to the Vale of Venus with its cascades and its small, marble tablet in the upper cascade wall—to a friend, this one the "faithfull Ringwood, an otterhound." He has circled around and sees love from a different perspective. No furtive glances now, an adult, he is emboldened to look on Venus directly.

To his astonishment, just beyond the Vale of Venus is a replica of the Praeneste, the forecourt of the Temple of Fortuna in Italy where ancient Romans sought oracles to learn their fate. The hero's story reaches a climax for here he will discover the boon. His journey and reflections reveal precious knowledge about his future and the good that he, like Prometheus carrying the torch, will bring back for the good of others.

But there is something more. Atop the Praeneste is the disquieting image of the *Dying Gladiator* and the balustrade from which early in his journey the hero had looked out over the river to the fields and hills beyond. He has come a long way, encountered challenges, but persisted. His landscape journey has been about gaining new perspectives, finally seeing clearly what was before but dimly perceived. Perhaps Kent, in hiding and then revealing the gateway to the Temple of Fortune, was recalling his own long sojourn in Italy that changed his perspective and fortune.

Next the hero pauses in the amphitheater formed at the bank of the river. Mercury, made of lead, delivers his message. Bacchus and Ceres allude to prosperity. The sacred journey is almost complete. Our hero climbs a final hill, conquering the last obstacle. Home is now in reach. Joseph Campbell reassuringly reminds us, "Each who has dared to harken to and follow the secret call has known the perils of the dangerous, solitary transit. . . . We have not . . . to risk the adventure alone; for the heroes of all time have gone before us. . . .Where we have thought to be alone, we shall be with all the world."

RIGHT Kent's placement of the Praeneste is praised as a clever use of limited space, but it also reminds those following the Rousham path that through the journey of life we come to understand what was previously hidden.

BELOW Up the steep slope and across the bowling green to the house, our young hero returns home changed. He is now a man.

Claude Lorrain's painting *Landscape with Aeneas at Delos* combines the open, Arcadian countryside with classical structures.

Stourhead

Wiltshire, England

The pioneering landscape design introduced by John Aislabie and William Kent offered new perspectives by extending the view and using asymmetrical and curving lines. At Stourhead, Henry Hoare set Augustan Age literary images and references to English history in a planned natural, parklike setting. In so doing he created a means to contemplate and indeed anticipate England's future. His contemporaries and future visitors have declared Stourhead to be one of the most engaging of European gardens.

He was just beginning what was to be a highly successful career as banker and financier when, at only twenty years of age, he inherited the Wiltshire property from his father. Three years of travel in Italy stimulated his interest in painting and he began collecting the works of Nicolas Poussin, Gaspard Dughet, and Claude Lorrain, whose *Landscape with Aeneas at Delos* would serve as model for the primary scene at Stourhead.

His design revolves around a planned natural lake two miles long and covering twenty acres, created by damming the River Stour where two valleys converge. On the hills surrounding the lake, following Alexander Pope's advice to plant trees "in large masses as shades are in a painting," Hoare used firs and beeches for color contrast. The skyline thus created makes the slopes seem even steeper. The trees are grouped in such a way that the landscape is not seen all at once but as a series of pictures. As in the paintings he collected and admired, Hoare placed at lakeside or in the hills various structures, each serving as focus for a view.

While the landscape plan appears to adhere to the new design principle of asymmetry, in fact there are two cross-axes across the lake that point to the two interwoven themes of the garden: the events leading to the founding of the Roman Empire as recounted in Virgil's *Aeneid* and Britain's growth as nation and empire.

At the western end of the east-west axis is the primary focal point at Stourhead, a replica of the Pantheon in Rome designed by architect Henry Flitcroft. Sitting on a hill above the

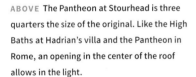

lake where it is reflected in the water, it is beautifully sited with a Romanesque bridge in the foreground. Nearby the Gothic Cottage associates by proximity the Roman and British Empires.

At the eastern end of the lake, the village of Stourton and the parish church with its square tower are incorporated in the scene as if to say that the bedrock of the British Empire lies in its small villages. Hoare was delighted with this view, likening it to a Gaspard Dughet painting. In the foreground of the "painting" and as a final touch, he placed the High Cross which he acquired in 1780. For four centuries it had dominated the market square in Bristol at the crossroads in the center of town. The base of the cross is four octagonal piers with ogee arches. Above are two tiers with alcoves containing the statues of English monarchs, the top a pinnacle and cross. Views from the hills above the lake juxtapose the Pantheon and the High Cross, the classical and the Gothic, Rome and Britain.

ABOVE The Pantheon at Stourhead is three quarters the size of the original. Like the High Baths at Hadrian's villa and the Pantheon in Rome, an opening in the center of the roof allows in the light.

ABOVE, RIGHT Henry Hoare's grandson Richard Colt Hoare inherited Stourhead. He added the leaded and arched windows to make the cottage appear more Gothic.

The north-south axis across the lake contrasts with the historical references of the east-west axis. It uses the *Aeneid* as an allegory for the storms that rock and endanger a nation, of the intervention of a calming force, and of peace earnestly sought. On the south side, the Temple of Apollo recognizes the god whose vengeful actions led to the Trojan War. Across the lake there once arose from the waters a sculpture of Neptune with his four horses that were, according to Hoare "very fine and full of spirit," recalling the opening scene of the *Aeneid* in which Neptune quells a great storm.

The grotto, a much-celebrated feature of Stourhead, lies in a straight line across the lake on its north side. While some eighteenth-century gardens included grottoes for lighthearted amusement, at Stourhead the grotto contributes to the iconography and is meant to be taken seriously. Approaching from the walking path requires a hike down the steep hill where plantings increasingly hide the surrounding views so that upon arrival the visitor, undistracted, feels fully the cool and calm. Words from Book I of the *Aeneid* are inscribed above the grotto entrance: "Inside are sweet waters and seats of living rock—the house of nymphs."

LEFT In 1773, the town fathers of Bristol, believing that with increased pedestrian traffic and horse-drawn vehicles the medieval market cross posed a danger, had it taken down. Eventually it was given to Henry Hoare who placed it, as seen here, at Stourhead.

RIGHT The view to the other side of the lake from the Temple of Apollo once included Neptune and his horses, now sadly disappeared, no one knows how or why.

Two figures convey the grotto's message. The River God is a replica of the sculpture of the god of the Tiber who pointed Aeneas in the direction of Rome. The Reclining Nymph invites repose, a message reinforced by the couplets of Alexander Pope inscribed at her base:

> Nymph of the Grot, these sacred springs I keep
> And to the murmur of these waters sleep.
> Ah, spare my slumbers, gently tread the cave
> And drink in silence or, in silence, lave.

Other structures reinforce the message. The Temple of Flora with its Latin inscription "Keep away, anyone profane, keep away" is the first building on the counterclockwise, circuitous route. Saint Peter's Pump covers the springs that feed the river. King Alfred's Tower, with its commanding view of the countryside, pays tribute to Alfred the Great, the Wessex king who defeated the Danes in a decisive battle near the tower's location.

The created topography of Stourhead, including the lake and plantations, is in the new planned natural style. The garden buildings and sculpture follow the older rules of garden design with their straight axes that end in focal points, although visitors often miss the axes since they cross the water of the lake. In bringing together the old and the new, Henry Hoare created a landscape that is intellectually cohesive and aesthetically satisfying. The planting of hills around the irregular lake together with the architecture and positioning of the structures create pictures worthy of the painters Hoare admired and collected. In Stourhead, he seems to have followed Apollo's command to Aeneas: "You must prepare great walls for a great race."

TOP LEFT The all-but-hidden entrance to the grotto emphasizes its separation from the world around.

TOP RIGHT The River God is the work of John Cheere, a well-known eighteenth-century sculptor.

RIGHT Fresh springs flow on either side of the Reclining Nymph, a copy of an antique statue of Ariadne acquired by the Vatican in the sixteenth century.

6 Place-Making

Extended democracy and extended views: Capability Brown's "planned natural" reverberates beyond Britain.

EIGHTEENTH CENTURY

WHEN WAR ENDS, people turn their attention to home. So it was in England early in the eighteenth century. True, there were still vexing political issues at home, but by 1714 the War of the Spanish Succession was settled and people were able to concentrate on family, home, and local community. Peace brought affluence. Sugar, shipping, finance, government office, and African slaves all contributed to burgeoning fortunes. New money was poured into the building of country houses and the designed landscapes around them. The English called it place-making.

There were incentives to direct energy and resources to country estates. The Civil War, the Protectorate, the Restoration, and the Glorious Revolution of the previous century had greatly strengthened the power of Parliament. Throughout the eighteenth and nineteenth centuries one had to be a landowner to vote in county elections. It was the landed gentry—those able to live off the income from their tenant farmers—who got to the House of Commons, and the elected tended to be those with the largest estate in the district. So powerful did some families become that the local seat in Parliament went from father to son and then to future heirs. Money all too frequently changed hands to make this possible. Place-making was about the landscape, but it was also about making a place for oneself and family in the social, economic, and political structure.

Upward mobility was possible because the lines between classes were porous. Money was crucial, though one also had to be decently mannered and spoken. The Test Act required membership in the Church of England. It helped to be at ease with classical languages and literature and to have traveled, especially in Italy. A family history of violence or gambling could act as a stumbling block, though not unconquerable. Marriage into a titled or moneyed family was the quickest way to improve one's standing. By 1813 Jane Austen would memorably describe this road to power and success in her opening sentence of *Pride and Prejudice*: "It is a truth universally acknowledged that a single man in possession of a good fortune must be in want of a wife." Of course, it worked both ways and there were landscape designers and landowners who profited by "good" marriages.

> Art should never be allowed to set foot in the province of nature, other than clandestinely and by night.
>
> —WILLIAM SHENSTONE

The intersection between literal place-making one's house and grounds and the metaphorical one of making a place for oneself and family in the social hierarchy is the house itself. Whether a Castle Howard on thousands of acres

Lake and lawn, Blenheim Palace.

In his 1748 painting *Mr. and Mrs. Andrews*, Thomas Gainsborough captured the landed gentry complete with gun, hunting dog, ha-ha, and the necessary land.

or a modest estate on only a few, the house became the symbol and measure of position. The larger and more impressive the house, the greater the esteem in which the owner was held. Artists were commissioned to paint the great houses in the most flattering light, just as they did in portraits of people. These house portraits were hung on a prominent wall of the grand staircase next to the family's dowager duchess or military-hero great grandfather. The dramatic action of novel upon novel and now television series revolves around the efforts of the descendants of these eighteenth-century estate owners to hold on to house and land, essential because they give identity, status, power, and place.

The gardens and landscape around these great houses needed a designer who could create the most impressive setting for them. He was there, ready, willing, and able. If ever there was the right man in the right place at the right time it was Capability Brown. So successfully did he ride the crest of the wave in landscape design in the second half of the eighteenth century that he is recognized as the most important landscape designer in English history. Receiving commissions for at least 170 estate gardens and landscapes during his career, he left a style that has been copied and adapted around the globe for public parks and private estates to the present day.

He was born in 1716 in a small Northumberland village and, at his christening in the parish church, named Lancelot after his grandfather. The family were landowning farmers—yeoman farmers—who had been in the area for generations. He attended local schools and then at age sixteen went to work as gardener at the estate of the principal landowner in the area. He had no more formal education, nor did he travel in Italy.

Soon opportunities began to open for him, first nearby and then, in 1739, in Oxfordshire. He may have chosen to go south to alleviate his asthma, but as likely because the job opportunities were greater. He would have been aware that the deaths in the previous year of John Vanbrugh, Charles Bridgeman, and Henry Wise left a vacuum. Of the great English garden designers, only William Kent remained and he was not well. Brown saw that the field could use hard-working new talent.

A recommendation from his employer led to a position at an estate near Woodstock. The owner's wife was a distant cousin of William Pitt, Lord Chatham, and dear friend of Richard Temple, first Viscount Cobham of Stowe. Both were leading Whigs. Within two years Brown was employed at Stowe as head gardener in what can only be called a meteoric rise, for Stowe was England's most famous garden. Lord Cobham generously allowed Brown to take on other nearby commissions, offered to him because of the viscount's enthusiastic endorsement and his connections in Parliament and the Kit-Cat Club. One of these commissions came from Richard Grenville, Lord Cobham's nephew and heir.

The years at Stowe brought family happiness as well as career success. Brown courted Bridget Wayet from a respectable country family. They married in the church at Stowe and in the years following had five children. The death in 1749 of Lord Cobham prompted Brown to move, this time to Hammersmith, center of London's nursery business. His business thrived and earned a commission from Lord Chatham who was recognized as the greatest politician of the time. Lancelot Brown's crowning glory came when King George III appointed him as Royal Gardener at Hampton Court. He had made a distinguished place for himself professionally and socially.

The facts of his life suggest little about how he rose to such distinction, even in his lifetime to be called "immortal Brown." To be sure, he had good luck in the connections between people who furthered his career and in the publicity that came from the great writers of the day who celebrated his artistry. Beyond these assets his character and personality won for him friends and clients. He was ever-positive, seeing not the obstacles but the capabilities of the site, so much so that his patrons and friends gave him the nickname by which he was known and is remembered. In an era known for corruption, his patrons appreciated his honesty in returning to them unused funds. Like André Le Nôtre in France a century earlier, Brown was genial and quick-witted and never presumed upon a relationship with his superiors. People of every station liked him, calling on his landscape design skills but also making him their friend and companion. He was frequently found at the king's table, a guest at even the most intimate of family meals. A tribute by William Mason in the parish church where Brown is buried reads:

> But know that more than Genius slumbers here,
> Virtues were his which Arts best powers transcend.
> Come, ye Superior train who these revere
> And weep the Christian, Husband, Father, Friend.

Nathaniel Dance captured in his portrait the intelligence and humor of the genial Capability Brown.

As important, he possessed extraordinary business acumen and took an approach different from that of his predecessors. Kent, Vanbrugh, and Bridgeman designed only a few landscapes, each one different from the others. Brown, in contrast, developed a formula, key features of which were repeated in landscape after landscape. Further, the design style was minimalist with little ornament, sparing him the time-consuming job of designing, constructing, ordering, purchasing, and placing a large number of garden buildings and sculpture. A day on horseback surveying the property was enough for him to make his recommendations. He left meticulous notes for his engineers and gardeners, enabling him to move from one commission to the next, riding his circuit like a country preacher.

But even his character and entrepreneurial skills would not have made him successful had he not so perfectly understood the ambitions of his clients. They were about place-making, about house and property, about social, financial, and political status. The landscapes he designed highlighted the house and grounds in ways that made them appear large and impressive, often more than they actually were. Whether by intellect or intuition, he satisfied the yearnings of the great estate owners, enhancing their view of themselves in their own and others' eyes. Who would not want such a wizard to adorn their place?

Perhaps he was perfectly attuned to his patrons' wishes because he, too, had the same hopes and dreams. In 1767 he bought at Fenstanton, near Cambridge, a modest estate of which he was very proud. Through its purchase he achieved the status of landed gentry, an equal now of many of his patrons. There he enjoyed the last sixteen years of life. His gravestone in the parish churchyard of Saint Peter and Saint Paul identifies him as Lord of the Manor of Fenstanton. He had earned his place.

Stowe
Buckinghamshire, England

Alexander Pope ended his essay in verse *Of Taste, an Epistle to the Right Honourable Richard Boyle Earl of Burlington* by recommending Stowe as the standard of aesthetic excellence in garden design to which the young earl should aspire:

> Nature shall join you; time shall make it grow,
> A work to wonder at—perhaps a Stowe.

As early as 1719, twenty years before Capability Brown arrived, Stowe was recognized as the apex of English gardens for its iconography and its use of the new, open, asymmetrical design. Older geometric forms by the estate's earlier designers were softened first by Kent and then Capability Brown, proving that the styles of different periods can be pleasingly joined under the direction of an artist.

In landing a job at Stowe, young Brown was also obtaining the best possible education in landscape design. The owner, Sir Richard Temple, made first Viscount Cobham in 1718,

The family motto is worked into a pebble mosaic above a covered bench.

found respite from his active political career in the art of gardening, consulting with and often directing the gardeners at Stowe. A leading Whig, promoter of the power of Parliament and advocate of limited monarchy, he wanted an Arcadian landscape featuring the English countryside, one that would stand in stark contrast to the authoritarian designs of Versailles and Hampton Court with their axial roads leading to the heart of court and monarchy.

Richard Temple was not without a sense of humor. The family motto, taken from Psalm 84, "Templa Quam Dilecta" (How Lovely Are Thy Temples), alludes to both the family name and to the many buildings on the grounds of Stowe. His landscape iconography would include the ancients whom he admired, but even more, Whig ideals. Viewing the three dozen temples and other monuments, visitors to Stowe would be left with no doubt about Lord Cobham's political sympathies.

Not surprisingly, Lord Cobham hired the best of designers: John Vanbrugh, James Gibbs, Charles Bridgeman, and the recognized master, William Kent. At first the buildings and monuments were placed piecemeal around the property. There was an equestrian statue of George I and later statues of George II, Queen Caroline, and Saxon gods, a miniature villa in the popular Palladian style, and, after Vanbrugh's death, a pyramid in his memory.

A serpentine path connects Stowe's famous Palladian bridge to the Temple of Liberty, both structures designed by James Gibbs.

The earliest garden designs at Stowe were geometric and traditional. A great axial road bounded by allées of poplars leading from the house to the octagon lake were part of the older design and remained even though the viscount's ideas about garden design were changing. He became an admirer of the open landscape with its asymmetry and naturally curving lines. The Palladian bridge was completed in 1738, a year before Lancelot Brown was hired. When Brown arrived at Stowe, Kent was the official landscape architect but he was in poor health, designing and directing *in absentia*. It fell to the novice to carry out his plans.

Stowe deserves special attention as an early example of Capability Brown's contouring of earth, among his most noteworthy contributions to landscape design. Below the house terrace, Brown eliminated Charles Bridgeman's parterres and lake of elaborate geometrical design surrounded by clipped hedges in arched indentations, replacing them with a large lawn and contouring the slope to make gentle undulations. Instead of a consistently sloping ground, he used both concave and convex arcs ending in a concave curve next to the water, the earth finally rising to water level. The design ensures that no ground obscures the reflection of the house in the water.

TOP The great lawn created by Brown extends to the water's edge.

BOTTOM Alexander Pope was a frequent guest at Stowe. His poem "The Temple of Fame," a paraphrase of Chaucer's poem, was said to have inspired the choice of statues within the Temple of Ancient Virtue.

Brown also most likely exercised his skill at contouring in the Elysian Fields, the only non-geometric area of Stowe when he arrived in 1739. Kent had designed the area but Brown supervised its installation. Located on one side of the slightly irregular Alder River and crowning the small hill above is the elegant Kent-designed Temple of Ancient Virtue, inspired by the Temple of Fame at Studley Royal. Inside Homer, Socrates, Lycurgus, and Epaminondas stand facing one another in a circle as if in conversation. At one time, a ruined Temple of Modern Virtue stood nearby, its headless statue declaring Lord Cobham's thoughts about the morality of the time. Brown is believed to have contoured the earth from Kent's temple to the river below.

On the opposite bank of the river stands the Temple of British Worthies, an exedra designed by Kent. From their niches, busts of the great Whigs as well as other English leaders face the Temple of Ancient Virtue as if basking in the reflection of the ancients' virtues and shining forth their own righteousness. The two temples are connected upstream by a Kent-designed pebble bridge. The gentle contours of the earth, the informal grouping of trees, the water's edge stripped clean to allow a perfect reflection were to become the trademarks of a Capability Brown landscape, all features learned and the skills to install them honed while he was a gardener at Stowe.

Then, most notably, Brown created the Grecian Valley. He moved the Chinese House sited in the sixty-acre area to another location and masterfully contoured the flat stretch of land to appear as an irregular depression, planting cedar, yew, larch, beech, Scots pine, and sycamore trees on the opposing slopes to give the appearance of extra height. The effect, as with the Arcadian scenes of Studley Royal, Stourhead, and Rousham, bore no resemblance

The Temple of British Worthies honors those described in Pope's poem as "fabled Chiefs in darker ages born, Or Worthies old, whom arms or arts adorn."

to the real Greece or Italy. In this, Brown was well served by not having traveled in Italy as his predecessors had done because his designs are a pure celebration of the English countryside.

Possibly more than any other garden, Stowe is the intersection of styles, expresses many moods, and carries many messages. Represented in the three dozen temples and monuments is a variety of architectural styles, from a Palladian bridge to a Chinese house. It combines the older geometric style such as the allées of trees with Arcadian views as in the Grecian Valley. All is set within an asymmetrical landscape park of curving lines, great swards of grass, lakes, a river, contoured earth, and clumps of trees in what appear to be natural plantings and shapes. It is elegant, humorous, playful, serious, romantic, imaginative, and at places even angry. It celebrates contemporary literature and classical learning, erotic and filial love, virtue, vice, and political ideals. Over all is Brown's softening touch. Stowe is a lesson in combining styles, proof that periods of landscape design history can, with skill, be woven together to be aesthetically pleasing and more interesting because of the variety.

CLOCKWISE FROM TOP

The Temple of Victory and Concord stands at the head of the Grecian Valley.

The plaque above John Locke reads, "The best of all philosophers, [he] understood the . . . bounds of civil government [and] refuted the slavish systems of usurp'd authority over the rights . . . of mankind," a Whig sentiment if ever there was one.

Dramatist William Congreve was a member of the Kit-Cat Club as was Lord Cobham. Designed by Kent, the Congreve Memorial is the figure of a monkey studying his image in a mirror with the masks of tragedy and comedy at the base. The inscription reads: "Comedy is the imitation of life and the glass of fashion."

Neither trees nor ornaments distract from the house at Petworth.

Petworth

West Sussex, England

At Petworth, Capability Brown crystallized the landscape park formula that made him famous, and Petworth remains as the best preserved Brown landscape.

With the death of Lord Cobham in 1749, Brown determined his apprenticeship complete. He was already getting commissions in addition to his work at Stowe. As important, he had developed his own strong ideas that an independent business would allow him to realize. He had started work at Petworth House in West Sussex for the Wyndham family, headed by the Earl of Egremont. Now additional contracts called for a large lake to be created at Petworth near Half Moon Wood. Brown's own move south to Hammersmith would be convenient for his oversight of the work at Petworth, just south of London.

As landscape designer, Brown knew by reason or intuition to make the house the centerpiece, that it might be seen in all its glory, pleasing the owner and impressing visitors. He achieved this by clearing the land around the house of any distraction, installing instead a great green sward of grass. No trees were allowed close to the house, and certainly no fountains or parterres. Unheard of were foundation plantings. There would be no carriage road, axial or curving, in the rear of the house to break the clear expanse of lawn to the new lake.

In his use of grass, he was both following tradition and breaking with it. Turf had been admired and used since the Middle Ages and recent Arcadian landscapes included an expanse of lawn such as that surrounding the moon ponds at Studley Royal, the bowling green at Rousham, and the slopes cradling the lake at Stourhead. But with Brown, the lawn took on new importance, serving as does a mat around a painting.

At Petworth, as at other Brown sites, the lawn was made up of many varieties of short grasses and tiny flowers, most prominently the English daisy, *Bellis perennis*. It was mown by two methods. Armed with scythes, a long handled tool with a curved blade and grasped by two short handles projecting at right angles from the long pole, a team of men walked in a line, swinging their scythes back and forth in unison, thereby cutting a wide swathe. The size of these teams was a means of judging the owner's wealth. The second method of mowing was to allow sheep or other animals to graze, making the ha-ha a necessity, the men cutting near the house, the sheep doing their part on the far side of the ha-ha. At Petworth, Capability Brown set the ha-ha at a right angle to the house so that the walk or horseback ride to the lake would be unbroken. He insisted that the water's edge be cleared of the sedges and other plants, creating a most unnatural look in his planned natural design, but one that further enhanced the view of the house.

The serpentine line of Brown's lake appears to underscore the house.

ABOVE Brown used a belt of trees rather than walls or high hedgerows to bound property.

OPPOSITE, CLOCKWISE FROM TOP LEFT

A fine old sweet chestnut at Petworth.

Capability Brown often put a clump of trees on the top of a hill as at Petworth House. The iron fence and wall now mark the line of the ha-ha.

Capability Brown's equipment for moving large trees.

Around his newly created lake he thinned already existing mature trees into groups. To the southwest he installed "plantations of shrubs and plants of low growth that would not prevent the prospect." These, according to the nurseryman's bill, included altheas, bird cherry and double cherry, broom, ilex, lilac, laburnum, roses, spirea, sweet briars, and sweet bryony. On a knoll near the house Brown removed the existing formal garden, replacing it with a clump of cedars and chestnuts. He gave the land leading to the crest a gentle undulating form, adding single trees and small clumps on the downward slopes.

On his grand green carpets he placed trees, and there proved to have a painter's eye, though he himself resisted such an image, comparing himself instead to a writer "putting a comma here, coming to a full stop there." He had four approaches to using trees in a design. One was to plant a specimen tree to stand alone, sometimes of an unusual variety, but always green. Trees with plum-colored or yellow leaves were known in England in the eighteenth century, having been imported from the Americas, but Brown preferred the varying shades of green that were part of the traditional English landscape.

Because his clients were unwilling to wait years for the finished effect he invented a machine that allowed him to transplant huge trees. His men laid the uprooted tree onto a

cart, tying it firmly to a long horizontal pole connected to a gear. At the new planting spot, the pole was swung into an upright position for the tree to be lifted into place.

Another method he employed for designing with trees was to plant clumps of the same kind of tree, clearing underbrush beneath them to achieve a clean look A third approach was to group two or more species. These clumps and groups became a Capability Brown signature. A fourth use of trees was to plant belts to surround the property, blocking out views of village, farms, and even the parish church tower. The effect of the contoured land, the great expanse of lawn uncluttered by ornament, classical buildings, or Rococo follies, and the plantations of trees produced, within the apparent naturalness, a desired sense of order and control as well as satisfaction of the owner's vanity.

But Brown's design served yet another purpose, this one practical. Hunting had been the sport of the rich and powerful since the Middle Ages and so it was for the titled estate

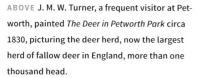

ABOVE J. M. W. Turner, a frequent visitor at Petworth, painted *The Deer in Petworth Park* circa 1830, picturing the deer herd, now the largest herd of fallow deer in England, more than one thousand head.

ABOVE, RIGHT A pheasant in the meadow at Boughton House, bordering a belt of trees.

owners and landed gentry of the eighteenth century. The seven-hundred-acre deer park at Petworth was once the site of a medieval hunting park, as was the case at other Brown sites. The property had in the fourteenth century been owned by Sir Henry Percy, Shakespeare's Hotspur. Henry VIII, briefly owner of Petworth, had a hunting lodge and banqueting hall that has recently been uncovered by archeologists. At Petworth and in other Brown-designed landscapes, the resemblance to the old hunting parks is striking.

Belts of woodland surrounding the property with a border of meadow harbored birds and smaller animals including fox and hare which would be hunted in the open fields. Partridges and pheasant nested at the edge of the woodland. The medieval bow and arrow was replaced by the gun. Then, at the end of the eighteenth century as guns had become shorter and lighter, the art of shooting flying birds became popular. Large shooting parties were preceded by attendants who beat the edge of the woods to drive hundreds of birds to flight, there to meet their end. So important was this activity to the estate owners that a law was passed limiting hunting rights to those with an income of £100 a year, the equivalent today of well over one million U.S. dollars. Game Acts of 1707 and 1725 spelled out severe penalties for poaching, even including hanging. A law forbidding the sale or purchase of partridge and pheasant, passed when Capability Brown was at work on Petworth, was meant to reserve these delicacies for the land owners and their guests, but it proved counterproductive, actually increasing poaching instead.

What Capability Brown did at Petworth and would do elsewhere was to make every spot one for viewing the landscape. The medieval gardener walled out the distant scenes, directing the focus within to such features as the central fountain. Italian Renaissance gardens "allow" the garden visitor to look outward, although the chief sights remain within the planned garden. The geometric French Baroque gardens locate key vantage points for the visitor walking the length to pause and look forward and back, sometimes beyond the formal garden. The Arcadian and Augustan gardens of the early eighteenth century provide opportunities to view the countryside beyond. Now Capability Brown opens the entire landscape so that any place offers a fine view.

Blenheim

Oxfordshire, England

King George III, entering Blenheim through Triumph Gate and seeing all at once and for the first time the lake, island, bridge and palace, turned to Queen Charlotte and exclaimed, "We have nothing to equal this!" Capability Brown meant the view to astonish, described by eighteenth-century publisher John Boydell as "a transition from nothing to everything."

Blenheim is not a country place as are Petworth and Stowe, but rather lies in the village of Woodstock. One minute the visitor is on the village street with its shops and pub, the next in another world, a picture complete with the primary features in an elegant and soothing relationship one to another. The lake, Brown's largest, looks widest at this point just as he intended. The island stands between the palace and the bridge, resolving the conflict of dual attractions. The belt of dark trees is the perfect backdrop for the shining lake reflecting the changing skies above.

Considered Brown's great masterpiece, Blenheim shows all his design sensibilities. He used expanses of turf, planted clumps, groups, belts, and specimen trees, contoured earth, and manipulated water. Throughout England, he channeled rivers, dammed streams, created cascades, made lakes where none existed, built islands in them, controlled the water level, fabricated shore lines, and cleared the water's edge, nowhere more brilliantly than at Blenheim. It was planned natural writ large.

The property at Woodstock in Oxfordshire had been the gift of a grateful nation to John Churchill for successfully leading the military campaign ending the French domination of Europe. Given the title Duke of Marlborough, he and the duchess, Sarah Churchill, would name their grand new home Blenheim after the location of the decisive battle that brought him victory and fame.

Brown was not the first landscape architect for Blenheim, making his design achievement even more impressive for it is surely the harder task to work around another's design than to start afresh. The Duke of Marlborough or, some say Queen Anne herself, chose John Vanbrugh to design the palace and surrounding property. But he and the duchess did not get along. Vanbrugh, the playwright and stage set designer turned architect, always wanted to work on the grandest scale. No longer confined to a small space, he took to heart "all the world's a stage" and designed accordingly.

The first view of Blenheim after passing through the entrance gate.

To cover the rather puny River Glyme and the marsh it created in the wide, deep valley through the property, Vanbrugh proposed a vast bridge. In the Palladian style popular at the time, the bridge was, as Sarah herself was to report, large enough to have "thirty-three rooms beneath." As the construction proceeded, she and Vanbrugh were increasingly at odds, she complaining frequently and vehemently about the expense. Finally, in 1716, when she declared his bridge "ridiculous," Vanbrugh's giant ego was seriously bruised. He stalked off, never to return.

At last Colonel Armstrong, the chief engineer, was summoned to manage. He created canals and a small lake that looked too small for the immense bridge, inspiring Alexander Pope's cutting jest, "The minnows, as under this vast arch they pass, murmur, 'How like whales we look, thanks to your Grace!'"

Brown's trees were always in scale with the scene. The weeping beeches on either side of the bridge at Blenheim are as impressive as the bridge and lake.

When it was clear that Armstrong had failed, Capability Brown was waiting in the wings. In 1764, he was appointed by the fourth Duke of Marlborough to take over the development of the Blenheim landscape. Ever-inventive, he had the perfect solution to the issue of scale, one that would solve simultaneously the two problems of the swamp and the oversized bridge. With uncanny accuracy, he dammed the river and flooded the valley, thereby creating an enormous lake and raising the water level by fifteen feet to the height where the arches of the great bridge spring. The old scene-dominating bridge would become a causeway, providing the needed roadway over the water, the view now featuring the water, trees, and palace. Confident though he was in his ability, Capability Brown must nonetheless have held his breath as the first water rushed into the newly created lakebed. The foundation of the bridge proved solid and, with its new look, held fast.

Brown ensured that the most magnificent view from the palace courtyard would be unobstructed. He grassed over the enormous Great Court on the side facing the bridge, producing a lovely contrast to the sun-colored stone of the palace. (Early in the twentieth century the courtyard was replaced with cobbles, making palace and courtyard resemble the grand courtyard at Versailles.) The gently sloping lawn leads the eye to lake and island with its slim Lombardy poplars standing at attention.

CLOCKWISE, FROM TOP LEFT

The island, now a bit overgrown, makes the lake look larger.

Brown controlled the water level of the lake within a two-foot range, achieved by means of pumps and overflow tanks disguised to preserve the illusion that the lake and its water level were entirely natural.

Viewers are deliberately deceived, believing the lake extends far into the distance.

To achieve the wonder of lake and island, Brown rechanneled the River Glyme, building two cascades to carry the water downward into the newly formed lake.

Most amazing was his disguise of the lake's boundaries to make the body of water appear larger. He constructed small peninsulas or spits and then planted them with trees, thereby concealing the edge of the lake. The viewer believes that the water extends far beyond when in fact its boundary is just behind the trees, a deceptive technique Brown would use time and time again to the satisfaction of owners.

For the shoreline as well as for roads, Brown used curving and serpentine lines which artist and satirist William Hogarth praised in his widely read essay *The Analysis of Beauty*. Published in 1753 just a decade before Brown began work at Blenheim, the essay describes straight lines as boring and denoting stasis, the stage before death. Hogarth argued instead that waving lines engender interest and convey energy and movement: "Forms of most grace have least of the straight line in them." Of all curving lines, he declared the serpentine made of two equal curves reversed in direction to be the "line of beauty."

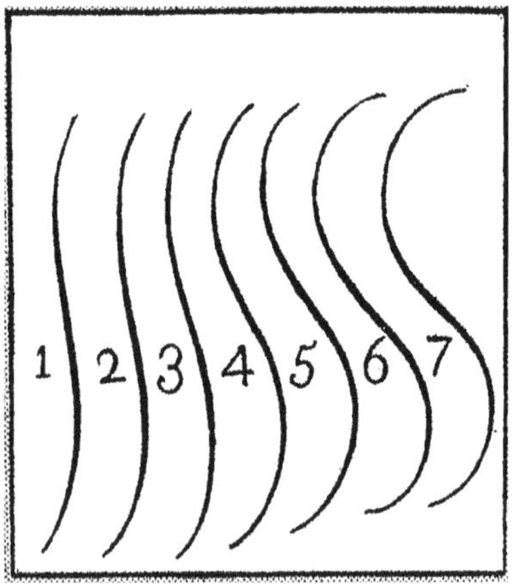

The line of beauty had been used in gardens from the beginning of the eighteenth century, most notably in the Serpentine in Hyde Park in London. With the circulation of Hogarth's essay the concept gained prominence. Brown used curved, sometimes serpentine, lines to reroute and reshape the river at Blenheim. He surrounded the property with a winding belt of trees and, inside, a carriage road that does not run parallel to the wood's edge. In using these ideas, Brown once again rode the crest of the design wave.

ABOVE Hogarth used his own painting *Country Dance* to illustrate the use of curving and serpentine lines to show vitality.

RIGHT An illustration from *The Analysis of Beauty* shows the construction of serpentine lines.

OPPOSITE The Thames winds its way through the valley below Nuneham.

Years before, when Capability Brown was just a boy, Sarah Churchill had declared that Blenheim was "a chaos that only God Almighty could finish." Eventually, true to the name his admirers had given him, he was willing to do God's work. He put to use all the tricks of the landscape architect's trade that he had learned and developed to a high art. Many then and now agree with King George III that the views he created at Blenheim are unsurpassed in England. Brown concurred, declaring of his transformed River Glyme, "Thames, Thames, you will never forgive me!"

Nuneham

Oxfordshire, England

Among the glittering literary circle of the eighteenth century, two poets—Oliver Goldsmith and William Whitehead—referred specifically to Nuneham Park. In so doing they illuminated the essence of the grand vision of Capability Brown with its glorious aesthetic features—and the price paid for it.

Nuneham was among Brown's last commissions, one in which he employed his talent and formula for using earth, water, and trees to make his landscapes appear to have been created by nature, not by the hand of man. It may have been one of his easier jobs, for the gentle hills overlooking the Thames Valley near Oxford needed no earth moving as at Stowe. The flowing river required no new lake as at Petworth, no swamp to be drained or dammed as at Blenheim. With its rich plantation of trees, the old deer park needed only selective pruning to open up the prospects. Brown added his trademark, a large lawn and additional clumps of trees.

The story of Nuneham begins almost thirty years before Brown's involvement in the 1770s, but not on a happy note. As Brown was just beginning work at Petworth, Simon Harcourt, first Earl of Harcourt, was embarking on a building project for his family seat. The old manor house was to be replaced by a new and grander house in a slightly different location. He determined, as had other English landowners, that the church and village of "tumble-down clay built cottages" would have to be demolished if the house was to have the proper setting. In his decision, he was joining a movement that had begun in England as early as the sixteenth century or even before.

Once social classes had been interdependent, each part contributing and essential to the whole. The landowner, whether hereditary nobility or landed gentry, acknowledged and admired the skills and knowledge of those who farmed his property, waited his table, or adjusted his cravat. Workers, in turn, recognized and accepted their role in society as both valued and dependent. But the late seventeenth century saw the beginnings of land becoming a commodity for buying and selling, a trend that would accelerate drastically with the Industrial Revolution and rend the fabric of society.

As land became a commodity, the villages were considered the property of the owner who could do as he pleased with them. The belting of property with woodlands to screen out the cultivated fields and village was often a part of the landscape park design, a feature exercised by Brown at Petworth and Blenheim. Nothing was to ruffle the pleasure of the owner's view.

The razing of hamlets to make way for great houses and their gardens was not new. Versailles and Vaux-le-Vicomte, to name but two, had required similar action. At Nuneham, Lord Harcourt tore down the medieval church, replacing it with a new Palladian-style church erected on a different site. He likewise demolished the village of Nuneham Courtenay, constructing a mile to the northeast two rows of semidetached houses facing each other across the main road. Gone as well was the old village green, the earl providing instead a small garden space to each new cottage. Brown himself had no direct hand in these operations at Nuneham, but like other estate owners, local officials, architects, and landscape architects, he must be labeled a co-conspirator for profiting financially and enhancing his reputation from his work on the newly cleared property.

Oliver Goldsmith does not name Nuneham Courtenay in his poem *The Deserted Village*, but the park and village have long been linked to the famous poem. He saw that obscuring the view of and on occasion obliterating the villages and farms contributed to the increasing rift between laborer and landowner. The poet called his fictional village Auburn and in the

The houses constructed for Nuneham Courtenay villagers as compensation for the seizing and destroying of their homes remain in use today.

poem laments the destruction of English villages, condemns the heartlessness of uprooting common people from their homes, and warns of the consequences. At least Lord Harcourt had relocated the population to new homes nearby and built a new church. But for Goldsmith, as undoubtedly for displaced villagers, these were not adequate compensation for the loss of their old village, church, and way of life.

Sweet Auburn! Loveliest village of the plain,
Where health and plenty cheered the labouring swain;
. . . Sunk are thy bowers in shapeless ruin all,
And the long grass o'ertops the mouldering wall;
. . . The man of wealth and pride
Takes up a space that many poor supplied;
Space for his lake, his park's extended bounds,
Space for his horse, equipage, and hounds:
The robe that wraps his limbs in silken cloth
Has robbed the neighbouring fields of half their growth;
. . . Ill fares the land, to hastening ills a prey,
Where wealth accumulates, and men decay.

Goldsmith shared a mindset with other poets and writers of the later eighteenth and early nineteenth centuries in celebrating the countryside without reference to antique civilizations. Romantic, often nostalgic, the writers captured the appeal of the green fields asleep in the sun, the cattle grazing, the plowboy shouting with joy, and the village with its graveyard beside the parish church. After the death of Lord Harcourt in 1777, his son, George Harcourt, caught up with the democratic ideas of Jean-Jacques Rousseau, hired Brown to transform the axial lines of his father's garden, lines closely associated with the absolutist French monarchy, into the flowing asymmetry of what was by then known as the landscape park.

While agreeing with his patrons to eliminate from sight the fields and villages, Brown highlighted the natural beauty of rural England. His designs did not rely on garden buildings or sculpture, and contain neither iconography nor moral lessons. Just as Goldsmith and other poets arranged words in the most pleasing way, Brown arranged water, earth, and plants to their best advantage.

Another eighteenth-century poet, in an amusing poem, caught the genius of and problem for Capability Brown. Poet Laureate William Whitehead was a frequent visitor at Nuneham and, using it as the setting for an encounter between Dame Nature and Brown, relates their imaginary argument about who should get credit for the beautiful landscape. Dame Nature argues that the lawn, wood, and water are her handiwork. Brown comes back, reminding her that it was he who "thinned, grouped, and scattered the trees," he who "bade the slopes fall with that delicate ease," and he who determined their placement in light or shade. They continue, but finally Dame Nature tires of arguing. Withdrawing, she has a last and satisfying thought, one that might serve as warning to all would-be landscape designers: "The world's little malice will balk his design; Each fault they'll call his, and each excellence mine."

An obituary for Brown, cited by Christopher Hussey, editor of *Country Life*, repeated the idea: "Where he was the happiest man he will be least remembered; so closely did he copy nature that his work will be mistaken [for nature]." His work did not in fact copy nature: he moved tons of earth to reconfigure the topography, creating artificial lakes and keeping their water at the same level in flood or drought; he planted trees at the top of hills, cleared the plants that grow naturally at the water's edge, and substituted a large expanse of mown turf for the tall meadow grasses and flowers. But compared to the old geometric patterns of topiary, axial lines, and trees planted in allées, Brown's designs seemed natural. As his work became associated with the rejection of authoritarian monarchy and the drive toward democracy, his style spread around the world.

Parc Jean-Jacques Rousseau

Ermenonville, France

The Reverend Charles Caleb Colton might have had Capability Brown in mind when, around 1800, he penned the phrase "Imitation is the sincerest form of flattery." Even before his death in 1783, Brown's landscape park design was copied and adapted so often throughout England that people thought it was Nature herself. French political and social philosopher Jean-Jacques Rousseau shared with Brown's Whig clients similar views on the evils of absolute monarchy and, understanding how an art form reflects the values of the culture, on landscape design. Rousseau's great friend, follower, and last pupil, the Marquis René Louis de Girardin set out to create a garden at his home in Ermenonville that would illustrate the new ideas of Rousseau about democracy and garden design. Only partially correctly, the garden just north of Paris would often be identified as the first English landscape park in France.

Venant d'herboriser dans les Jardins
d'Ermenonville au mois de Juin 1778.
Botanique.

Gathering Herbs at Ermenonville by artist Nicolas-André Monsiau is the last engraving of Jean-Jacques Rousseau made in his life.

Rousseau's essays, particularly *The Social Contract*, had made him the most talked-about philosopher in France in the heated years leading to the French Revolution. As the conflict intensified, Rousseau's house was stoned, driving him to seek refuge first in his native Switzerland, then in England at the invitation of sympathetic Scottish philosopher David Hume. Rousseau did not speak English, and his mental health was not good. Still, in two years of living in England, he could hardly have missed learning something about the famous Capability Brown and his work.

In his 1761 novel, *Julie, or the New Heloise*, Rousseau had described his own vision of the ideal landscape, as far in concept and design from the authoritarian gardens of the Bourbon kings as possible. Criticizing the current fashion, he posited that "the time is coming when people will no longer want anything which is found in the country in their gardens. . . . They will want in it only porcelain flowers, china figures, lattices, sand of all colors, and fine vases full of nothing." In contrast, in his garden "The carpenter's line never entered this place. Nature plants nothing by the line."

The imaginary garden of his novel is asymmetrical with "winding and irregular walks bordered by flowery thickets and covered with a thousand garlands of woody vines, with a limpid and clear stream, sometimes winding in almost imperceptible rivulets, sometimes running in larger brooklets over pure and speckled gravel which [makes] the water more transparent." He reminds his reader that birds, not men, were the original owners of the land. His ideal was nature unadorned, where the gardener acts not as laborer but as caregiver.

Girardin's inherited estate was not far from the great châteaux of Versailles and Chantilly. Educated and well-connected, he was interested in landscape design and had visited gardens in several countries including England. When he settled in Ermenonville he laid out his garden along the small L'Aunette River using a series of ponds united by the river's naturally serpentine line.

Hiring Hubert Robert, a Scottish gardener, as architect and one hundred English workers, he began construction in 1776. In the plans were such garden buildings as the Temple of Philosophy, deliberately unfinished to illustrate Rousseau's belief about the state of human

The inscription on Rousseau's tomb on the Isle of Poplars at Ermenonville reads: "Here Lies the Man of Nature and Truth." His body was moved to the Pantheon in Paris in 1794.

knowledge. Structures included a grotto, a rustic temple, and other effects evoking scenes from *Julie*.

Le Desert was the wildest part of the garden, complete with a small, thatched roof cottage. In May 1778 Rousseau visited and was captivated by the setting. At the urging of Girardin, he moved in and remained there until his death. He was buried July 2, almost two years after the Declaration of Independence in America and eleven years before the storming of the Bastille that began the French Revolution.

Girardin had prepared his tomb at Ermenonville on the little Isle of Poplars at the far end of the largest pond and described the setting and emotion: "The stream, the breeze that fans it, the flowers that gild the grass that borders its margin, the verdant, o'erhanging arch, its vocal tenants [the birds], the glittering inhabitants of the moving crystal; all whisper love, all speak his presence here."

It is true that Girardin used the concepts of the English landscape park as opposed to the geometric lines of the French Baroque garden, thereby expressing his opposition to absolute monarchy and his sympathy for the democratic cause. Like Brown, Girardin arranged nature to advantage, leaving all but unseen his own designing head and hand. But the underlying design principle was different. Unlike Brown who moved earth and would undoubtedly have moved heaven had his plan required it, Girardin believed in minimal intervention in nature. Like the painter whose keen eye can see in nature the form of a great outline on which to draw, he believed the designer could "manage light and shadow," provide "variety," and create a "beautiful assemblage of colours," while allowing "the happy negligence which is the peculiar characteristic of grace and nature."

The anti-geometric, asymmetrical, and naturally curving lines of Rousseau's nature and Brown's landscape park were soon being widely adopted. So enthusiastic were the French that the English landscape park design became known throughout Europe as the *jardin anglais*. What poetic justice that the first such landscape in France would be constructed to honor Jean-Jacques Rousseau, the perfect resting place for the man whose ideas about the nature of society were championed by the advocates of democracy in Europe and North America.

Hawkstone Park

Shropshire, England

The English landscape park design popularized by Capability Brown spread across England, then France and beyond. But by the end of the eighteenth century there were critics. The tame, manicured, neat, and clean work of Capability Brown was beginning to seem unnatural and boring. The medieval fears of the dangerous countryside were now so far in the past that they could be romanticized. The peace, welcomed at the beginning of the eighteenth century, now felt dull.

In 1757 English philosopher Edmund Burke had taken the English intellectual and artistic world by storm with the publication of his essay *A Philosophical Enquiry into the Origin of our Ideas of the Sublime and Beautiful*, followed by ten editions in the next thirty years. In it, Burke differentiated between two fundamental sources of human emotion that cause pleasure and dictate aesthetic taste. The Beautiful, inspired by sexual attraction, is intimate, soft, curving, gentle, round, and safe. In contrast, emotions engendered by the Sublime come from fear—ultimately the fear of death—and are to be found in the extensive, majestic, exciting, awful, and awe-inspiring. William Hogarth expressed the Sublime in this way: "Huge, shapeless rocks have a pleasing kind of horror in them . . . their vastness draws our attention and raises our admiration."

> Though [Hawkstone] wants water, it excels. . . . by the extent of its prospects, the awfulness of its shades, the horror of its precipices, the verdure of its hollows and the loftiness of its rocks. The ideas, which it forces upon the mind, are the sublime, the dreadful, and the vast. Above is inaccessible altitude, below is horrible profundity.
>
> —SAMUEL JOHNSON

Italian Baroque painter Salvator Rosa pictured these qualities of untamed nature. His works, showing scenes of storms, mountains, rocky precipices,

Rocky Landscape with Huntsman and Warriors by Salvator Rosa depicts the Picturesque ideal.

powerful cascades, and dead trees, set forth a different and, to many, appealing concept of beauty. Landscape designers and estate owners responded to this desire for excitement with what became known as the Picturesque style. Two men in particular articulated the new approach. Sir Uvedale Price wrote about landscape design, but his real commitment was to conservation. He advocated nature unadorned, and in his 1794 *Essay on the Picturesque* he argued that both the Sublime and the Beautiful were found in a landscape in the Picturesque style.

Anticipating Price's essay by only a few months, Richard Payne Knight addressed his famous poem *The Landscape* to his neighbor, Price. They shared similar negative views of, in Knight's words, "the improver's hand." Knight, like Price, hoped that we might

> Learn to cure or kill that strange disease
> Which gives deformity the power to please;
> And shews poor Nature, shaven and defaced;
> To gratify the jaundiced eye of taste.

He even had the nerve to question Hogarth's famous line of beauty, employed by Kent, Brown, the Marquis de Girardin, and others to channel bodies of water and lay out paths and carriage roads:

> In humbler art the self same laws obtain
> Nature in all rejects the pedant's chain;
> Binding beauty in its waving line,
> Destroys the charm it vainly would define;
> For nature, still irregular and free,
> Acts not by lines, but general sympathy.
> The path that moves in even serpentine
> Is still less natural than the pointed line. . . .
> The best of rules are those of common use
> Affected taste is but refined abuse.

Of the few remaining gardens in the Picturesque style, Hawkstone is the best example, with designed features to enhance the natural, sublime countryside. Rather like adventure films today, Hawkstone was meant to engender with its majestic views pleasurable thrills and almost but not quite heart-stopping moments. It was Sir Rowland Hill and his son, Sir Richard Hill, who developed the park at their home in Shropshire. Their intent from the beginning was for visitors to exclaim at the views and feel the thrills of the Picturesque landscape, Sir Richard building an inn nearby to accommodate the scene-seekers. Hawkstone soon became a honeymoon destination.

At the Moss Hut gingerbread and lemonade were sold for the refreshment of eighteenth-century tourists.

RIGHT The arch, a folly, is the daunting goal at Hawkstone.

OPPOSITE, CLOCKWISE FROM TOP LEFT

Two levels of Hawkstone Park are seen at the Swiss Bridge.

At Hawkstone, the grotto is carved from the rock at the top of the mountain.

The natural precipices become platforms for the daring to take in the extensive view.

The goal as glimpsed from the lowest level is a ruined arch that is only a folly but acts as the eyecatcher and inspiration for undertaking the journey. The rigorous climb leads through narrow passages and around bends, creating the sense of forsaking civilization in favor of natural wilderness with its attendant pleasurable anxieties. The sensations are intensified at the narrow Swiss Bridge eighty feet above the ground where the visitor must decide if he is brave enough to look down.

A path along the cliff's edge leads to the most extensive construction, a cave fashioned in the natural rock. The several rooms in the grotto, each with entrance and exit as in a maze, cause the terrifying, if momentary, belief that one is lost. Then victorious at last, the goal achieved, hikers look out over the glorious Shropshire countryside and congratulate themselves on their endurance and courage.

The Picturesque style was popular only briefly, its followers far outnumbered by Brown devotees. This was true in part because the English landscape held more opportunities to develop a Brownian design than a Picturesque one. Few estates had scenery on which to build like that at Hawkstone. In time the American landscape would better accommodate the Picturesque.

7 Gaiety *and* "Gloomth"

Rococo landscapes bring fantasies of faraway places and thrills for visitors.

EIGHTEENTH CENTURY

TODAY'S VISITORS to England's great eighteenth-century gardens are often surprised by what appear to be anomalies: Chinese pagodas and pavilions, Egyptian sphinxes and pyramids, Mughal domes and Arabian tents. Equally perplexing are the Italian grottoes and gothic ruins. What motivated owners and designers to put these seemingly out-of-place and out-of-century structures on their elegant grounds?

By the early 1700s England was ready not just for peace but for play. The previous century had been violent and restrictive. Continuing a practice that began in the sixteenth century, the serious Puritans, disapproving as they did of frivolity, promoted the Cromwell Parliament's ban on Christmas and saint's day celebrations. Soldiers were charged to find revelers. When they smelled a goose cooking, they followed the scent to the offenders. Theaters were shut down and the performances of masques in village streets outlawed. In the nation that had recently produced Shakespeare, people were not allowed to enjoy themselves. Yet happily by the early 1700s the harsh laws were changed and the English were recapturing the activities that had given pleasure in the past and discovering new ones. As if denied the joys of childhood and youth, they were making up for lost time in lighthearted, whimsical, imaginary delights.

Artists in every medium found satisfaction in humor and imagination. The witty and not-a-little-naughty drawings of visual satirist William Hogarth were enormously popular. *The Beggar's Opera* by John Gay made fun of the upper crust and was rewarded with what at the time was the longest theater run in British history. John Vanbrugh called his first comedy *The Relapse, Or, Virtue in Danger* and later wrote *The Provoked Wife*, both filled with brilliantly funny repartee. William Congreve's play *The Way of the World*, considered among the best of eighteenth-century comedies, and Alexander Pope's *Rape of the Lock* satirized domestic conventions and values. Together Congreve and Vanbrugh created Her Majesty's Theatre on Haymarket as a performance venue for opera and later Restoration comedies and other entertainment, including pantomime, dance, opera, juggling, and even animal acts.

> A hid Recess, where life's revolving day
> In sweet Delusion gently steals away.
>
> —HORACE

So important and successful was wit in eighteenth-century literature that it has sometimes overshadowed the more serious and indeed scholarly work of the poets, essayists, and dramatists. Alexander Pope, who called wit

Grotto, Painshill.

Chinese pavilion, Cliveden.

"nature to advantage dress'd," translated into verse the first books of Virgil's *Aeneid*. Samuel Johnson compiled his *Dictionary of the English Language*. Jonathan Swift, dean of the Anglican cathedral in Dublin, was a student of theology and writer of sermons in addition to the humorous essay *A Modest Proposal* and the fanciful *Gulliver's Travels*.

Landscape designers, too, sought to put humor, whimsy, and fantasy into their art. And, like their associates in the other arts, they were literate, sophisticated, and intellectual. Operating on many levels at the same time, they incorporated weighty concepts with elements to feed playful imagination and engender laughter. After all, what better place to have fun than in the garden? Landscape designers used two primary means to inject the spirit of play into their creations: their expanding knowledge of the world and the slightly frightening experiences that Edmund Burke praised in his theory of the Sublime.

Lands newly visited by Europeans figured prominently in garden design. The chief travel destination remained Italy, but a few bold souls ventured farther afield. The voyages of discovery continued with new plants a major goal. Missionaries, especially Jesuits, spent time in China, returning with tales to tell. Others went to Asia to seek their fortune, the English with the East India Company. Still others served in the army or navy. Samuel Johnson decided with his secretary James Boswell to visit Scotland including the Outer Hebrides, thought then to be wild and uncivilized though they found it otherwise. From their travels each produced a journal, both enormously popular with the reading public.

Many other travelers also wrote about and sketched scenes from their journeys, enabling those at home to participate vicariously. The knowledge of foreign cultures was often grossly inadequate, superficial, incomplete, and wrong. But their romantic and fantastical visions were just the stuff of which imaginative play is made. Like Hadrian who filled his villa landscape with remembrances of his travels, eighteenth-century garden owners and designers included reminders of pleasurable travel or images of travel about which they could only dream. China had a special appeal. Garden buildings inspired by Chinese design popped up in gardens everywhere, not only in England but throughout Europe, features called chinoiserie.

Another source for imaginative play in the garden was akin to Edmund Burke's Sublime. Anticipating the Picturesque style, landscape designers introduced eerie elements to induce harmless fear and a little thrilling dread. Horace Walpole coined a word for it: "gloomth." Children have always incorporated spine-tingling, goose-bump-producing experiences in their adventurous play. The dark cave, the abandoned building, the strange and slightly frightening person—all may be part of the narrative they create. Eighteenth-century gardens provided such experiences for adults. Grottoes inspired by those in Italian gardens found a place in many a garden. Some, such as that at Stourhead, were meant to be treated seriously as part of the garden's iconography. But many were just an amusing diversion. Follies resembling medieval watchtowers could be found on hillsides and ruined abbeys at the water's edge. Perhaps most odd was the hermitage where a local was hired to play the part of a strange recluse. Without movies, spy novels, television, and electronic games, eighteenth-century Englishmen and women used their garden props to make an afternoon stroll more entertaining and an evening stimulating and downright fun.

A portrait of Yongzheng, the second Qing emperor, reading a stitched-bound book.

Yuanming Yuan (Garden of Perfect Brightness, Old Summer Palace)

Beijing, China

If eighteenth-century English landscape designers had been able to visit the newly built imperial palace Yuanming Yuan instead of just imagining it, they would have felt an instant affinity for the asymmetry of design, the planned natural look, the centrality of water in man-made lakes, and the "borrowed" scenery. They would have wondered at the constructed mountains with their forest plantations. The very features that the English designers were introducing on the great estate gardens and parks had long been present in Chinese gardens.

But for all they had in common, the English were innovators while the Chinese were conservators of design conventions just as they were of other Chinese beliefs and values. While William Kent and Capability Brown were challenging the older geometric gardens and revolutionizing landscape design in England, the Qing emperors were incorporating centuries-old Chinese garden traditions in Yuanming Yuan.

A primary value of Chinese mandarin culture was that of active participation in the nation's great literary tradition. The English derived power and identity from their land and expressed their station in landscape design. The Chinese scholar-bureaucrats understood that for them power and identity derived from reading ability and so they honed their knowledge of literature, especially poetry. They used their gardens for study, writing, intellectual discussion, and meditation. As literati, they incorporated their knowledge in their gardens, giving each garden and garden feature a poetic name, inscribing poetry on stones and walls, and recreating scenes as described by great poets and writers.

Also greatly revered, the Chinese scroll paintings inspired garden design. As in the landscape scenes depicted in paintings, at Yuanming Yuan irregular and curving lines predominated. Forty garden buildings dotted the landscape, but unlike the houses on eighteenth-century English estates, none was allowed to stand out. Designed though they were, the views were meant to look natural, the hand of the designer humbly hidden.

Yuanming Yuan was originally a retreat from the summer heat of the city but shortly became the principal residence and place of work for the three Qing dynasty emperors

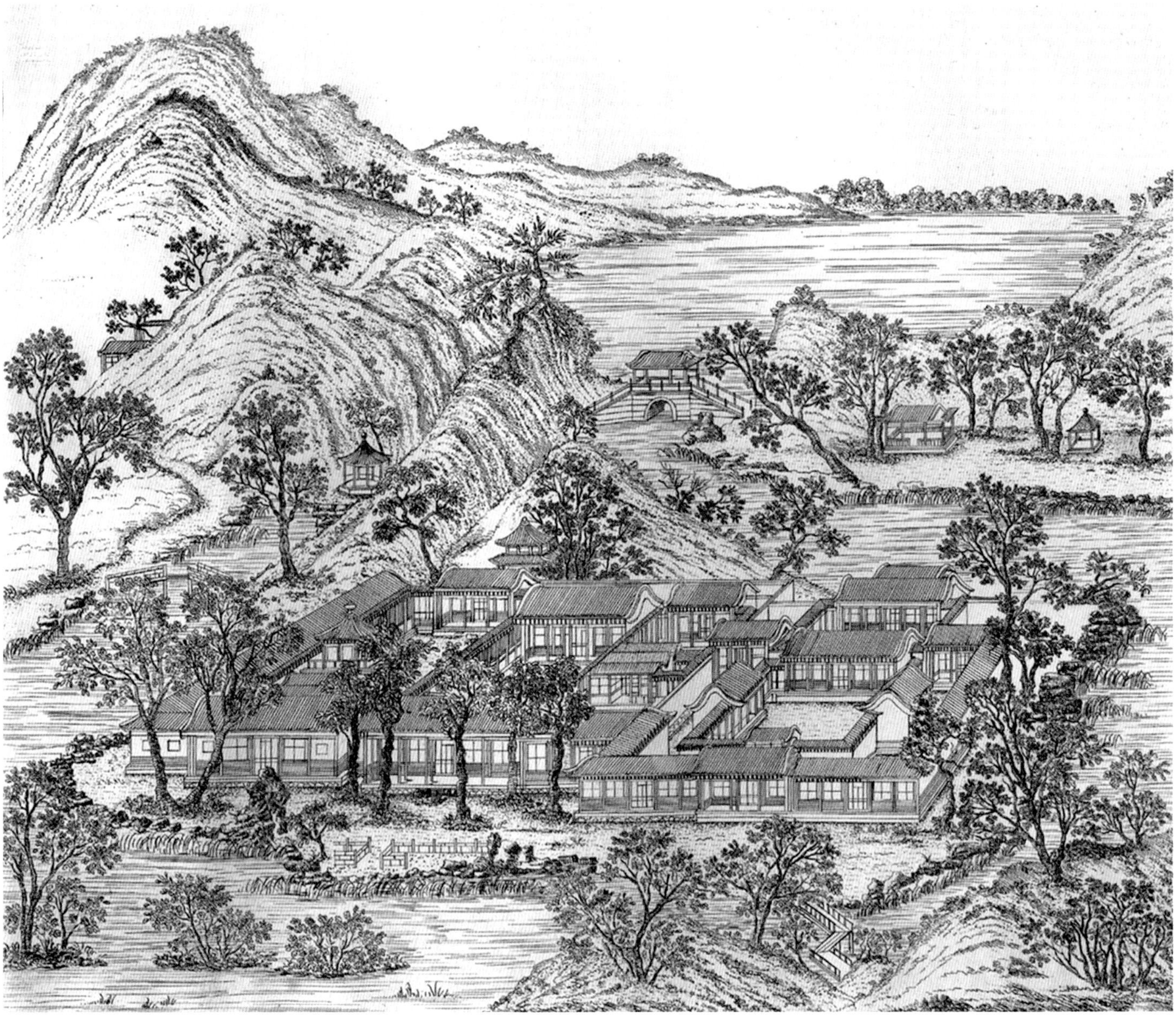

A view of the Old Summer Palace at Yuanming Yuan with designed mountains and lake and the characteristic arched bridge.

who developed it, instituting 135 years of governing from a garden. Sadly the Garden of Perfect Brightness lies in ruin, all but obliterated by the British High Commissioner, Lord Elgin, in 1860 during the Opium Wars. The site remains a symbol to the Chinese of foreign aggression and destruction. It remains for landscape designers a quintessential imperial Chinese garden.

The stone boat landing and a pavilion remain at Yuanming Yuan.

How has China managed to so revere and adhere to its past, in cultural values and landscape design? The answer lies largely in its written language of characters that are a kind of pictograph. For example, the Chinese word for garden requires in calligraphy thirteen strokes and is composed of the words for pavilion, lake, a plant or rock, and an enclosure.

Unlike English in which mastery of only twenty-six letters allows even a small child to crack the reading code, there are forty thousand characters in classical Chinese. To be functionally literate a person must know two thousand characters and three thousand to read and write the language at a level needed for high positions. Historically only the leisure class had time to master so many characters. While throughout Chinese history there were peasant revolts, none until the twentieth century achieved lasting change because the illiterate did not have the requisite skills to govern. Soon the old governing class—the mandarins—came back into power, reintroducing and reinforcing their closely held values including those about what constitutes beauty in landscape design.

Bridges at the Old Summer Palace.

Shizilin Yuan (Lion Grove Garden)

Suzhou, China

Water, rocks, garden buildings, bridges, mosaics, paths, courtyards, trees, shrubs, flowers—all these features of European landscape design have their counterparts in Chinese gardens. But the grassy lawn, cherished by Western culture from the Middle Ages until today, was unknown in traditional Chinese design. The grazing of sheep and cattle lies at the foundation of European culture, the lawn an idealized form of pasture and meadow. China, however, had no grazing culture, relying instead on fish, pigs, and poultry including ducks for food, and traditional Chinese garden design revolves around water and only a little land.

Suzhou, the "Venice of Asia," is laced with canals.

Rocks whose shapes suggest lions have given Shizilin its affectionate name, Lion Grove.

Suzhou, an ancient city on the Yangtze River delta near Shanghai, is the location of a collection of classical Chinese gardens developed over centuries by wealthy mandarins. It was and is a wonderful place for gardens since the desired water is readily available.

Among its oldest and most renowned gardens is Shizilin, "Eighteen Scenic Spots of Heaven," built in the middle of the fourteenth century by a Buddhist monk and his Zen followers. It is a scholar's garden, honored in the eighteenth century by several visits from Qing Emperor Qianlong and by thousands of tourists before and since.

Water in the form of lakes, ponds, protected inlets, and waterways is the largest garden feature of Shizilin as it is in most Chinese gardens. Small boats for transportation of people and goods and for recreation glide silently through its waters, goldfish dart beneath, and lotus and lilies grace the surface.

Of equal importance to ponds and waterways are the rocks, representing the mountains of the Chinese landscape. Those at Shizilin and other gardens in Suzhou come from the bottom of nearby Lake Tai, the soft sandstone worn into interesting shapes by centuries of eroding water. Shizilin has come to be referred to as Lion Grove or Lion Forest because

This view at Shizilin shows traditional Chinese garden features: water, lotuses, rocks, a pavilion, and two bridges, one zigzag, the far one of stone gently arched.

many of the rocks look like lions, though continued erosion has made the image apparent only to the imaginative.

Because water is at the center of Chinese landscape design, bridges are also a prominent feature. High arched bridges allow large boats to pass freely beneath. Small sites, where foot traffic and small carts are the norm, may have wooden or stone, high arched, or gently curving bridges. Most distinctive is the zigzag bridge. The oft-repeated but possibly apocryphal explanation is that the earliest Chinese believed that bad spirits could travel only in a straight line. What is clearly true is that changes of direction force strollers to slow their pace and, turning first left and then right, see the garden from different perspectives. Often without side railings, the zigzag bridge demands concentration on the moment, a Zen Buddhist value. The zigzag also serves to stabilize the bridge, especially where the bottom is soft mud in which the piles of a straight bridge might shift.

In addition to the zigzag and arched bridge, Shizilin illustrates other traditional Chinese means of directing and focusing a view. Round and fan-shaped windows serve as frames. Tracery or grille windows are designed in an infinite variety of patterns, making the view

LEFT Is an opening such as this at Shizilin meant only as a window through which one peers, or as a doorway leading to another courtyard? The visitor decides.

RIGHT Semiprivate tracery windows are simultaneously beckoning and deterring, making that seen beyond even more desirable.

beyond noticeable and intriguing by what is revealed and by what is partly hidden. As when the shade of an airplane window remains up when others around are closed, the dark interior makes the sun and green on the other side appear even more prominent.

In featuring water, rocks, bridges, and windows, Shizilin contributed to the pattern of the Chinese garden, inspiring future designers in Suzhou and elsewhere in China. Eighteenth-century English designers, adopting what they believed were hallmarks of Chinese gardens, failed to pick up on many of the features found at Lion Grove and other Chinese gardens. We can only speculate how the English and European adaptations of Chinese design—chinoiserie—might have looked had they done so.

A sixteenth-century painting of the Garden of the Humble Administrator by Wen Zhengming.

Zhuozheng Yuan (Garden of the Humble Administrator)

Suzhou, China

Eighteenth-century English writers celebrated in prose and poetry not only the art of gardening but specific gardens. Artists painted the great estates and their designed landscapes. So also did Chinese writers and painters immortalize their country's gardens.

Of the forty gardens in Suzhou, the Garden of the Humble Administrator has more than any other attracted the attention and commanded the admiration of artists. Sometimes translated as the Garden of the Unsuccessful Politician, its roots extend back to the twelfth century. But Zhuozheng Yuan became widely known in the sixteenth century when Wang Xiancheng, imperial envoy and Suzhou native, retired to this location after a tempestuous career. Wang sought the contemplative life, to be fed by literature and nature, and to that end began to build the ideal setting for his meditation. His friend, the famous poet and artist Wen Zhengming, also from Suzhou, wrote about and painted Wang's garden. During the eighteenth century, writer Cao Xueqin, who is said to have lived in the house during his teenage years, used Zhuozheng Yuan for the garden description in the classic Chinese novel *Dream of the Red Chamber*.

An interlocking series of lakes, small ponds, islands, and waterways, Zhuozheng Yuan has forty-eight structures including pavilions, bridges, pagodas, and viewing platforms. Fine old trees and smaller shrubs soften the lines of rocks, willows show their leaves in the glassy stream, and lotus blossoms light the water's surface.

While eighteenth-century English writers were composing poems and crafting essays about gardens, the Chinese were following an ancient convention by adding verse to their gardens. Scroll landscape paintings always included an accompanying poem, the Chinese characters rendered in elegant calligraphy. The logical extension of the custom was to have inscriptions in a garden. In Zhuozheng Yuan there are dozens of tablets and tall and narrow steles with commemorations and literary quotations.

Uniting poetry and landscape design is an ancient Chinese practice, adopted in England in the eighteenth century and still seen today in exhibits such as those at the New York Botanical Garden featuring flowers mentioned by Emily Dickinson with lines of her poetry or that of Alhambra gardens with the writings of Federico García Lorca.

ABOVE Poetry or other inscriptions complement the scenes in Chinese gardens as here at Zhuozheng Yuan.

OPPOSITE, TOP The lake, bridge, and pavilion attract painters and writers today as in the past.

OPPOSITE, BOTTOM Today photographers find Zhuozheng Yuan a place to practice their art. The lotus, symbol of peace and harmony, raises its bloom upward while ever-present goldfish seek food on the water's surface.

Paths and courtyards at the Garden of the Humble Administrator also excel in the ancient craft of mosaic. While the eighteenth-century English landscape designers were building pebble benches such as that at Stowe and grottoes as at Stourhead, Chinese artists were gathering pebbles from nearby riverbanks and lake shores, painstakingly sorting them by color, size, and shape, and making an infinite variety of pictures for their courtyards. Patterns were given poetic names such as Plum Blossom on Cracked Ice, Satin Dogwood, Crabapple in Diamonds, and Square Golden Coin. Some were abstract designs, others depicted animals or flowers.

Zhuozheng Yuan excels in another Chinese art form. Throughout the garden are hundreds of miniature gardens called penjing or penzai, representing scenes from nature, beloved Chinese paintings, or poetry. The Chinese equivalent of Japanese bonsai, they are constructed on trays called pens. Arrangements of a single artificially dwarfed tree or a grouping of rocks and plants may include small figurines of people, bridges, and pavilions. In the Suzhou tradition, the small trees may be pruned in a variety of shapes but often that

ABOVE The artistic arrangement of stones in this penjing at Zhuozheng Yuan may remind the visitor of the famous Three Gorges in the Yangtze River.

OPPOSITE Mosaic patterns at the Garden of the Humble Administrator.

of clouds. Penjing frequently represent contrasting ideas such as yin and yang, light and darkness, precision and abandon, change and permanence, solid and pliable, or vertical and horizontal. Mastering the art form takes a decade and the dwarfing demands daily attention for years. The patience required of the craft is itself illustrative of the seemingly unchanging culture of classical China.

ABOVE An artist lays out the pattern at the Master-of-Fishing Nets Garden.

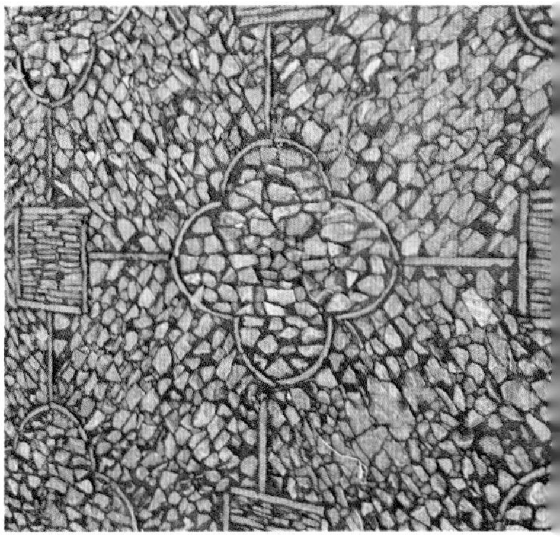

Wangshi Yuan (Master-of-Fishing Nets Garden)

Suzhou, China

Wangshi Yuan is only one-acre square, the smallest of Suzhou's gardens but some would say the most impressive. Built in the eighteenth century by a retired bureaucrat, it captures the essence of the Buddhist belief that withdrawing from the secular world and looking ever more deeply inward leads to enlightenment. The garden looks inward, as do other Chinese gardens, for they were designed for relaxation, rest, tea, edifying conversation, poetry readings, musical performances, contemplation, and meditation.

An entrance portal leads visitors through long, narrow hallways, helping them make the transition from one partially hidden courtyard to the next. As in the labyrinths of medieval Europe, they draw the pilgrim deeper within both physically and spiritually. Various buildings—a library, viewing platforms, pavilions, and courtyards—surround the central pond.

The shoreline of the pond is surrounded by rocks and plants and is itself sinuous. At no place can one see the whole. The rocks with their crevices and spaces juxtapose substance and void in a way that, according to Maggie Keswick, scholar of the Chinese garden, is "much admired by sophisticated viewers (but quite alien to the untutored Westerners)." Wangshi Yuan also exemplifies the Chinese design tradition of creating scenes within scenes, just as in meditation each revelation leads to another. Doorways beckon. Mirrors reflect the image from a pavilion's opposite side.

Visitors flock to Wangshi Yuan especially in spring when the peonies for which it has long been famous are in bloom, white the Chinese favorite. In all shades of red, pink, yellow, and white, peonies made their way to England in the eighteenth century where gardeners immediately fell in love with them, making them a mainstay of their gardens.

The Peony Study courtyard at Suzhou is revered, not only in Asia, but in the United States, for it served as model for the Astor Court at the Metropolitan Museum of Art in New York. Soon after President Nixon visited China in 1972 and Chinese-American cultural exchanges began, the museum engaged garden designers from Suzhou to build a Chinese garden using traditional materials, techniques, and tools including an eighteenth-century Chinese kiln to make the tiles.

Chinoiserie, which swept Europe and England, missed many of the subtleties of Chinese design. Europeans in the eighteenth century were looking outward to the wider world and expanding their horizons, both as nations and as individuals. Americans, too, were extending their territory and their fortunes. China and Chinese gardens encouraged another kind of expansion, that of refined taste and inner consciousness.

ABOVE The reflective water calls the viewer to reflect on life's meaning.

RIGHT The *bas relief* on the entrance portal depicts the tradition of welcoming guests.

ABOVE, LEFT Rocks at Wangshi Yuan encourage contemplation of empty spaces.

ABOVE, RIGHT The moon gate at Master-of-Fishing Nets Garden is but one of many in Chinese gardens.

RIGHT Mirrors reflect the opposite view and, at the correct angle, the viewer as well.

ABOVE The courtyard at Suzhou's Master-of-Fishing Nets Garden was the model for this, the Astor Court at the Metropolitan Museum of Art in New York City.

RIGHT *Paeonia lactiflora* is native to Tibet and northern China. Its many layers call Chinese admirers to contemplation.

Trompe l'oeil, the deceive-the-eye technique, here in the Wrest Park temple, is also used on the exterior of buildings for columns, quoins, niches, and sculpture.

Wrest Park
Bedfordshire, England

When fashionable Jemima Marchioness Grey became mistress of Wrest Park she was intent on having her home and its surrounding grounds look up-to-date. Following the new interest in all things Chinese, she had, according to the inventory taken on the duke's death in 1740, "a red . . . tea table, a Teapot Stand and Slops bason, eight large Tea Dishes and Saucers ditto, all blue and white China." Most expensive was the hand-painted Chinese paper of birds, flowers, trees, and figures for the dining room walls.

Turning her attention in 1758 to the ninety-two-acre park and gardens, she hired increasingly well-known Capability Brown to soften the lines of the formal gardens. True to form, Brown made irregular the straight sides of the canals and planted trees as clumps and groves rather than as allées. But he left much of the former design in place at the insistence of his strong-willed patroness.

ABOVE The elegant Chinese pavilion at Wrest Park, beautifully sited near the bridge.

RIGHT The original chinoiserie bridge of timber had to be replaced in 1876 with this one of stone.

A primary structure remaining from the older garden is the temple meant for hunting parties and suppers. The interior features painting techniques that have been used in garden design on the exterior of buildings as well as within. Corinthian columns, winged cherubs, urns, busts, herms, and full-sized statues were rendered at Wrest Park not in stone or wood but in paint by French artist Louis Hauduroy. Employing the art of trompe l'oeil, he made his columns and ceiling appear three dimensional. Painted in shades of gray—a technique called grisaille—his sculpture looks made of marble or stone.

Horace Walpole, a proponent of planned natural, called the temple "frightful." His opinion notwithstanding, Jemima was almost satisfied with the gardens of Wrest Park. She wanted only one more touch to show how *avant-garde* she was. She and her husband added two iconic examples of Chinese derivation. The first, installed in the 1760s, was a high arching wooden bridge; the second structure, placed on the canal bank near the bridge, a Chinese pavilion.

The question scholars have continued to debate since the eighteenth century is the degree to which Chinese design influenced the asymmetrical, planned natural style of Kent and Brown that swept England and Europe. Was it the primary source of inspiration for the landscape park design, simply one source among many, or had it little influence, just happening by coincidence to have characteristics of the changes already in motion? The French called the style *jardin anglo-chinois*, thereby seeming to give equal weight to English and Chinese influence. Horace Walpole, English patriot that he was, vigorously defended the English claim that the changes were made independent of Chinese design.

Sir William Temple would have disagreed with Walpole. The owner of Stowe, Temple had served with the East India Company and while in Asia visited China. In his 1685 essay *Upon the Gardens of Epicurus*, he wrote that the Chinese "way of thinking seems to lie as wide of ours in Europe as their country does" and that Chinese landscape design differs from the European way of planting "in certain proportions, symmetries, or uniformities." Rather, he wrote, they

ABOVE Stowe's Chinese house has been moved to different locations over the years. It was first in the garden's Grecian Valley and now stands near the Palladian bridge.

RIGHT A true Chinese pagoda has for good luck an uneven number of floors, the Kew Pagoda ten.

design "without any order or disposition of parts that shall be commonly or easily observed.... They have a particular word to express it... and, where they find it hit their eye at first sight, they say the '*sharawadgi*' is fine or is admirable." The seventeenth-century Chinese garden writer Ji Cheng described it this way: "There is no definite way of making scenery; you know it is right when it stirs your emotions." In 1712, writer Joseph Addison cited Temple's essay, thereby fueling interest in Chinese design and that of gardening in particular, and in 1738 Richard Temple built a Chinese house at Stowe, the first in England. Soon others followed.

Then, just after midcentury, William Chambers, who had himself lived in China for two years, published *Designs of Chinese Buildings, Furniture, Dresses, Machines, and Utensils: to which is annexed a description of their temples, houses, gardens, &c*. It was from a Chambers design that the Chinese pavilion at Wrest Park was built. He soon was designing the great Pagoda of brick and wood at Kew Gardens. Octagonal in shape, its ten floors rising over 164 feet, the Pagoda has been the trademark of Kew Gardens since its construction in 1762.

At the same time, missionary and painter Jean-Denis Attiret, SJ, went to China, there becoming the official painter for Emperor Qianlong, accompanying him in battle and recording the scenes. He sent copies of his extraordinary paintings back to Europe where they were widely circulated. The bridge at Wrest Park is strikingly similar to those in Father Attiret's paintings.

English estate owners, captivated by these stories and pictures of China, began filling their houses with Chinese lacquerware and porcelain, even calling their dishes "china." Like Jemima Marchioness Grey, in their gardens they built pagodas, bridges, and pavilions. But their choice of Chinese garden features was selective. They embraced some features, especially the asymmetry, the curving lines of the water's edge, the "natural" plantings, the bridges, and the pavilions, while ignoring other features—the dominance of oddly shaped rocks, mosaic paths, tracery windows, and variously shaped door frames. Most significant and jarring for those familiar with real Chinese gardens, the eighteenth-century landscape designers set the features they did adopt from China into their beloved English greenswards.

How much they recognized that their version of Chinese gardens was fantastical must have varied widely. Those who had been to China may have recognized wild imagination at work in English gardens; those who studied closely the reports coming out of China may have had an inkling of the anomalies; and those who, having heard but vaguely about what they called the Far East may have thought they were replicating the real China. Ultimately the greatest authenticity was to be found in the shrubs and flowers from China, including the rhododendrons, plum trees, chrysanthemums, and peonies that became integral and finally synonymous with the English garden and landscape.

And what of the debate as to the degree of influence of Chinese landscape design on that in England and Europe? Perhaps the best answer comes from scholar Rudolph Wittkower who suggested that the English embraced chinoiserie because they felt an affinity for the asymmetry, the natural lines, the hidden views, and the plants that characterized Chinese gardens. The design reflected a changing culture that was rejecting the previous axial, geometric style in favor of one that spoke more of the new source of power to be found with Parliament and the landed gentry. As well, the fantastical Chinese look fed their playful imagination.

Taj Mahal
Agra, India

China was not the only East Asian culture to be included in eighteenth-century English gardens. Buildings and decoration from Turkey, Egypt, and India were also popular.

In the same years that England was engaged in civil war, halfway around the world in Agra, India, the fifth Mughal emperor Shah Jahan was assuaging his grief over the death of his beloved wife with the construction of her mausoleum. The tomb itself and the surrounding garden reflect Muslim, Persian, and Indian design traditions, as Shah Jahan was a Muslim, his wife Persian, and his mother Hindu. The Taj Mahal was quickly recognized as a great architectural achievement. Often with their families, Englishmen in the employ of the military or the East India Company as well as other European travelers began visiting the increasingly famous Taj Mahal, bringing back tales of its beauty and romance. Soon there were Mughal-inspired buildings and gardens throughout Europe, just as Chinese buildings multiplied on European and English estates.

The *charbagh* or garden setting for the Taj Mahal is the Persian paradise garden form found in the Islamic gardens of Alhambra, in other Moorish gardens, and in the Christian gardens of medieval Europe. The quadrants (*char* meaning four and *bagh*, garden) are divided by the four rivers flowing out of Eden in the form of wide rills at right angles from the central pool. Unlike the Muslim custom of situating the tomb in the middle of the garden, the Taj Mahal lies at one end, a Hindu tradition. The pool is visually tied to the tomb itself through the repeated use of white marble. The almost still waters of the rill leading to the tomb reflect its ethereal beauty. Raised paths lead the visitor forward. Tall cypresses line the walkways, echoing the four slender, 130-foot minarets at the corners of the Taj Mahal, climbed by the Muslim *muzzerein* to call the devout to prayer. Beside the paths are sixteen sunken parterres, once filled with roses, daffodils, and fruit trees and later converted by the English to extensive lawns.

The Taj Mahal sits atop a tall plinth measuring 180 feet on each of its four sides. When viewed at ground level the fields and river behind it disappear, making the lacy marble tomb seem to float in air. Here the designer excelled in his decision to exclude from view undesirable elements, a useful technique for landscape designers even on a modest scale.

A paradise garden form leads the visitor to the tomb itself.

WATER AT WENTWORTH, YORKSHIRE.

WATER AT WENTWORTH, YORKSHIRE.

Sezincote
Gloucestershire, England

Sezincote is the last remaining Mughal-inspired house and garden in western Europe. Located in the Cotswolds near Oxford, it was the 1805 creation of the Cockerell family. John Cockerell, having gone as a young man to India where he made a fortune with the East India Company, bought the property known as the Home of the Oaks. Upon his death his youngest brother who had been with him in India inherited Sezincote. It was he who hired another brother, well-known architect Samuel Pepys Cockerell, to build a house with Muslim and Hindu elements designed to recall the sixteenth-century Indian culture of Emperor Akbar who sought to unite both traditions.

The design for the estate was one produced by collaboration. The owner knew India; the architect designed the house; painter Thomas Daniell designed the sculpture, the bridge, and garden buildings, and Humphry Repton, successor to Capability Brown, was consulted for the landscape.

The extent of Repton's involvement at Sezincote is unclear. It was Repton's practice—and his great contribution to the craft of landscape design—to present an owner with a book bound in red Moroccan leather in which he showed by means of overlays two scenes of a landscape, one as it presently appeared, the other the way it would look after his proposed changes. Repton produced no "Red Book" for Sezincote, though there exists a Repton sketch with overlay.

In 1808 in his notes for the design of the Brighton Pavilion, also of Mughal design, Repton describes the influence of Sezincote on him and hence on the famous pavilion:

> I had been consulted by the proprietor of Sezincote, where [the owner] wished to introduce the gardening and architecture which he had seen in India. I confess the subject was then entirely new to me: but, from his long residence in the interior of that country, and from the good taste and accuracy with which he had observed and pointed out to me the various forms of ancient Hindu architecture, a new field opened itself, and, as I became more acquainted with them. . . . I was pleased at having discovered new sources of beauty and variety which might gratify that thirst for novelty, so dangerous to good taste in any system long established because it is much safer to depart entirely from any given style than to admit changes and modifications in its proportions that tend to destroy its character.

OPPOSITE, TOP Trees obscure the bridge and lake at Wentworth, a country estate, in this "before" overlay by Humphry Repton.

OPPOSITE, BOTTOM Repton's "after" shows his proposal to remove the grove and install a curving path around the property to open the view of water and bridge.

At Sezincote, the setting for the Indian elements illustrates all of Repton's design preferences: the curving paths, lawns, tree clumps and belts, serpentine streams, and a small lake complete with island, which he learned from Brown. But combined with the Indian elements, there is an exotic feel. As in the Augustan gardens that placed classical elements within an

English pastoral setting, Sezincote freely uses the images and figures of India—a temple, a bull, a snake— in a landscape park design, successfully creating a picture very different from the unadorned vista favored by Brown or the Picturesque such as that at Hawkstone.

While a student at Oxford, twentieth-century British poet laureate John Betjeman was a frequent visitor at Sezincote, later putting into verse his memories of the romance of house and garden.

RIGHT Features such as the pond and island are miniaturized versions of Capability Brown elements today without Brown's clean water line.

BELOW "The bridge, the waterfall" of Betjeman's poem and a stone snake entwined around a stone tree trunk introduce the visitor to the theme: India.

RIGHT Betjeman found Sezincote's half-Tudor, half-Indian style true of garden as well as house.

BELOW, LEFT He wrote of an Indian temple and pool set in the lush green of England.

BELOW, RIGHT "And there they burst on us, the onion domes." Betjeman called Sezincote the "supremest landscape-gardener's art."

In this portrait by Godfrey Kneller, is Alexander Pope puzzling over the next lines of his humorous epic *The Rape of the Lock* or his design problem at what he called Twit'nam?

Pope's Grotto

Twickenham, England

If garden buildings suggesting China and other cultures evoked the romance and delight of foreign lands, the grotto was meant to arouse a different set of feelings. Unlike Italy where the grotto served as a cool place for relief from the intense heat, England with its frequent rain and chilly weather had no such need. Rather the eighteenth-century grottoes were meant to produce a sense of the mysterious. Especially when toured at night by candlelight, they produced at least a little thrilling terror. The fear upon entering the cave, the wonder at the views framed by openings, and the interior rooms hinted at a buried past.

Decorating grottoes became a popular pastime, as needlework or stamp-collecting were in other eras. Gentlemen and ladies, often with time on their hands in their country homes, delighted in making patterns, collecting materials, and affixing the stones and shells to the walls, thus leaving their mark for posterity. Many of the grottoes were but mediocre, others works of art, but all were intriguing.

Alexander Pope must have had the "aha" moment when he hit upon the solution to the landscape design problem he faced at his country home in Twickenham in the London borough of Richmond upon Thames. He wanted to connect two pieces of his property separated by the busy London road. A bridge would not do as it would obscure the straight view to the garden. An underpass was clearly the answer, but how boring to disrupt the guests' experience of the lovely property by taking them into a dark, dank tunnel! Never one to be satisfied with the mundane, he would apply his quick and witty mind to the challenge.

Perhaps inspired by the caves described in Virgil's *Odyssey* on whose translation Pope was working, he conceived of turning the tunnel into a grotto, with all the thrills a real cavern might present. Light would come in at both ends, but in between? A shiver of terror, a little chill, followed undoubtedly by witticisms from the host would turn the moment reassuring and lighthearted. Emerging at the other end after such an adventure would make the peaceful calm of the adjacent garden all the more pleasurable.

In his grotto he would have niches and side chambers and eventually cover the walls with pebbles, rocks, flint, spar, mundic, stalactites, crystals, Bristol and Cornish diamonds, marble, alabaster, snakestone, spongestone, and shells gathered from far shores. Admirers and friends including Hans Sloane of the Chelsea Physic Garden sent treasures for the walls and ceiling. The grotto would remind some visitors of those of Italian Renaissance villas that they had seen on their grand tour.

Most ingenious was the inclusion of small bits of mirror in angular forms embedded in the wall and ceiling, creating, as Pope himself explained, a *camera obscura*, a phenomenon known from ancient Greece and China. Light coming through the narrow entrance into the

RIGHT The boat landing on Pope's property on the bank of the Thames in Twickenham.

BELOW, LEFT Rose quartz here takes center stage among the many other kinds of rocks in Alexander Pope's grotto.

BELOW, RIGHT The grotto, now lit by electricity, once required candles and torches of fire which cast eerie shadows on the walls.

darkened grotto and striking the surface, projected "on the Walls . . . the River, Hills, Woods, and Boats, forming a moving picture in their visible Radiations."

Samuel Johnson, never without an astute analysis, described Pope's famous tunnel and in doing so laid down a challenge for all landscape designers. "A grotto is not often the wish or pleasure of an Englishman, who has more frequent need to solicit rather than exclude the sun, but Pope's excavation was requisite as an entrance to his garden, and as some men try to be proud of their defects, he extracted an ornament from an inconvenience, and vanity produced a grotto where necessity enforced a passage."

Dr. Johnson, right about so much, was wrong about one thing: Englishmen were to build grottoes on their grand estates throughout England, an anomaly perhaps, as were many features of the eighteenth-century English garden, but one relished and beloved.

Strawberry Hill

Twickenham, England

When Horace Walpole bought the pair of small attached houses on the Thames in Twickenham, he declared it a "little plaything-house, the prettiest bauble you ever saw." He would play in and with this house and land with intensity and creativity for fifty years and in doing so give a name to a wholly new style of architecture, Strawberry Hill Gothick. He would also have the chance to make concrete his strong opinions about landscape design, expressed in his now-classic *A History of Modern Taste in Gardening* in which he praised the landscape park style just coming into fashion in England.

A sophisticated and witty man of letters, Walpole was also a collector of both the fine and decorative arts. Strawberry Hill would house his art, and he was determined to create a unique setting for it. Delighted with his new property in this fashionable area of rural retreats for wealthy Londoners, he celebrated Strawberry Hill's prospects, its convenience, its "dowagers as plenty as flounders," and "Pope's ghost, skimming under the window by a most poetical moonlight."

His vision for the transformation of the plain houses was rooted in two concepts. The first was his love of fantasy, encapsulated in his book *The Castle of Otranto*. Described as the first gothic novel, its appeal is that of the Sublime as defined by Edmund Burke, engendering feelings of terror and astonishment.

The second governing concept lies in his patriotic beliefs. The son of Britain's first prime minister, he had studied the antique languages and literature at Eton and King's College, Cambridge, and had made the grand tour of Italy. But he preferred the traditions and art of medieval Gothic as the epitome of English culture and history.

In his decision to celebrate the English Middle Ages he was joining other estate owners and landscape designers of the eighteenth century. Lord Cobham had his Saxon deities in the landscape at Stowe, Henry Hoare put a Gothic cottage next to the Pantheon at Stourhead, and others had similar garden buildings or sculpture. But Walpole brought a new interpretation, one of humor through exaggeration.

Walpole began by clothing the buildings with a fantastical facade, inspired by *The Three Princes of Serendip*, the fairy tale from which he coined the word "serendipity." He planned a series of surprises, some with a touch of mystery. Like much chinoiserie, his design was based not on reality but on his literary and poetic imagination with no pretense that it was otherwise. The entrance hall and grand staircase make clear that his was no attempt at historical recreation as the ceiling and walls are clearly trompe-l'oeil, made of paint and paper, not stone and wood.

For the interior of Strawberry Hill, he wanted a mood he described as "gloomth," likening it to the feeling in old abbeys and cathedrals. But outdoors he wanted only "the gaiety of nature." As soon as construction on the house was started, Walpole began laying out the gardens. In his book *A History of Modern Taste in Gardening*, published in 1780, he praised

OPPOSITE An illustration from Walpole's Gothic novel *The Castle of Otranto*, published in 1790.

RIGHT The chimney pots were modeled after the interior of cathedrals and abbeys, including Westminster Abbey. The gray English skies enhance the romance

BELOW "Gloomth" inside, "riant" gaiety without.

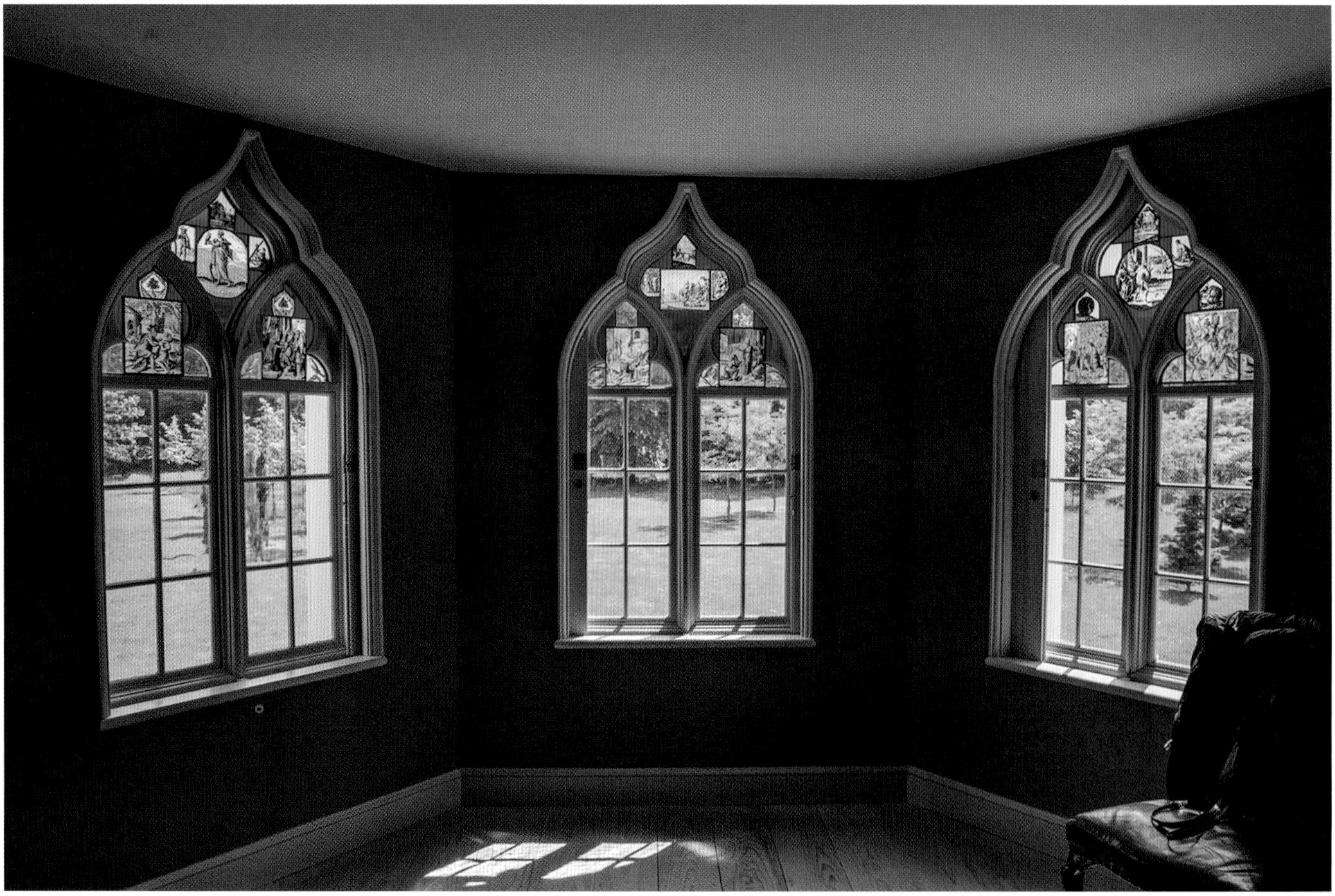

TOP Beside the house and enclosed within a medieval screen is the Prior's Garden.

INSET The Walpole-designed fanciful bivalve bench of wood was re-created in the 2012 restoration at Strawberry Hill.

the new style of William Kent and others who eschewed the formal geometrical lines, parterres, and topiary of the past in favor of asymmetry and curving lines. True to his national loyalty, he argued that Chinese gardens were not the source of these innovations, but he nonetheless used the Chinese term *sharawadgi* for the aesthetic achievement of his garden. Following his Gothic theme, he built the Prior's Garden alongside the house, enclosed at one end by a wattle fence, at the other by a gothic screen.

Then he set about laying out and planting "an open grove . . . a field, a serpentine wood of all kinds of trees and flowering shrubs and flowers. . . . The lawn, the town and church of Twit'nam . . . with meadows of my own down to the river." A lime grove filled the side yard. Lilacs, jonquils, and acacias were among his plants, and trees that would, in the words of his gardener, "hang down somewhat *poetical*." All this he adorned further with a Chinese bridge, a chapel in the woods, a rustic cottage, and a shell bench of his own design.

In Walpole's lifetime, Strawberry Hill became a tourist attraction. At first he enjoyed showing off the house, his art collection, and gardens. But when the number of visitors became overwhelming, he issued tickets, only admitted people in small groups, and strictly forbade children. The last was rather a shame for perhaps children, above all other visitors, could most appreciate the fantasy world he had created.

Painshill

Surrey, England

At Painshill, Charles Hamilton created a garden with the Rococo features that celebrated foreign lands and the follies so loved in the eighteenth century for imaginative play. In doing so he displayed three important skills of the landscape designer. First, he successfully managed smooth and pleasing transitions from one landscape scene to another, probably the most difficult challenge a landscape designer faces. He artfully arranged his focal points so that within a relatively small space one view flows to the next with ease. Wildly different garden buildings, each creating a different mood, are sited so that a single view may include two or more, yet the effect is not jumbled or contradictory but calm and unified.

Second, Hamilton, himself a painter, was a master at framing views. From the interior of garden buildings or by the placement of plants and trees, he focused the viewers' sight on particularly artistic and appealing scenes.

Third, Hamilton planted Painshill with what was at the time the most outstanding collection of trees and plants in England. He was a regular customer of Peter Collinson at his London nursery and John Bartram in Philadelphia through whom he acquired his extensive collection of North American trees. A first-rate horticulturist, he planted his acquisitions in the right conditions of soil, water, and sun, all arranged to show them in their most complimentary light.

Educated at Westminster and Oxford, he, like others of his age, had enjoyed the grand tour including Italy. Upon his return he began searching for property where he could exercise his interest in landscape design and horticulture. The same South Sea Bubble fiasco that had sent John Aislabie home to York to create his beautiful Studley Royal water garden forced the previous owner of Painshill to sell his estate. Beginning in 1738, Hamilton acquired the house and eventually 250 acres of surrounding land. As he began to realize his vision for the landscape, Horace Walpole noted, "He has really made a fine place out of a most cursed hill."

Except for the walled garden that protected his young plants, the general layout he chose was, like those of his contemporaries Kent and Brown, that of planned natural. At the heart of his design unifying all the diverse elements is a fourteen-acre lake. Believing as did Alexander Pope that "half the skill is decently to hide," Hamilton made each view of the lake, whether at water's edge or in the Surrey hills surrounding it, such that at no point could the entire lake be seen. Along the curving banks and in the gently rolling hills, he situated his garden ornaments. Symbols of far-flung lands were brought together at Painshill. So were those of times past.

A tightly planted fir walk high above the lake provides the needed transition from the reality of the outside world to the magical world of Painshill. It leads to the hill with the most prominent of Hamilton's garden buildings, the Gothic Temple with slender buttresses, a patterned stone floor, and quatrefoil clerestory windows. He used ogee arches for the temple's openings and then repeated the motif in the painted fan-vault ceiling of the building.

ABOVE The ten-sided Gothic Temple, made of wood, is sited to be glimpsed from several points in the landscape. On the north and south sides vision is controlled, but on the east and west it is open to focus the view as Hamilton wished.

RIGHT, TOP This open side of the Gothic Temple framed by ogee arches directs the view.

RIGHT, BOTTOM Miraculously, the Turkish Tent sitting atop a great greensward and backed by majestic oaks rather than the red Arabian sands is, although an anomaly, felicitous.

The ogee arch, formed by two arcs pointing in opposite directions, is of Arab origin and was adopted widely in medieval England. It was a brilliant choice for it visually unites the Gothic Temple with Painshill's most exotic element, the Turkish Tent.

Seen from the interior of the Gothic Temple and framed by the arches is the lake and adjacent hill topped with what Hamilton declared was his favorite structure. The Turkish Tent was constructed in brick and plaster, with a lead roof, and draped with white-painted, blue-fringed canvas. A bench deep within gives respite from the sun as do Arab tents, but here more frequently sheltering from cold English rain. It encourages the hiker to linger and relish the serenity of the Gothic Temple opposite and lake below. Framing the view, the canvas tent sides were described in 1763 by Sir John Parnell as "drawn up in festoons like Darius' tent."

Between the two hills crowned with the Gothic Temple and the Turkish Tent is, at the lake below, Painshill's famous grotto, most likely designed by Hamilton himself. Looking like a rocky outcrop natural to the site, the grotto connects two small closely adjacent islands. It was built with a brick base and faced with oolitic limestone quarried near the city of Bath.

LEFT The Painshill Grotto, appearing as one structure, connects two small islands.

RIGHT The eye travels from the cool interior of the grotto, across the lake and bridge, up the hill to the Turkish Tent.

The cave's opening beckons the adventurer into its mysterious depths. Only inside does the visitor realize the ingenuity of the construction. The most elaborate and spectacular of the eighteenth-century English grottoes, it has many rooms and views across the lake, framed by the hanging "stalactites."

Other nearby islands in the lake are joined by a Chinese Bridge. Far from appearing jarring so near the grotto, the bridge is the perfect complement, the exterior of the grotto resembling the rocks of real Chinese gardens. How much Hamilton understood this himself is unclear. Increasingly information about China was coming into England and Hamilton was well read, but it is possible his well-honed artistic taste led him to the compatibility of the grotto rocks with the Chinese bridge design without knowledge of real Chinese gardens.

In the Peninsula Plantations Hamilton planted exotic North American trees that turned color in autumn, a new sight in eighteenth-century England. He used a serpentine planting scheme, recommended by Philip Miller at the Chelsea Physic Garden, with beds on either side of a grassy path and a bed in the middle featuring an American redbud (*Cercis canadensis*). The bed was planted in layers, the tree surrounded by flowering shrubbery of middle height such as lilacs (*Syringa* species) and broom (*Cytisus* species). Around these were roses and spirea and other shorter flowering plants. At the border of the grassy path, violets, daffodils, and primroses made a showing. Artist William Hogarth said the serpentine planting scheme at Painshill "leads the eye a wanton kind of chase."

On the lake shore, and to hide Hamilton's brickworks, is the Ruined Abbey, framing views of the lake and opposite shore and romantically recalling England's past. On the hill adjacent, Hamilton had a vineyard of Pinot Noir and Pinot Meunier, producing an excellent sparkling wine that was mistaken by a French visitor for an expensive champagne.

TOP, LEFT The sides of the Chinese Bridge resemble the pattern of Chippendale furniture, a contemporary fashion in interior design.

TOP, RIGHT Sited next to the vineyard, the Ruined Abbey is the last of the follies Hamilton created. Perhaps his imaginary monks were wine makers.

BOTTOM The hermitage was inhabited briefly by a monk-for-hire who, being found inebriated in the nearby pub, was abruptly released from his vows and job.

Hidden in the woods was the hermitage, another garden building evoking a medieval and mysterious past. Again, Hamilton has provided frames to view the shrubbery, a planting innovation he is credited with initiating, as well as "borrowing" the view of distant fields. But Horace Walpole called the hermitage "the ornament whose merit soonest fades." By identifying garden features that may delight the visitor with surprise but that "soon lose their charms to their surfeited master," Walpole raises an important point for the landscape designer to consider. Humphry Repton went further: "Deception may be allowable in imitating the works of nature . . . but in works of art, every trick ought to be avoided. Sham churches, sham rivers, sham bridges, and everything which appears what it is not, disgusts when the trick is discovered."

In 1786, the year of Charles Hamilton's death, Thomas Jefferson and John Adams visited Painshill as part of their tour of English landscape gardens. Adams wrote in his diary, "Paines Hill is the most striking piece of art, that I have yet seen." Many visitors past and present agree.

8 Three Men, Two Nations, One Passion

EIGHTEENTH CENTURY

In the age of revolution, edible gardens influenced the course of history.

THEY WERE CONTEMPORARIES and they shared a passionate, decisions-determining interest in horticulture. For Joseph Banks, it was his only interest. King George III loved agriculture and horticulture so much he came to be known as "Farmer George." Thomas Jefferson said, "There is no occupation so pleasant to me as the cultivation of the earth."

Each man contributed to a new design idea that had but brief popularity in the eighteenth century. Today, however, people seek foods grown without pesticides and the environmentally aware want locally grown produce to reduce the fossil fuel required for transport. Others look for heirloom or unusual fruits and vegetables. For all, the answer lies in the *ferme ornée*, the ornamental farm, the edible garden as it is variously called, now one of the most advocated, written about, and executed of garden plans. Combining vegetables and flowers, ornament and utility makes sense in our small and therefore multipurpose gardens.

Moreover, horticulture played a role in important political events of the times. Jefferson was the third president of the United States and King George III ruled longer than any other British monarch before Victoria. Both led their nations at a momentous time in history. The embattled farmers of Massachusetts may have, as Emerson correctly reported, "fired the shot heard 'round the world" but plants and seeds also played a role, one usually and mistakenly ignored by historians. Landscape design reflects a culture. In this case it helped to *shape* the culture.

The lives of Thomas Jefferson, King George III, and Joseph Banks coincided almost exactly. The king was born in 1738, just five years before Jefferson and Banks. He died in 1820 as did Banks, six years before Jefferson. The king and Banks were close friends and associates, at times seeing each other daily. Jefferson, presented at the English court, was understandably received only briefly and coolly. He may or may not have met Banks, though they certainly knew each other by reputation. But his life and role as national leader intersected profoundly with those of George III and Joseph Banks.

> The greatest service which can be rendered any country is to add a useful plant to its culture.
>
> —THOMAS JEFFERSON

Marie Antoinette's *ferme ornée*, Versailles.

LEFT A portrait of Thomas Jefferson when he was secretary of state under George Washington, by Charles Willson Peale.

RIGHT Joseph Banks, seated, with Daniel Solander, protégé of Linnaeus, and Bora-Boran Mai, the second Pacific Islander to visit Europe.

Had Thomas Jefferson not written the Declaration of Independence and the Virginia Statute for Religious Freedom, served as governor of Virginia and secretary of state, vice president and then president of the United States, negotiated French support in the early years of the new republic, purchased for the United States the vast Louisiana Territory, founded the University of Virginia, or been an accomplished architect and inventor, he still would have gone down in history for his role in introducing new landscape design principles and advancing the knowledge of horticulture in his new nation. His knowledge of and devotion to horticulture may well have contributed to his diplomatic and political success.

Joseph Banks was the son of wealthy English parents. At school Latin and Greek instruction passed him by. Instead he applied his quick mind to plants, first roaming the fields around his Lincolnshire home and then those near his schools Eton and Oxford. Later he dogged the heels of Superintendent Philip Miller at the Physic Garden when his widowed mother moved to Chelsea. He soon became known as one of England's most knowledgeable naturalists and botanists.

Then, in 1768, the chance of a lifetime came his way. The great explorer James Cook, commanding HMS *Endeavour*, was to explore the South Seas. Without hesitation, Banks signed on as naturalist for the three-year voyage, knowing that hundreds, perhaps thousands, of new plants awaited his discovery there.

George III in a portrait by Allan Ramsay.

King George III ascended the throne at age twenty-two. Like Banks and Jefferson and so many others in the eighteenth century, he was besotted with agriculture and horticulture, critics accusing Farmer George of spending so much time pursuing agriculture that he neglected other kingly duties. In his own time and subsequently he has been evaluated variously. Was he the tyrant that Americans believed him to be or was he merely doing his duty in enforcing Westminster's laws regarding taxation? For a long time he remained adamant about not losing the American colonies but finally acquiesced. Could it be that horticulture played a role in his willingness to surrender?

John Whipple House

Ipswich, Massachusetts

When Thomas Jefferson developed his ideas of the *ferme ornée* he began with the several and varied traditions of American colonial garden design that were both utilitarian and decorative. John Whipple House is an early example of the utilitarian.

New England winters were harsh. When the baby came down with whooping cough in the middle of a seventeenth-century January night, it was critical that his mother had grown and dried scarlet pimpernel. All summer she would plant, tend, and harvest this and other medicinal herbs to prepare potions to cure the diseases winter was bound to bring. And she needed her garden near the house, enabling her to keep an eye on both baby and stew pot as she planted and weeded. Practicality, not aesthetics, was the prime consideration for those carving a living out of the wilderness.

The earliest American settlements were forts, evolving eventually into fortified communities. Only after many years—a century in some locations—was it possible to let down the guard and enjoy a relatively safe and peaceful existence. Only then were flowers and other ornamentals introduced. Some, such as the useful and attractive calendula, feverfew, pot marigold, tansy, and gallica rose 'Apothecary', fulfilled both criteria.

Captain John Whipple built the first rooms in his Ipswich, Massachusetts, home in 1677. His son and grandson each made additions until, with fourteen rooms, local residents called it "the Mansion." Medicinal and culinary herbs interspersed with flowers occupied the beds in the front of the house. Sweet-smelling lilacs, able to withstand cold weather and biting wind, framed the front door at John Whipple House then as they do today.

The vegetable garden and orchard were also planted near the house, customary in most colonial American gardens for practical reasons. The housewife's or kitchen garden as it was variously called was located in the front, back, or side yard depending on the house's orientation to the sun and other conditions such as wind or ocean spray. The land was cleared around the house for some distance since dangers lurked in the forest. Seeing hostile Indians from a distance allowed time to bolt the doors and load the musket.

Fences encircled gardens to protect from hungry animals, wild or domestic. Split timber was the available material. Building upon memories of England, the colonists laid out their gardens geometrically, often using the paradise form with quadrants around a central point. Paths of gravel or crushed shells gave easy access to the planting beds. Colonial gardens such as that at John Whipple House were the beginning of the *ferme ornée* in America.

RIGHT The mostly medicinal herbs complement the plain New England architecture of John Whipple House.

BELOW The rail fence and planting beds seen from a second story window at Whipple House.

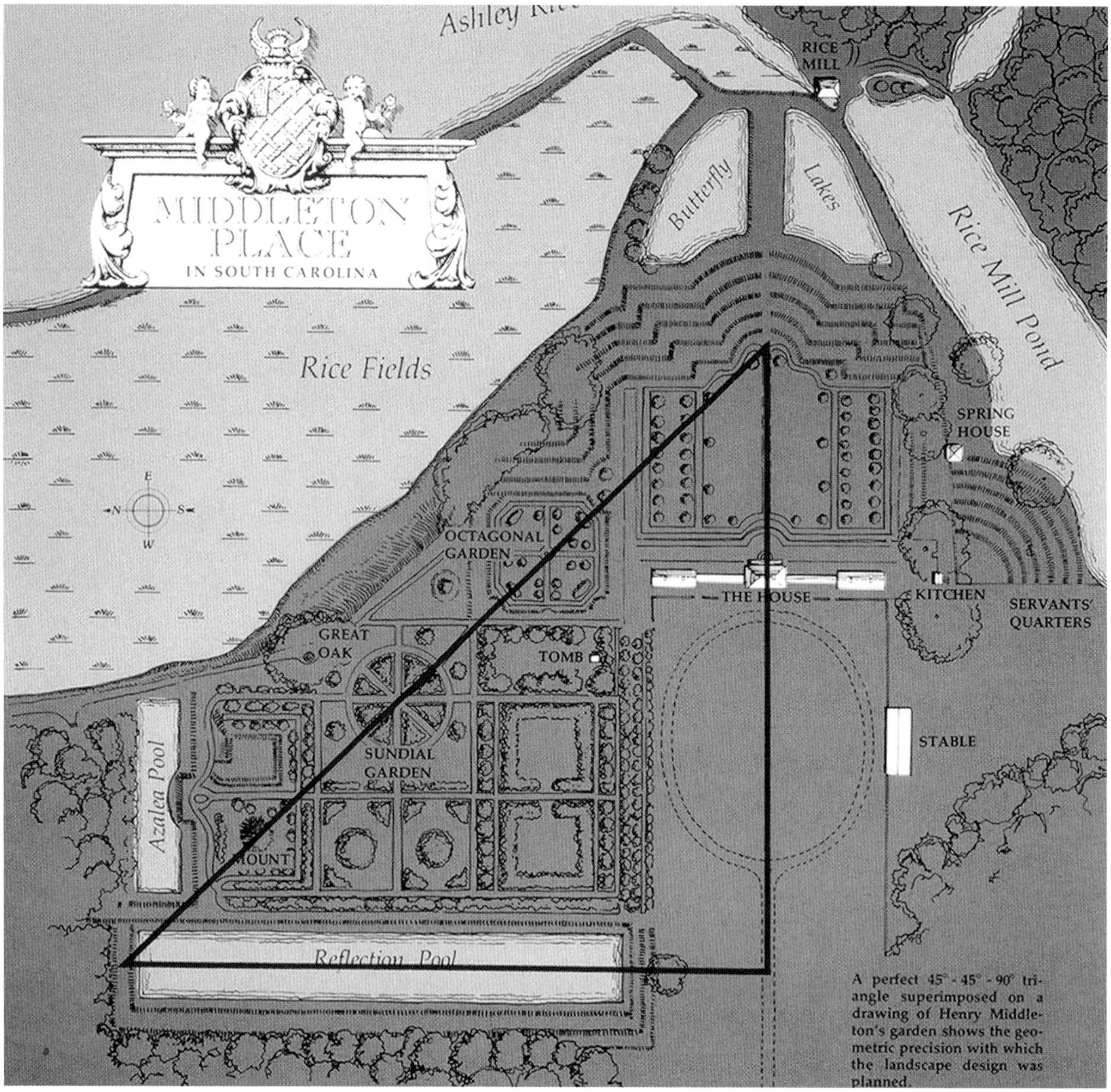

A triangle forms the basis of design at Middleton Place where the eighteenth-century garden remains the oldest surviving European-style landscape in America.

Middleton Place

near Charleston, South Carolina

The Middletons of South Carolina were to the American South as the Adamses were to New England and the Roosevelts to New York. A leading family for generations, they were plantation owners, growing rice in the coastal region near Charleston. Henry Middleton inherited the property from his father in 1741 and began creating the gardens. Following André Le Nôtre's principles of symmetry, balance, order, and focal and vantage points set

TOP, LEFT Spanish moss (*Tillandsia usneoides*), an epiphyte, drips from the live oak (*Quercus virginiana*) in the octagonal garden at Middleton Place.

TOP, RIGHT Middleton Place's graceful and pensive wood nymph has lived in the garden since 1810.

RIGHT The enchanting butterfly-shaped garden at Middleton Place is perfectly symmetrical.

within a precise geometric form, he used one hundred slaves for a decade to construct his sixty-five-acre garden.

The house stood atop a forty-foot bluff, a topographical feature unusual in the low country of the Carolinas, commanding a straight view to the Ashley River. Henry Middleton, with the help of an English gardener, extended this axis in the opposite direction, using it as one leg of the right triangle. The second side was formed by a reflection canal, the third by a line through the centers of three smaller geometric gardens with shape-defining hedges, some pruned as trapezoids. Flowers, simple topiary, birdbaths, and urns adorn these gardens, all surrounded by the magnificent live oaks native to the area.

The butterfly-shaped garden has astounded visitors since its creation. A bowling green bordered by the flower beds and divided by an axial path leads from what was once the house's center to the grassy terraces and symmetrical, man-made lakes that suggest the blue wings of the butterfly.

Designed to be purely ornamental, Middleton Place is a study in peacefulness and prosperity. It was not so with the Middleton family. Henry Middleton was a member and, for a few days, presiding officer of the Continental Congress, resigning when the talk of seeking independence from Britain became serious and intense. His son took his place and countered his father's position by signing the Declaration of Independence.

Mount Vernon

Mount Vernon, Virginia

For generations American schoolchildren learned that George Washington was "first in war, first in peace, and first in the hearts of his countrymen." First in Washington's heart was his home, Mount Vernon, overlooking the Potomac River near the nation's capital that bears his name. Here Washington rested from presiding at the Continental Congress, leading the army in the War of Independence, and serving as first president of the United States. Here he returned to his beloved family, his honored staff, and to farming that was his first profession and his declared first interest. The designed landscape, its utilitarian purpose set within an aesthetically pleasing plan, the *ferme ornée*, illustrates traits of Washington himself and characteristics of the new republic.

His design for the approach to the house is an interesting combination of styles prevailing in Europe and America in the eighteenth

OPPOSITE Generals Lafayette and Washington at Mount Vernon in a painting by Thomas Rossiter.

century. Immediately in front of the symmetrical house is a turf circle, itself surrounded by a circular carriageway allowing his many and frequent guests to arrive easily at the main entrance. The two roads that feed into the circle are likewise geometric and symmetrical, but they incorporate the serpentine lines that were becoming popular in England and Europe. A bowling green lies between the roads. Oak and hickory trees, now of great size, line the roadway. Sadly, the American chestnuts that Washington planted fell to blight in the twentieth century. The house is flanked by curving porticoes ending in small buildings that form a semicircle, contrasting with the serpentine lines of river and carriage road.

ABOVE The Potomac River can be seen through the porticoes.

OPPOSITE Ha-ha, lawn, specimen trees, and shed of Washington's design as a "repository for dung," the first known structure in the United States devoted to composting.

The east lawn between the house and river was designed in the planned natural style of Capability Brown, complete with a ha-ha that kept the farm animals from the house while ensuring an unbroken view to the river. When Washington in his travels up and down the eastern seaboard encountered new trees or shrubs, he came home with saplings including the eastern redbud, dogwood, and mountain laurel for planting at Mount Vernon.

Committed though Washington was to creating a beautiful home and landscape, his first interest was in making the property that he had inherited a profitable farm. There was the large Mount Vernon community of family, employees, and slaves to feed and many other needs to be met. Putting his considerable organizational and entrepreneurial skills to

work, he established a highly successful farm and ancillary enterprises including fisheries, a gristmill, and a distillery. Livestock were work animals as well as providing meat, butter, milk, wool, leather, and, importantly, fertilizer. Writing to his neighbor and friend George Fairfax on June 20, 1785, Washington declared, "When I speak of a knowing Farmer, I mean one who understands the best course of Crops . . . and above all, Midas like, one who can convert everything he touches into manure as the first transmutation towards Gold."

Trained as a surveyor, Washington laid out on either side of the house extensive vegetable and herb gardens and orchards. The lower garden on the south side was the kitchen garden, bounded by warm brick walls and espaliered fruit trees lining the walks as wind breaks. Head vegetables such as broccoli, cabbage, cauliflower, and lettuce were featured. Adjacent was the orchard for apples, apricots, cherries, peaches, and pears.

The upper garden to the north featured a large greenhouse and a botanical garden that served as nursery and research station for new plants. The garden outside of the orangery combined ornamentals and vegetables, a style that was gaining popularity in England, France, and the United States. A parterre next to one side of the orangery features the fleur-de-lis honoring France for support of the American cause. Seeing it on his visit to Mount Vernon, General Lafayette must have been pleased.

Old traditions and new ideas are woven together in the gardens of Mount Vernon, just as they were in the new American republic. The geometric forms honored the older traditions; the landscape park represented the new democracy. Both republic and garden were eminently practical, places to put hand to plow. Washington, a man of taste, successfully arranged his garden to be as beautiful as it was productive.

RIGHT The stylized lily has been the symbol of France since the reign of Charlemagne.

BELOW With its tool house and espaliered fruit trees, the kitchen garden provided vegetables that Martha Washington declared were “the best part of our living in the country.”

Father Junípero Serra portrayed in bronze at the Carmel Mission.

San Carlos Borromeo (Carmel Mission)

Carmel-by-the-Sea, California

Had Thomas Jefferson turned 180 degrees from his sights on England and France magically to look west across the North American continent he would have seen another colonial effort, this one founded by a Spanish Franciscan missionary from Mexico. In 1771, just as independence from England was in the East Coast air, Father Junípero Serra founded the second of what would be twenty-one missions in California to Christianize and "civilize" the Esselen Indians and make firm the claim by Spain to the area. The architectural style of the missions would become the inspiration for future California buildings and their furniture. The layout and ornament of the mission gardens, which included elements of the *ferme ornée*, likewise influenced future landscape and garden design. Two centuries after the founding of the missions, they would be understood as an early stage in the long history of immigration from the south.

Located on the Monterey peninsula near San Francisco, the mission San Carlos Borromeo was named by the recently canonized Junípero Serra to honor the sixteenth-century cardinal and archbishop of Milan. Known for his care of the poor, San Carlos Borromeo (of the same family who built Isola Bella on a Borromeo-owned island in Lake Maggiore) had roundly criticized his colleague Cardinal Gambara for the expense of Villa Lante, declaring that the money should have been used instead for a hospital.

The first years of the California mission saw change and growth. Moved from the original site to a hillside a half mile from the sea, the buildings at the new location were at first log, then adobe. But the greatest change to the mission in the early years was not that of buildings. In 1784 Father Junípero Serra died at the Carmel Mission and was buried in the church.

It was almost a decade before the mission, its church, other facilities, and gardens were made permanent and beautiful. Manuel Ruíz, a master mason from Mexico City, was assigned the job of designer to build a stone church. While English and European landscapes were being changed by the new ideas of Capability Brown, the California missions, including San Carlos Borromeo, relied on older monastic traditions. Ruíz incorporated Moorish elements and in doing so paid homage to Father Serra and his birthplace in Moorish Mallorca.

Like medieval monasteries, the mission of San Carlos Borromeo is enclosed. But unlike many other California missions, the quadrangle is a trapezoid. At its heart, a quatrefoil fountain with tile floor supplies water to the compound, brought from the Carmel River by a simple canal.

TOP Bells call the mission community to worship. The inner courtyard seen here is constructed with the requisite fountain and a cloister as protection from the elements.

BOTTOM Like Alhambra, the Carmel Mission is a study in sun and shade. Thick adobe walls protect interior rooms from the intense heat.

INSET Prickly pear cactus has three edible sections: the pad, the flower petals, and the fruit. It is also used medicinally to treat diabetes, high cholesterol, obesity, and viral infections. Decorative, it is a *ferme ornée* in itself.

On one side lies the basilica, made of sandstone quarried from the nearby Santa Lucia mountains. Lime from abalone shells collected on the beach provided an essential part of the mortar. The church features a Moorish window made from a combination of a circle and a square placed at an angle. The bells are reached by an external staircase, the surrounding walls lush with colorful bougainvillea.

As well as medicinal herbs, foods such as apples, cactus, corn, culinary herbs, grapes, and olives are grown within the enclosure. Bougainvillea, roses, and other decorative flowers make the Carmel Mission a *ferme ornée*.

The Mexicans, who founded and operated the California missions, were to become one of the largest and most influential of U.S. immigrant populations. With their counterparts from all over the world on the East and West coasts, they would contribute to the American mosaic and give the nation beautiful and popular architectural and garden forms.

Jeffersonia diphylla, or twinleaf, is the only plant named for Thomas Jefferson.

Monticello
near Charlottesville, Virginia

When notable American botanist Benjamin Smith Barton addressed the American Philosophical Society in Philadelphia in 1792, he assigned a new botanical name to a native Virginia plant. He called it *Jeffersonia diphylla*, justifying his action with these words: "I have had no reference to his political character, or to his reputation for general science and for literature. My business was with his knowledge of natural history. . . . especially of botany and zoology, the information of this gentleman is equaled by that of few persons in the United States." Thomas Jefferson would not have been displeased, as horticulture was for him a consuming interest, a passion that ran throughout his long life.

The perfect choice to bear the name of Jefferson, the twinleaf has two opposite and equal leaves, separate yet connected. Thomas Jefferson himself had two sides, the one scientific and empirical, the other artistic and imaginative. At Monticello, his beloved Virginia home, he would utilize the landscape design known as the *ferme ornée*, the ornamental farm, which he described as "articles of husbandry" interspersed with "the attributes of a garden."

Jefferson had a great and rare gift that he employed in all dimensions of his rich life. He paid close attention to particularities but always placed these within universals. He famously demonstrated this ability in the Declaration of Independence. Beginning the argument not with objections to the stamp and tea tax, he set the logic for separation from Britain within the framework of "self-evident" truths, "all . . . created equal," "unalienable rights," and "life, liberty and the pursuit of happiness."

So it was in his approach to horticulture and landscape design. He sought and understood the larger picture. He favored landscape design that spoke of his democratic principles. He advocated and practiced farming methods including contour plowing which took account of ecology but also declaring that in "point of beauty nothing can exceed the waving lines." In his horticultural explorations and experiments he looked for ways new plants could aid the economy and better people's lives such as when, despite the threatening objections of rice growers, he tried growing upland rice. Brought from the South Seas by Captain Bligh,

ABOVE The small reflecting pool is located perfectly to show the house in its waters. The dark red cockscomb (*Celosia* cultivar) seen here was among Jefferson's favorite flowers.

OPPOSITE A curving path with flower beds on either side encircles the green turf lawn on the southwest side of Monticello.

this strain of rice would, he hoped, encourage growers to move from the malaria-infested swamps near the coast.

Tom Jefferson was only twenty-three when he began converting the five-thousand-acre tobacco plantation he had inherited into his *ferme ornée*. He was inoculating cherry trees even before he began building the house on the "little mount," and soon he was adding white oak and tulip poplars. Observing the plants on his property breaking dormancy, blooming, and dying back, he began recording in his garden and farm journal each stage of their growth. He would maintain and enlarge his records at Monticello for almost sixty years, noting the date of plantings, when vegetables "came to table," what flourished or failed, and under what weather conditions. With knowledge of surveying acquired from his father, he began

drawing plans for ornamental and vegetable gardens, vineyards, and an extensive orchard.

He decided to put the house on the top of the hill and chose the style of Italian Andrea Palladio as his architectural model, a style that was then popular in England. It was ideal for Monticello because it allowed views in all four directions of the Virginia countryside.

His first design effort for the gardens at Monticello followed the European geometric style that was in favor at the time. But a trip to England in 1786 changed his mind. Ambassador to France from the brand new United States, he was sent from Paris to England to join John Adams in negotiating with the English. A lull in the proceedings freed him and Adams to visit sixteen English gardens about which he had read, including Stowe, Blenheim, and others designed by Capability Brown, as well as Painshill, Kew Palace, and Stourhead.

Always perceptive, he understood that the new style of gardening was more than a new fashion, that the landscape park style with its curving approach roads was more representative of participatory democracy than were the old axial, allée-lined roads pointing to a central power. An admirer of other aspects of French culture and not wanting to offend in any way the country he was courting for support for his new nation, he never openly criticized French gardens. Yet he did offer his critique of a German garden designed in the French geometric fashion but with a *jardin anglais* section: "[It] show[s] how much money may be laid out to make an ugly thing, what is called the English quarter, however, relieves the eye from the straight rows of trees, round and square basins which constitute the mass of the garden." Of England he wrote, "The gardening . . . is the article in which it surpasses all the earth. I mean their pleasure gardening. This, indeed went far beyond my ideas."

He thought how he might use these new English ideas at Monticello and eventually was the first to adopt the landscape park style for an American garden. He laid out his plan to his granddaughter: "a winding walk surrounding the lawn . . . with a narrow border of flowers on each side." He was to revise the plan, planting ten-foot oval flower beds at intervals on either side of the path, each containing one kind of flower, and including in the scheme both local woodland treasures and exotics brought from distant shores. Here he could plant his "belles of the day, [which] have their short reign of beauty and splendor, and retire, like them, to the more interesting office of reproduction." Hyacinths and tulips were superseded by belladonnas, they in turn by the tuberoses. Flowering trees as well as mighty elms, walnuts, and weeping willows provided needed shade and aesthetic pleasure, trees that he described as planted in "clumps."

Inspired by garden ornament he had seen in England, he sketched more than twenty ideas including a grotto embellished with pebbles from the Rivanna River which lay at the bottom of Monticello mountain and where he planned to put the quotation from Alexander Pope that he had seen at Stourhead. He got as far as building an elegant pavilion in which he would read, rest, and contemplate his garden and the Virginia hills. But his other plans for decoration at Monticello were abandoned when responsibilities to his new nation demanded his time, first as secretary of state under Washington and vice president under John Adams, then as president himself. Away most of these years, he could only write home and direct his daughter and later granddaughters as when, in 1793, his daughter Martha Randolph wrote of insect damage in the vegetable garden. He advised, "This winter we will cover our garden with a heavy coating of manure. When the earth is rich it bids defiance to droughts, yields in abundance and of the best quality. I suspect that the insects . . . have been encouraged by the feebleness of your plants; and that has been produced by the lean state of the soil." In so analyzing the problem and its solution, he was anticipating the advice that horticulture and agriculture experts give today: feed the soil, not the plant.

Even when he was absent from Monticello, he was, in these years and ever after, working on his vegetable garden, orchards, and vineyards, advising family and slaves, and gathering seeds and plants from afar. At age seventy-six, he described his own eating habits to a doctor, "I have lived moderately, eating little animal food, and that . . . as a condiment for the vegetables, which constitute my principal diet." While he, his family, endless guests, and servants certainly dined on his garden produce, he also purchased household food from his slaves who were allowed land to farm for their own benefit.

But for Jefferson, the extensive plantings at Monticello were above all an experimental station where he could try new plants with the hope that they would thrive, providing income for farmers in the region. In the orchard there were 150 varieties of fruit and nut trees. Ever hopeful about the vineyard, Jefferson replanted it at least six times, trying thirty-six varietals, but disease, insects, and neglect during his absences took their toll. Another disappointment was olives. Although he tried numerous varieties, none survived the Virginia winters.

The crowning glory of Jefferson's *ferme ornée* was his vegetable garden, one thousand feet in length. Here on a terrace carved from the sloping hillside he grew seventy species of vegetables started from seeds gathered from many places, some acquired by purchase, others by exchange, still others from plant expeditions.

Among Jefferson's sources were the nurseries of John Bartram and Bernard McMahon in Philadelphia, Peter Collinson in London, the Jardin des Plantes in Paris, and dozens of

RIGHT The vineyard, today re-created at Monticello.

BELOW The vegetable garden, the pavilion, and in the distance the mountain Jefferson named Montalto. Threatened by developers in the 1970s, the eight-acre twin of the "little mount" was purchased by the Thomas Jefferson Foundation for fifteen million dollars, the same price Jefferson paid for the Louisiana Purchase.

correspondents near and far. Not least of these was the Comtesse de Tessé, devoted horticulturist and aunt of General Lafayette whom he met while serving as American ambassador to France. They corresponded until her death in 1813, she sending him plants and seeds including those of white heliotrope (*Heliotropium arborescens*) and Chinese golden rain tree (*Koelreuteria paniculata*) which he declared he cherished "with particular attentions, as it daily reminds me of the friendship with which you have honored me." It was the first grown in America. He in turn sent her a beautyberry (*Callicarpa americana*), a persimmon tree (*Diospyros virginiana*), and a sweetshrub (*Calycanthus floridus*). Lafayette and Jefferson were dear and lifelong friends, bound by a common commitment to democracy, to horticulture, and to Madame de Tesse.

With the Louisiana Purchase in 1803 now-President Jefferson acquired from France the entire area today comprising the middle of the country, instantly doubling the nation's size. Immediately Jefferson set about assembling an exploring party of thirty-three to map and describe the new territory, the party to be led by U.S. Army officers William Clark and Meriwether Lewis. The chief goals were to find a route westward, secure relationships with the Indian tribes inhabiting the area, establish U.S. sovereignty over the vast territory, and research the natural resources including plants. To that end he sent Captain Lewis to Philadelphia to study botany for nine months under the direction of Benjamin Smith Barton. Departing in May 1804 and returning over two years later, the expedition brought plants, seeds, drawings, reports, and maps of the newly acquired territory.

Among the Lewis and Clark Expedition seeds were those from three Indian tribes who hosted the party in the Dakotas, including sunflowers from the Hidatsa, beans from the Arikara, and Mandan red corn, all subsequently planted at Monticello. There Jefferson also grew red peppers (*Capsicum annuum* 'Corno di Toro') from Mexico; French tarragon (*Artemisia dracunculus*) for which Jefferson may have acquired a taste while ambassador, perhaps at Madame de Tesse's table; and white eggplant (*Solanum melongena*) from North Africa.

At age sixty-eight, Thomas Jefferson wrote to a friend: "I am still devoted to the garden, but though an old man, I am but a young gardener." In his admission he recognized that from the science of horticulture there is always something yet to discover and that the art of garden design is by its very nature a reflection of ever-changing culture. Both his intellect and imagination remained keen until his death on July 4, 1826, the fiftieth anniversary of the signing of the Declaration of Independence.

We can only wonder at his achievements in many fields and at his impact on generations and nations. We can only speculate as to how his consuming interest in horticulture shaped his life and thought. Did his knowledge and interest help him to break into the society of Paris when he was but an unseasoned new ambassador? Did his friendship with Madame de Tesse, formed from their shared interest, contribute to Lafayette's favorable impression of the leaders of the new United States? Did his commitment to gaining knowledge of new plants and the economic possibilities for cultivating them stimulate western settlement of the expanding United States? Is his *ferme ornée* the basis of our edible garden today and our current rethinking of what constitutes healthy eating? Thomas Jefferson was a primary shaper of American society. His passion for horticulture and landscape design helped shape him.

Royal Botanic Gardens, Kew
London, England

The stated purpose of the voyage of HMS *Endeavour* was to document, from the shores of Tahiti, the transit of the planet Venus. But the hidden object was another: to determine if there was truth in the vaguely rumored tales of Terra Australis, a yet-unexplored southern land. The voyage proved to be an early step in the creation of the world-renowned research institution, the Royal Botanic Gardens, Kew. The vision behind Kew and its scientific achievements changed the course of political and economic history.

Banksia serrata, a plate from *Banks' Florilegium*.

The ship's captain was Lieutenant James Cook, charged by the voyage's sponsors—King George III, the Royal Navy, and the Royal Society—with keeping the second purpose a secret, lest other nations, especially the Dutch, rival the claim Britain would have to any newly found territory. Even the ship's sailors were kept in the dark until the departure from Tahiti.

Twenty-seven-year-old Joseph Banks, appointed by the king as the official botanist for the voyage, outfitted the ship from his own fortune for the task of documenting the plant life he expected to find. *He* would not make the mistake of Columbus and Magellan who had brought back no specimens and no drawings from their explorations. To that end he hired his own staff: Daniel Solander, Finnish naturalist Herman Sporing, a scientific secretary, and two artists, one of whom was Sydney Parkinson. Banks also supplied the *Endeavor* with a library of more than one hundred books for botanical research and artists' supplies including microscopes, lenses, razors, chemicals for preserving specimens, wax, and several kinds of salt in which to keep seeds. To Cook's annoyance, the captain's quarters were appropriated by Banks for his research station. John Ellis, a merchant and amateur naturalist, wrote to Linnaeus that "No people ever went to sea better fitted out for the purpose of Natural History, nor more elegantly."

As the ship made its way along the South American coast and around Cape Horn to Tahiti, Banks, by his collecting, was already making botanical history. Then, departing from Tahiti, Captain Cook steered the *Endeavour* around the coast of New Zealand and west. Reaching the east coast of Australia, the ship set anchor in what Cook was to name Botany Bay

ABOVE The pleasure gardens surrounding Kew Palace are geometric.

OPPOSITE Queen Charlotte's Cottage at Kew.

for the rich specimens gathered there. Sailing northward and hugging the coastline, the ship was almost wrecked near the Great Barrier Reef and had to remain for seven weeks of repair while Banks, Solander, and Sporing found a trove of botanical material. Throughout the journey artist Sydney Parkinson drew each specimen, noting its colors. Upon return to London, Banks had each drawing painted in color and then hired eleven engravers to make copperplates for future printing.

Finally, after three long, often dangerous, and always adventure-filled years, the *Endeavour* docked once again on English shores. Everyone was eager to hear what the returning crew had seen, done, and learned. With his charm and knowledge, Joseph Banks soon became London's most talked-about and sought-after speaker, lecturing for the Royal Society where he was a member and later, for forty years, president.

Soon after the voyage, King George III began garden plans for the smallest of the royal palaces. Known as the Dutch house, Kew Palace was conveniently located on the outskirts of London. There the king settled his family, displayed pieces from his extensive art collection, and indulged his interest in the new plants flooding into England from the Americas and around the world.

Lovely as this setting was, it was not long before Farmer George was introducing vegetables into the scheme. Tomatoes were planted but a stone's throw from the palace itself. Soon there was a whole garden in the *ferme ornée* style, designed and planted for both beauty and productivity. The king's consort, Queen Charlotte, supported his enthusiasm. Her way of participating was to develop her own romantic rustic cottage a short walk from the palace itself, a place to retreat for a quiet afternoon alone or picnic on the lawn with the family.

As the romance with farming and rustic village life grew, the *ferme ornée* became stylish and was adopted elsewhere. Within a few years Charlotte's counterpart, Marie Antoinette, taken with the country retreat at Chantilly, built her Petit Hameau, a little village surrounding a pond, on the grounds of Versailles. Instead of the traditional French parterres, her little hamlet featured meadows and vegetable gardens to adorn the rustic buildings that included a farmhouse, dovecote, bakery, boudoir, and grange that served when needed as a ballroom.

Sir Joseph Banks Centre for Economic Development at the Royal Botanic Gardens, Kew.

But in England Kew was more than a place to play at country life. With adequate land and water, and nurseries nearby in Twickenham and Hammersmith, Kew Palace provided the perfect location for King George to develop his interest in and knowledge of horticulture. Now he needed someone to oversee his efforts and develop the plant collection. Who better than knowledgeable and agreeable Joseph Banks?

King George and Joseph Banks were a good match for they shared not only a passion for horticulture but a particular focus and purpose. Theirs was not only scientific curiosity about botany, but a belief in the potential economic benefits that agricultural development held. Their belief was a realistic one because early in the century London nurseryman Thomas Fairchild, a correspondent of Linnaeus and fellow researcher of the sexual characteristics of plants, had succeeded for the first time in intentionally creating an artificial hybrid. By means of a feather, he cross-pollinated a sweet William and a carnation. The resulting plant, called by other botanists Fairchild's Mule, opened the door to endless possibilities for new plants whose weaknesses could now be eliminated and desirable characteristics strengthened.

At first Banks was an informal adviser to the king, but that did not hinder his all-out effort on behalf of England. His vision was to collect seeds and plants from around the world, determine the desirable characteristics, develop the best possible plants, and dispatch them to the places in the British Empire where they would be most lucrative. To that end he supported William Bligh in bringing breadfruit from Tahiti to the West Indies. Soon plants as various as spices, mango, cotton, orchids, flax, tea, and bananas were being transported

Banks's discoveries are recognized in the Australia and New Zealand section of today's Kew.

across oceans and around the capes. He also set about establishing botanical gardens in far-off places including Calcutta where local plants could be strengthened for transport and imported plants tested and nurtured.

Banks's role at Kew was formalized by his appointment as superintendent and he continued his effort to bring economic benefit to the British Empire. By the time of his death in 1820, he had set Kew on the path it was to follow until the present day. The Royal Botanic Gardens, Kew, became the world's most renowned botanical collection and research institution, rivaled in importance today only by the New York Botanical Garden. Joseph Banks's interest and leadership is recognized and honored in the Sir Joseph Banks Centre for Economic Development at Kew.

And what of the intersection of the lives of George III, Joseph Banks, and Thomas Jefferson? During the 1770s opposition in Britain to the war in America was building to a crescendo. Whig leader William Pitt, Lord Chatham, made an impassioned speech before Parliament about what he described as "the gathering storm," arguing that the war was costly and would be interminable. Pitt reminded his countrymen and king that America "is a double market—the market of consumption, and the market of supply." Pursuit of the American war would give "millions, with naval stores, . . . to your hereditary rival [France]."

Pitt appealed to his longtime friend and landscape designer Capability Brown, then head gardener at Hampton Court, to act as intermediary with the king and to convey his profound opposition to the American war. Although Brown agreed with Lord Chatham that the war was, in Brown's words, "unfortunate" and "disgraceful," he "shared private hours" with the king. Some weeks later Brown reported that he had fulfilled the requested mission: "To-day, and indeed many opportunities, have occurred of late in which I have had very favorable conversations with the King—no acrimony, nor ill will appeared." For a long time George III resisted abandoning the war, but eventually, in 1779, British General Charles Cornwallis surrendered to George Washington.

Did King George cave to pressure from the Whigs or did he decide to put his effort and money into the economic development of the rest of the increasingly vast British Empire? Americans have often used the term "Farmer George" pejoratively, implying that this sophisticated man was but a country bumpkin. But the king was astute indeed to make horticulture his passion and focus. Thomas Jefferson's interest in horticulture was a thread woven throughout his life, political relationships, and decisions, affecting developments in colonial America and then the United States. Similarly with King George III, horticulture contributed mightily to his thinking and decisions, consequently influencing the development of the British Empire and, by extension, world history.

9 Designing *for* Democracy

Landscape designers help forge a new American identity.

NINETEENTH CENTURY

IN THE HUDSON RIVER VALLEY of New York in the mid-nineteenth century and then in New York City itself, landscape designers did more than reflect the culture. They actually *shaped* the culture, blurring the lines between ordinary working folk and the rich and powerful and paving the way to a new identity for the young nation. The confluence of artists and social reformers led by Andrew Jackson Downing would give Americans expanded aspirations. Downing's work in turn would lead his partner, architect Calvert Vaux, and Frederick Law Olmsted to express clearly and concretely a bold new vision for America. The landscape design they championed, the places they practiced their art, and most of all the purpose to which it was directed affected not only landscape design but the social fabric of America, giving rise to the appellation by which the United States would be known around the world, "the land of opportunity."

The American Revolution of the 1770s was a political revolution of the most important consequence, but it was not a social revolution. The men (and they were all men—white, free, and property-owning) who had sat in the Virginia House of Burgesses when Virginia was a colony were the same who represented the new state of Virginia. The great families of Massachusetts, Pennsylvania, New York, and other colonies similarly continued their leadership. And the rest of America's people? They were thought of and perhaps more importantly thought of themselves as "a nation of woodsmen" (so described in *Harper's New Monthly Magazine*), their chief occupation that of chopping trees to carve farms and settlements out of a wilderness. The purchase of the Louisiana territory in 1803 increased pioneering opportunities, reinforcing America's prevailing identity.

When, in 1815, Samuel and Eunice Downing named their youngest child Andrew Jackson after the hero of the Battle of New Orleans, they could not know how much their son would fulfill the legacy of the woodsman from Tennessee who, as seventh president of the United States, would be known as the first populist president and champion of the common man. Nor could the Downings predict that their child, Andrew Jackson Downing, would, through his profession of landscape designer, his skill at writing, and his deep commitment to populist values, become a leading light in extending the benefits of democracy.

> Plant spacious parks in your cities, and unloose their gates as wide as the gates of morning, to the whole people.
>
> —ANDREW JACKSON DOWNING

A place for everyone: Central Park, New York City.

As he grew up in the mid–Hudson River Valley, young Downing learned the family nursery business. When his father died, his older brother took him on as partner. Charming, intelligent, and articulate, he found himself advising Highland Gardens customers, the owners of the grand estates that graced the river's banks, about their choice and arrangement of trees and orchards. He was a good salesman and soon proved to be something more.

But the story of his life, work, and contribution begins earlier. He was just a boy, attending the local academy near his home, studying painting, drafting, and surveying, when a new spirit began to emerge in the Hudson Valley. Writer Washington Irving was the herald. As a child, Irving had been sent to the Hudson Valley to live with family friends during the summers when cholera gripped New York City. In the valley he came to love the wide and bountiful river and the mountains covered with virgin forests that cradled it. Then as a young man he went to Europe to write a history of the reconquest of Spain, actually living in Alhambra. But it was less his history of Spain than his accompanying short stories, *Tales of the Alhambra*, that captivated the European and then the American reading public. When he returned to buy a home in the Hudson Valley, it was as a celebrity. Soon his stories of the valley, *Rip Van Winkle* and *The Legend of Sleepy Hollow*, made the home he called Sunnyside a popular tourist destination. His success paved the way for the literary flowering of New England, emboldening James Fenimore Cooper, Nathaniel Hawthorne, Herman Melville, Ralph Waldo Emerson, Henry David Thoreau, and many other Americans to write. They discovered that they could write well.

Visual artists in the Hudson Valley were likewise giving Americans a new identity. Painting had in the early years of the republic been confined to two subjects. One was portraits of the founding fathers and the rich who could afford to engage such painters as Charles Willson Peale and Gilbert Stuart. The second subject of painting was events in American history such as *The Death of General Warren at the Battle of Bunker's Hill* by John Trumbull.

Then in the early 1800s, Hudson Valley artists opened their doors and began painting the scenes around them, the river, the Catskill Mountains, autumn colors, storms, and sunsets. Asher Durand, Jasper Cropsey, Frederic Church, Albert Bierstadt, and Thomas Cole had no need for access to the rich and famous nor direct experience of the events leading to nationhood. The landscape outside was nearby and accessible. As their reputations grew, these Hudson River school painters expanded their horizons traveling across the country and then overseas, capturing with canvas, brushes, and oil paints the beauty and majesty of the landscape. Following their lead, other Americans soon tried their hand at the visual arts.

It was onto this stage that Andrew Jackson Downing came. Delivering trees from his family nursery to the estates on the river, he soon knew all the great families of the valley and married into one of the old and respected Dutch families. His wife Caroline was a De Wint, her mother a niece of U.S. President John Quincy Adams. As the Downings developed the increasingly successful nursery business, Andrew Jackson Downing was forming ideas not only about how to be a successful grower but how gardens should look. Aesthetics became increasingly important to him.

Perhaps inspired by his valley neighbor Washington Irving, Downing at age twenty-six wrote *A Treatise on the Theory and Practice of Landscape Gardening adapted to North America*

OPPOSITE *Kindred Spirits* by Asher Durand pictures poet William Cullen Bryant and painter Thomas Cole admiring the naturally Picturesque scenery of the Hudson Valley.

with a view to the Improvements of Country Residences. The book's endlessly long title would not have predicted its success, but a success it was. Soon it was said to be on every parlor table in America. The next decades would see eight editions, and it remains in print now, more than 175 years later.

What could Andrew Jackson Downing possibly have written that brought him such instant fame? He put forth two tenets, developed in the book with practical and sound advice to make them real. First, true to his name, he promoted the idea that one did not have to be a Roosevelt, Livingston, Delano, or Vanderbilt to have a beautiful garden. In his book he showed ordinary folk in the Hudson Valley how they could replace the natural meadow with its foot-worn path through the tall grasses that led to the front door of their modest farmhouses. His guide suggested simple but elegant front yards of turf and shrubbery, winding paths, judiciously placed trees, and an occasional ornament such as a stone urn planted with flowers. In doing so he gave his neighbors of modest means an expanded vision of themselves, just as were the widening school of artists and writers. He was promoting a means of upward mobility.

Downing's second tenet was that society benefits when people put down roots. He agreed with the analysis of French diplomat and historian Alexis de Tocqueville that Americans are restless, always looking for new opportunities. But he held that communities benefit when people establish homes in which they expect to live for a long time. He believed that when they plant trees for their grandchildren to climb, they also invest time and energy in schools, churches, government, and other local institutions. He believed that as people work at improving their homes, gardens, and land, society becomes more stable and prosperous.

In his book as well as other writings and activities, he set the stage for social reformer Frederick Law Olmsted whose landscape designs were as numerous and extensive in the United States as those of Capability Brown a century earlier in England. Downing and Olmsted transformed the look of America and as they did so were key players in inspiring American beliefs and values.

Andrew Jackson Downing.

Montgomery Place
Annandale-on-Hudson, New York

Flush with the success of his popular book, Andrew Jackson Downing embarked on another writing venture, that of editing, writing articles, and answering readers' questions for a new monthly journal, *The Horticulturalist*. In the October 1847 edition, he wrote an extended article about Montgomery Place and in doing so identified what he considered to be a superb landscape design and expressed his preference for the Picturesque style.

At the time, there was no official profession of landscape architect, no formal training and no licensing, so the role Downing played in designing a number of gardens including those at Montgomery Place is not known. A modest man, he did not claim ownership where he might have done so, but as a close friend and neighbor of the influential Livingston family, owners of Montgomery Place, as well as their supplier for trees and shrubs, he likely offered his design advice. His extensive writing about the design elements he admired remains our best source of knowing what he valued and advocated.

It is not surprising that Downing felt an affinity for the Picturesque for it was the style of nature herself in the Hudson Valley. Towering spruce and pines, untamed woodland, craggy mountains, high bluffs overlooking the wide river, rushing streams that fed the river: these were the very embodiment of the Sublime as lauded by Edmund Burke whose philosophy Downing had studied. A reader as well as a writer, Downing was knowledgeable about landscape design in England and knew of the Picturesque style that was then popular.

Downing himself had a kind of Picturesque appearance and manner. His dark hair worn loose on the neck, strong brows, and piercing black eyes enchanted the ladies who often mistook his roots as "Spanish." Although considered charming, he was serious and intense. His own character, the events of his life, and his historical moment of time and place formed an ideal union.

The allée becomes a stately wood leading to the lawn surrounding the house at Montgomery Place.

The wrap-around porch offers several views of the Hudson River and mountains on the west bank.

His essay on Montgomery Place begins with a description of its surroundings: "For twenty miles on the eastern shore the banks are nearly a continuous succession of fine seats." With small river landings, each estate boasted extensive pleasure grounds, old woods, and views across the river "with its numberless bright sails and steamers" to the Catskill Mountains on the west bank.

The Montgomery Place property is bounded on the west by the Hudson River "broken with small islands into an outline unusually varied and picturesque," on the north by " a wooded valley in the depths of which runs a broad stream rich in waterfalls," on the south by an oak wood in the center of which is a private drive, on the east from the post road "a long and stately avenue of trees, like the approach to an old French château," which gives way to a tall wood, in turn succeeded by the lawn "which opens with increased effect . . . after the deeper shadows of this vestibule-like wood."

The back terrace of Montgomery Place looks across the river to the Catskill Mountains.

Specimen trees of hemlock, lime, ash, and fir supplied by the Downing nurseries grace the house's north side, a perfect place to watch the "spectacle of rare beauty, the sunset fade into twilight." The columns and arches of the house's generous porch frame views of the river and distant hills of "azure, purple, violet, pale grayish-lilac and the dim hazy hue of the most distant cloud-rift."

The four hundred acres of Montgomery Place contain miles of trails. In Downing's day there was a flower garden and conservatory, but most remarkable were the features that took advantage of the natural terrain and plantings.

The Morning Walk begins on the western terrace of the house leading past a small pond and down to the river, then curves along the bank for "a great distance with overhanging cliffs crested with pines [that] frown darkly over it; sometimes thick tufts of fern and mossy-carpeted rock border it, while at various points, vistas . . . of the beautiful river burst upon the eye."

The Wilderness features a long wooded valley, "much varied in surface, swelling into deep ravines" with a stream that has "all the volume and swiftness of a mountain torrent. But the peculiarity of 'The Wilderness' is in the depth and massiveness of its foliage. . . . with native trees, thick, dark and shadowy."

TOP Sawkill Creek incorporates into its name *kill*, the Dutch word for stream, acknowledging the heritage of the Hudson River Valley.

BOTTOM Fallen trees enhance the sense of the Picturesque.

Soon the hiker comes to the waterfall of Sawkill Creek on the northern side of the property which "here rushes in wild foam and confusion over the rocky fall, forty feet in depth." Sawkill Creek was known far and wide for its beauty, General Lafayette coming to see it on his farewell tour of the United States in the 1820s. The "shadowy" path leads to the lake, "a natural mirror in the bosom of the valley" where birches and maples mixed with evergreen spruce and white pine are reflected in the lake.

Downing concludes his description of Montgomery Place by noting that:

> The remarkably natural beauty which it embraces has been elicited and heightened everywhere in a tasteful and judicious manner. There are numberless lessons here for the landscape gardener; there are an hundred points that will delight the artist; there are meditative walks and a thousand suggestive aspects of nature for the poet; and the man of the world, engaged in a feverish pursuit of its gold and glitter, may here taste something of the beauty and refinement of rural life in its highest aspect.

Mount Auburn Cemetery
Cambridge, Massachusetts

Mount Auburn was the first rural cemetery in the United States, important in itself and because it paved the way for public parks. It owes its purpose to the nineteenth-century preoccupation with death and takes its form from the philosophy of transcendentalism.

Like the Hudson Valley, Boston was in the early years of the nineteenth century feeling secure and confident. The old New England stoicism in the face of hardship was giving way to optimism. The new philosophy of transcendentalism, articulated and championed by Ralph Waldo Emerson and Henry David Thoreau, was taking hold. Rejected was the stern theology of John Calvin and the emphasis on rationalism in Unitarianism. Influenced by philosophy in the Romantic tradition such as that espoused by Jean-Jacques Rousseau and Marquis Girardin at Ermenonville, the transcendentalists held that mankind and nature are one, intuition should be one's primary guide in life, and contemplation in a natural setting is instructive because it is in nature that God shows Himself.

This new approach to life affected the understanding of death. In the early 1800s and before, burials took place in family plots on farms or in the increasingly crowded churchyards or public burial grounds of the cities. Unsanitary practices polluted the water, causing disease. While the Grim Reaper was just as frequent a visitor to Boston as previously, by the 1820s a gentler notion of death was espoused, emphasizing life beyond the grave as a continuation of life on earth and death as a natural part of the life cycle. Above all, death was seen as the great teacher, revealing life's meaning, value, and purpose.

But understanding from death came only with reflection. Elaborate mourning rituals served as reminders that death was an occasion for contemplation of the eternal verities. This changed understanding of death required a new setting for burial, one that beckoned the grieving to visit the graves of their loved ones who had "passed on to the other side," there to meditate on life and death. Built in 1804 near Paris, Père Lachaise was just such a burial ground. It would be a model for the new Boston cemetery.

It was Jacob Bigelow who initiated the action to establish Mount Auburn. A physician who taught at Harvard, he envisioned a rural setting after that romanticized by the poets where nature was at its most beautiful, where sorrowing families could inter their deceased loved ones, return periodically to "commune" with them, be comforted by nature, and, as expressed by Wordsworth, "muse in solitude." Gathering a group of such prominent citizens as Daniel Webster and Justice Joseph Story who had lost his wife, parents, and five children in a fifteen-year period, Bigelow and his committee then met with the newly formed Horticultural Society of Boston. All agreed with the vision of establishing a public "rural" cemetery.

They found their ideal property near Cambridge where Harvard students hiked, calling it Mount, after the land's highest point, and Auburn, after the village in Oliver Goldsmith's poem *The Deserted Village*. Mount Auburn as described by Justice Story in his consecration speech is "beautifully undulating in its surface, containing a number of bold eminences, steep acclivities and deep shadowy valleys," a Picturesque setting.

The graves appear at places almost like the natural outcropping of rock, a look that must have pleased the transcendentalists.

The plan was conceived by Dr. Bigelow but largely carried out by Henry A. S. Dearborn, then president of the Horticultural Society of Boston. Dearborn took advantage of the natural contour of the land and of the large old trees growing on the eighty-acre tract. He created winding and interesting pedestrian paths and avenues for carriages throughout, giving access to all parts of the cemetery. Three points of interest form an isosceles triangle, but true to the spirit of naturalism, no axial roads connect them: rising some 120 feet above the Charles River is Mount Auburn on which was erected a medieval tower honoring George Washington; the chapel designed by Bigelow in a gothic style is surrounded by towers reminiscent of the minarets of a mosque; and two small lakes separated by only a narrow piece of land are located at the intersection of the two shorter sides of the triangle. Graves are not lined row upon row as in military cemeteries but rather as nature dictates, one small family grouping nestled in a protected concave formation, another nearby set at an angle and facing another direction. A collection of specimen trees adorns the hillside and lake edge, among them fir, oak, cypress, beech, maple, cedar, and sweetgum.

The symbolism of the weeping trees would not have been lost on grief-conscious nineteenth-century visitors to Mount Auburn.

Jacob Bigelow called Mount Auburn "an attractive and consoling association of the garden and the grave," where people were urged to come, especially after church on Sunday, to stroll the winding paths, ponder nature and the morning sermon, enjoy the trees and flowering shrubs, view the State House of Boston from the top of the hill, contemplate their own mortality, and find God in nature.

As Boston was burying its dead at Mount Auburn, all too soon the decision was made to dedicate the great battlefield at Gettysburg as a memorial to fallen Union soldiers of the Civil War. Mount Auburn founding committee member Edward Everett gave the dedicatory speech. (Abraham Lincoln's address was intended as only a few brief remarks.) Towns and cities began to believe that having a "rural" cemetery was an essential element to being considered progressive. Mount Auburn was their model. It also led Andrew Jackson Downing to one of his most notable projects and his only surviving landscape.

4 *Advertising Sheet of Mag. of Horticulture.*

ADVERTISEMENT.

PROFESSIONAL LANDSCAPE GARDENING.

The numerous applications and inquiries made of the undersigned respecting his professional terms in giving designs for laying out grounds, in forming new residences, or in embellishing or improving old ones in accordance with correct principles of taste, have induced him to publish his list of prices, as below. It is proper, also, to state, that when extensive improvements are required, in places at a distance, within a certain time, it is desirable to receive notice by letter, a week or two in advance, as, otherwise, previous engagements might give rise to disappointments.

For a design for the grounds of a villa residence, (the survey, or plan of the place, in its existing state, being furnished) . . .	$50 00
For the same, with the working drawings, details of ornamental structures, &c. complete, and the principal outlines staked out on the ground, and lists of trees and shrubs furnished . . .	100 00
A design for the grounds of a cottage residence	30 00
For the same, with details, working drawings, lists of trees, &c., &c.	60 00
*** The travelling expenses are to be added to the above, when the place to be visited is more than fifty miles from New York.	
A design for a flower garden	10 00
A sketch, with working drawings for any ornamental garden building of rustic work, a gate lodge, gardener's house, or green-house	15 00

When a professional visit is required at any place, to give an opinion, to suggest, superintend, or carry out any improvements in the buildings, garden, or grounds, the charge is $15 a day (of six hours,) while at the place, and travelling expenses.

A. J. DOWNING.

Botanic Garden and Nurseries,
Newburgh, N. Y., June 1, 1842.

A. J. Downing's advertisement for landscape design appeared in Hovey's *Magazine of Horticulture*, vol. 8, 1842.

Springside

Poughkeepsie, New York

Matthew Vassar, a mid-Hudson brewer and entrepreneur, was disappointed when the local citizens did not respond to his repeated advertisements for cemetery plots on property he had bought in the city of Poughkeepsie. Ever on the cutting edge, in 1851 he had hoped to establish a rural cemetery modeled on Mount Auburn. Like Mount Auburn, the property he chose had "undulating hills, groups of forest trees of luxuriant growth. . . . curious mound formations of rocky character studded . . . with oak, hickory, chestnut and evergreens," according to the *Poughkeepsie Eagle* in 1850. Additionally, there were meadows, about ten acres laid out in an apple orchard, and "rivulets," all "susceptible to tasteful embellishment." Failing to sell cemetery plots, Vassar decided to make the property of forty-four acres into his own residence with numerous farm buildings, calling it Springside. It would be a *ferme ornée* and a forerunner of the planned community concept.

Naturally he turned for the design to Andrew Jackson Downing, his famous neighbor across the river in Newburgh. Sadly, he would all too soon suffer another disappointment, this one far greater than the first and one he would share with the nation.

Downing had first advertised his design services in 1842. Previously landscape design was not a paying profession, architects and nurserymen including it in their primary work. But Downing, now a celebrated author of books on design, recognized that people would pay for landscape design and so made known his availability.

Vassar and Downing went to work on Springside, planning the buildings and grounds. Downing suggested the layout of avenues, walks, and drives. Buildings included the residence, barns, a carriage house, ice house, dairy room, granary, apiary, and aviary "for wild and domestic fowls," a spacious conservatory, the gardener's cottage, a log cabin, and the porter's lodge.

For the landscape, Downing drew upon the ideas of both the Sublime and Beautiful as defined by Edmund Burke and on which Downing expounded in his *Treatise*. Numerous springs on the property were put to use for ornamental fountains, the wooded knolls and natural rock outcroppings for the Picturesque scenes. Curving avenues following the natural topography created "bold horizontal lines and the broad, free stretches of richly wooded intermediate distance contrasting and yet in harmony with the home landscape." Native trees were judiciously thinned into groups or clumps; evergreens were planted beside the roadways.

Springside would be a contrast to most other great estates as described by Downing himself:

The only remaining building at Springside, the porter's lodge or gatehouse is board-and-batten, a style Downing used in designing other Springside buildings, helping to make the style popular and prevalent in the Hudson Valley in the nineteenth century.

> The failure consists . . . in a certain incongruity and want of distinct character in the treatment of the place as a whole. They are too large to be kept in order as pleasure grounds, while they are not laid out or treated as parks . . . the lines of the farm and the ornamental portion of the grounds meet in a confused and unsatisfactory manner, and the result is a residence pretending to be much superior to a common farm and yet not rising to the dignity of a really tasteful country-seat.

For Springside, Downing would adhere to his principles of unity, variety, and harmony. Unity, he held, prevented discordancy, giving a wholeness to the composition. Variety "belonging more to the details than to the production of a whole," creates intricacy and "a

Matthew Vassar continued the Hudson Valley progressive tradition by founding Vassar College in 1861. It was the first women's college in the United States to have a curriculum identical to that of a men's college. Vassar believed that the students should be surrounded by fine art and thus built a collection of the work of Hudson River school painters that can be seen in the college art museum today.

thousand points of interest." Harmony presides over variety, supposing contrast but not so exaggerated as to disturb. Downing illustrated his three principles:

> If unity only were consulted, a scene might be planted with but one kind of tree, the effect of which would be sameness; on the other hand, variety might be carried so far as to have every tree a different kind, which would produce a confused effect. Harmony, however, introduces contrast and variety but keeps them subordinate to unity, and to the leading expression and is, thus, the highest principle of the three.

Perhaps the original plan to make the property a rural cemetery modeled after Mount Auburn remained in Downing's vision, for the effect of the finished landscape is similar. One visitor, reported the Poughkeepsie *Eagle*, described Springside as "elevated summits gently sloping into valleys, forming the natural openings for the roads to girdle the hills and knolls." But Springside was more. It was a true *ferme ornée* that included the mystery of the forest in the Picturesque tradition, glimpses of the Hudson River, and elegant and beautiful ornament and plantings, all woven together with the cultivated fields, orchards, and buildings of the productive farm, "Surely," declared the *Eagle*, "Paradise could scarcely have been lovelier."

Tragically, Andrew Jackson Downing was not to see its completion or that of his other prestigious commissions. On July 28, 1852, he boarded the *Henry Clay*, a steamship that

ABOVE Springside is an early example of a planned community designed as a harmonious whole, here pictured in paintings by Henry Gritten from 1852.

began in Albany and stopped along the river to pick up passengers bound for New York City. Downing was going to Washington D.C. where he was designing new grounds for the White House, the Capitol, and the Smithsonian Institution. As the boat neared the city there was an explosion and fire. Eighty passengers perished. Downing drowned trying to save a friend. Only thirty-six years old at the time of his death, he was mourned and eulogized throughout the nation as one whose unwavering commitment to the common man and his belief in the ability of people to beautify their surroundings had advanced the cause of democracy. An editorial in *The Horticulturist* said simply, "He taught us how to live."

For his outstanding talent, his leadership in landscape design for public spaces, and his innovative establishment of a commercial value for design services, Andrew Jackson Downing is known as the father of American landscape architecture. Today Springside remains as the last surviving landscape definitely identifiable as the work of Downing, his last commission all but complete at his death, now appropriately preserved as a National Historic Landmark.

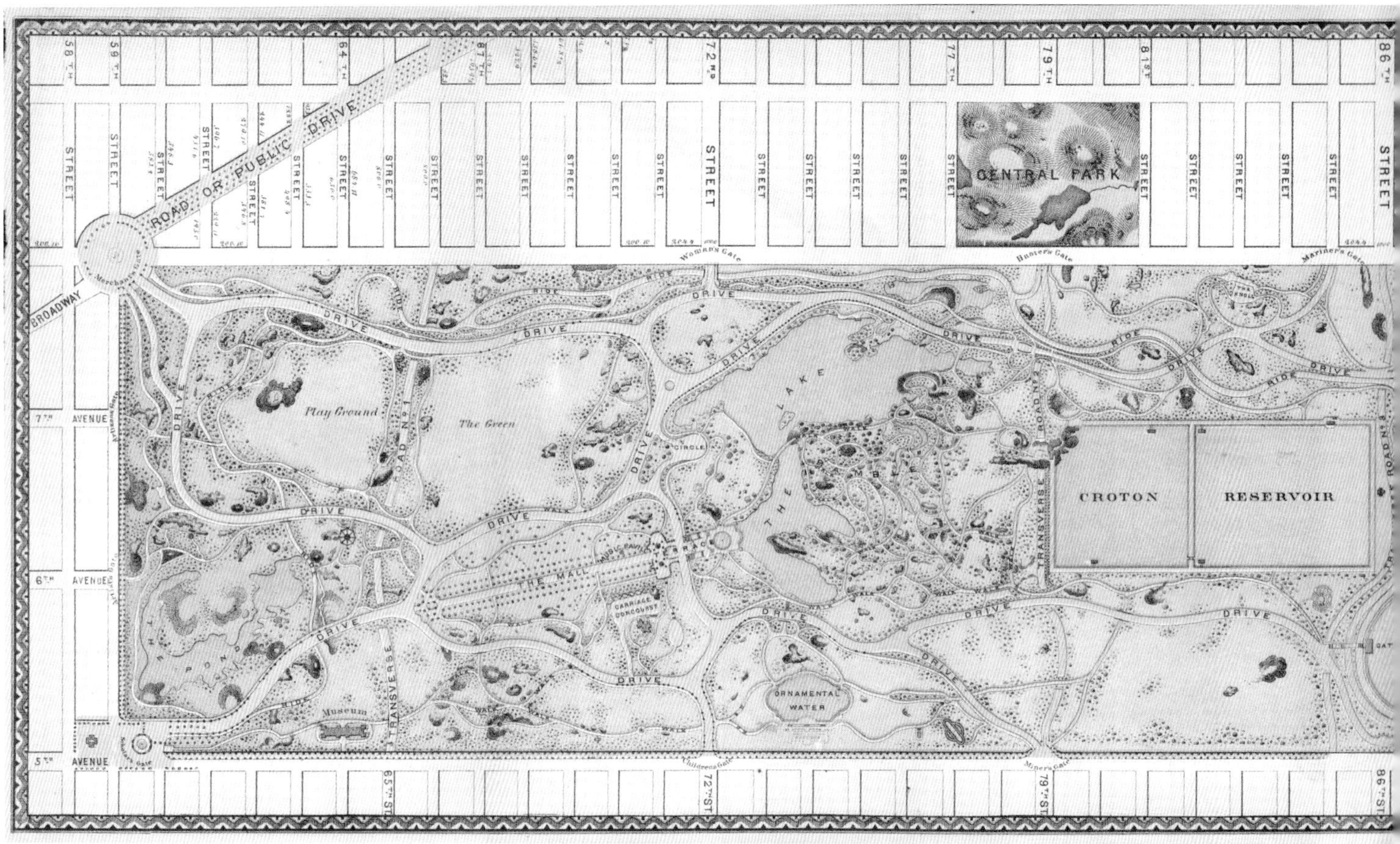

The Olmsted and Vaux plan they called Greensward won the competition to design Central Park. This rendering dates from 1868 or 1869.

Central Park

New York City, New York

In the decade before his untimely death, Andrew Jackson Downing had challenged New York City to build a park for the burgeoning population of immigrants pouring in to escape revolution in Germany and the potato famine in Ireland. The few small parks that then existed in the increasingly dense city were meant mainly for strolling in one's finery on a Sunday afternoon after church. These parks, which Downing called "paddocks," were far from adequate for the needs of the newcomers living in crowded tenements who had taken to going for picnics and games to the Green-Wood Cemetery in Brooklyn.

Downing called instead for a large park in the center of Manhattan that would provide a place for these new Americans to benefit from recreation and the restorative power of nature. His idea was that people of all walks and stations in life could walk, eat, rest, visit with one another, exercise, and breathe fresh air. The setting of thousands of trees would transport park visitors from the adjacent city into another world. His death in 1852 prevented his continued leadership in the effort to build such a park, but his design for democracy did not die with him.

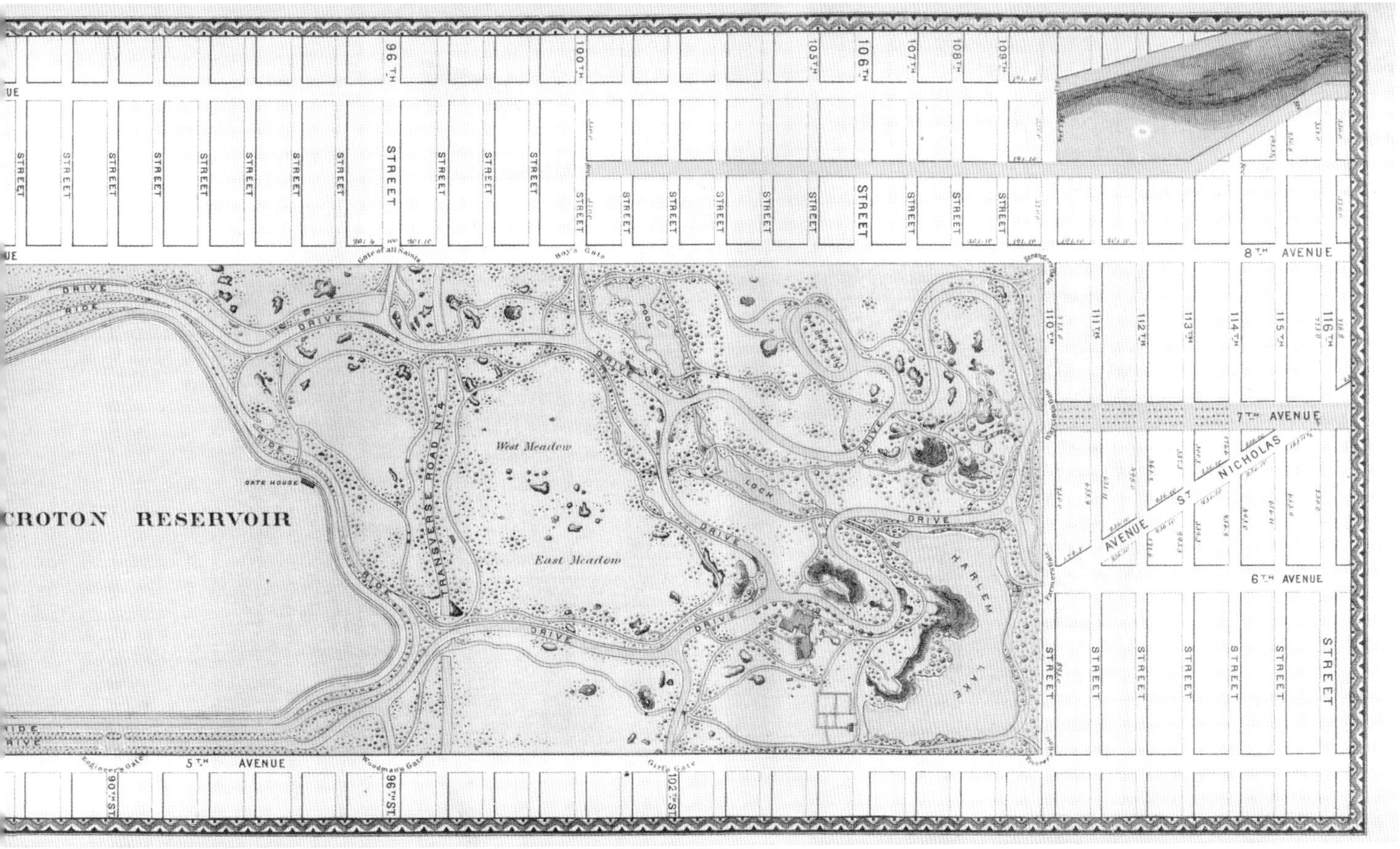

His business partner was prepared to carry on his vision. An architect, Calvert Vaux had been persuaded to leave his native England in order to join Downing in the Newburgh, New York, office in what was expected to be a good move for them both. In addition to Hudson River estates, they were hired to design in Newport, Rhode Island, where some of the country's richest families were building homes. Even more prestigious were commissions in Washington D.C. where, at the urging of President Millard Fillmore, plans were afoot to connect and beautify the White House grounds, the Capitol, and the newly established Smithsonian Institution. Vaux had been in the United States only a year and a half when Downing drowned. His reputation not yet established apart from Downing, he pondered his options.

By the 1840s, plans based on the Downing concept for a large park in New York were moving forward. A large, elongated rectangle of 778 acres had been purchased. It was not ideal. Denuded of its forests during the American Revolution, the ground was rocky with huge, immovable boulders. Individuals and indeed a community of three hundred free African-Americans had to be evicted. There were two reservoirs that supplied water to the city.

Frederick Law Olmsted, hired to oversee the clearing of the park land, was an unlikely candidate for the job. He had no experience in managing seven hundred men, a workforce that would shortly grow to one thousand. His past careers had included clerk in his father's

Architect Calvert Vaux, bookish and shy, was never the front man for either Downing or Olmsted, but his exquisite taste and imaginative design contributed mightily to the success of both his partners.

Hartford, Connecticut, store, sailor on a commercial ship to Asia, farmer first in upstate New York and later on Staten Island, and off-and-on journalist. It was that work that led to his being hired for the Central Park job, not because of his literary qualifications—these were thought to be a detriment—but because it connected him to important New Yorkers. As a young man he had written a well-received account of his walking tour with his brother through England. In the 1850s Olmsted made two trips to the South to analyze the economics of slavery. In his published articles, he reported that, contrary to popular belief and to the rationale used to justify slavery, he did not find slavery an efficient and profitable economic system. In his travels he had visited a German community in Texas that, without slaves, was raising cotton more profitably than were southern slave owners. Always a man of human sympathy, he became a passionate abolitionist. His writings brought him admiration in the New York publishing business and, by extension, among other powerful New Yorkers.

When the job to superintend the clearing of land for Central Park was announced, Olmsted was desperate. He was in debt to his father and had no real prospects for paying work as his efforts in journalism had brought acclaim but little income. So anxious was he to get the job that he mounted a huge campaign, gathering letters of endorsement from all the right people. It worked. He was chosen.

As Olmsted organized the work crew and began clearing the land, the committee argued about design. Calvert Vaux was keen to get the job that undoubtedly would have gone to Downing had he lived. He was appalled that the designer might be chosen without a competition as was the practice in England. He proposed the idea to members of the committee who eagerly took up his recommendation and announced the contest to design what was now called Central Park. Studying the map supplied to the candidates, Vaux recognized its inadequacies. He turned to Frederick Law Olmsted, for who knew the topography better than the man who had supervised every inch of its clearing?

Naming their plan Greensward after English grassy lawns, Olmsted and Vaux submitted their entry. It was based on the Picturesque and Romantic styles promoted by Humphry Repton in England and popularized by Downing in the United States. Largely asymmetrical, it had only one geometric area. The axial promenade for military parades was but three quarters of a mile long with no triumphal arches. They placed it diagonally in the center of the park to encourage people to come to the park's heart rather than remain on the periphery. The plan for the park featured grassy slopes and meadows, flat fields for games, bodies of water for small boats and winter skating, and miles of winding paths for walking, rolling hoops, and pushing baby prams. By the end of the century bicycling was also a popular activity. These paths as well as the bridle trails were designed to suit the natural features that Olmsted had come to know so well. The plan accommodated with relative ease the innumerable and immovable outcroppings of rock.

Central Park has hundreds of private spots such as this one where Mike has just proposed to Casey and where she said yes.

In presenting their plan, Olmsted and Vaux once again turned to the inspiration of Humphry Repton, adapting his idea of the Red Book showing with overlays both current views of a property together with the proposed changes. The "before" images were Mathew Brady daguerreotypes of the most unattractive of the Central Park land. In contrast, lovely sketches in pencil and watercolor by Vaux showed the park as it would look when finished to their design. They won the competition hands down. Now Olmsted had a proper job and Vaux's future was secured.

Their first challenge was to find a way for carriages and trucks to transverse the park, for it was unrealistic to expect delivery carts and individuals to travel the long distance around the park to get from the east to the west side of Manhattan. Four such routes were required because the many horse-drawn vehicles were dangerous, noisy, and unsightly. The solution they proposed was a stroke of genius. They lowered the carriage roads eight feet below the surface so that the traffic was unseen from the higher level, rather like the ha-ha with which Vaux and Olmsted were familiar, each having walked the English countryside.

Thirty-four bridges spanning these carriageways are a prominent feature of Central Park, most attributed to Vaux, the architect. Each is designed differently to complement the mood of the specific site.

ABOVE Olmsted and Vaux could not have anticipated New York's ubiquitous yellow taxis, but the sunken roadways that once hid horses, carts, and carriages from park visitors still do their job.

OPPOSITE Bridges of various materials and styles, some over water, others over carriageways or bridle paths, are graceful and inviting.

The original plan, before the Greensward submitted by Olmsted and Vaux, called for no water except that of an occasional fountain. Olmsted, following in the footsteps of Capability Brown, created a lake out of a low and swampy area. Clay pipes directed runoff from the carriage roads and paths into the basin. To keep the water level, a series of sluices guided excess water to New York's East River. The goal was for the lake to be seven feet deep in summer to accommodate rowboats but only four feet in winter for the safety of ice skaters.

And ice skate they did. The first official sport in Central Park opened in December 1858. The first day three hundred came to skate, a week later ten thousand. It was the must-do activity for every New Yorker, young and old, rich and poor, fulfilling Downing and Olmsted's fondest hopes for the park. It also presaged another use for the park as a place where men and women could meet without chaperones, a guidebook proclaiming that "many a young fellow has . . . skated himself into matrimony on the Central Park Pond!"

True to the plan's name, great lawns of green grass cover the park for resting, reading, and picnicking. Garment workers, clerks, ship stevedores, deliverymen, cooks, and nannies were only a few of the nineteenth-century city residents who found in Central Park a place to stretch out for an afternoon nap on their day-off once a week. Olmsted and Vaux provided hundreds of such spots.

CLOCKWISE FROM TOP LEFT

Looking south from Gapstow Bridge the hiker sees the famous Plaza Hotel.

Vaux's Driprock Bridge is made of red brick and New England sandstone.

Beautiful cast iron Bow Bridge is an early Vaux bridge.

The cast iron Gothic Bridge by Calvert Vaux.

At the same time that skating was initiated in the park, baseball was gaining popularity as a sport, thanks to a team of upper-crust fellows who called themselves the New York Knickerbockers. Soon sixteen area teams formed the National Association of Base Ball Players. Little boys began to dream of a future playing ball, but first they had to practice. Nowhere else in the crowded city could they find both space and the assurance they would not also be breaking expensive windows. Central Park was a godsend to them, their parents, and their neighbors.

All of these and many other activities such as summer concerts and Shakespeare plays are accommodated in the park. The demand for more bridle trails required that Olmsted and Vaux install miles of new paths, separating pedestrians from horseback riders, just as the sunken transverses separated carriages and horse-drawn wagons from the walkers. The miracle is that each of these functions was placed in such a way as to maximize the

RIGHT Today there is skating at the Wolman Rink where ice is guaranteed despite warmer winters.

BELOW, LEFT Yellow tulips and deep pink azaleas nod to the original plan for "pleasure gardens." Although it is only April, New Yorkers take advantage of the greensward and the first warm days to sunbathe.

BELOW, RIGHT Another equalizer, the national sport of baseball has for over a century brought together its New York devotees from all walks of life.

views of nature within the park. Each path revealed around the bend a stately tree, each Vaux-designed bridge was perfectly reflected in the water below. Above all, Central Park was a magical forest of some 240,000 trees planted between 1859 and 1863. Olmsted chose and placed them with the utmost care, aware of the change of colors of the deciduous trees through the seasons and the shades of gray, blue, and dark green of the evergreens which gave an illusion of distance.

Central Park has had its ups and downs. In the years following its completion, it was allowed to deteriorate as the city had other priorities and failed to recognize the maintenance needed for a landscape. In the 1960s the park fell into the hands of drug dealers and graffiti

Cherished by New Yorkers as they gird their loins for winter, autumn trees provide a brilliant finale to the park's year-round show. The 106-acre reservoir, surrounded by a jogging path, bears the name of the park's famous and beloved neighbor, Jacqueline Kennedy Onassis, thereby assuring that it will never be filled in to serve another purpose.

"artists." Fortunately, nearby resident, landscape designer, and preservationist Elizabeth Barlow Rogers took charge, making her mission the revitalization of Central Park. At first singlehandedly, then as the first Central Park administrator, she formed the Central Park Conservancy, a private, not-for-profit corporation. Through her extraordinary leadership, hundreds of volunteers cooperate with city officials and agencies to care for the park. Today, as at its inception, the park continues, in Olmsted's words, "to supply to the hundreds of thousands of tired workers . . . a specimen of God's handiwork that shall be to them, inexpensively, what a month or two in the White Mountains or the Adirondacks is, at great cost, to those in easier circumstances." The populist and democratic beliefs of Andrew Jackson Downing, Calvert Vaux, and Frederick Law Olmsted that governed the design for Central Park have been sustained for more than 150 years in New York City, inspiring the creation of public parks everywhere.

Buffalo Park System

Buffalo, New York

The advertisement placed in the *Nation* soon after the founding of Olmsted, Vaux and Company in 1865 read:

> LANDSCAPE ARCHITECTS. The undersigned have associated under the above title for the business of furnishing advice on all the matters of location and Designs and Superintendence for Buildings and Grounds and other Architectural and Engineering Works including the Laying-out of Towns, Villages, Parks, Cemeteries and Gardens.

In the city of Buffalo, New York, Olmsted and Vaux were able to make concrete these extravagant promises. There they designed and developed not only a park but a system of three widely spaced parks connected by wide multipurpose boulevards for which Olmsted coined the word "parkways."

Buffalo in the nineteenth century was among the fastest growing and most progressive cities in America. The Erie Canal, opened in 1825, joined Buffalo with Albany and the Hudson River. Providing the first means of transporting goods without portaging to and from New York City to the Great Lakes, the canal reduced costs by ninety-five percent.

The way for western expansion was opened and Buffalo became its hub. By midcentury the railroad was in operation as well, attracting entrepreneurs. In 1881 the first hydroelectric generating station was inaugurated, harnessing the might of nearby Niagara Falls.

Business was not the only achievement of nineteenth-century Buffalo. Nearby Seneca Falls was the site of the convention that launched the women's suffrage movement in America and the area remained at its heart with many supporters among both women and men in Buffalo. Forward-looking city leaders founded the Albright-Knox Art Gallery which since 1862 has made its mission the collection of contemporary art. The leadership of Buffalo was of a mindset to embrace eagerly a giant leap forward in city planning and park development.

Millard Fillmore, a native of Buffalo, is buried at Forest Lawn Cemetery. He was the U.S. president when Downing and Vaux were chosen to design the Capitol and White House grounds and it was he who recommended Olmsted and Vaux to the Buffalo park committee.

Olmsted was at first shown three possible locations for a Buffalo park. Instead of selecting one, he presented a plan for three parks, each with a distinct purpose. He knew that the parks, located on the edge of the semicircle farthest from the city center, would soon be surrounded by the growing population. Social reformer that he was, Olmsted would provide green space to every neighborhood, rich and poor, colonial descendants and newly arrived immigrants.

The center of his system is Delaware Park, with 350 acres the largest park, meant for respite from the busy and noisy city, with a natural-looking but totally man-made lake, its serpentine edges planted with willows and other gentle trees. The Albright-Knox Gallery stands at one side, just as the Metropolitan Museum is adjacent to Central Park. The effect is as Olmsted intended, peaceful and serene.

Delaware Park invites strolling, resting on the grass, meditation, conversation, or a visit to the Albright-Knox Gallery.

Adjacent to Delaware Park is Forest Lawn Cemetery. Founded fewer than twenty years before Olmsted and Vaux began work in Buffalo, it follows the precedent set by Mount Auburn in Cambridge, Massachusetts, as a place of beauty where the bereaved come for comfort and other visitors come to enjoy nature. Olmsted saw Delaware Park and the quiet and contemplative "rural" cemetery forming a contiguous park.

A second park, the fifty-seven-acre Parade, was designed for military parades, active sports, and large gatherings. A two-story refectory housed festive events such as Oktoberfest in the nineteenth-century neighborhood of German immigrants.

The smallest of the three parks located on a bluff above the city, Front Park looks down on the place where Lake Erie narrows as it feeds into the Niagara River. Olmsted recommended that here the city should hold its formal ceremonies, welcome important guests, and show the world the magnificence of Buffalo. Today a superhighway divides communities, causes pockets of poverty, and impedes the view of the lake.

Perhaps most visionary was the system of connecting parkways. Olmsted and Vaux had considered the idea for some time, and a trip to Paris had confirmed for Olmsted the wisdom of their approach, he declaring the Champs-Élysées "the most magnificent urban or interior town promenade in the world." The concept for Buffalo was that a person could go from one park to the next without leaving green space. Two hundred feet wide, the parkways with separate bridle

and walking paths, carriage and service roads, were lined with elms, the medians adorned with flowers and shrubs. Periodic circles and fountains further enhance these elongated parks.

Consistent with New York City's experience of Central Park, the property adjoining the Buffalo parkways became highly desirable with elegant homes facing them. A special financial arrangement with the builders provided the city with adequate revenue for the development and maintenance of the parks and parkways.

Olmsted named Buffalo "the best planned city, as to its streets, public places and grounds, in the United States if not the world." One felicitous result of the progressive design was that the city attracted such prominent architects as Frank Lloyd Wright and H. H. Richardson whose work further affirmed Buffalo's elegance and sophistication.

TOP, LEFT Today neighborhood children, most African-American, play in the water at Parade Park.

TOP, RIGHT Buffalo is working to reroute traffic in order to return the Olmsted and Vaux concept and view.

BOTTOM The Buffalo parkways designed by Olmsted and Vaux became the model in hundreds of U.S. cities.

Biltmore

Asheville, North Carolina

Frederick Law Olmsted was a man of sixty-six when young George Washington Vanderbilt called him to the mountains of North Carolina to design the gardens and landscape for the house and two-thousand-acre parcel of surrounding land. It would be Olmsted's last great commission for a private residence, and it was his alone for he and Calvert Vaux had parted ways. At Biltmore, as the estate was named, Olmsted joined formal, geometric

In 1895 Olmsted returned to Biltmore for John Singer Sargent to paint his portrait amidst flowering dogwood and mountain laurel. The sessions proved too hard on the aging Olmsted so his son, wearing his father's clothes, stood in for him.

gardens with his favored Picturesque style, setting all within a grand forest. His work was a great artistic triumph and equally a triumph of spirit, for his health, always precarious, was rapidly declining, his memory failing. But with the fortitude he had displayed in the past, he worked, often feverishly, completing what critics have declared to be a masterpiece.

Fortunately, the working conditions for Olmsted were copacetic. He had worked for the eight Vanderbilt siblings on several of their properties, in Newport, on Staten Island, and in Maine. George W. Vanderbilt, the youngest of the family, was but twenty-five when he purchased the North Carolina property, but he was already a man of taste, having traveled to Europe on five occasions with his father to buy paintings. Money was no object for an heir to one of America's largest fortunes, and the family tradition was to spend freely on house, landscape, and gardens. Vanderbilt knew that he was engaging the nation's foremost landscape architect. By the time Olmsted began his work at Biltmore he had designed the campus at Stanford University on the West Coast, the Arnold Arboretum and Back Bay Fens in Boston on the East Coast, and countless campuses, parks, and residences. Most important, he had completed the work begun by Downing in the nation's capital. Vanderbilt gave Olmsted *carte blanche*.

The property proved less tractable than the owner. Surrounded by the Great Smoky Mountains and Blue Ridge Mountains, Biltmore's views were awe-inspiring, just the setting for Picturesque treatment. But generations of farmers had cleared the land of trees with no attempt at renewal, leaving the woods, in Olmsted's words, "miserable" and the eroded hillsides "unsuitable for anything that can properly be called park scenery."

The house designed by Richard Morris Hunt was also a challenge for Olmsted. It is a grand French château, modeled after those in the Loire Valley. Olmsted admitted, "I am nervous, and this is because I am not quite at home when required to merge stately architectural work with natural or naturalistic landscape work." His answer to both problems was to propose formal gardens near to the house, a planned natural treatment in the Picturesque style farther away, and all surrounded by a regenerated forest.

TOP, LEFT Familiar since his early travels with the vast lawns surrounding the great estates of England, Olmsted set Biltmore similarly.

TOP, RIGHT The great Rampe Douce at Biltmore, reminiscent of those at Vaux-le-Vicomte and Chantilly, unites the château and landscape and provides an easy gradient for those ascending or descending the hill.

BOTTOM Terrace walls break the strong mountain winds, allowing visitors to linger over the magnificent views of the mountains and forest. The corner pavilion anchors the terrace and connects it visually to the mansion.

For the approach road, Olmsted eschewed the straight allée as too pretentious even for a Vanderbilt. Democrat that he was, he sought to give enormous, ornamented Biltmore a simple but elegant setting. Winding three miles from the entrance of the property to the house, the road presents the visitor with a series of views, each revealed in turn as the road bends. Finally the trees part, revealing the magnificent house and even more magnificent mountains that serve as backdrop. Capability Brown would have approved Olmsted's handling.

Across the lawn and facing the house is the Rampe Douce, bracketing the esplanade which serves as forecourt, joining the architecture of house and landscape. On the hill above, a small temple and statue of Diana, goddess of the forest, further complement the architecture of the house. In the interest of further wedding house and landscape, Olmsted strongly suggested to Vanderbilt and Hunt that a great viewing platform should tie together the majesty of the house with that of the forests and mountains, one that would afford a panoramic view. To Olmsted's satisfaction his suggestion—indeed almost a requirement—was accepted. He further insisted on a small corner pavilion or "Tea House" called by art critics a masterstroke.

Olmsted installed formal gardens near the house, the patterns similar to those of the grand gardens of Europe. A long pergola, a conservatory, and two walls protected the fruit trees and tender flowers. They also provided a place for family and guests to "take the air" when weather prevented their enjoying the paths and carriage roads farther afield. In this plan Olmsted took a page from Capability Brown who at Petworth, Nuneham, and other places installed a pleasure garden near the house for inclement days and a peripheral road around the extensive properties for a carriage or horseback ride when the weather was agreeable.

Below the formal gardens a shrub garden of rhododendrons, azaleas, and kalmias leads to the planned natural wooded glen. Using winding paths and rustic structures, Olmsted made the transition from the straight lines of the geometric garden to the Picturesque style with remarkable success. A small lake with two small islands also recalls the techniques perfected by Capability Brown, the disguised boundaries of the lake making it appear larger than the reality.

Perhaps most visionary of all his ideas was the proposal to establish the Pisgah Forest to serve as a model of forest conservation. Vanderbilt eagerly agreed, purchasing surrounding land until his holdings totaled almost two hundred square miles. At Olmsted's recommendation he hired a skilled forest manager trained in France in the most advanced theories of forestry. The soil was rejuvenated with manure from the farm, thousands of trees were planted, and later the Biltmore Forest School was established, the first in the United States, where scientific ideas about forest management were pioneered. After Vanderbilt's death in 1914, his widow sold 85,000 acres to the U.S. government to preserve the land and forest.

Biltmore proved to be among the last of Frederick Law Olmsted's efforts at social reform, this one in ecology and responsible land use. He, Andrew Jackson Downing, and Calvert Vaux left an indelible mark not only on American landscape but on the social fabric of the nation as they designed for democracy.

TOP As at Italian Renaissance villas and French Baroque châteaux, the formal gardens below the house are best viewed from above where their design is most clearly evident.

BOTTOM Humphry Repton, Uvedale Price, Richard Payne Knight, and Andrew Jackson Downing, all advocates of the Picturesque school of design, would have been at home in this area of Olmsted's landscape at Biltmore.

10 Bedding-Out *and* Getting-On

Industrial Revolution affluence, acquisitiveness, and ocean travel make flowers the colorful centerpiece.

NINETEENTH CENTURY

NOW, AT LAST, it is about flowers, *all* about flowers and their colors. After centuries in which shades of green in trees, shrubs, hedges, and turf dominated garden design, in the nineteenth century flowers of myriad shapes, textures, and above all colors became the very definition of a garden. So strong was the attachment to flowers that it has not abated today, more than a hundred and fifty years later.

Flowers occupied the attention not only of garden designers in the nineteenth century but also artists and craftsmen in all media. Professionals made flowered wallpaper and flowered fabric for interior decoration. Chintz with its gaudy florid patterns was the popular fabric for dresses and drapery. Milliners adorned hats and bakers decorated cakes with real flowers and those crafted from silk or sugar. Both professionals and amateurs painted innumerable pieces of china with every possible combination of flowers. Kate Greenaway, Arthur Rackham, and Walter Crane were among the many Victorians who instructed children about flowers through their imaginative books and illustrations.

Lovers also put flowers to use, developing an unspoken language based on flowers and sending flower messages to the object of their affection. Different from the use of flowers as religious symbols in the Middle Ages, the Victorian code conveyed sentiments hard to express in words. Flowers spoke of love and its counterpart, loneliness, and the Romantic poets made full use of the metaphors. Having "wandered lonely as a cloud" Wordsworth was pensive: he recalled the host of golden blossoms beside the lake and found his "heart with pleasure fills, and dances with the daffodils."

In the sixty-three years of Queen Victoria's reign, three developments made flowers the center of garden design and so much else. The first was innovation in the transporting of plants, easing their ocean voyage. At the beginning of the century plants aboard ships were subject to salt spray on deck or lack of sun in the hold below. Extreme changes of temperature and a crew untrained and indifferent also contributed to the tender plants' vulnerability. Most succumbed, leaving those few that did survive exorbitantly expensive.

> In those tropical forests where the beasts of prey roam grow many a beautiful and delicate flower.
>
> —MARY KINGSLEY

Stud bed of succulents, National Botanic Gardens of Ireland.

ABOVE For an 1883 portrait by Carl Rudolph Sohn, Queen Victoria wears her "widow's weeds"—mourning black and white—which she wore for the forty years of her reign after the death of her beloved consort, Prince Albert. But her gardens and those of other Victorians were made all-colorful with flowers.

RIGHT Here writer and illustrator Elizabeth Scott Gordon turns a thistle into a Scotsman in her book *Wild Flower Children*.

OPPOSITE So hardy is the London plane tree that it accounts for half of the city's street trees.

Then Nathaniel Ward, an English physician and amateur botanist, came by chance on a solution. His collection of ferns was dying as a result of the London air polluted from coal dust and sulfuric acid. He also kept moths and insects in sealed bottles. Lo and behold, a bit of soil and a few seeds of grass attached to a fern spore germinated and thrived in the closed bottle. Several years later when the seal on the bottle rusted, the plants died. Making the connection, Dr. Ward built wooden planting cases with glass panels to allow in light but not polluted air. Experimenting to determine just how much water was needed, he soon found his plants quite healthy in their enclosed environment.

When he published his findings in 1842, entrepreneurs immediately grasped the commercial potential of "Wardian cases." Now plants could travel on deck absorbing the sunlight

The London plane tree (*Platanus acerifolia*) is thought to be an eighteenth-century cross between *Platanus occidentalis* and *P. orientalis*. It was able to survive the fierce air pollution created by the dust from coal that fired nineteenth-century factories and heated homes. In 1952 a dense smog covered London for days and it is estimated that some twelve thousand people died of lung problems as a result. The Clean Air Act of 1956 took steps to reduce pollution through the use of cleaner coals, electricity, and gas, an early action in what became the environmental protection movement.

yet protected from the salt spray, their watering no longer dependent on uninterested sailors. Dr. Ward tested his case by shipping ferns to Australia via Cape Horn. They survived the journey of several months in good form as did Australian plants making the reverse trip.

Then, late in the century, transportation of plants was aided by the development of ocean-going steamships that shortened the voyage from months to weeks or mere days. Soon the terrariums aboard steamships were breaking the monopoly of agricultural goods as plants were moved from one area of the world to another with efficiency and success. Soon, too, the nurseries of Hammersmith, Philadelphia, Halifax, and elsewhere were burgeoning with exotic flowers brought from the corners of the earth.

The second development leading directly to flowers as the centerpiece of the garden was England's affluence. The success of the British Empire and the ease of transportation brought natural resources to England and simultaneously provided markets abroad for British goods as never before in history. The machines of the Industrial Revolution were mass producing thousands of new goods at prices more and more people could afford. Those who profited by the increased commercial activity had money to burn. Victorian design became elaborate and complex to satisfy the desire to spend. Fringe was added to lampshades

An 1866 advertisement in *Curtis's Botanical Magazine* for the new-fangled invention the lawn mower, testifying to its use by royalty. To own such a machine would certainly indicate that, by association, one was getting-on.

and sofas; fish-scale shingling and wooden "gingerbread" to the exterior of houses; and ribbons, factory-made pearls, and silk flowers to dresses. Meals became long and rich with many courses—and gout became the prevailing disease. A different piece of silver for serving and eating each dish was designed, manufactured, and eagerly acquired. Conspicuous consumption was evident in eating and everywhere else.

Among the ways Victorians spent their new money was on their gardens. For those seeking to improve their social status, house and garden were a natural way to display their newly acquired wealth. After all, in England the quality of "place" had long been the measure of station. Victorians who succeeded in raising themselves and their family in the judgment of society were declared to be "getting-on."

One Industrial Revolution invention aiding gardeners was the lawn mower. In 1830 Frank Budding, watching a machine that shaved the pilling from machine-made knitted material, realized the technology could be adapted to cut grass. With his invention, it was no longer necessary to pay a team of men to scythe. One man—the paid gardener, the homeowner, or his son—could do the job. Now a greensward was within reach not just of the nobility or landed gentry but everyone. So linked was the green lawn with success and identity that Englishmen took this garden feature with them wherever they went to live in the empire and elsewhere, however unsuited it was to the climate. Just as the nineteenth-century love of flowers has stayed with us until today, so a green lawn signals success to many, especially perhaps American men, and hence the sight, ridiculed in many a cartoon, of the huge ride-on mower with pot-bellied driver proudly cutting his few square feet of lawn.

A related development was the "lawn fountain" or sprinkler, wrought of iron in elaborate designs. The sight of this invention casting its water in mesmerizing patterns on the newly mown grass that provided endless play for children signaled to the passer-by that the homeowner, clearly with running water and indoor plumbing, was getting-on.

The two inner rectangles are the same shade, but the bottom one can appear to be darker because it is surrounded by a lighter shade than the top one. This phenomenon can be demonstrated by the use of any combination of colors.

The sprinkler also helped in maintaining the new "exotics"—plants brought from abroad—purchased to adorn nineteenth-century gardens. Scotsman Robert Fortune, only one of many plant collectors, brought back from China weigela, double-flowering ornamental peaches, forsythia, Japanese anemone, and bleeding heart to name but a few. From Mexico the dahlia, desired for its long period of bloom and its rich and varied colors, sold first in the United States as early as the 1830s. Only ten years later an English nursery was offering more than one thousand dahlia varieties. All these and hundreds of other flowering plants were purchased and planted because, in addition to being beautiful, they were a sign of prosperity.

The third nineteenth-century development making flowers the prima donnas of the garden was the new color theory that gave artists including garden designers an utterly new way of thinking about and practicing their art. Early in the century German poet Johann Wolfgang von Goethe posed ideas about color based not on the science of optics but on experience. "Newton's error," he declared, "was in trusting mathematics over the sensations of the eye."

Then Michel Chevreul, a French chemist working with the Gobelins tapestry company in Paris, made a curious observation. Many clients, having chosen colors for their custom-made tapestries, complained that the end result was not as they had envisioned. Chevreul conducted experiments in color contrast and came to believe that human perception of a color changes depending on the colors that surround it. Chevreul published his findings in French in 1839, and they were translated into English in 1854. Artists in all media were fascinated. As a result, some—most notably the Impressionists—developed new ways of using color. New understanding of color stimulated painters to use their brushes, oils, and watercolors differently. Gardeners, too, used the newly imported and colorful flowers in new combinations and patterns.

The wide variety of flowers made available through better means of ocean transport, the affluence generated by the Industrial Revolution, and the new interest and inventiveness of those using color made the nineteenth century the era in which flowers took center stage in garden design. The Victorians were devoted to their long-reigning queen, but it was to be the flowers of her era that outlasted even the beloved Victoria in popularity.

This wrought iron Wardian case at the Baltimore Museum of Art might have been in the conservatory of a fine house.

National Botanic Gardens of Ireland

Dublin, Ireland

Although Dr. Ward's planting case was highly functional, it was homely. It spawned offspring, however, that were handsome works of art. Some of these would hold pride of place in modest parlors, others would make a huge footprint on a property of many acres. The smallest of these terrariums were made of glass, tin, and wire to house only a single delicate plant, perhaps an orchid.

Larger conservatories with iron frames nurtured hundreds of specimens from all climates of the world. Gardening under glass became a pastime for the hobbyist, a sign of fashion for those who could afford a greenhouse, and a means for serious research at botanical gardens. The National Botanic Gardens of Ireland was and is one such important garden, its graceful glass and iron buildings of special beauty matched by the value of the horticultural research generated there.

Eighteenth- and nineteenth-century inventions that greatly improved the manufacturing of glass made the Dublin conservatory possible. England became the center for glass manufacturing, and glass became more and more a medium for architecture. Two horticulturists and landscape designers who contributed to the building of the large glass conservatories were John Claudius Loudon and Joseph Paxton. Scottish botanist Loudon invented in 1816 a wrought iron sash bar (muntin), making possible curvilinear glass houses with domes, including that in Ireland. Joseph Paxton designed the amazing Crystal Palace for the Great Exhibition of 1851. Providing almost one million square feet of space for fourteen thousand exhibitors to show the latest technology of the Industrial Revolution, the palace with its long central dome-shaped roof was made almost entirely of glass.

The National Botanic Gardens was begun in 1795 with the purchase of a house and land by the Dublin Society. Its first curvilinear house, built in 1843, was opened formally by Queen Victoria in 1849. The aquatics conservatory to house a giant Amazonian waterlily (*Victoria amazonica*) soon followed. The palm house, built in 1862, was originally made of

The exquisite building of iron and curved glass provides a home for delicate exotics at the National Botanic Gardens of Ireland.

wood and glass. Unstable, it was brought down by strong gales some twenty years later and replaced by one with an iron frame. Additional glass houses were added including ones for cactus and fern. Early in its history the National Botanic Gardens of Ireland made its mark as a research institution by identifying the fungus responsible for the potato blight that gave rise to the Great Hunger in Ireland. Researchers in Dublin also made history by germinating the first orchid seed in cultivation. Today the National Botanic Gardens houses some twenty thousand plants and millions of dried specimens.

At the same time other glass-domed conservatories were being constructed in Europe and Britain. The Royal Botanic Gardens, Kew, in London was the greatest of them with its Palm House and specialized greenhouses for plants from the far reaches of the globe. Early in the next century Kew would be rivaled by the Enid A. Haupt Conservatory at the New York Botanical Garden.

Gardening under glass provided an efficient means of keeping exotic plants alive and thriving in hostile environments whether on board ship or in the polluted air of nineteenth-century industrialized cities. The botanical gardens with their iron and glass hothouses not only protected the plants but stimulated the public's interest in these newly introduced plants. Interest in horticulture increased as riotous flowers became the center of attention, adding to sumptuous Victorian life.

ABOVE Palms and succulents thrive in the National Botanic Gardens of Ireland.

RIGHT The conservatories are a safe and elegant home for plants away from their native habitat.

RIGHT The Palm House at the Royal Botanic Gardens, Kew, in London was designed by Decimus Burton and built by Richard Turner who had earlier built the Dublin glass house.

BELOW The Enid A. Haupt Conservatory, the symbol of the New York Botanical Garden, opened in 1902.

Cliveden

Buckinghamshire, England

Londoners flocked to the Crystal Palace to see in the Great Exhibition of 1851 the inventions that created the nation's vast new wealth. It was also a good place to be seen, to meet potential business partners, to show off new clothes, and to hear the latest gossip. Among the topics for conversation were the new glass conservatories at Kew and Dublin and the huge mansion under construction a short distance northwest of London. Designed by the architect of the Houses of Parliament Charles Barry, the new Cliveden replaced the previous house that had burned just months after the second Duke of Sutherland had purchased it. There Victorian garden design would be epitomized in a display of wealth. The estate would also be connected to the Italian Renaissance, a natural wedding since both periods were times of enormous confidence and oversized egos.

Most characteristic of Victorian gardens was the practice of "bedding-out" in which bright flowers, usually spring bulbs followed by annuals, were planted *en masse* in elaborate or simple patterns. Gardening manuals laid out designs for circular, oval, square, or rectangular beds that might include hearts, fleur-de-lis, the family crest, or the year of the house's building. Later, industries adopted the practice, displaying at the entrance to the corporate headquarters the company's name, letters, or logo in beds of meticulously planted flowers.

Larger gardens required hundreds, indeed thousands, of several different kinds and colors of flowers in order to complete a pattern. At Cliveden, six triangular parterres bounded by hedges on both sides of a long greensward cover four acres, making it one of Europe's largest examples. The bedding-out designs were meant to be seen from the upper stories of the house.

Cliveden is now a hotel. The Victorian gardens are eye-catching with their patterns of flowers in the colors of the Union Jack.

Another good place to view the parterres and flowers at Cliveden is the balustrade that Lord Astor, a subsequent owner, purchased from the Villa Borghese gardens in Rome at the end of the nineteenth century. Made of travertine stones and brick tiles in the early seventeenth century, it is counted among Cliveden's most prized possessions. Its bold carving of benches, eagles, dragons, and river gods fits Cliveden perfectly as both eras—the one in which it was made and the one in which it was brought to England—could hardly be thought of as timid. The same could be said of its owners, Lord Astor and his American wife, Nancy Langhorne, a naturalized British citizen and the first woman to serve in Parliament.

ABOVE The parterres with their colorful bedding plants viewed from the roof of Cliveden.

RIGHT A colony of Mediterranean snails, stowaways on the Italian balustrade when it was brought to Cliveden at the end of the nineteenth century, still survive despite harsh English winters.

ABOVE A topiary peacock at Cliveden conveys pride of place.

OPPOSITE, TOP Named the Fountain of Love, the Cliveden fountain makes an ironic entry for the house that in the early 1960s was the site of the Profumo Affair, a sexual scandal that brought down Prime Minister Harold Macmillan and his government.

OPPOSITE, BOTTOM At Cliveden today, replicas of the iron gates from 1894 prevent uninvited visitors from getting lost in the maze's intricate pattern of tall yew hedges.

Colorful Victorian beds were often punctuated by precisely pruned topiary in geometric shapes such as the yew pyramids at Cliveden. Trees or shrubs shaped with shears into animal or bird forms were also popular. Many a gardener grew old in the lengthy process of growing and clipping these elaborate living sculptures.

"Hard" sculpture had a revival in Victorian England. Capability Brown and the Picturesque school of the eighteenth and early nineteenth centuries had eschewed garden sculpture, especially of classical figures, confining landscape ornament for the most part to urns and planting boxes. But with Victorian wealth and the concomitant love of all adornment, sculpture of marble, stone, or molded concrete was once again in fashion, now, in keeping with the times, oversized and elaborate. Coade stone, a mixture of grog, quartz, flint, glass, and clay fired over a period of several days, was highly prized as a material for garden ornament as it is a beautiful and strong ceramic, lasting indefinitely.

With enormous confidence in themselves and holding the belief that their empire had superseded that of Rome, Victorians saw no reason to limit themselves to reminders of past glories. Lord Astor was a leading collector of sculpture, which can be seen today at Cliveden. The great shell fountain, designed by American Thomas Waldo Story, stands at the entrance of the long allée of lime trees leading to the mansion. It features three life-sized, voluptuous women, cavorting sensually in the water of an enormous shell made of Carrara marble.

Ironwork, a finely honed art form in the nineteenth century, was the complementary accompaniment to Victorian gardens, valued in part because it could by wrought in ornate patterns. Iron formed the frame of the glass conservatories and smaller decorative Wardian cases and was likewise used in garden gates, arbors, fences, tables, chairs, and benches.

Having been a guest at Cliveden on more than one occasion in the 1930s, Harold Nicolson, co-creator of the great garden Sissinghurst, described Cliveden as "great sofas in vast cathedrals." Writing to his wife, Vita Sackville-West, he declared, "How glad I am that we are not so rich. I simply do not want a house like this where nothing is really yours, but belongs to servants and gardeners. There is a ghastly unreality about it all . . . I enjoy seeing it. But to own it, to live here, would be like living on the stage of the Scala theater in Milan." In an era that lauded conspicuous consumption, that feeling may have been precisely what the owners of nineteenth-century Cliveden sought for themselves and hoped their guests would experience.

Gardens that unite the railway lines and station, Princes Street, Edinburgh Castle, and the National Galleries allow residents to take advantage of lengthening summer days.

Princes Street Gardens

Edinburgh, Scotland

Scotland in the eighteenth and nineteenth centuries was a study in contrast. The period has been named the Scottish Enlightenment for it boasted some of the finest minds in the world, among them Adam Smith, David Hume, Sir Walter Scott, Robert Lewis Stevenson, Robert Burns, and James Boswell. Robert Fortune and William Forsyth were but two of many renowned Scottish botanists and plant collectors of the era.

Scotland's capital city, Edinburgh, was called the Athens of the North. But in its heart, in the valley below Edinburgh Castle, was a slum that encircled the stagnant and putrid Nor' Loch. In the sixteenth century, it was the site for "trial by douking," a practice for determining if a person was a witch. Once the castle's chief defense as well as a lake of great beauty, it had over the years become polluted and unsanitary causing misery to the impoverished dwellers nearby.

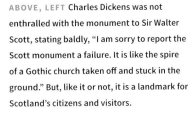

Public outcry called for a new town to replace the squalor and danger. Work was begun in 1767 but it took a century to transform the area into the cultural and commercial center it became and is today. Most of the changes took place in the nineteenth century and it is the Victorian style that gives the area its character. Consistent with progressive thinking in Scotland at the time, the new design was a model of city planning.

New residences were erected along Princes Street. The Royal Scottish Academy was constructed in 1822 and the Scottish National Gallery of Art opened in 1859. Nor' Loch had been drained and now the gardens were installed. Sloping from the high ridge to the bottom of the former lake basin, the gardens incorporate the railway lines that were the city's hub. Princes Street in the twentieth century was gradually transformed from a residential area into a lively commercial center with shops and other business enterprises.

ABOVE, LEFT Charles Dickens was not enthralled with the monument to Sir Walter Scott, stating baldly, "I am sorry to report the Scott monument a failure. It is like the spire of a Gothic church taken off and stuck in the ground." But, like it or not, it is a landmark for Scotland's citizens and visitors.

ABOVE, RIGHT The softness, delicacy, and bright colors of roses contrast with the massive gray rock foundation of Edinburgh Castle above.

True to the Victorian love of sculpture, the gardens' focal points are monuments that celebrate Scotland's luminaries. John Knox, Robert Lewis Stevenson, and David Livingstone are but three of many, but the centerpiece is the monument dedicated to Sir Walter Scott, the beloved nineteenth-century novelist and poet, author of *Ivanhoe*, *Rob Roy*, and *Lady of the Lake*.

Enlivening the gardens are, of course, flowers, their cheerful colors welcome after the long nights of Scottish winter. Of all the flowers beloved by the Victorians, none was more admired, collected, and displayed than the rose. Special gardens were designed for the array of rose cultivars available. Not lending themselves to patterns as do annuals, roses were often grouped by colors, the designer either knowledgeably or intuitively using the new color theories of harmonizing or contrasting colors, such as pairing pink and red roses or dark red and white roses. In the Princes Street Gardens, roses are often planted with lavender to grace the steep banks.

The mechanism for the Edinburgh floral clock is set inside the adjacent monument dedicated to artist Allan Ramsay. Made in 1903 of parts salvaged from a church, the mechanism included only an eight-foot-long hour hand that had to be manually wound each day. The minute hand and a cuckoo were added soon after. The mechanism was updated in 1934. During World War II, the planting designs commemorated wartime events and victories. In 1953, electricity was installed to operate the clock and a house for the cuckoo was built for the life-sized replica of the bird that makes an appearance to chirp every fifteen minutes.

TOP The circular stud beds bloom each spring with bulbs, which are then replaced with summer annuals.

BOTTOM The annual design of the floral clock has celebrated such events as the Queen's Golden Jubilee in 2012, the centenary of Robert Louis Stevenson, and the one-hundredth anniversary of the Princes Street Gardens. Here the design calls attention to Edinburgh's designation as a Fair Trade City.

Circular flower beds spaced at regular intervals and forming a straight line are called stud beds after the fasteners of a man's dress shirt. Here massed annuals display colorful and ingenious patterns. They serve to connect the sculpture in the long narrow garden of Princes Street. Victorian gardeners often mounded such beds so that the height at center is greater than at the circumference, a practice seen today in some rotary traffic circles.

Of the numerous Victorian patterned flower beds, the floral clock at Princes Street Gardens may be the most famous and enduring. Inspired by the carpet bedding planted to honor King Edward VII at the time of his coronation in 1902, it is one of the oldest floral clocks in the world. Located on a slope next to heavily frequented stairs, the clock has kept Edinburgers on time for well over one hundred years. Every year the pattern is redesigned and replanted with thirty thousand small bedding plants to bring attention to the annual theme. Because they are low growing and contained, hens-and-chicks, sedums and other succulents, lobelias, and begonias are frequently used.

Princes Street Gardens is an example of early town planning, one factor in its being named a World Heritage Site. Today the original Victorian planting style that complements the Victorian monuments and buildings of Edinburgh continues. The floral clock has been adopted far and wide from Australia and New Zealand to Mexico, Ukraine, and Iran. Patterned carpet bedding and stud beds adorn city parks, center medians between roads, and public monuments. It is these uses for which the grand display of riches in bedded-out Victorian gardens is most suited today.

Annapolis Royal Historic Gardens

Annapolis Royal, Canada

Annapolis Royal, Nova Scotia, may be a long way from London, but the city and its residents participated fully in the Victorian prosperity of the British Empire. The Canadian city founded in 1605 was the first English-speaking settlement in North America and became an important port. As did other parts of the empire, Nova Scotia adopted the garden design styles popular in England at the time. Annapolis Royal Historic Gardens feature the history of Nova Scotia including its Mi'kmaq Indian and French Acadian settlements, British colonial rule, and its nineteenth-century designation as a Canadian province.

On a smaller scale and with a less formal layout than Cliveden, the Historic Gardens sparkle with brightly colored beds of exotics and annuals in the Victorian section. A popular Victorian shape preserved today at Annapolis Royal is the long and narrow ribbon bed. Exotics such as coleus were much sought and proudly displayed.

As its name implies, Nova Scotia was largely settled by Scots, many driven from Scotland during the eighteenth- and nineteenth-century Highland Clearances. In this cruel action, small tenant farmers, called crofters, were driven out by the landowning lairds who believed sheep farming would be more profitable. Those who could scrape together the cost

Salvias, snapdragons, marigolds, begonias, and other annuals are bedded-out in the Victorian section at Annapolis Royal, here seen thriving in the shade of the dramatic but poisonous castor bean plant (*Ricinus communis*).

of passage to begin life anew in the New World brought seeds and cuttings, their farming and gardening skills, and their preferred landscape styles. Heather and heath which cover the Scottish Highlands may have been among their possessions, a reminder of the home they had been forced to leave.

In Nova Scotia, the English garden style and choice of flowering plants fit easily into the climate and soil. So also did the English penchant for large lawns. But it was not so in many other parts of the world where the British set their flag. As they established schools, churches, hospitals, and other institutions of British society, so they also took their customs surrounding family, home, and landscape. In garden design nothing was more ingrained in the English soul than the lawn, the very symbol of prestige and place. Kept ever lush and green in England by the incessant light rain and mist, the lawn was unsuited for many places where it eventually found its way, places such as New York or southern California where summer days are scorching. A close second to the lawn in affection are annuals and exotics that also require innumerable gallons of water. Ecology-aware people are questioning this practice and suggesting more environmentally compatible alternatives to the omnipresent English lawn and Victorian use of annuals.

Flowers popular in the nineteenth century and grown today in the Victorian section of the Historic Gardens at Annapolis Royal include blue althea, cleome, and tiger lilies as well as sunflowers, white roses, and zinnias.

TOP TO BOTTOM
Blue althea or rose of Sharon (*Hibiscus syriaca*).
Cleome or spider flower (*Cleome* species).
Tiger lily (*Lilium lancifolium*).

TOP, RIGHT Colorful heather and heath in some of their many varieties are gathered in a bed at Annapolis Royal.

BOTTOM, RIGHT The bright ribbon bed is set in the ever-present English turf.

11 Searching *for* Earthly Paradise

Arts and Crafts artists challenge factory production; painters, old cottages, and ancient values inspire Gertrude Jekyll.

NINETEENTH AND EARLY TWENTIETH CENTURIES

IT WAS APRIL 1864. The town fathers of Bradford, England, were atwitter with the news that John Ruskin, great British art critic and author of *The Seven Lamps of Architecture*, had accepted their invitation to come and advise about the building they proposed. In the industrial heartland, it would proclaim Bradford's preeminence in the woolen trade and reflect the power and wealth of its leading citizens. But instead of praising their plans, Ruskin excoriated them for developing their industry on the backs of underpaid men and women who labored for long hours, six days a week, in the dangerous and unsanitary spinning and weaving factories. Making matters worse, families were forced by poverty to put their young children to work. Laws against child labor were beginning to be passed in England, but when Ruskin came to Bradford, children as young as nine were still allowed by law to work sixty hours a week, day or night.

John Ruskin looked behind the glitter of Industrial Revolution wealth to the pain and suffering that produced it. And he saw more. Beyond the monetary poverty, he saw the poverty of spirit in the indignity, boredom, and diminished self-worth of factory workers. With the new industrialization the earlier organic nature of society was lost. The old reliance of a property owner on the skills of his tenant farmers did not apply in factories where one unskilled worker—injured, ill, dismissed, or dead—could always be replaced by another. Ruskin saw this breakdown of the dependence of one social class on another and admonished Bradford's leaders for their selfish and cruel greed, accusing them of worshipping, at the peril of their fellow men, the "Goddess of Getting-on."

Ruskin was not alone in his criticism. Charles Dickens wrote one novel after another about the abuses perpetuated by industry. Karl Marx and Friedrich Engels changed the course of history with their theories about bourgeois values and their prediction of a consequent uprising of the proletariat.

> Nothing but Art is moral:
> Life without Industry is sin, and
> Industry without Art is brutality.
>
> —JOHN RUSKIN

Within the arts community in England, Ruskin sympathizers made up what would come to be called the Arts and Crafts movement. Artists William

Herbaceous border, Cliveden.

Morris, Dante Gabriel Rossetti, and Edward Burne-Jones were among those who took up Ruskin's cry. They believed that the new industrialization was destroying both the artistry of objects and the joy that craftsmen have in creating handmade goods. They were appalled at the degrading factory practice of dividing labor into small and uncreative segments rather than allowing the worker the satisfaction of making the whole item.

With Ruskin and others, they looked back to the Middle Ages when, for the building of a cathedral, every stone was hand-hewn, every vestment hand-embroidered, the cover of every Bible or prayer book hand-tooled in leather or metal repoussé and its contents illuminated by pen and painter's brush. They believed that unlike the factory workers of nineteenth-century England, these worker-artists rightly enjoyed enormous satisfaction and pride in their one-of-a-kind products. They nostalgically imagined the time when craftsmen were artists and themselves applied their artistic talents to painting and drawing, as well as to designing tapestries, stained glass, fabrics, wallpaper, ceramic tiles, book covers, typefaces, and illustrations.

Gertrude Jekyll would become the doyenne of gardening of the Arts and Crafts movement. In chronology she was Victorian; Queen Victoria was only six years into her long reign when Gertrude was born in 1843. But the values she held and garden style she developed ran counter to those predominant in Victorian culture. Over the course of her long career she was employed as garden designer by the owners of many a grand estate, but she took her inspiration from the gardens of simple cottagers. She rejected bedding-out as a vulgar display of new wealth. Professionally trained as an artist, she likewise rejected the garish colors and commonplace patterns of these beds, applying instead her sophisticated knowledge of color and design. A first-rate horticulturist, she brought new subtlety to the ways plants are grouped in flower beds by studying and then following their natural growth patterns. This knowledge and artistry distinguished her designs for the herbaceous borders that would become her most admired contribution to landscape design.

William Nicholson painted Gertrude Jekyll as she was nearing eighty years old, the portrait commissioned by architect Edwin Lutyens.

Commissioned to design hundreds of gardens, she could never be said to follow a set formula. However efficient it might be, there would be no assembly line for Gertrude Jekyll. Nor would there be even a hint of nouveau riche. Rather she would, through her garden design, give houses and their owners a dignified past, just as her colleagues in the Arts and Crafts movement recalled in their work England's history before the Industrial Revolution.

Her genius lay in uniting her two great skills, those in horticulture and art. She began learning both in childhood. Born into a prosperous, large, and close-knit family of seven children, she was allowed to join her brothers in roaming the fields, woods, meadows, and hamlets of Surrey where the Jekylls lived. She picked wildflowers, studied their growing habits, and trained her eye to observe minute details in nature.

LEFT *The Cornfield* is but one of many paintings in which John Constable used a spot of red, usually in the foreground, giving Jekyll ideas for flower borders and beds.

RIGHT From J. M. W. Turner, Jekyll learned about grouping colors, seen here in a Turner painting of 1835, *Burning of the Houses of Lords and Commons*.

As an adult, she continued her intense interest in nature, designing garden beds with extraordinary detail, using her precise knowledge of plants, their needs, habits, and life cycles.

The second gift she brought to landscape design came from her training and talent as an artist. At age nineteen she was granted permission by her progressive parents to enroll in the recently established South Kensington School, now the Royal College of Art. Having painted watercolors since childhood, she was here professionally schooled. As she trained her eye, she put her hand not only to drawing and painting but to the crafts she loved and that were celebrated by fellow Arts and Crafts artists. She designed wallpaper and fabric, made pottery, and worked silver. She was especially accomplished at embroidery. But fine work requiring keen eyesight was not to be her future. Her myopia worsened and so, in part by necessity, she turned her artistic talent to gardening.

In art school she learned the new color theories, copying the paintings of J. M. W. Turner and John Constable, both of whom she greatly admired. From Turner she learned to group hot colors and cool colors. She employed this technique in the herbaceous border, the gardening feature that would become her signature piece. Here she would put the reds, oranges, and golds in the middle, the pale lavenders, blues, and grays at the ends. From Constable, Jekyll learned the value of a spot of red to draw the eye, another useful tool in designing an herbaceous border. Jekyll's encyclopedic knowledge of flowers and her sensitive use of color gave her gardens a rare subtlety and artistry.

Fortunate indeed for Gertrude Jekyll and for those past and present who admire architecture and landscape design was the partnership she formed with Edwin Lutyens whose skill would one day make him the most renowned British architect of the age. Their long

Helen Allingham's *The Dairy Farm near Crewkerne, Somerset* romanticizes the old cottage and its garden as did Wordsworth: "The lovely Cottage in the guardian nook / . . . with its own dear brook, / Its own small pasture, almost its own sky!"

friendship and collaboration is legendary. Most would have pronounced them unlikely partners, he just out of architecture school when they met and twenty-six years her junior.

After art school she had returned to live with her widowed mother in Godalming, Surrey. The story goes that Jekyll and young Lutyens attended the same party but did not speak. Then, as she was departing, she invited him to tea. He accepted, thus beginning their discovery of just how much they shared common sympathies, values, and aesthetics. Gertrude had begun to plan for the house she would put on the property next to her mother's home, property where she had already started the garden. Now she hired young Lutyens as its architect. As the house at Munstead Wood was planned and built, so also was the relationship between Aunt Bumps, as Lutyens was to call her, and Lut-Lut, her fond name for him. They were to work together on 120 houses and their gardens.

At this time they also began their famous drives together in pony cart through the country lanes and back woods of Surrey looking for old cottages and gardens, cottages that with their thatched roofs and exposed timbers were survivors of the medieval period admired by Arts and Crafts sympathizers. The gardens they loved were created and tended by the cottagers themselves rather than by the staff as at a grand estate. There they would find althea, foxgloves, hollyhocks, honeysuckle, roses, and other cottage plants arranged informally, often with an intuitive artistry for color, form, and texture.

In admiring these cottages and gardens Jekyll and Lutyens were joining the poets and artists of the Romantic movement as well as Arts and Crafts adherents who idealized life in England's villages and countryside. Paradoxically, it was a sign of "getting-on" when one could afford to buy such a house and transfigure the little plot of land surrounding it into a living replica of the popular paintings of Helen Allingham.

By the late nineteenth century, in large part because of Jekyll's advocacy, cottage gardens had become fashionable. They bore but little resemblance to earlier cottage gardens for the focus had shifted from utilitarian herbs and vegetables to the aesthetics of garden planting. Flowers planted tightly together, apparently with neither rhyme nor reason, dominated, countering the Victorian practice of "bedding-out" where colors and patterns were highly controlled.

As the popularity of cottage gardens took hold in England, village contests for the prettiest blossom or flower arrangement were established, contests that became fiercely competitive. England was becoming as much a nation of gardeners as of shopkeepers. Clergy and Arts and Crafts moralists including Jekyll helped to justify the intense attention on gardens and flower contests by making a link between virtue and gardening. Samuel Reynolds Hole, dean of Rochester Cathedral and founder of the National Rose Show, pronounced gardening, a "pleasant and profitable occupation of leisure hours, [that] will keep [our] brother from drunkenness [more effectively] than all the pamphlets every printed." Jekyll declared that the garden "teaches patience and careful watchfulness; it teaches industry and thrift; above all it teaches entire trust." John Ruskin and William Morris were among those who approved the cottage garden for joining creative work and moral rightness.

Jekyll's designs brought together her own talents and interests with the beliefs and values of the romantic and anti-industrial sentiments popular in England at the time. She would have called it a providential intersection between her life history and the historical moment. Contributing to her enormous success as a landscape designer was her output as a garden writer. No one was more prolific. Author of dozens of books and hundreds of articles on gardening, old houses, and interior decoration for such prestigious magazines as *Country Life*, she detailed with clarity and charm her philosophy, her designs ideas, and her extraordinary knowledge of plants and their habits. Her writing style is folksy as if she were speaking over the fence to the neighbor next door. She wrote regular newspaper columns and, until in her eighties, answered personally the dozens of queries she received weekly. Her most well-known book is *Colour Schemes in the Garden*, but all are filled with keen observations and sage advice.

Gertrude Jekyll's designs varied in style, capitalized on the nineteenth- and early twentieth-century love of flowers, and gave the sense of a solid past and permanence to the houses and gardens where she worked. In the rapidly changing world of the Industrial Revolution, it was just what homeowners desired. As her predecessor Capability Brown a century before had hit upon a landscape design style that spoke perfectly to his clients and their time, so Gertrude Jekyll understood the longings of her era. She became as famous, admired, and beloved as he. A tour of England today is to see his influence and hers side by side, their landscape and garden designs very different but together predominating so that their work has become the very definition of England.

Anne Hathaway's Cottage and Gardens

Stratford-upon-Avon, England

Actress Cornelia Otis Skinner, in a charming 1925 poem, speculated about what was on William Shakespeare's mind as he walked the mile from his home in Stratford-upon-Avon to the town of Shottery. Was he composing lyrical poetry or working out an intricate plot? "Or was the Poet wondering, as he chewed his blade of grass, / If he should walk that night with Anne or choose some Stratford lass?"

Whatever the dilemma of his courting days, William Shakespeare did in fact choose Anne Hathaway as his bride. The twelve-room cottage with visible timbers and thatched roof in Shottery was Anne's childhood home. It was the supreme ideal of the medieval house and garden for Arts and Crafts artists and sympathizers.

Begun prior to the fifteenth century, the house remained in the Hathaway family until the mid-nineteenth century. When they acquired it in the late 1800s, the Shakespeare Birthplace Trust determined that the garden would be planted as a cottage garden. The trustees chose as designer Gertrude Jekyll's friend and colleague Ellen Willmott, distinguished English horticulturist, influential member of the Royal Horticultural Society, and recipient of their first Victoria Medal of Honour. She sponsored expeditions to discover new plants

ABOVE Nineteenth-century cottage gardeners found their ideal at Anne Hathaway's Cottage.

BOTTOM, LEFT Potatoes stuck with feathers and then strung, move with the breeze to scare away the birds, a method recommended by a Victorian book on cottage gardens.

BOTTOM, RIGHT Perhaps it was a rose like this at Anne Hathaway's Cottage that Shakespeare had in mind when he asked his famous question and supplied the answer: "What's in a name? that which we call a rose / By any other name would smell as sweet."

and herself cultivated thousands of species. Some sixty plants have been named for her or her home, Warley Place.

At Anne Hathaway's Cottage, Willmott used dahlias, delphiniums, foxgloves, globe thistle, hollyhocks, lavender, lupines, oxlips, poppies, primroses, rosemary, and violets. Planted near the house for convenience, culinary and medicinal herbs and vegetables were also part of Ellen Willmott's design as they would have been in the Middle Ages and in the Tudor gardens of Will and Anne Shakespeare's day. Anne undoubtedly did her share of weeding and picking, just as would the daughter of a nineteenth-century cottager.

Roses predominate at Anne Hathaway's garden as they did in most nineteenth-century cottage gardens. Yellow, red, and apricot are among the colors of roses that climb the brick walls, cover the arbor, and rise above the shorter plants, serving visually to tie together vegetables and flowers. Anne Hathaway's garden served as a model for those romantics seeking to replicate on their own property the old-fashioned cottage garden. Gertrude Jekyll, through her books, gave them precise instructions on how to do it.

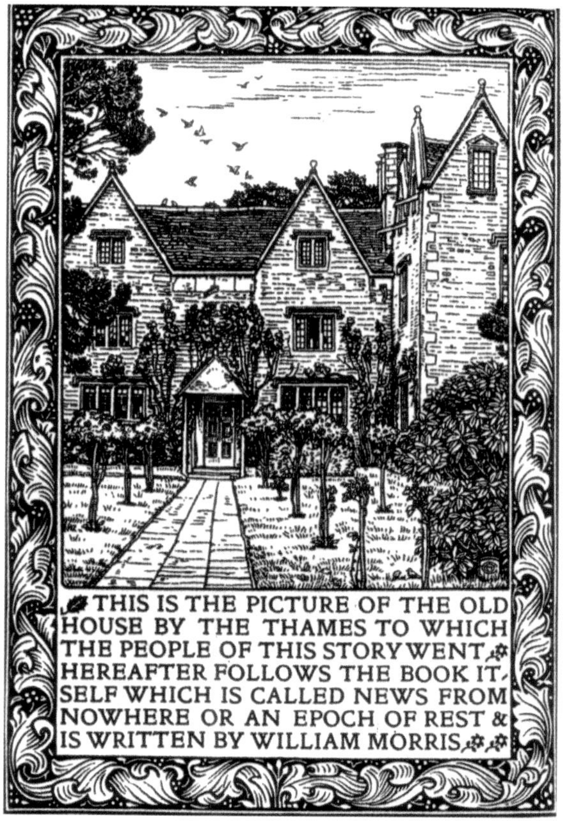

In Morris's 1893 utopian novel, *News from Nowhere*, he pictured Kelmscott and its entry garden.

Kelmscott Manor

Oxfordshire, England

Kelmscott proved to be just the place poet and artist William Morris was seeking. He wanted a home for his family, a workshop for himself and friends among the Arts and Crafts community, and a place to plant a cottage garden that would supply ideas and models for his flower and plants designs.

Studying the estate agent's description of the centuries-old house in Oxfordshire, he believed it would be the home he had once seen in a dream. His visit confirmed that the house was "heaven on earth." He was equally pleased with the garden, which was surrounded by high walls and hedges, "fenced," as he said, "from the outside world," as were medieval gardens.

He found it comforting that Kelmscott Manor had been owned for three hundred years by a farming family, work he called "useful" in contrast to "useless toil" in factories. It conformed to his Arts and Crafts ideal of the old house of hand-hewn stone and wood and had just the right ambiance for creating and decorating with his beautiful fabrics, tiles, embroidery, and books.

As with most cottage gardens, roses were everywhere, connecting different garden sections. Of special note is the Yard at the back of the house bounded on one side by a service wing where dairy workers made butter. Fronted by a cloistered walk like those of monasteries in the Middle Ages, the facing wall of the paved courtyard is romantic with roses and other cottage flowers and shrubs.

He made few changes to the garden's layout, only enhancing it with colorful cottage flowers. Set within boxwood frames as in medieval gardens, the flowers included acanthus, aconites, asters, bachelor's buttons, bluebells, crocuses, dianthus, hollyhocks, irises, narcissus, peonies, poppies, primroses, scabiosa, snakehead fritillaries, snowdrops, and violets. Above all there were Madonna lilies and wild tulips (*Tulipa sylvestris*) which are found stylized in his wallpaper, tiles, fabric, and book designs.

Fruits and vegetables were also part of Kelmscott gardens and models for Morris's art. The orchard of Victorian apples and plums was underplanted with bulbs and small flowers, with the effect of the millefleur of medieval tapestries. The medlar, a popular Victorian fruit excellent for jam, was among the trees in the orchard at Kelmscott Manor. He incorporated the artichoke, a striking sight in the vegetable garden, into one of his most famous designs. When Kelmscott's gardener employed the medieval method of trellising raspberries, Morris was pleased and encouraged use of the similarly ancient practice of lashed fencing made from local ash and hazel. All of these would make their way into his designs.

Illustrator Walter Crane described Kelmscott Manor and its cottage gardens as demonstrating William Morris's "return to simplicity, to sincerity; to good materials and sound workmanship." In the house and garden Morris had hoped to find the ideal place to live and work. The gardens provided ample subjects for his art. Here he would formulate his ideas of socialism to correct the ills of Victorian society which so appalled him. Sadly, it was not to be his haven in the heartless world. His family life deteriorated when his wife, Jane, had a long and complex affair with Rossetti, their friend and fellow Arts and Crafts artist and poet. But despite the problems, Kelmscott remained Morris's favorite house and garden. He would title his most famous book of poetry *The Earthly Paradise*. Perhaps as he wrote, he had Kelmscott in his line of vision, wishing it had been so for him.

TOP, LEFT Morris himself clipped the yew hedge bounding a side of the front garden into Fafnir, the dragon of his Icelandic translations.

TOP, RIGHT The berry patch at Kelmscott may well have given Morris his idea for his popular pattern "Strawberry Thief."

BOTTOM Morris often worked roses—their shapes and colors, petals and foliage—into his designs.

The courtyard, Munstead Wood, where Jekyll used both geometrically pruned shapes such as these spheres and hedges and also freely growing shrubs and trees.

Munstead Wood
Surrey, England

Munstead Wood was Gertrude Jekyll's haven, her home, laboratory, and studio. Here she perfected the art that brought her commissions, fame, and a lasting place in the history of landscape design. Here she designed and planted an herbaceous border, formulated her beliefs about seasonal beds, and learned how to make the transition from garden to woods. Here she would live from the house's completion in 1897 until her death in 1932.

At Munstead Wood she wanted to achieve comfort, simplicity, and the quiet she needed to work effectively. She also wanted the values of the Arts and Crafts movement to be evident. The house, designed by Edwin Lutyens, is constructed of warm honey-toned Bargate sandstone available nearby, dark old timbers, and weathered roof tiles. Casement windows enhance the impression of age. A modest entrance and small courtyards with ironstone cobbles create the "cottage in the woods" for the "serenity of mind" she sought. Munstead Wood has been described as having the feeling of a convent, and so it does, just the place for contemplation and concentration, just the place for an Arts and Crafts artist.

On the north side of the house is a courtyard, enclosed on three sides by the house, the fourth side opening onto the garden. Above the Lutyens-designed and Lutyens-named bench hangs a swag chain for *Clematis montana* echoing the lines of the visible timbers. Jekyll believed that water in the garden is essential, whether in a formal or natural shape. At Munstead Wood the pool is simple like the plantings that surround it, its geometry conveying the order and peace that she desired.

Studying the life cycle of plants in Surrey, Jekyll became convinced that it is impossible to have a garden bed that is beautiful in all seasons. Rather she advocated seasonal beds that put forth a magnificent display for a few weeks and then recede as a focal point, being allowed to rest, decay, and die before their resurrection. It was a lesson learned from observing plants and one compatible with her religious convictions about human life.

Parallel to the house in the lower garden is her herbaceous border, two hundred feet long by fourteen feet wide. Here she employed the techniques that would secure her fame as a border designer. The color scheme she had learned from studying the paintings of

Brightly colored Ghent azaleas line a woodland path for the pleasure of late spring visitors.

J. M. W. Turner: hot colors of red, yellow, and orange in the middle, cool lavenders, grays, and soft pinks at the ends, enlivening white throughout. Tall flowers next to the eleven-foot Bargate stone wall, itself adorned with flowering shrubs and climbers, were planted on earth mounded to make them appear even taller. Ground-hugging plants formed the border, and middle-height flowers held place in-between. Plants were grouped in clumps or drifts as if they were growing naturally. She used perennials and annuals, plants native to the region, and exotics, a favorite being yucca.

Hydrangea petiolaris, *Actinidia chinensis*, *Rosa banksia*, and a fig tree hug the walls of the North Court. The visible timbers and casement windows give a medieval feel reinforced by the clipped hedge in the foreground.

At Munstead Wood Gertrude Jekyll developed one of her greatest design interests and skills, that of linking surrounding woodlands with the garden. She generally positioned the more formal and geometric features—walls, pools, and flower beds—near the house with the wilder or natural elements such as woodlands and ponds farther away. When she purchased the Munstead Wood property it was semiwoodland with Scots pines, Spanish chestnuts, oak, and birch trees. She planted woodland bulbs such as snowdrops under the trees in a scheme that used many near the house and at the woods' edge, then more sparsely as the trees were more dense. From the woods to the garden each few steps found the plantings more clearly those of garden rather than woods. Paths were made of materials that would naturally occur in the woods.

Gertrude Jekyll lived by herself at Munstead Wood, but she was rarely alone. Her mother lived a short walk away on adjoining property and when she died, Gertrude's brother

TOP Successful transitions are the sure sign of a master gardener. Here Jekyll's gently winding path through the woods leads up stone steps to her garden at Munstead Wood. The huge cat topiary looking toward the house is sculpted from yew, one of her favorite plants.

BOTTOM Jekyll's detailed plan for the Munstead Wood herbaceous border.

Herbert moved with his family into the house. Other Jekyll siblings visited with their children who, as adults, affectionately remembered their famous aunt. Friends including luminaries William Morris, William Robinson, and Ellen Willmott were guests. Her dear friend, collaborator, and architect for Munstead Wood, Edwin Lutyens, came often with his family. And she was never bored. In the garden that she had begun soon after purchasing the fifteen-acre property in 1883, she was always studying new plants and their habits and developing her ideas about the aesthetics of a garden. In her herbaceous border, her seasonable beds, and the transitions from woodland to garden she developed the garden design features that are synonymous with her name.

Jekyll substituted flower-planted terraces for the previous sloping banks at Upton Grey.

Upton Grey Manor

Hampshire, England

When Charles Holme retired from the wool and silk trade in Asia, he founded what was to be the most important magazine of the Arts and Crafts movement, *The Studio: An Illustrated Magazine of Fine and Applied Art*. He also bought several properties in the charming Hampshire town of Upton Grey including the fifteenth-century manor house. He hired architect Ernest Newton to make extensive renovations and alterations to the Tudor house. Gertrude Jekyll, sharing as she did Holme's Arts and Crafts sympathies, was the obvious choice to be landscape designer.

All of this was unknown to John and Rosamund Wallinger when they bought the manor house at Upton Grey in 1983. Having had six owners in the years between Holme's ownership and theirs, the house and surrounding gardens had become derelict and even the villagers had forgotten the manor's distinguished past. The Wallingers knew only that the house was listed on the national register of historic buildings. Research identified owner and architect but nothing about the gardens. Then Rosamund came across an intriguing footnote in a

LEFT Might John Wallinger be anticipating the pleasure of a tennis game on the grass court of the lower lawn when he completes the required daily deadheading?

RIGHT Instructions for planting dry walls, a Jekyll hallmark, are included in her books.

document related to the house: "Garden possibly by G. Jekyll." She knew little about Jekyll except that she was a famous gardener. Dogged research produced the information that Jekyll had indeed designed the gardens at Upton Grey and that her plans existed. With the news, the Wallingers realized that under the out-of-control vines, brambles, and stinging nettles there lay a national treasure.

The University of California Berkeley owns the Gertrude Jekyll papers including the plans for Upton Grey. When a copy of Jekyll's detailed plan arrived at last with every plant and its location identified, the Wallingers began restoring the disconsolate gardens to the glory they had once known. Faithfully following Jekyll's directions, they recreated what is now recognized as the best restored of all the Jekyll gardens. It illustrates Jekyll's planted walls and terraces, gentle steps, a sunken garden, herbaceous borders, and even a wild garden, all features for which Jekyll was known, as well as her wizardry in making a garden appear to have a venerable history.

When Jekyll began her planning for Upton Grey Manor there was a long and steep bank in front of the house. She hated banks. She would obliterate this one, creating at the lower level a sunken garden nearest the house with an adjacent turf area for bowling and lawn tennis. Terraces were supported by dry stone walls that she planted generously with more than twenty kinds of plants, among them alyssum, anemones, antirrhinum, arabis, arenaria, buxus, centranthus, dianthus, hemerocallis, irises, penstemons, poppies, sedums, and veronica.

The steps leading from the house to the lower garden were crucial to the success of the design. They had to be inviting, not daunting, a need for which she may have been especially aware at Upton Grey as she was herself in her mid-sixties when designing the gardens. She made the risers as short as possible and the treads as wide as the space allowed. When faced with the same challenge at other sites, she included landings to provide a place to pause.

Jekyll's sunken, formal garden has only straight lines. On each side in the center of the

Peonies and *Stachys byzantina* complement the roses.

space is a two-tiered square stone structure, replete with rock-hugging plants, moss, and lichens to enhance the impression that the structures are as old as the Tudor beginnings of Upton Grey Manor. Trapezoidal flower beds on each side frame the scene.

Throughout the gardens Jekyll put her artist's eye to use. Did she think of Turner's paintings when she planted the borders with the hot colors in the middle and cool grays and lavenders at the ends, or had the practice become so much a part of her work by this time in her life that she no longer consciously recalled its source? Did her spot of red, especially at the front of a border to draw the eye, remind her of John Constable whose paintings she had copied so many years before while in art school in London?

Sundials were favored by Jekyll as a garden ornament. They served as a focal point. They acted as a useful reminder to the tarrying gardener before wristwatches were made to withstand the moisture of the garden. And they were a means of teaching gentle moral lessons, bearing as they did maxims in Latin, English, French, or German such as "Count only sunny hours," "Trifle not, thy time is short" and "Lead, kindly light."

The borders and beds of Jekyll-designed gardens rarely had empty spaces, despite the natural life cycle of plants that die back after blossoming. She achieved this perfection in two ways. Anticipating the time each plant would go dormant, she planted something

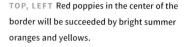

nearby that would be coming into bloom after its neighbor was spent. Hostas, she advised, are just the thing for hiding the dying leaves of bulbs. And she always had pots of plants on the verandas and in the courtyards that she could press into service when needed to fill in blank spaces in the borders.

Jekyll countered the formal garden at Upton Grey with a wild garden that by the Wallingers' time would be the only surviving and faithfully restored example of this type by Jekyll. Iron gates, a stone apron, and grassy steps in a semicircle provide the transition from formal gardens and house to the planned natural wild garden. Mown paths wind through the plantings of taller grasses, rambling roses, shrubs, bamboos, and trees until ending at the pond, itself surrounded by artfully placed rocks and water-loving plants. Cowslips oxlips, primroses, and snowdrops were the flowers in the woods and fields Gertrude roamed as a child with her brothers: these she planted with anemones, fritillaries, muscari, and scilla in the wild garden at Upton Grey, these the Wallingers have faithfully and skillfully restored.

TOP, LEFT Red poppies in the center of the border will be succeeded by bright summer oranges and yellows.

BOTTOM, LEFT Jekyll applied to the art of gardening painter John Constable's technique of adding a spot of red to draw the eye.

OPPOSITE, TOP RIGHT At Upton Grey the sundial is framed by an array of flower colors, shapes, and textures.

OPPOSITE, BOTTOM RIGHT Jekyll kept potted hostas as well as other plants in reserve to fill an empty space in the herbaceous border.

ABOVE A beautiful gate leads to grass steps and then into the woodland below.

RIGHT Yellow flag thrives at the boggy edge of the pond at Upton Grey in the only surviving wild garden designed by Jekyll.

Royal Horticultural Society Rock Garden at Wisley

Surrey, England

Gertrude Jekyll did not need to travel far from her home to design and plant a large rock garden for the Royal Horticultural Society at Wisley, for it also is located in Surrey. "Rockeries" were all the rage in England in the late nineteenth century. Unlike many rock gardens that are a jumble of ill-placed rocks and randomly chosen plants, hers at Wisley would be a model of good design, based on her knowledge of both geology and the growing conditions required by alpine plants.

The interest in rock gardens grew out of two nineteenth-century developments. The great botanical greenhouses of Kew, Dublin, and elsewhere displayed the appealing alpine plants that visitors saw and then coveted for their home gardens. The nurseries began stocking these plants and expeditions to Switzerland were organized from which participants returned with their case of tiny gems. In their home rockeries they sought to create an artistic and nurturing home for their horticultural treasures. Through her books and articles, Gertrude Jekyll would teach them how.

Another motivation for creating rock gardens was the new science of geology. As increasing numbers of people traveled to remote locations around the globe and observed different geologic formations, some began to speculate and then study how these came about. In 1795, Scotsman James Hutton, an important figure in the Scottish Enlightenment of nineteenth-century Edinburgh and who is recognized as the first modern geologist, published his theory that the earth was older than previously thought. He argued that at least some mountains were formed from volcanic lava deposits and that the earth was continuing to change. Hutton's work was followed by the first geological map of the United States.

Soon the study of geology was at the center of the scientific curriculum in Germany and elsewhere. Sir Charles Lyell's *Principles of Geology* was published in 1830. Charles Darwin formulated his theory of evolution through study of the distribution of fossils around the world. Swiss-born geologists Louis Agassiz at Harvard and Arnold Guyot at Princeton became legends for their research and teaching. From the advances made by these men and others in the understanding of geology, ordinary people began looking anew at rock formations.

When Gertrude Jekyll arrived at Wisley she found the chosen site to be a gently sloping hill. She was pleased for she identified the ideal location for a rockery as "a natural knoll of sharply rising ground or rather a kind of promontory thrust out from the wood." For Jekyll, the choice and placement of rocks was crucial. She believed that they should be large, positioned with the largest face down, follow a predetermined and uniform stratification plan, and never moved. "Every stone in the garden should bear the semblance of having been in its place from time immemorial," she wrote in *Wall and Water Gardens*. The paths through the garden should:

OPPOSITE, TOP Materials for paths and steps must harmonize with the materials of the garden. Above all Jekyll warns of the dangers of using gravel for the paths.

OPPOSITE, BOTTOM Water from the rock garden falls into the stream below.

be cut through the heart of the knoll, gently turning with steep banks right and left. . . . In forming such a rock garden . . . the rock-builder must use all his skill, so that the lines of the work shall not only be good in themselves but shall not jar with anything that comes before or after, or with any view of the half distance that can be seen from any portion of the garden scheme.

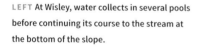

LEFT At Wisley, water collects in several pools before continuing its course to the stream at the bottom of the slope.

RIGHT Jekyll advised larger plants like this yellow gorse for the highest points to convey unity, dignity, and simplicity.

After shaping the ground and placing the rocks, the next matter of importance is to have "a solid planting of suitable small shrubs crowning all the heights," preferably those with dark foliage. She recommends as "neat of habit" andromedas, heaths, Spanish gorse, and especially the alpine rhododendrons, "all of a scale that they do not overwhelm the little plant jewels that are to come near them." It is these crowning shrubs that "decide whether the rock-garden is to be a thing of some dignity or the usual rather fussy mixture."

Water is always a desirable addition in a rock garden if it can be managed. Winding down through the rocks, it provides moisture to the trailing plants growing in the crevices, as well as being a charming design feature. "Few things are more delightful than the reflection in still water of overhanging rocks clothed with masses of blossom," Jekyll wrote.

Her knowledge of plants and their requirements is once again evident. She noted that the mountain chains of Europe are made of either limestone or entirely of granite and that each has a flora proper to itself. To ignore this information, she warns, "is only inviting failure." In designing the rockery for the Royal Horticultural Society and in her writing about rockeries, Jekyll proved herself to be not only an artist, but aware of the new science of geology and of the conditions needed to succeed in growing alpine flora.

Seen from the mainland across the three-mile stretch of blue water is the Holy Island of Lindisfarne. Medieval monks and later Gertrude Jekyll and Edwin Lutyens made the crossing by boat. Those who today travel to the island use a causeway but must be aware of the tidal schedule lest they find themselves and their car underwater.

Lindisfarne (Holy Island)

Northumberland, England

Holy Island lies off the east coast of England, just south of the border with Scotland. No place could have been more appealing to Arts and Crafts adherents and practitioners than the medieval site of the Lindisfarne Priory. Here, beginning in the sixth century, monks lived under the Benedictine Rule of Life, a rule that emphasizes the relationship of the individual to the community. Here they gathered for prayer in the eight daily offices, fished, farmed, and gardened. And most notably, with vellum, fine pens and brushes, colors made of insects, plants, and minerals, and gold and silver metals, the monks painstakingly copied, illustrated, and illuminated manuscripts of the Four Gospels and other sacred Christian writings. *The Lindisfarne Gospels* is one of the world's most treasured works of art, in the nineteenth

LEFT The castle caps Holy Island's highest crag.

RIGHT Descendants of Jekyll-planted flowers hold fast today on the cliff at the base of Lindisfarne Castle.

century inspiring William Morris to use similar medieval themes, designs, and colors. On Holy Island, Gertrude Jekyll and architect Edwin Lutyens collaborated on castle and gardens.

Like their counterparts in Ireland who fashioned the Book of Kells, the monks were by their lives and art defending civilized life in the face of barbarism. Finally, in AD 793, the Lindisfarne monastery was destroyed by brutal Viking raids. Fortunately at least some of the manuscripts were saved. The priory was later reestablished, surviving until the suppression of the monasteries by Henry VIII in the sixteenth century.

At the same time that the monastery was dissolving, a small castle was built atop the highest point of Holy Island, adjacent to and arising almost vertically from the sea. It served various military purposes until it came on the market at the turn of the twentieth century. It was August 1901 when Edwin Lutyens wrote to his wife about dinner with their friend Henry Hudson, editor of the prestigious *Country Life* magazine and advocate of the Arts and Crafts philosophy and aesthetic: "He has offered for a castle!!" At the bottom of the letter Lutyens scrawled, "too funny." Of course Hudson hired Lutyens to make the extensive renovations he wanted in the castle. For these two pre-Raphaelite sympathizers, the romance of Lindisfarne Castle on Holy Island where the apex of handmade art had been reached was irresistible. Did they associate the medieval monks who safeguarded civilization with themselves, fighting the ugly and ruthless factories?

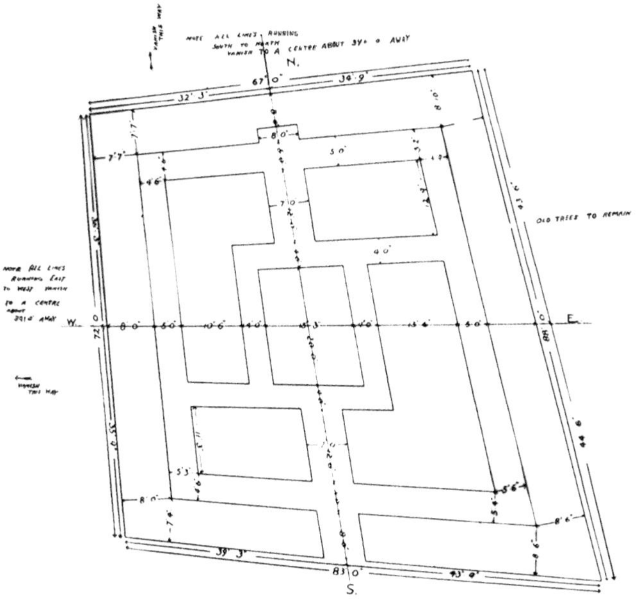

TOP The front wall is lower, allowing views of the castle from the bench on the opposite wall. The gate, with its semicircular apron of beach pebbles set as chevrons, halts sheep in search of a new taste treat.

BOTTOM Lutyens's plan for the garden, its shape designed to give the best view from the castle.

Who else but Gertrude Jekyll could design the gardens? Summoned by Hudson and Lutyens, she arrived to a new challenge. Always an active gardener, she was physically strong but the steep and rocky sides to the castle where she wanted to plant were impossible to reach by foot. Knowing the plants that would take hold in walls and crevices, her solution was to pellet the crag with their seeds fired from a large fowling gun. For plants, she lowered a seven-year-old local boy in a basket from the upper battery of the castle, a memory he undoubtedly carried for life.

For the meadow below, Lutyens drew plans for an enclosed garden, using two already existing walls. Wanting it to appear larger from the castle, he put to use his knowledge of perspective drawing, making the garden trapezoidal with the longest side nearest the castle and sides tapering to a back wall shorter in length. To accomplish this, Lutyens had two vanishing points to create an illusion of greater depth when viewed from the castle. Paths and planting beds within follow the same lines. His interior design suggests the "carpet" pages of the Lindisfarne Gospels, their shapes now planting beds.

Jekyll made a planting plan for the enclosed garden. With her usual meticulous care, she detailed a range of colors and textures with a special eye to the summer months when the Hudsons would be vacationing on the island. It took some experimentation to find plants that could withstand the sea air and mist. Along the east wall are espaliered fruit trees and vegetables including artichokes and kale. The west wall is planted with Bourbon and hybrid

The wall between the bench and castle rise frames the view.

tea roses in shades of pink, and climbers including the thornless 'Zephirine Drouhin.' Along the border at the foot of the roses are sturdy lupine spires side by side with delicate blossoms of mignonette. Fuchsia dominates the north wall surrounded by anemones, gladiolus, helianthus, hollyhock, monarda, and santolina. A Lutyens-designed bench centered on this wall looks toward the castle. The opening on the south wall is framed by a variety of sweet peas.

With their dazzling colors, the flower beds within the walled garden are like illuminated manuscripts. Perennials include calendulas, campanulas, centaureas, chrysanthemums, delphiniums, phlox, and white poppies. Clematis achieve extra height on hazel frames. In these island beds the plantings are graded in height to repeat the line of the lower southern wall. Connecting it all is *Stachys byzantina* or lamb's ear, which the British also call the saviour's flannel, a gentle reminder of the object of devotion for the monks who once worshipped through their prayer and art on Holy Island.

Gertrude Jekyll's obituary in *The (London) Times* in December 1932 acknowledged "her contribution to the complete transformation of English horticultural method and design, [and to] that wide diffusion of knowledge and taste which has made us almost a nation of gardeners. Miss Jekyll was also a true artist with an exquisite sense of colour." Her gardens magnificently illustrate these virtues.

The path might be an illuminated T from the Lindisfarne Gospels.

Lindisfarne's is the cottage garden dreamed of by the Arts and Crafts adherents who looked nostalgically and romantically back to the what they believed was the earthly paradise of the Middle Ages. They remembered the monks of Holy Island as those who kept alive civilization in the face of barbarism. Ruskin, Morris, Burne-Jones, Hudson, Lutyens, Gertrude Jekyll, and other artists of the Arts and Crafts movement saw themselves as having the same morally right mission, that of defending art and civilization against the evils of the Industrial Revolution.

12 Lush *and* Fleeting, Spare *and* Lasting

French Impressionism and Japanese garden design: the passing moment, enduring contemplation.

FOURTEENTH TO NINETEENTH AND EARLY TWENTIETH CENTURIES

A landscape [painting] is only an impression, instantaneous, hence the label they've given us—all because of me, for that matter.

—CLAUDE MONET

When creating a garden, let the exceptional work of past master gardeners be your guide. . . . When making a garden deep spiritual concentration is required.

—FROM *SAKUTEIKI*

CLAUDE MONET, the quintessential French Impressionist painter, and Gertrude Jekyll, leading light of English gardening, were contemporaries born before the middle of the nineteenth century and living well beyond World War I. Both were painters and masters of color, and both were afflicted with myopia. They cherished their homes, their families, and the domestic routines interspersed with the work to which each was devoted. They loved collecting and used the decorative arts to enhance their surroundings. They welcomed guests and made them comfortable. And they loved their gardens, both based on the cottage tradition.

Both recognized the brevity of a moment in nature, she advising gardeners to accept the seasonal changes, he painting a scene many times to capture the moment as the light changed or the wind shifted the position of the waterlilies on the pond. Monet's garden, Giverny, provided endless models, not of human figures but of flowers and trees. His irises, roses, and other cottage flowers were eventually superseded by waterlilies. He became a giant in art history and Giverny one of the world's most visited gardens, receiving annually a half-million Monet admirers. Forgoing his studio, he painted *en plein air* in order to capture a moment in time. His was not the strictly representational art of the past, but rather the impression of a fleeting instant. Ultimately the garden and his paintings of it would be his haven for meditative solace in the spirit of the Japanese gardens that he had come to admire.

He spent his childhood in Le Havre, absorbing the pearly and ever-changing skies of the coast and the light and shade at play in the verdant Seine valley. Always drawing, he went as a young man to Paris for formal study of painting. But there he grew impatient with the traditional methods and was encouraged to strike out in his own style by his new-found friends Édouard Manet, Pierre Auguste Renoir, Alfred Sisley, and Frédéric Bazille among others, including Paul Cézanne and Camille Pissarro who would also join the Impressionist movement.

In 1870, he married his model Camille Doncieux. Almost immediately they were forced to leave France for London to escape the Franco-Prussian War

Waterlilies abound at Giverny and in the gardens of Japan.

Claude Monet's painting *Impression, Sunrise* inspired the name given to the movement he is credited with founding.

which had Paris under siege. There he continued his study of painting and, like Gertrude Jekyll before him, was inspired by the paintings of John Constable and J. M. W. Turner. A year and half later and after a brief stay in the Netherlands, Monet and Camille returned to France, now to settle in Argenteuil, on the right bank of the Seine near Paris, a popular destination for artists. There he painted, gardened, became a father, and with Camille entertained friends. At first the subject of his paintings was people, portraits of Camille and depictions of family and friends in the daily occupations of their lives in their houses, their gardens, and at the waterside.

At the same time he was struggling to make a success of his career. The traditionalist critics had made him and his compatriots the laughing stock of the art world, using the word "Impressionism" as a term of contempt. Having been rejected by the juried exhibition of the Salon de Paris, in 1874 the Impressionist painters mounted their own show. Well over three

Renoir captured Monet painting his garden *en plein air*.

thousand people visited the exhibition but it was not a financial success. The critics continued their sneers.

In addition to his financial problems, Monet had a greater worry: Camille was seriously ill. He was thankful to accept a commission to paint the rotunda of the Château de Rottembourg from Ernest Hoschedé, an art dealer and early admirer. Could either the Monets or the Hoschedés have anticipated what a momentous decision this was to be for both families? Ernest spent months doing business in Paris, leaving his wife, Alice, and Monet together.

The commission finished, Alice and Ernest Hoschedé with their six children and Camille and Claude Monet with their two sons set up housekeeping together at Vétheuil. Camille died some months later and Ernest, bankrupt, fled to Belgium, leaving Alice and Monet together to care for the eight children. These years gave Alice time "to compare her overgrown child of a husband with Monet, the simple but reliable man." They married after Ernest's death in 1892.

In the meantime, businessman and art dealer Paul Ruel Durand was confounding his friends by purchasing the work of the Impressionists and advancing them funds. Increasing numbers of people in the art world were taking a second look and beginning to find virtue in the style of Monet and his fellow artists. With their increasing prosperity, Monet and Alice began looking for a new house to accommodate a studio for Monet and the needs of the growing children. One day, on a train passing through a little town northwest of Paris, Monet got a momentary glance of a pink farmhouse that appeared abandoned. Returning, he saw that this house had all they required and property for the garden that he so desired. In 1881 they moved in. He would live, paint, and garden at Giverny for the remaining forty-five years of his life.

These were the events of Monet's young life that shaped his way of seeing the world and his work as artist and gardener. At the same time an historic event occurred halfway around the world that would shape his life history and have a profound impact on his garden and paintings.

Japan had been all but closed to the West for two hundred years as a means of resisting Catholic missionaries and unfair trading practices. Only the Dutch had been allowed a trading post on a small artificial island near Nagasaki. Carl Peter Thunberg had served the post as botanist and physician. As a result of his time there he published *Flora Japonica*. Then, in 1823, German physician and botanist Philipp von Siebold took the position. He began to teach Western medicine and in turn learned from the Japanese about the flora and fauna. He was allowed to go to the mainland to look for plants, eventually collecting some twelve thousand specimens. But in 1829 he was discovered to have a map of northern Japan, a practice strictly forbidden by the government. Siebold was expelled and returned to the Netherlands. He settled in Leiden and gave his collection to the University of Leiden botanical garden, making it the first collection of Japanese plants in Europe. It was opened to the public

Monet painted Camille in a Japanese kimono.

in 1831. Von Siebold was honored by having many plants named *sieboldii* or *sieboldiana*, including clematis, fern, hosta, magnolia, malus, maple, orchid, primula, prunus, sedum, tsuga, and viburnum.

From information brought back by Thunberg, von Siebold, and Dutch traders, Europeans learned enough of Japan to long for the opportunity to trade with these Pacific islands. The United States, too, looked to Japan when, at midcentury, California was annexed, giving the United States a Pacific-facing port. To utilize this route to Asia the coal-powered steamships needed a place to refuel. It was rumored that Japan was rich in coal, and businessmen imagined trade as lucrative as that with China. President Millard Fillmore appointed Commodore Matthew Perry to lead a small naval fleet to force Japan into a relationship with the United States.

Perry was successful, despite carrying an official letter to the Japanese emperor who by this time was but a figurehead, real power being held by the military Tokugawa shogunate. After the presentation of gifts and a veiled threat of superior firepower by the Americans, agreement was reached. A series of treaties followed. Japan, its natural resources, and goods were now available to the West, and U.S. ships could find harbor and fuel in Japan's ports.

The opening of Japan in 1854 spurred a fascination in Europe with all things Japanese, just as a century earlier China had captivated Europe. Japonism or japonisme became the nineteenth-century equivalent of chinoiserie. Gilbert and Sullivan set their popular light opera, *The Mikado*, in Japan and Puccini wrote his tragic opera *Madame Butterfly*. Japanese silk, lacquerware, pottery, and porcelain dishes appeared in houses large and small. Japanese teahouses took their place alongside classical buildings in French châteaux, English estates, and in the gardens of American magnates.

Monet was among those whose interest was sparked by the once-impenetrable culture. In Holland, where he and Camille had gone for a few months after leaving England, he came by chance on a series of Japanese woodblock prints tucked in a bowl beneath a Delft porcelain merchant's counter. Enchanted with the lines, the subjects, and especially the bright colors, he bought the bowl and the grocer threw in the prints without charge. It was the beginning of a collection that Monet developed and studied throughout his life. He would add elements that he found in Japanese art to his gardens and his paintings but in his own style, with no pretense that he was replicating what might be seen in Japan. As the paintings of the Impressionists became admired and finally eagerly sought, Monet's fame grew. Would he be to japonism what Father Attiret had been to chinoiserie, an interpreter of the foreign land that only a few visited, leaving some to believe that in his unique expression he was showing the way Japanese gardens actually looked?

Had Monet traveled to Japan, he would have seen a different reality in Japanese garden design. While he was revolutionizing the art world by recording on canvas ever-changing moments and creating his lush cottage garden at Giverny, Japanese gardeners were honoring the past with uncluttered forms, simple in appearance and pointing to eternal truths.

Monet kept the exterior of the house a soft pink and had the shutters, trim, and later the iron and wood of the garden painted the green he specified.

Giverny
Giverny, France

Monet, his wife, Alice, and their eight children settled into the old farmhouse that would be called simply Giverny after the nearby town. He lost no time in starting the garden. On the property were a few old orchard trees, beautiful when flowering, and a meadow with wildflowers. Flowers planted by a previous occupant tangled with an abundance of weeds. Wild irises grew beneath ancient pollarded willows.

With the children's help, Monet planted aromatics, chrysanthemums, poppies, and sunflowers whose blooms he would bring inside to paint when it was raining. At first he grew a few vegetables—lettuces, peas, radishes, and spinach—near the house, but soon acquired a large plot in the village for the kitchen garden.

Over the months and years the Clos Normand, as he called his garden, took form in the cottage style Monet loved. Following the French tradition, it is geometric in layout, but planted with a riot of textures, shapes, and especially color. In some places he grew flowers whose colors lie in close proximity on the color wheel, at other places colors that stand opposite. As did Impressionist painters, he used white to brighten and highlight. Next to the house, Monet's pillar roses are underplanted with mostly monochromatic colors, pink tulips in spring with just a touch of blue in forget-me-nots that echo the sky above, followed in summer by geraniums and cottage pinks.

Most noted in Monet's time as now is the Grand Allée. One-hundred-seventy-two feet long, it is composed of successive iron arbors. As Monet dictated, the plantings and

TOP Red and purple are immediate neighbors on the color wheel.

BOTTOM Monet used white to brighten his garden as did the Impressionists in their paintings.

color schemes change with the seasons, each creating a new feeling and multiplying opportunities for him to capture fleeting time. In spring an abundance of pink roses mount and cover the arbor arches. In autumn when the roses die back, the focus shifts to the path below as orange, red, and yellow nasturtiums almost meet in the middle of the twenty-two-foot-wide path.

As Monet was developing and painting the Clos Normand and selling his paintings of Giverny, he was continuing to collect Japanese woodblocks, ultimately owning 231 by thirty-six artists including Hiroshige, Hokusai, and Utamaro. Among the subjects were Commodore Perry's opening of Japan, chrysanthemums, peonies, and moments in time like a crashing wave or rain on a bridge.

Then in 1889, another event would change Monet's life, garden, and painting. A world's fair was held in Paris, the Exposition Universelle de Paris, celebrating the one hundredth anniversary of the storming of the Bastille, the event that began the French Revolution. The exposition was a grand affair with all kinds of attractions. Countries from around the world built sample houses to show their culture, new machinery was demonstrated, and America's

LEFT In *The Roseway at Giverny*, Monet interpreted the arbor's fall colors.

RIGHT In early spring the roses are just beginning their annual climb to the top of the arbor. Tall perennials line the path in the cottage border.

Buffalo Bill performed. The crowning glory was the newly opened Eiffel Tower rising above the Champ de Mars pavilion, built to celebrate beautiful France. At one end of the pavilion was an art exhibit that included three Monet paintings. At the other end were Joseph Bory Latour-Marliac's hybridized waterlilies. Descendants of Monet believe that it was here that Claude Monet saw the plant that would dominate the rest of his life as gardener and painter.

Latour-Marliac had been captivated as a young man by the idea that lush, large, and colorful tropical waterlilies might be crossed with the hardy lilies native to Europe. After a decade of trying, collecting seeds from distant shores, and cross-pollinating them, he finally produced his first hybrid in 1877. It was not as he had hoped the union of tropical and hardy lily but rather that of a northern waterlily with another hardy lily, one from the more temperate south. But instead of being white or yellow as were the native French waterlilies, this one was red. Red! Further work encouraged Latour-Marliac to take his small collection of hybrids to Paris for the exposition "to see if possibly they might attract some notice from amateurs." Indeed they did, winning for him a first prize.

For Monet there were two happy results from the exposition. His paintings began at last to sell, freeing him and Alice from the constant worry about money. Always planning his garden, he was able to wed his longtime interest in Japanese arts including that of the garden with his new fascination with waterlilies. He began plotting the addition of the pond, island, and bridges at Giverny.

In 1893 he bought adjoining property across the road. To the distress of neighbors, he made a pond by damming a small stream of the River Epte and built the now famous Japanese bridge in line with and extending the view from the Grand Allée. On the island and the banks of the pond he planted bamboo, irises, and willows. Over the bridge he would one day grow purple and white wisteria. And in the pond? The waterlilies he collected there would be immortalized in his painting.

The years of success as a painter were also the years of sadness for the family. After the death of his beloved stepdaughter Suzanne he never again painted a human figure. He was turning inward, looking from the "reflection bridge" of Japanese legend into the mirror pond.

He extended the pond by purchasing additional land and adding to his collection of waterlilies. Then, in 1911, Alice died, a loss followed all too shortly by the death of his son. And once again a world event intersected with his life history, this one also near. World War I brought the fighting so close to Giverny that he could hear the cannon and saw the wounded soldiers daily. He grieved, did what he could to help, and remained at Giverny for the four long years of the war. Now he found a measure of solace in the huge canvases he was painting of waterlilies in order "not to think more of the horrors being endlessly committed," paintings that would one day hang in the Orangerie in Paris.

He was painting not only the pond's surface but its depth, including underwater roots and dying lilies, sometimes appearing peaceful and beautiful, sometimes disturbed and angry. Although he never visited Japan, he was appropriating the very purpose of Japanese gardens that are meant for meditation. His waterlily pond became his Zen garden as he pondered both the joys and sorrow, goodness and tragedy of his own life and of the world. Like the Buddhist monks who tend the Japanese gardens, his painting of the waterlilies and pond became a life commitment, engaging him until his death in 1926.

TOP A weeping willow points downward to the second and smaller Japanese bridge, the pond, and waterlilies.

BOTTOM Monet painted many views of the bridge, this one in the late 1890s.

Although the rock garden at Saihō-ji has no water, it is easy to imagine a stream wending its way downward through the rocks.

Saihō-ji (Kokedera or Moss Temple)

Kyoto, Japan

In the early years at Giverny, Monet planted his lush garden where he could study and then paint the rich and ever-changing forms and colors of nature. But with the addition of his Japanese garden at the close of the nineteenth century, he increasingly focused on the mystery of the waterlilies, their beauty, and the dark, always-moving stems below the surface. Had he been able to visit Japan he would have experienced gardens that, like his waterlilies, foster reflection and meditation. But rather than lush and fleeting, Japanese gardens are simple and give testimony to ancient verities.

Saihō-ji, one of the oldest gardens in Japan, is lean and subdued. By its very simplicity it fosters a contemplative mood. Located near the ancient capital, Kyoto, it was originally a Shinto shrine but was converted in the twelfth century into a Buddhist monastery. Then in the mid-fourteenth century it was reconstructed, some believe under the direction of the famous Buddhist priest and gardener Musō Soseki, though he presided at Saihō-ji but briefly. The garden is said to represent Buddha's paradise on earth.

Its design is based on advice found in *Sakuteiki*, a garden design manual written in the eleventh century that is possibly the oldest such book in the world. It is among the treasures of art and poetry in the Heian period when Japan was establishing art forms independent from those of China.

The manual begins with the words "the art of setting stones." These words describe the focus and genius of Japanese garden design and set the path for future gardens. It was in stones that heavenly spirits came to earth to reside, their beneficence bringing health and prosperity. It was advisable therefore to treat stones with the greatest respect, "following their request." This included honoring their original position whether horizontal or vertical. The most splendid stone was selected as the Main or Guardian Stone to be set first. Then Bracketing Stones and a Fore Stone are laid. "If there are stones that 'flee,' then there should be stones that 'chase' after; if there are stones that lean, there should be those that lend support; if some proceed, then others should acquiesce; if some face up, then others should face down; and to balance with stones that stand upright there should also be those that recline."

At Saihō-ji the dry cascade, a designed landscape, is thought to be the oldest dry garden in Japan, presaging the later Zen Buddhist gardens. It follows the stone-setting principles outlined in *Sakuteiki*:

Of the many mosses at Saihō-ji, some are soft, some coarse, some spongy.

> According to a man of the Sung Dynasty, stones taken from mountains or riverbanks have in fact tumbled down to the base of a mountain or valley floor from above, and in doing so have become reversed. Some are upright while others lie flat. Still, over time they will change color and become overgrown with moss. This weathering is not the work of man. Because the stones have weathered naturally, they can be set or laid in the garden as they are found in nature without impediment.

Rocks divide the dry-cascade "stream" into three, a process repeated as it flows downhill, representing the spread of Buddhism.

The pond at Saihō-ji is shaped like the Japanese character for heart. Three small islands

Tree trunks frame the view of the mossy bridge and islands in the pond.

are connected by simple bridges. Originally the ground was covered with white gravel, but flooding and neglect have produced Saihō-ji's most famous characteristic. The forest floor and bridges are covered with 120 varieties of moss. So prominent is this feature that the garden is popularly called Kokedera or Moss Temple. The soothing shades of green stand in contrast to the riotous colors of Giverny. Only in fall when the maples turn red is a color other than green seen at Saihō-ji. The effect of the monochrome is one of solitude, peace, and reverence for nature, all promoting meditation on life's mysteries.

Buddhism began in India in the sixth century BC when the wealthy young Prince Siddhartha left the palace to seek the meaning of life. On his travels he met sickness, old age, death, and finally a truth-seeker who set him on the path to becoming Buddha, the Enlightened One. His followers spread his practices throughout Asia and developed three branches of the religion. Buddhism came to China in the first century AD and to Japan in the eighth century AD where Zen Buddhism emphasizes concentration and meditation.

Horizontal stones line the pond's edge, following the curve of the bridge. Fall brings once-a-year color as the maples turn red.

The art of setting stones reaches perfection at Ryōan-ji.

Ryōan-ji
Kyoto, Japan

Ryōan-ji is also a Buddhist temple in Kyoto with monastery, lake, islands, and trees. Its most famous feature is a dry garden of such balance, harmony, and mystery that it is recognized as one of the world's great art treasures. In a rectangular area thirty-three by ninety-eight feet, the dry garden consists of white gravel that is raked lengthwise, with fifteen stones and boulders arranged in five island groups of five, two, three, two, and three. Carefully managed moss grows around each grouping. The surrounding wall, backed by a weeping cherry and other deciduous and tall evergreen trees, is essential to the scene. It is made of clay boiled in oil that has over the centuries seeped out to create a beautiful patina.

TOP Ryōan-ji dry garden is an abstract rendering of scenes like this in the early sixteenth-century *Landscape of the Four Seasons* by Kangaku Shinso, Sōami.

BOTTOM Flowering quince (*Chaenomeles* species) is native to Japan and is found on the grounds of Ryōan-ji and elsewhere throughout the country.

The borrowed scenery behind the wall changes with the seasons and highlights the rhythms of nature especially for those whose daily responsibility is to tend the garden. While people come to Ryōan-ji to meditate, it is the act of raking the stones and other maintenance tasks that are meant to be the occasion of meditation, just as in Christianity the faithful are to make daily tasks their vehicle for prayer.

Ryōan-ji was traditionally thought to have been created in the early sixteenth century by the artist Kangaku Shinso, also known as Sōami, but modern scholars dispute the claim. What is clear is that the abstract art of the dry garden resembles Japanese islands and water depicted in his screen paintings. The idea of a *dry* garden representing water may seem an anomaly, but in Zen Buddhism the contrast provides a subject for meditation.

Shapes frequently found in Japanese paintings and landscape design are the tortoise and crane. Both are symbols of longevity, a belief that comes from an ancient Chinese legend of Horai, an archipelago populated by immortal beings who flew on the backs of cranes, the islands held aloft on the back of huge tortoises. *Sakuteiki* advises: "Ponds should be constructed in the shape of a tortoise or a crane. . . . Ponds may also be made in the shape of felicitous words written in kana script."

The balance achieved at Ryōan-ji reflects harmonious proportions: the dry garden and wall occupy the bottom half of the view from the main hall of the house of the abbot (the monastery head), and the trees behind comprise the upper half. The design follows the advice found in *Sakuteiki* based on the rules of geomancy or, as it is currently called in the West, *feng shui*, which holds that all things are related and their placement therefore affects our *qi* or life energy.

Over the centuries Ryōan-ji has had many interpreters who have sought its deepest mysteries. Most discussed and written about is that only fourteen of the fifteen stones can

be seen at once. Many have said this feature is a reminder of the Buddhist concept that only the Enlightened who have reached a state of perfection can see them all at the same time. Some have seen in the rock groupings an ocean with islands, similar to the geography of Japan itself. Others believe the design shows a tiger leading her cubs across a river. Still others have seen in the design of Ryōan-ji the pattern of the stars. A modern scientific analysis, using a model of shape analysis (medial axis transformation), argues that the empty space is implicitly structured to appeal to the unconscious preference for axial symmetry. But Elizabeth Barlow Rogers is correct in concluding that "Neither mathematical explanation nor allegorical meaning can be attached to it. To achieve either would rob it of its enigmatic quality and thereby make it less satisfying from a Zen perspective, as the inexplicability it offers is fundamental to Zen experience and an intrinsic factor in its design."

While the dry garden is Ryōan-ji's most well-known feature, the grounds surrounding it are also beautiful. Originally the home of a wealthy administrator, the property was founded as a temple in 1450, damaged in the Ōnin War, and rebuilt shortly after. The site includes a teahouse, monks' quarters, and those of the abbot. The pond, harboring mandarin ducks, has two small islands. In front of the teahouse is another landmark of Ryōan-ji. A water basin for rinsing hands and mouth before entering the tearoom requires crouching which, like the Japanese practice of bowing, is a sign of humility. The inscription can be translated as "I know only satisfaction," a Zen Buddhist belief that we have within ourselves all that we need.

Although asymmetrical, Ryōan-ji has the same effect as geometric Vaux-le-Vicomte in reducing stress. Its harmony of elements ensures that those meditating are able to relax and concentrate on their reflections.

In 1624 a visitor declared Katsura to have "the finest view in Japan."

Katsura Imperial Villa

Kyoto, Japan

"Far away, in the country village of Katsura, the reflection of the moon upon the water is clear and tranquil." So reads a line in the eleventh-century Japanese classic *Tale of Genji*. A century before England was reveling in Augustan literature and creating Rousham, Stourhead, and other gardens to recount images and stories from classical Greece and Rome, in faraway Japan Prince Toshihito was starting a garden based on the literature *he* adored. In building the imperial villa (also known as the Katsura Detached Palace) he created one of Japan's most beautiful stroll gardens, a perfect setting for recalling the many loves, unrequited and fulfilled, of the noble Genji. A central pond, completely surrounded by a belt of trees, is shaped like a flying crane and one of its islands like a tortoise. As we have seen, both figures are revered in Japanese lore and Prince Toshihito was following *Sakuteiki* where it is advised that "ponds should be constructed in the shape of a tortoise or a crane since water will take on the shape of the vessel it enters." Early Shinto garden practices are merged with the beliefs and sense of beauty of Zen Buddhism.

A path of 1,760 stepping-stones leads the stroller around the garden, a new view revealed around each bend. Principal among the destinations along the route are the teahouses. At one time there were five, now only four, each separate from the main building and from each other, each in its own isolated spot surrounded by the peace of nature. Here the tea ceremony, an important part of Buddhist practice, was performed. The precise ritual demonstrates the four virtues of harmony, respect, purity, and tranquility. It is meant to be transformative as it focuses the participant on *sabi*, the inner spiritual life, and *wabi*, the outer life with its imperfections, the acknowledgment of which is the first stage to enlightenment. Each teahouse looks onto a tranquil scene of pond and trees, some pruned into cloud shapes, a classic feature of Japanese gardens.

The traditional entry gate of bamboo, unfinished wooden posts, and thatched roof continues the Buddhist theme of rusticity and imperfection. From origins in the Shinto temple that was always kept open for worshippers, Japanese gates are never closed. The path itself is a model of Japanese design. Individual stones set into moss or short grasses guide the stroller. Straight and curved lines define areas; varied materials including stones, tiles, and river pebbles are carefully and artistically laid by hand.

Bamboo and twig fencing is a feature of most Japanese gardens, used to enclose a garden or simply to screen one view from another. Patterns vary. The fence at Katsura is simple. Others have vertical as well as horizontal bamboo, some crisscrossing diagonally. The hand-tying of twigs to support them is itself an art form.

CLOCKWISE FROM TOP LEFT

Attention to detail is a virtue of Japanese gardens as in this path's meticulously placed stones.

A Katsura gate is modeled after temple gates that mark the transition from the mundane to the sacred.

Imagine "Shining" Genji, son of the emperor, meeting his beloved concubine, Lady Kritsubo, in this romantic Katsura setting.

Bamboo is one of nature's strongest materials. This fence will last for many years..

As the passage from the *Tale of Genji* suggests, moonlight has its fascination for lovers in Japan as it does elsewhere. The path is lit with carefully placed stone lanterns. A feature of most Japanese gardens, they are located to be functional, not merely decorative. At water's edge the lantern on a sunny day or moonlit night is reflected in the water, doubling its impact.

Visual artists as well as dry garden designers have represented swirling ocean waters in their work, this one by Hiroshige.

Tōfuku-ji

Kyoto, Japan

The opening of Japan brought a passion for all things Japanese to Europe and the United States, and the reverse was true in Japan. Interest in the West grew with every ship that sailed into a Japanese port bearing products and styles from overseas. Life began to change in traditional Japan in the late nineteenth-century Meiji period when the emperor was restored to power. Among the garden designers was Mirei Shigemori who sought to resolve the tension between changeable Western culture and the enduring traditions of Asia.

Born in 1896, Shigemori's early education included the ancient Japanese arts of the tea ceremony, flower arranging or ikebana, and ink-and-wash landscape painting. As a young man, he studied Japanese painting at the Tokyo Fine Arts School where he was attracted to the modern design that was beginning to come out of the West. Soon he was pursuing the study of garden design, proving himself a prodigious scholar by producing, in his early forties, the twenty-six-volume *Illustrated Book on the History of the Japanese Garden*.

Shigemori's first major landscape design commission, on the eve of World War II, was Tōfuku-ji near Kyoto. Built in the first half of the thirteenth century, the Buddhist temple burned in the fifteenth century but was rebuilt on the original plan. Over the years buildings were added to the first abbot's quarters and monks' residence. At its height Tōfuku-ji had fifty-three sub-temples and was recognized as one of the five great temples of Kyoto. After a devastating fire at the end of the Meiji period, the temple was again rebuilt and in the 1930s Shigemori was hired to design the gardens. As advised in *Sakuteiki*, there would be

TOP The eastern garden's raked stones are a traditional form, yet also suggest movement and change.

BOTTOM The checkerboard pattern of moss and stone has a strongly modern feel.

four gardens on the corners following the rules of geomancy. The ancient garden manual sometimes calls the directions simply east, west, north, and south, but as often refers to the animals associated with the guardian gods: "to the east of the house is the Blue Dragon. . . . to the west is the White Tiger. . . . to the south is the Scarlet Bird. . . . The hill to the north is the Black Tortoise."

The southern garden in front of the abbot's house, called the *hojo*, represents the islands of Japan. Its four natural stone formations lie on a bed of finely raked gravel, symbolic of the eight rough seas. Five moss-covered rocks form a backdrop in one corner. The eastern garden is a dry garden with seven cylindrical stones that were foundation stones for the old temple. They rise above the raked gravel "ocean" surrounded by a moss field in the pattern of the constellation Ursa Major, the Great Bear of Heaven.

The western garden has a gravel base laid out like waves. Low squares of severely pruned azaleas alternate with equal sized stones, a large version of what would become Shigemori's signature piece. The northern garden features a checked pattern of moss and stone, bordered by roof tiles and tightly pruned shrubs. The stones' regular placement close to the observer becomes random and more sparse in the distance. They are from the original temple path, honoring the abbot's request to follow the Zen Buddhist admonition not to waste. Beyond, colorful maples point to the Tsūten-kyō bridge at Tōfuku-ji.

In 1868 the capital of Japan was moved from Kyoto to what is now Tokyo, but Kyoto remained vibrant. Traffic between the two cities was heavy; the most popular road, the Tōkaidō. Fifty-three stations, the number determined by Buddhist lore, provided resting places for sojourners. The wide and at places tree-lined road was meant for pedestrian traffic, the primary means of transportation. Guidebooks to the sights along the Tōkaidō became popular as novelists, poets, and artists made these the subject of their art. Among the most famous was the nineteenth-century painter Hiroshige. His colorful prints included thirty-six scenes of Mount Fuji and the fifty-three stations of Tōkaidō. One of his prints pictures the Tsūten-kyō bridge at Tōfuku-ji, a popular view on the Tōkaidō road.

Hiroshige's *Red Maples at Tsūten Bridge*, a view seen from Tofuko-ji.

Claude Monet was an admirer and collector of Hiroshige prints. It is easy to see their appeal for the Impressionist painter with their bright, clear colors, and tiny specks of paint for the leaves of trees, drops of water, and flower petals. Like Hiroshige, Monet followed nature's seasons. In his garden at Giverny and in his paintings, Monet placed elements of the two cultures side by side.

Shigemori found similarities between modern Western and traditional Japanese design. Both value simplicity. Both use abstract forms to convey ideas. He successfully fused the two traditions, demonstrating that change can be harmonious with an honored past.

13 Bringing Home "Abroad"

Wealth and travel in the Gilded Age inspire garden designs from Italy, England, France, Japan, and Mexico.

LATE NINETEENTH AND EARLY TWENTIETH CENTURIES

MARK TWAIN CALLED the late nineteenth century the Gilded Age. America at one hundred years was affluent and gaining a measure of polish. The New England writers, Hudson River painters, and landscape designers such as Downing and Olmsted had helped to refine the country's aesthetic taste. But to many who were impatient for education and high culture, there seemed a long way to go. Higher education in the liberal arts was concentrated in the East Coast Ivy League. Johns Hopkins was founded in the centennial year, Berkeley and Cornell were then but infants, Stanford and the University of Chicago yet to be conceived. Most colleges and universities focused primarily on agriculture, education, or religion.

America's great cultural institutions were also but gestating. The Metropolitan Museum of Art in New York opened in 1872, the Boston Museum of Fine Arts four years later. The Art Institute of Chicago and the Metropolitan Opera would follow at the end of the decade. One day there would be money from the wealthy industrialists to fund these and many other educational and cultural institutions in America and with them would come a flowering of culture. But first the visionaries and potential philanthropists had themselves to be educated. With ease of ocean travel and growing fortunes they turned to Europe to expand their knowledge. Only a few went specifically to study garden and landscape design, but many returned with an awakened appreciation of the art form and sought to apply what they had seen to their own properties. In garden and landscape design as well as in other aspects of intellectual, artistic, and cultural life, they were bringing "abroad" home.

> The garden lover, who longs to transfer something of the old garden-magic to his own patch of ground at home, will ask himself . . . : What can I bring away from here? And the more he studies and compares, the more inevitably will the answer be: "Not this or that amputated statue, or broken bas-relief . . . but a sense of the informing spirit."
>
> —EDITH WHARTON

John Adams, America's second president, had once written: "I must study politics and war that my sons may have liberty to study mathematics and philosophy. My sons study mathematics and philosophy, geography, natural history, naval architecture, navigation, commerce and agriculture in order to give their children a right to study painting, poetry, music, architecture, statuary, tapestry and porcelain." As if to fulfill his great-grandfather's prophesy, when he graduated from Harvard

Pegasus strikes his hoof at Powerscourt.

Mary Cassatt painted *Lydia Crocheting in the Garden at Marly* in 1880 while studying art in France.

in 1858 young Henry Adams did what other young men his age were doing: he asked his parents for money to go abroad. In his case he wanted "to begin at a German university the study of the Civil Law—although neither [I] nor they knew what the Civil Law was, or any reason for . . . studying it."

Young Adams may have been vague about his purpose, but he did understand that scholarship was at its apex in Germany. New subjects like geology, chemistry, and biblical studies known as historical criticism not yet in American college curricula were being taught, and he had a feeling he should be exposed to them. Who would not benefit from three years at the universities of Heidelberg or Munich, Oxford or Cambridge?

As students flocked to England and Germany, American painters flooded Paris. Thomas Jefferson once said that every man has two countries, his own and France. That proved true for nineteenth-century artists. In the mecca of the art world would-be artists were able to study with many different teachers, paint in various indoor studios and out-of-doors in both the city and countryside, learn about exhibitions, and meet those who controlled the entries and the judging. Writer Henry James summarized the influence of France on American art: "It sounds like a paradox but it is a simple truth that when to-day we look for American art, we find it mainly in Paris. When we find it out of Paris, we at least find a great deal of Paris in it." Winslow Homer, Mary Cassatt, Thomas Eakins, John Singer Sargent, James Whistler, Childe Hassam, and Edward Hopper were only a few of the hundreds of Americans who studied and practiced their art in Paris from the mid-nineteenth century to 1914. Some like Cassatt spoke French and were integrated into the French art world, she establishing lifelong friendships with the Impressionist painters. Others were satisfied to confine their associates to those in the English-speaking community of Paris.

Writers also, following Washington Irving and James Fenimore Cooper, went to Europe. Edith Wharton and T. S. Eliot established residence, she in France, he in England. Neither returned to live in the United States. And then there was Henry James, who not only went to Europe to write but made Americans in Europe the subject of his novels.

As James's characters reveal and history bears out, hundreds of other Americans traveled in Europe for a variety of reasons, some well-conceived, others, like young Henry Adams less clear, staying from a few weeks to years. Some like Strether, James's protagonist in *The Ambassadors*, who had tired of the social strictures of his small American town, found freedom in Europe. Others believed that Europe provided the next level for "getting-on." The propitious union of an American fortune with titled aristocracy was one way of doing so.

But whether man or woman, young or old, rich or not-so-rich, student, writer, artist, or mere traveler, they seemed all to make their way to Italy at one time or another in their time abroad. Henry James may have settled at Lamb House in Rye, England, but he had frequent sojourns in Italy, especially Venice and Florence. Edith Wharton's influential *Italian Villas and Their Gardens* was published with illustrations by Maxfield Parrish in 1904. American art historian Bernard Berenson made his home Villa I Tatti near Florence.

The English, too, continued to go to Italy where they found both classical antiquity and the Renaissance. Perhaps taking a lesson from Emperor Hadrian himself, they sought to bring home reminders of their experiences for their own pleasure and to impress their acquaintances with their newly acquired knowledge. What better place to show the world their sophistication than in their gardens?

And so, like garden designers since antiquity, travelers of the late nineteenth and early twentieth centuries incorporated elements from abroad into their landscapes. They looked primarily to Italy, but just as eighteenth-century designers had folded what they perceived as Chinese into their landscapes, many designers now included the traditions of newly opened Japan. Some confined their garden design to that of a single culture. Others created separate sections or rooms, each featuring a different cultural tradition. Although many failed aesthetically, a few succeeded in their integration of more than one culture in a single garden area.

But by the early 1900s change was in the air. In America the graduated income tax ratified in 1913 and antitrust laws expanded in 1914 reduced fortunes, making foreign travel and elaborate gardens less possible for many. And in Europe there were rumblings as Germany and England flexed their military muscles. The outbreak of World War I in August 1914 sent travelers rushing for home, there to remain for many years. Europe in the aftermath of the war was hardly a desirable vacation spot. Only the wealthiest could afford travel during the worldwide Depression of the 1930s, and World War II brought an end to the era of the grand tour and with it the designing of gardens reminiscent of travels abroad. Fortunately some gardens remain to remind us there was once a Gilded Age.

Powerscourt

County Wicklow, Ireland

It was Queen Elizabeth herself who in 1603 granted Powerscourt Castle and its surrounding forty thousand acres to Richard Wingfield, an expression of gratitude for his military success. It was an appropriate gift, for Powerscourt had been an important strategic site for the Anglo-Normans as early as the twelfth century. For 350 years, descendants of Richard Wingfield owned Powerscourt where their international travels and interests would be reflected in the gardens. In the mid-eighteenth century, just south of Dublin

TOP At Powerscourt the Italianate pebble mosaic landing unites the architecture of the house and garden, and looks from Victorian flower beds and topiary to the Irish mountains of County Wicklow.

BOTTOM Life-sized winged horses, symbols of the Wingfield family, and an iron gate open to the circular lake. Water from the jet rises one hundred feet in the air, echoing the tall, columnar trees in the landscape.

on hills where sheep and cattle once grazed, the first viscount built a new and grand villa in the popular Palladian style. In the nineteenth century the seventh viscount made real the great gardens that his father had but imagined for Powerscourt.

As in the Italian gardens on which Powerscourt is modeled, terraces take the visitor from the villa and its veranda on the highest level to the lowest level, Triton Lake. The eye follows a wide axial walk to a pair of winged horses, the lake, and the distant mountains. Pebble mosaics like those at Hadrian's villa and in Italian Renaissance gardens form the first landing downward to the lake. On either side of the pathway, flower beds and architectural topiary common to both Victorian and Italian gardens convey a sense of order. At the center of the lake, Triton is modeled after Bernini's fountain in Rome. Head back, he blows the conch shell before delivering his message in the Deluge, sounding the horn for the waters to retreat. Renaissance villas including the Medici villa at Fiesole began to extend the view beyond the garden walls. By the nineteenth century the distant views were integral to landscape design. Those at Powerscourt are among the most beautiful.

Another popular feature of Gilded Age gardens, the Japanese garden, completed in 1908, was the last major addition to the landscape. Perhaps time had served to educate about Japanese gardens because the Powerscourt Japanese garden has an authenticity not found in many earlier Japanese-style gardens in Europe. Occupying land that was once a bog, it is first viewed from high above, in the crenellated Pepperpot Tower. Hikers descend through the American Garden, so named for the specimens of *canadensis* conifers, many rare and planted from seed.

Entering the Japanese garden, strolling visitors are guided downward along a winding path by stone lanterns. Delightful little Japanese bridges cross the bubbling stream. Brightly colored azaleas and dark red Japanese maples dot the surrounding land. The centerpiece is a pagoda. Chinese windmill palms (*Trachycarpus fortunei*), cultivated in China and Japan for thousands of years and brought to Europe in 1830, encircle the garden. The idea governing the design is that as the pilgrim moves to the garden's center, he discovers his inner self and while moving outward and up, he gains knowledge of the world.

LEFT Here a stone lantern, one of many at Powerscourt, marks the path over the bridge to the Japanese pavilions.

RIGHT The Bamberg Gate from the German cathedral is almost 250 years old.

Uniting these and other parts of the Powerscourt landscape are black wrought iron and gold-painted gates, some original, others replicas from Germany, Italy, and England. Among their motifs are the rose, thistle, shamrock, and musical symbols including heralding angels. The Bamberg Gate leading into the walled garden is especially interesting for its use of forced perspective, making the view beyond appear longer than it actually is. It is but one of the appealing perspectives for visitors to Powerscourt.

Sutton Courtenay Manor

Oxfordshire, England

"Uncle Bob," Lord Wantage, included not only the manor house but the little village of Sutton Courtenay located on the Thames in Oxfordshire in his 1895 wedding present to Sir Harry Lindsay and his new bride. There young, beautiful, and charming Norah would develop a garden greatly admired by those in the aristocratic circles in which the Lindsays moved. Through these connections she built a successful landscape design business and a reputation as one of the period's great designers. The garden provided Norah the ideal setting for her parties to which everyone wanted to be invited. Her style both employed and challenged the design conventions of the Arts and Crafts movement and included garden features she had discovered on her tours of Italy.

The wedding gift of Sutton Courtenay was generous and needed, for although the extended Lindsay family owned many properties in Scotland and England, Harry Lindsay

LEFT The beautiful Norah Lindsay, painted in 1891 by George Frederic Watts.

RIGHT The earliest part of five-gabled, two-winged Sutton Courtenay Manor is Norman and was the eleventh-century venue for entertaining King Henry I.

was not in line to inherit any of them. Sutton Courtenay comprised fifty-four acres, with six houses, barns, stables, and other buildings. The idea was that, in the tradition of English estates, rental income from the houses would support the Lindsays. They moved into the manor, made it their home, and there raised two children, Nancy and Peter. They loved to entertain and Norah became known as a glittering hostess for her intelligent and witty conversation, her musical talent, and her beauty. Amidst their busy lives, Harry developed skills in refinishing antiques, Norah in gardening.

Like Gertrude Jekyll whom she admired, Norah also made the colorful herbaceous border her signature piece, but she incorporated into it ideas of the wild garden as promoted by garden writer William Robinson. Born in India where her upper class Anglo-Irish father was in military service, Norah Lindsay may have formed her design preferences early by playing with her sister in the garden of cornflowers, hollyhocks, sweet peas, and verbena, shaded by the feathery and free-flowing neem trees (*Azadirachta indica*).

At Sutton Courtenay, Norah planted flowers not in the Jekyll sequence of tall in the back of a border to short in the front but rather as they might grow naturally with some tall flowers in the middle and front, permitting them to fall forward into the lawn or path. She added further variation in height with urns that were always brimming with flowers. Not committed to grouping flowers in clumps or drifts, she encouraged their mixing, as she said, in "inspired untidiness," a complement to the medieval buildings of Sutton Courtenay in the spirit of old cottage gardens. Her friend Lady Diana Cooper wrote, "Flowers literally overflowed everywhere and drifted off into the wilderness." Norah welcomed what she called "arrivistes," the "newly arrived," plants that had seeded themselves. Although she followed no customary rules, all agreed that she had an exquisite sense of color.

ABOVE The "boys" from nearby Oxford, enchanted by Norah, loved the Lindsay-hosted parties on the nearby Thames. Sir Henry Channon wrote in his memoirs: "Sutton Courtenay, roses, the river and the youth of England splashing in the Thames, and Norah, the sublime Norah, Russian ballet, food in the courtyard, Chopin, color, gardening, a riot but a healthy riot of the senses."

RIGHT Dark green foliage often served Norah Lindsay as backdrop for flower blooms whose colors were, in combination, both cheerful and soothing.

The fastigiate trees in the background, reminiscent of Norah's visits to the Italian countryside, offer contrast to the broad topiaries, the one on the right, a Welshman's hat.

Travels to Italy inspired another one of Norah Lindsay's contributions to design. There she fell in love with the tall Italian cypresses standing watch in formal gardens and over the countryside. She also liked the effect of the precisely shaped topiary shrubs. She would use both columnar trees and topiary to give a sense of order to her otherwise run-riot gardens.

Sadly, after a decade the Lindsays' marriage began to fail. Harry and Norah drifted apart as he spent more and more time away from Sutton Courtenay. Finally, they divorced and Norah was left wondering how she would support herself. Visitors' compliments for her gardens made her realize that she had a special eye and gift. But how, at age fifty-one, could she make her skill profitable? It was Norah's mother, now married to the Earl of Clarenden, who supplied the answer. Through her connections with aristocracy, her daughter began to receive commissions. Soon Nora was in great demand with design work in England at Cliveden, Trent Park, Blickling Hall, Ditchley Park, Mottisfont Abbey, and overseas at, among other places, Serre de la Madone, the French home of Lawrence Johnston, creator of Hidcote, with whom she and her daughter, Nancy, became close friends. In these and other gardens, Norah Lindsay made her contribution to landscape design in the twentieth century.

Stan Hywet
Akron, Ohio

When in 1928 Gertrude Sieberling wanted to abolish the garish orange and maroon flowers that dominated her English garden in Akron, Ohio, she was advised by the house's original landscape architect to employ Ellen Biddle Shipman for the task. Warren Manning declared Shipman "one of the best, if not the very best, Flower Garden Maker in America." Such a designer was just what Mrs. Sieberling sought.

The house had been built a decade and a half earlier for F. A. Sieberling, the founder and president of the Goodyear Tire Company. His home was Ohio but like many of his contemporaries he was educated abroad, in his case at Heidelberg University. When he returned to Ohio, he established a rubber tire business. Originally making bicycle tires, his company moved quickly to supply the new automobile industry, creating a fortune for its founder.

He and Gertrude began plans for what would be a sixty-five room mansion to accommodate their six children, the staff, and his brother and seven sisters on their frequent

LEFT The first edition of *The Secret Garden*, the enduring classic that inspired the garden at Stan Hywet and many others since.

RIGHT Stan Hywet's broad lawn and curving, tree-lined entry road were modeled after features common to English estates.

visits. To arrive at a style for the house the Sieberlings and their architect visited three great Tudor houses in England: Compton Wynyates, Ockwells Manor, and Haddon Hall, all with walled gardens.

The land on which the Sieberling house was built was named Stan Hywet, meaning "stone quarry" in Old English, for the business that had once occupied the property. Manning's design for the landscape, based on the approach common in English estates, included a broad lawn, a wild garden at the quarry site, meadows, horse-riding trails, and even an oh-so-fashionable Japanese garden on the 3,500-acre property.

Of all the parts of the Stan Hywet landscape, Gertrude most loved her enclosed garden, taking an active role in its design. According to family lore, *The Secret Garden* by popular writer Frances Hodgson Burnett, published in 1911 just when the house was being planned, inspired its design. Burnett herself had been peripatetic like so many of her generation, born in England, immigrated to the United States but with extended stays in Paris and Italy, later in life moving back and forth between England and the United States. It was in England that she saw walled and secret gardens that would provide the setting for her classic tale, though she might have seen *giardini segreti* in her travels in Italy as well.

At Stan Hywet, the secret, walled garden with its two water pools and sculpture was Gertrude's place for meditation, perfect for a break from the demands of the active children, numerous guests, and staff. To make the seclusion complete, Shipman added trees such as yellow laburnum and white dogwood to prevent any viewing from outside the walls.

It was Shipman's planting scheme of flowers that would dramatically change the garden's character. Like Gertrude Jekyll, she was meticulous, designating 3,400 plants and 112 different varieties of perennials, annuals, and bulbs for the new look in Stan Hywet's English garden. Following the wishes of Gertrude Sieberling, Shipman used soothing blues, lavenders, pinks, and pale yellows to achieve peace and calm. Although only an armchair

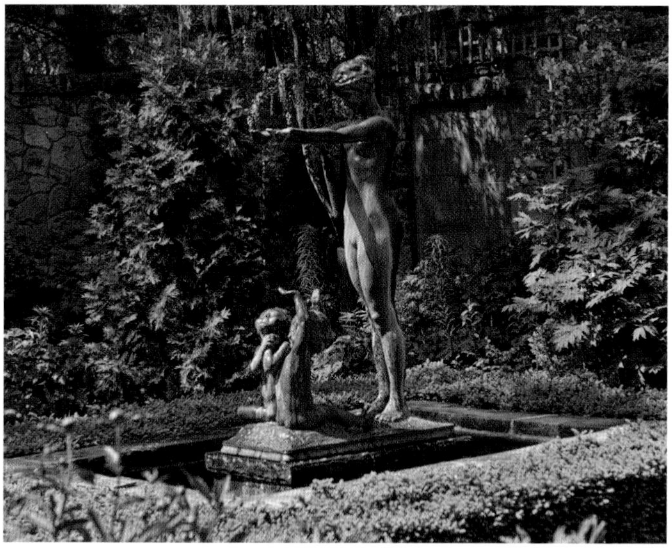

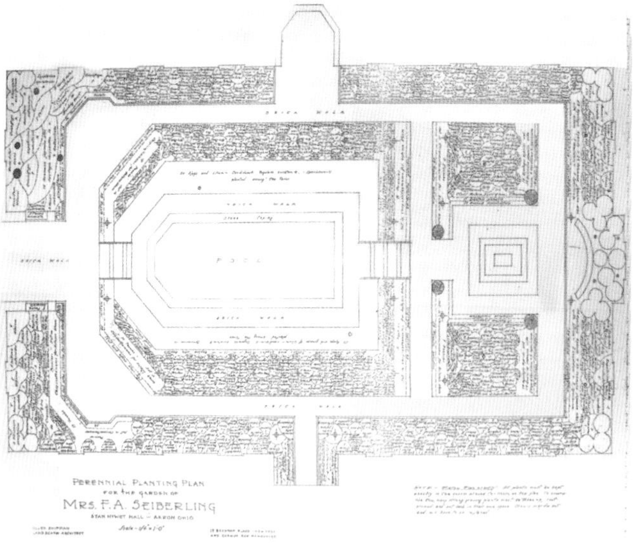

ABOVE *The Water Goddess,* installed in 1916, is the work of American sculptor Willard Dryden Paddock.

TOP, RIGHT Ellen Biddle Shipman's plan for the secret garden is detailed and precise.

BOTTOM, RIGHT Espaliered trees soften the stone wall, the framing rose trellises Gertrude Sieberling's idea.

traveler herself, Ellen Biddle Shipman looked to England, inspired originally by Jekyll's color schemes. Her herbaceous borders at Stan Hywet between the walls and the low hedge bounding the pools may be likened to an Impressionist painting or a stained glass window.

Later the house and garden would become important in another way. Daughter-in-law Henrietta Buckler Sieberling brought together at Stan Hywet two men who would become known to the world as Bill W. and Dr. Bob. We know they met in the Gate Lodge and perhaps in the secret garden as well, as they began to lay plans for the founding of Alcoholics Anonymous. Now open to the public, Stan Hywet is a pilgrimage destination for garden aficionados and for those in recovery.

The focal point of the Italian terrace is the mighty *Oceanus and the Three Rivers* fountain.

Kykuit

Pocantico Hills, New York

Upon arriving at Kykuit, just north of New York City, many visitors express surprise. While certainly grand by ordinary standards, the house is modest compared to other mansions in the United States and the great European villas, châteaux, and castles. The paradox is that it was built by the person who was unquestionably the richest man in the world, his fortune counting for one and a half percent of the entire American economy and his name becoming a synonym for great wealth. His house and landscape incorporate the international knowledge and interests of the sophisticated yet unpretentious family.

John D. Rockefeller came from modest beginnings. His rise as founder and president of Standard Oil would have suggested he might build on an enormous scale, but he had other values and ways to spend his money. His would be no Victorian house and garden of conspicuous consumption, no vulgar display of wealth. A devoted Northern Baptist all his life, he is acknowledged as a prime creator, along with Andrew Carnegie, of modern philanthropy. Rockefeller foundations and trusts support medical research, education, the arts, and a host of other charitable causes.

The forty-room house of local stone sits high above the Hudson River. Eclectic in design, it underwent periodic changes from its initial form to assume a Classical Revival Georgian character. The gardens similarly are eclectic, drawing on garden and landscape traditions from several cultures. Originally the Rockefellers hired Frederick Law Olmsted as landscape architect, but John D. was not happy with the plans, hiring instead architect William Welles Bosworth who, among other commissions, had designed the Massachusetts Institute of Technology campus. Following his work at Kykuit early in the twentieth century, in the 1920s he oversaw the restoration of Versailles, the Château of Fontainebleau, and Reims Cathedral, projects Rockefeller funded.

The forecourt on the west side of the house is Italian. Geometric shapes, symmetrically placed pools and trees, and low trimmed hedges define the lines. A straight path leads from the center of the house to the large Oceanus fountain of white Carrara marble, its lower basin twenty feet in diameter. It is a copy of the sixteenth-century sculpture by Giambologna in the Boboli gardens in Florence.

Beside the house lies the enclosed garden, a pair of bronze swans presiding. Charming small gilt creatures—a crab, frog, dragon, and fairy—are at home in the waters. A rill

flows outward from their pool, punctuated by periodic shallow and circular basins with jet sprays. Just outside the enclosed garden is an asymmetrical garden, remarkably successful in combining elements from European and Japanese garden traditions. High on a steep and rocky hill is the circular Temple of Love. In its center is an eighteenth-century copy of the Medici Venus, the original a Hellenistic marble sculpture in the Uffizi Gallery in Florence.

A grotto is tucked below in the rocky hillside. From it a gentle stream winds its way down a slight slope, its surroundings designed with Japanese elements. In contrast to the hewn-rock temple base, the rocks in the Japanese section are smooth and placed as if by nature herself, just as they are in gardens in Japan. Weeping trees are reflected in the water. Completing the picture are bronze Japanese lanterns, part of the original design.

The Rockefellers must have found this section of the garden especially pleasing for only a year after its completion they added a much larger Japanese garden on a lower site. To insure its authenticity Ueda and Takahashi, both trained at the Imperial Palace in Tokyo, were employed to work with Bosworth. A teahouse overlooks a pond. An enclosed dry garden modeled after Ryōan-ji, stone lanterns, Japanese gates, and the winding paths of Japanese stroll gardens contribute to the scene. A stream with stone and mortar bed flows over two thousand feet, catching the overflow from other water features in Kykuit's gardens. Azaleas, bamboo, flowering cherries, pines, and thread-leaf maples along with low spreading juniper and grasses cover the steep easterly bank above the pond while shrubs and ornamental trees lead to the house's main lawns on the western side.

Today, the Rockefeller tradition of support for good causes continues at Kykuit as elsewhere. The house and gardens are open to the public. The family has long welcomed hikers and horseback riders to the grounds of the 250-acre estate. The sculpture collection of third-generation Nelson Rockefeller, governor of New York and vice-president of the United

TOP In the enclosed garden between topiary pyramids are a rill and circular pools recalling the Court of the Lions at Alhambra.

BOTTOM The Medici Venus at Kykuit in the Temple of Love is one of many copies of this most popular antique sculpture.

A graceful bridge crosses the recirculating stream in Kykuit's Japanese garden.

States, is placed around the grounds as well as in the house. The property beyond the gardens immediate to the house is used for food production for the estate residents and patrons of the Stone Barns Restaurant on the grounds, thus promoting the idea of locally grown foods. Cultural events and educational activities including the Agricultural Literacy Academy are held at Kykuit, another Rockefeller philanthropic legacy.

The Hinoki bark gate frames the view to the Zen dry garden modeled after Ryōan-ji. Roof tiles stand vertically to form the path bounded by log piles.

Bertram Goodhue's elegant rendering of his design for Balboa Park.

Balboa Park

San Diego, California

While the English and Americans were bringing the design traditions of Italy, England, and Japan to their home gardens, a development in California would popularize another style of architecture and landscape design, and through it not only reflect but in fact shape American culture. For this new development the planners and designers looked for ideas neither east nor west but south to Mexico. "Abroad" would take on an extended definition.

The new development began in the southern California city of San Diego, in 1910 a city of only forty thousand people. There leading businessmen sought to launch a world exposition to rival that in San Francisco, both celebrating an amazing achievement, the 1915 opening of the Panama Canal. In San Diego, the planning committee determined that the style of architecture and landscape design for their exposition should refer to the state's Spanish mission history as well as recognize the Hispanic culture that connects southern California and Panama through Mexico and Central America.

Fortunately the city had the open land needed for the exposition. An ancient tradition adopted by Mexico from both Aztec and medieval Spanish culture, the ejido was land set aside for common use. In 1834 the Mexican government, which then controlled the area, so designated a tract of 47,000 acres in what is now San Diego.

Soon Alta California, as southern California was known, was ceded to the United States in the Mexican-American War of 1848. Two years later California gained statehood, San Diegans became U.S. citizens, and the city began to grow.

Twenty years after San Diego became U.S. territory its leaders presented a resolution to the city council to establish a public park. They were not to be outdone by New York City where Central Park was but a decade old. The location would be 14,000 acres of the ejido, but for a long time it remained mostly open space with a few private groups and individuals establishing and maintaining small gardens.

One was Kate Sessions who later became known as the mother of Balboa Park. She operated a nursery within the park, open to the public, where she nurtured both native and exotic plants. One she introduced was the now widely used ceanothus or California lilac. Generous to the city, she donated trees and plants for the city's beautification and is credited as a pioneer in establishing the vegetation that characterizes California today.

ABOVE The California Bell Tower has become the city's symbol.

RIGHT Moorish influences in the Alcazar garden at Balboa Park.

When the town fathers began planning for their grand exposition, they conducted a contest to name the park. From the entries they chose Balboa Park, honoring Vasco Núñez de Balboa who, having crossed Central America from east to west, became the first European to view the Pacific from the Americas. Now work on the exposition could begin in earnest.

The city leaders looked to Bertram Goodhue, an East Coast architect. It must have seemed to some an odd choice as he was known as the designer of neo-gothic churches. But he had shown his versatility in creating the beautiful byzantine Saint Bartholomew's Church in New York City and demonstrated his ability to use Spanish architecture styles in Hotel Washington in Colón, Panama. In San Diego he would prove that skill again, this time by choosing for Balboa Park the highly decorated Churrigueresque style of Spanish Baroque and Spanish colonial architecture.

The park is formed by a long promenade, El Prado, along which the major exposition buildings were located. Most prominent, the California Building with a bell tower

The Botanical Building is now over one hundred years old.

One might mistake southern California for southern Spain, so similar is the Casa de Balboa to the Partal at Alhambra.

two hundred feet high was the center of the exposition and remains the focal point of the park today. Beneath the tower lies the Alcazar garden, fashioned after the Moorish gardens of Seville, Spain, with tiled pool and fountain, parterres with flowers in the interstices, geometric beds, and, for shade, a pergola with climbing roses. The Casa de Balboa reinforces the Spanish flavor with its architecture and reflecting pond.

Another major feature of Balboa Park is the domed Botanical Building, reflected in the long lagoon at its entrance. Constructed of wood for the 1915 Exposition, it is one of the largest lath structures in the world, housing more than two thousand cycads, ferns, orchids, palms, and other tropical plants as well seasonal displays.

In creating Balboa Park, Bertram Goodhue gave the city a cultural identity. Spanish revival architecture and its attendant gardens became popular in the Southwest and elsewhere. It opened the eyes of the United States to cultural diversity, especially to the growing number of immigrants from Mexico and Central and South America. The Hispanic heritage shaped U.S. national consciousness, becoming one of the most visible and bright stones in the national mosaic.

Filoli

Woodside, California

Mr. and Mrs. William Bowers Bourn II wanted a country house on the peninsula where they would join other wealthy San Franciscans who had built estates there in the years following the devastating 1906 earthquake. Having made a fortune as owner of the Empire Gold Mine, a winery, a water company, and its reservoir, Bourn chose a site for the house on the southern end of what is now known as the Crystal Springs Reservoir. It reminded him of the estate in Ireland that he and his wife had purchased and developed as a wedding gift for their daughter.

Like many Americans of the period, William Bourn studied abroad, at Cambridge. After all, the University of California Berkeley had opened for classes only two years before and Stanford had not yet been conceived when he was ready for higher education. His time in England allowed for the obligatory tour of Europe, including Italy and France. The gardens of their home would recall these happy days before Europe was devastated by World War I.

The house the Bourns built was eclectic, exuding the confidence of the successful in the Gilded Age. Basically red brick Georgian, it is U-shaped, recalling the form of English Renaissance country estates. A noteworthy feature is the Spanish red-tiled roof, a nod to California's Mexican history brought to public attention by the 1915 California Exposition in San Diego. The Bourns instructed the architect to respect the trees already on the property of over seven hundred acres, especially those near the house.

They hired Bruce Porter as landscape architect as they shared with him an appreciation for California's natural landscape and wanted views of the surrounding hills incorporated into the design. The sixteen-acre formal garden between two parallel north-south walks is made up of rooms that each have a distinct character referring to a European experience. Plantswoman Isabella Worn supervised the garden, over the years adding a rich variety of plants including camellias, magnolias, rhododendrons, roses, and other plants not native to the area. William Bourn's university days are recalled in the English Renaissance knot garden. Here plants of different shades of green and gray appear to be woven together, the spaces in the pattern filled with colored gravel.

The English knot garden at Filoli recalls a garden feature popular in medieval and Tudor England.

The Jesse Tree Garden is a reminder of the famous medieval stained-glass window at Chartres Cathedral that depicts the lineage of Jesus on a columnar vine-like tree. While at Cambridge, William Bourn probably would have seen the medieval Jesse Tree windows at York Minster, Canterbury, and Wells cathedrals in England, and in his European travels those at Chartres and Sainte-Chapelle in Paris.

ABOVE The twelfth-century Jesse Tree window at Chartres Cathedral.

TOP, RIGHT Boxwood at Filoli represents the Jesse Tree vine, which shows Jesus's family tree. Red and blue annuals are planted as in the stained glass.

BOTTOM, RIGHT Irish yews stand in for Italian cypresses at Filoli.

The sunken garden at Filoli could be found in England, France, or Italy.

As did other Gilded Age travelers, the Bourns brought home Italian concepts such as garden parterres, clipped hedges, geometrical designs, water features, and fountains. Like an Italian casino, a garden house at Filoli provides respite from the sun. Filoli's much-photographed centerpiece is the sunken garden with its shallow reflecting pool, lead putti, olive trees pruned to a vase shape, defining hedges, and sculpted yews leading the eye to the California hills.

William Bourn named his northern California estate by using the first letters of each phrase of his creed: Fight for a just cause, Love your fellow man, Live a good life. Filoli provided him, his family and friends, and thousands of visitors a place to recall past travel pleasures and take in the beauty of the California countryside.

Old Westbury Gardens

Old Westbury, New York

For beautiful Margarita Phipps, her garden was a case of bringing her childhood home to her new home abroad. English, she married American John Shaffer Phipps. Both were heirs to great fortunes, hers from the Grace shipping lines, his from Carnegie Steel where his father had been a partner. When they married they determined they would build a grand house and develop gardens in the English style. They chose Long Island, a convenient commute to New York City. Once Quaker farms and fields, the area would become known as the Gold Coast for the mansions built there by America's nineteenth-century industrial tycoons. Eventually the Phippses acquired over three hundred acres for vegetable fields, an orchard, meadows, a dairy, and later a tennis court, polo field, golf course, and swimming pool.

They hired English architect George Abraham Crawley who used American brick and limestone and English stone slab roof tiles to build the house in late seventeenth-century English style. It proved a perfect setting for the family's antique furniture and their collection of paintings by Thomas Gainsborough, Joshua Reynolds, Henry Raeburn, and others.

It was natural that John and Margarita would give the garden and landscape planning special care. His father, Henry Phipps Jr., a generous philanthropist, gave to his native city of Pittsburgh the Phipps Conservatory and Botanical Gardens. She grew up at Battle Abbey in Sussex, site of the Battle of Hastings, whose garden elements she would recreate on Long Island.

Extending from the south side of the house is a wide veranda. Symmetrical staircases parallel to the house take the visitor down to the lower level where a broad greensward extends outward as in English estates. The lawn, bounded by a hemlock hedge, narrows to the Grand Allée which is divided by a black and gilded ornamental gate with horses, foxes, horns, and dogs, symbols of the sport the Phippses enjoyed.

To the east of the house is a small serpentine lake of irregular banks surrounded by a woodland path with viewing spots. At the far eastern side is a lovely Temple of Love, reminiscent of early eighteenth-century English gardens. Atop its ionic columns is a delicate wrought iron dome dappling the sunlight as in the adjacent woods and connecting visually at the west end of the lake with the pool pavilion, the iron entry gate, and the gate at the end of the allée.

The Phipps family was lively with three sons and a daughter. The garden was the children's

Capability Brown would have disapproved of the topiary at Old Westbury, arguing instead for an unbroken lawn to give full view of the house.

setting for imaginative play. Each boy had his own log cabin, little Margaret an English cottage complete with thatched roof. Inside her playhouse were the necessary furnishings, chairs and a small table set for tea, a rocking horse, dolls, a teddy bear, books, and a grown-up chair for watchful nanny. Outside, the English cottage garden of perennials might be Anne Hathaway's except for the Japanese lilac tree, flowering dogwood, and lacecap hydrangeas. The horticultural anachronisms would not have troubled the Phipps children or the thirty British children given a safe home at Old Westbury during the years of the World War II German bombing of London. Was the thatched cottage for them a comforting reminder of the peaceful England they once knew?

No respectable English garden would be without roses. At Old Westbury, the complex pattern of interlocking circles and squares laid out by architect Crawley recalls seventeenth-century English parterres such as those at the Old Palace at Hatfield. Beds, bounded by tiny hedges of Heller Japanese holly (*Ilex crenata* 'Helleri') contain a wide variety of old and new roses. The rose garden's showpiece is a dodecahedral sundial with the rampant lion, ancient symbol of British royalty, here grasping the globe. Beyond the rose garden and beside a walled garden lies the Ghost Walk, a replica in hemlock of the dark yew vault at Battle Abbey where Margarita and her sisters once played.

TOP, LEFT The Temple of Love provides a resting place for walkers and a meeting place for lovers.

BOTTOM, LEFT Taking center stage in June are blue and purple delphiniums surrounded by pink fairy roses in the cottage garden of the thatched-roofed playhouse.

RIGHT A weeping beech (*Fagus sylvatica* 'Pendula') and flowering shrubs including shell pink, smooth, and Ghent azaleas, quince, and rhododendron serve as backdrop to the roses.

Edith Wharton's novel *The Age of Innocence* tells the story of courtship and marriage in rule-bound New York society of the 1880s, made complicated for the novel's characters by the presence of a European countess with different—and fewer—social restrictions. It won Wharton a Pulitzer Prize for fiction, the first awarded to a woman. It is not surprising that director Martin Scorsese choose Old Westbury as the setting for his film of the famous book. But for the happy John and Margarita Phipps, busy with family, friends, business, and philanthropic activities, there appear to have been no difficulties such as those encountered by Wharton's characters.

Iford Manor
Wiltshire, England

For young Harold Peto the prospect of an extended stay in Italy was not the occasion for joy as it was for most Gilded Age travelers. His father, a wealthy baronet and builder, having lost his fortune, was forced to sell first their Suffolk country home and then their London house. The cost of living in Italy would be less than in England, and Harold's father had fourteen children to support. But the move would have its advantages. While living in Italy Harold developed a love of classical and Renaissance architecture and garden design and honed the exquisite taste for which he became known.

As a young man he returned to England to begin his training as an architect and, at age twenty, entered into a partnership with Ernest George, establishing an office where Edwin Lutyens would be among the assistants. The partnership lasted almost twenty years, but in that time Peto found himself at odds with architectural forms popular in England in the late nineteenth century, preferring instead the Italian Renaissance style and its attendant decorative arts.

When the architectural firm was dissolved, Peto agreed not to practice architecture in England and so went to France, there to design Italianate villas for wealthy expatriate Americans. In these years his interest in landscape design increased and he began what would become a remarkable collection of sculpture and *objets d'art* to adorn both house and garden. His desire to own his own home grew as well. He wanted a place to house his collection and put into practice his philosophy of uniting house and garden by developing them simultaneously.

In 1899 he found the place of his dreams, an eighteenth-century house with Palladian facade on a hillside overlooking a river. What, in England, could be more Italian? He purchased Iford Manor and began its transformation. Here he would bring to an English setting Italian tradition and art. "If the relative spheres and successful intermarriage of formal and natural gardening are better understood today than ever before, that desirable result is due to the efforts of no one more that Mr. Peto," wrote Avray Tipping, architectural editor of *Country Life* magazine.

TOP, LEFT Iford on the hill above the River Frome in Wiltshire.

BOTTOM, LEFT Has the soldier stood guard since the days of Roman Britain?

RIGHT The *Dying Gladiator* draws the visitor up an Iford road to the cloister.

Eschewing what he thought of as the too-quaint-by-half cottage style that focused almost exclusively on flowers, he sought instead the dignity of the old Italian villa and its gardens. "Old buildings or fragments of masonry carry one's mind back to the past in a way that a garden of flowers only cannot do. Gardens that are too stony are equally unsatisfactory; it is the combination of the two, in just proportion, which is the most satisfying," he wrote in *The Boke of Iford*. At Iford he would display his collection of artifacts in an Italian design but enriched with lush plantings that English weather makes possible.

The approach to Iford Manor sets the stage. Flowering plants line the retaining wall channeling the River Frome. The gently arched medieval bridge supports a statue of a Roman sentry. Another road leads to the cloister where music is performed on summer nights, the bounding wall featuring the *Dying Gladiator* not unlike the sculptures of the same subject at Rousham and the Rometta in the Villa d'Este.

On one of several hillside terraces, a colonnade becomes the setting for Peto's art collection. Placed among irises, lavender, and topiary along the open court are two stone sarcophagi, one adorned with a della Robbia swag, another a bas relief of a fierce boar hunt; a bronze statue of the she-wolf nursing Romulus and Remus; antique stone basins and Tuscan pots; the busts and full statues of saints and Romans; a bench created from two Corinthian capitals; and a stone bird atop a sheaf of wheat. Peto has tucked a small courtyard with a narrowed entrance on another terrace. His open columns and poles with swag rope give a feeling of an enclosed Italian *giardino segreto*. Here, on the walls under a canopy of wisteria, he placed pieces of his collection. At another site, geometric topiaries protect the putto fountain between them, all surrounded by simple Doric columns, tile, and stone walls.

A stone eagle perches on one wall
as if resting but briefly from his flight.

LEFT Topiaries reflect Peto's skill as architect. The bas relief above the fountain may be the gospeler Mark whose symbol is the lion.

BELOW Who would not chuckle at the Dog-by-the-Tuscan-Pot scratching himself or be enchanted by the delicate and romantic rose entwined around a stone pillar?

The long walk is an outdoor museum for Harold Peto's collection. A lion commands from the tall column.

Harold Peto's gardens at Iford have been called Arcadian, but they are not so in the same way as early eighteenth-century landscapes. Set in idyllic countryside, sculptures at Studley Royal, Stourhead, and Rousham make similar references to antiquity. They convey serious messages learned from Latin literature. In contrast, Peto's display holds a lighthearted charm, recalling not an imperial past or future so much as the pleasure of trips to Italy.

Harold Peto's achievement at Iford is rooted in the Edwardian era, named for Edward VII who acceded to the throne upon the death of his mother Queen Victoria in 1901. It was a time of relative peace in Europe and America, with financial prosperity for the upper classes who seem to our present day to have given excessive time and attention to their clothes, to sports, especially tennis, fox hunting, polo, horseracing, and yachting, and to entertaining with picnics and garden parties in summer, lengthy dinners and musical soirees in winter. Life was not to be taken too seriously and the unpleasantness below the surface could rather easily be ignored. If eighteenth-century gardens provided a setting for contemplation and exploration of the great and eternal questions, Iford, as did other Gilded Age gardens, provided a setting for vivacious women and high-spirited men to engage in witty and carefree pastimes.

Peto created at Iford his own serene world, surrounded by the things and styles he loved. He had brought home from Italy the bas reliefs and statues that Edith Wharton deplored, but placed them with such a sense of balance and elegance that she surely would have agreed that he had captured the "informing spirit" of Italian gardens. The old Italian gardens, she wrote, "to be a real inspiration must be copied not in the letter but in the spirit. . . . A piece of ground laid out and planted on the principles of the old garden-craft will be, not indeed an Italian garden in the literal sense, but what is far better, *a garden as well adapted to its surroundings as were the models which inspired it.*" In England, Harold Peto at Iford succeeded in doing just that.

"In Flanders fields the poppies blow
Between the crosses, row on row."—John McCrae

14 The Poppies Grow

Designers of five beloved gardens find solace in opposing the industry that led to war.

TWENTIETH CENTURY

IDEALISTIC YOUNG MEN of both sides went gaily off to war outfitted with swords. They met with guns instead, guns that in August 1914 when World War I began were expected to be silent by the end of September or early October at the latest. Nor had they reckoned with the cannons, made in Germany by Krupp Industries but sold to and used by both Allies and Central Powers. Dubbed Big Berthas, these cannon churned the earth between the army lines, making a wide swath of deep mud that rendered impossible a move forward by either side, thereby deadlocking the western front. The tragedy was that neither side won nor lost. The men were dug into trenches for four seemingly interminable years, many to be buried forever in the dead earth.

More than thirty million military and civilians died in the Great War, making it one of the deadliest in history. Only new military tactics and tanks capable of moving across the muddy fields broke the stalemate, giving victory at last to the Allies. But it was a pyrrhic victory. A generation of young men had been cut down—dead, poisoned by mustard gas, or forever maimed—leaving hearts and minds weary and broken. English country villages would never be the same again, as evidenced by the names commemorated on tablets in parish churches, more names than village rooftops as families lost both father and sons.

And, tragically, the pain was to be renewed only a generation later. The gay, wild, and free years of the Roaring Twenties with the ever-present spirit of the bon vivant were but a distraction from the storm brewing again in Europe. The punitive Treaty of Versailles ending World War I proved counterproductive, giving rise to disaffection and unrest in Germany. The Depression of the 1930s left people struggling and discouraged. Adolf Hitler harnessed these feelings to his own evil ends.

How does one bear such enormous loss, relieve the sadness, or heal a broken spirit? Where does one look once more for hope? Some took to drink, others to religion. Many poured their energy into volunteer organizations. Highclere Castle and Great Dixter were among the English country estates that were turned into hospitals for the wounded. Artists turned to their crafts. Wilfred Owen wrote poems before his death at the Battle of Verdun and Benjamin Britten set Owen's poems to music in the *War Requiem*. Rupert Brooke wrote his poem "The Soldier," and T. S. Eliot "The Waste Land." Francis Poulenc composed the dolorous *Lenten Motets*.

> Friend, be very sure
> I shall be better off with plants that share
> More peaceably the meadow and the shower...
> Soldiers may grow a soul when turned to fronds.
>
> —WILFRED OWEN

Other artists found comfort in creating gardens, making a different kind of trench, one that would nurture new life and bring forth signs of renewal and resurrection. Gardens have always been a source of comfort. Emperor Hadrian in his villa near Rome, the Duke of Marlborough at Blenheim, General Dormer at Rousham, and George Washington at Mount Vernon are among those who, returning home from war, found their gardens restorative. None needed the renewing power of the garden more than those who lived through the violence of the twentieth century.

The designers of five beloved gardens created during the war years were inspired by the Arts and Crafts movement and style. They understood on the deepest level that the suffering of World War I was tied to an industry whose motive was not society's best interest but profit and that turned out the high-powered weapons that caused the massive destruction. All looked back to John Ruskin and Gertrude Jekyll who lauded the time before gunpowder was introduced and before the Industrial Revolution. Gardens would be reassuring reminders of what they believed was a less savage and barbarous time, havens in the too often cruel and violent world.

Hidcote
Gloucestershire, England

For Major Lawrence Johnston, the tiny English village of Hidcote Bartrim was to be his safe port after the storm of war. There he developed the "garden of rooms," each area demonstrating a different design principle and displaying a different kind of plant. The creation of garden compartments as at Hidcote poses a design challenge. The transitions from room to room must be handled as skillfully as in a house. Having a special purpose and focus, each room will have a different style, furnishings, and color scheme, yet the flow from one room to the next must be smooth. The challenge is especially great where rooms are adjacent as at Hidcote, affording no opportunity for gradual change.

The son of a wealthy American widow who with many others in the Gilded Age lived in Europe as an expatriate, Laurie Johnston was born in Paris and spent his childhood in France. As a young man he matriculated at Trinity College, Cambridge. The Christopher Wren–designed library would have been a daily sight as he studied for his "second" in history, one of many Cambridge influences fine-tuning his already developed aesthetic taste.

After graduation he became a naturalized British citizen, joined the Imperial Yeomanry, and went off to fight in the bloody battles of the Anglo-Boer War. It was in South Africa that he discovered the joy of plant exploration. In 1907 his mother bought Hidcote, a comfortable but unpretentious stone house and three-hundred-acre farm in the Cotswolds. After military service he settled there with her, intent on turning the almost bare land into a garden. He started with only two stands of beeches and a cedar of Lebanon (*Cedrus libani*), planted too close to the house but also too fine a specimen to remove.

The majestic cedar of Lebanon, seen here at Hidcote, is a favorite tree of English gardeners.

War again intervened. As a major in the Northumberland Fusiliers during World War I, Johnston was twice wounded, once so badly that his body was set aside for burial. He was rescued from being buried alive only at the last moment. Promoted to major, he was second in command of his regiment and would be known as Major Johnston for the rest of his life.

After the war he pursued his growing interest in horticulture by participating in extended plant expeditions to South Africa, Mount Kilimanjaro, and Yunnan, China, where he collected rare specimens. At the same time he was building a network of gardening friends with whom he exchanged seeds and plants. Beyond this, we know little of this shy man. Unlike his prolific English contemporaries including Gertrude Jekyll, Nora Lindsay, Vita Sackville-West, Harold Nicholson, and Christopher Lloyd, he left few notes or plans. He was not active in the Royal Horticultural Society. Only a few letters have come to light. Whether he was retiring by nature or his war experiences made him so we cannot know.

We deduce from Hidcote itself the sources of its creator's design. Certainly the principles of Gertrude Jekyll and Edwin Lutyens are present: a strong backbone, separation into rooms, semicircular steps, seasonal beds, monochromatic color schemes, and herbaceous borders. The overall look is that of an English Arts and Crafts garden, but there are features that allude to Italian and French styles. A tiny stream-crossing with but a single stepping-stone reminds the visitor of Asian simplicity.

TOP The red borders, the pavilions, the steps, and the hornbeam Stilt Garden lead to a view of the hills and valley beyond the iron gate.

BOTTOM The Long Walk is bisected by a small stream. Spacious, it contrasts with the tightly packed garden rooms.

The Terrace Garden's delicate plants will be protected with glass panels inserted in the iron frame before wet winter weather arrives. Here Johnston nurtured alpines and succulents from Chile, Ireland, Morocco, Spain, New Zealand, Japan, China, and the Himalayas.

He began with two axes, forming a T. The Long Walk runs north to south. The east-west axis extends from the Old Garden of Borders in the east through the Stilt Garden. Here a wide allée of hornbeams, precisely pruned into a rectangular "roof," ends at iron gates with a view to the Vale of Evesham. The croquet lawn and theater parallel this succession of spaces as if to emphasize its importance.

Around these axes Johnston nestled twenty-nine small garden rooms. The Pillar Garden is formal and architectural with a lush herbaceous border. The Wild Garden is luxuriant with an untamed abundance. The Alpine Terrace Garden and Dry Garden each highlight a geographic area and a particular kind of plant. Into these rooms Major Johnston put an enormous array of plants, many that he had collected from around the world. Varieties of allium, campanula, clematis, dianthus, lavender, hypericum, penstemon, and symphytum are among the plants that bear the name Hidcote. A yellow climbing rose and a red verbena are named for him.

In the Pillar Garden, the tall architectural yews anchor the riot of perennials including the dark purple *Lavandula angustifolia* 'Hidcote' which was developed here.

ABOVE However different they may be, the Dry Garden is compatible with the adjacent Pillar Garden room.

RIGHT Trimmed yew rather than stone walls surround the circular pool, the roofed opening its entrance.

Major Johnston brilliantly transitioned from one garden room to the next. Unlike other Arts and Crafts designers, he used few walls, relying instead on plant material including holly, hornbeam, and yew, sometimes planted together. His tall hedges pruned in architectural forms serve like the walls of a house, with narrow or wide doors giving a glimpse of the appeal beyond or drawing the visitor within.

In 1948 Hidcote was the first garden to be accepted by the National Trust. Today, seventy years later, with thousands of annual visitors, Hidcote remains an inspiration for landscape designers and plant collectors.

Dumbarton Oaks
Washington D.C.

A few residences are associated in the public mind with an important event. Versailles, for example, will be forever linked to the Treaty ending World War I. The name Dumbarton Oaks recalls for most people not a house or garden but the conference that led to the creation of the United Nations. Robert Woods Bliss and his wife, Mildred Barnes Bliss, were instrumental in calling and hosting the conference at their Georgetown estate in 1944.

They also created one of America's most admired gardens, the work of the nation's first female landscape architect, Beatrix Farrand. At Dumbarton Oaks, in cooperation with Mildred Bliss, she designed and supervised the installation of an Arts and Crafts garden that brilliantly met the challenges of the hillside slope and the needs of the Blisses. It is considered her best work.

The famous conference could have been held in Paris, the city that first captivated Mildred Bliss. The daughter of a U.S. congressman from New York, she had gone to finishing school in Paris. She loved the city and might have stayed forever but for one, then another, event, one personal, one international. The first was her developing love for her stepbrother, Robert Bliss. His father and her mother, both widowed, had married when Mildred was eighteen. A graduate of Harvard, Robert Bliss was to be a career diplomat. Soon after they were married they moved to Paris where Mildred was completely at home with the international scholarly, intellectual, and artistic community. She could acquit herself in six languages, was among the cognoscenti of music and art, and under the tutelage of Bernard Berenson began what would become a distinguished collection of books and manuscripts.

For her war work, Mildred Bliss was awarded France's highest civilian honor, the Chevalier of the Légion d'honneur; she is seen here wearing its official sash.

But their good life was rudely interrupted by World War I. Robert and Mildred Bliss decided to remain in Paris for the duration, he fulfilling his diplomatic duties, she discovering and applying her considerable talent for organizing to various relief efforts including an ambulance corps that she and Robert supplied with vehicles. She was instrumental in the founding of the Comité des Enfants de la Frontière for war-orphaned children. She worked side by side with French citizens and American expatriates, including Edith Wharton, a longtime family friend.

Beatrix Farrand at her desk with her dog in her lap.

As the war drew to a close, Robert Bliss prepared to return to the United States. Mildred was less eager, writing in the last days of the war, "I have grown to care so much for Paris and for certain friends I can't imagine ever living away for long—Oh, there goes a cannon." But she acceded to Robert's plan to return home and his dream of a country house in the city. They found the ideal place in the Georgetown section of the District of Columbia. The large, rambling house set back from the road would need extensive remodeling, but Robert and Mildred were attracted by the charming orangery and the stately oak trees.

The house sits atop a hill, with surrounding land falling sharply down one hundred feet to Rock Creek. Creating a garden would be a challenge of the greatest magnitude. Far from being a deterrent, it was one that energetic and imaginative Mildred Bliss eagerly embraced. In 1920 the Blisses began to conceive the surrounding gardens. She wanted garden rooms such as she had seen in Arts and Crafts gardens in Europe. Her love of Italian gardens with their hillside terraces would influence their plans for Dumbarton Oaks. She was confident that wedding these styles with delicate French ornament of iron, wood, and stone would be aesthetically pleasing.

Soon, however, she wisely realized that she needed professional help in executing her plan; the sharp contours especially requiring expert knowledge. She turned to Edith Wharton's niece, Beatrix Cadwalader Jones, an acquaintance of her family in New York society and the person her mother had employed for the landscape design of their summer place on Mount Desert Island, Maine.

Beatrix, to be known professionally after her marriage to Yale professor Max Farrand in 1940 as Beatrix Farrand, proved to be the perfect selection. She was familiar with the gardens and garden traditions that Mildred loved. "Aunt Edith" had, after all, taken her on trips to Europe, introducing her to and simultaneously critiquing the great gardens. Beatrix had studied with the renowned botanist Charles Sprague Sargent at the Arnold Arboretum in Boston, had won twenty-one design commissions including from Ellen Wilson, the first wife of President Woodrow Wilson, for the White House Rose Garden and from John D. Rockefeller for a section of his home, Kykuit. While working at Dumbarton Oaks she was a member of the otherwise all-male committee to found the American Society of Landscape Architects.

The design challenge for Farrand lay in meeting the requirements of the Blisses including large and small areas for entertaining, tennis courts, and a large swimming pool, as well as vegetable and cutting gardens. Modest leveling was required at Dumbarton Oaks, but Farrand's changes in the topography were minimal. The general plan was for formal areas near the house, with sections away from the house becoming planned natural. But the land dictated a flexible scheme. Crabapple Hill occupies a contoured area just below the North Vista, the highest level that extends from the veranda of the house. On the side of the house, a formal Italian-inspired terrace garden includes an urn garden with rose gardens below.

At almost the lowest level is Lovers' Lane Pool with its grassy amphitheater seating fifty guests for evenings of music, poetry, or theater. Mélisande's Allée, at the lowest level, is bordered by a straight line of silver maples although the path between the trees is winding.

Farrand made the North Vista appear longer by narrowing the width from the house's veranda to the hillside looking down toward Rock Creek.

Nearby, also on a lower level, are the cutting and vegetable gardens. The transitions from one room to another are pleasing, accomplished with brick or stone walls, hedges, short allées, grassy slopes, winding paths, and steps as well as terraces.

Never has there been a more felicitous relationship between client and professional designer. Bliss and Farrand came from the same social class with many experiences and friends in common. They had seen and been influenced by the great European gardens and were sympathetic to the values and design features of the Arts and Crafts movement. Their working relationship lasted for twenty-three years, their friendship for a lifetime.

As Mildred and Robert Bliss prepared to leave their house and garden and their collections of art and books to Harvard University and for the visiting public, they had inscribed a stone monument commemorating the genius of Beatrix Farrand. Dumbarton Oaks would stand in the future as it had in the past for the virtues they admired—scholarship, good taste, elegance, the arts including that of garden design, the civility of Europe without the horror, destruction, and brutality of war, and peace among nations.

ABOVE The formal urn garden looks down to the rose garden and then to terraces below after the manner of Italian Renaissance gardens.

RIGHT The steep incline to the swimming pool above can be seen from the cutting garden.

ABOVE A bench echoes the curve of the land. Farrand herself designed many Dumbarton Oaks ornaments—stone urns, latticework, gates of iron or wood, and outbuildings that serve as toolsheds, as well as this beautiful bench.

RIGHT Two landings on the symmetrical steps make the steep decline less daunting. The shaded bench invites a pause to enjoy the view and a little rest.

The amphitheater by Lovers' Lane Pool is backed by romantic wisteria.

Vita Sackville-West and Harold Nicolson outside South Cottage, at Sissinghurst.

Sissinghurst
Kent, England

Poet and novelist Vita Sackville-West and Harold Nicolson, diplomat, biographer, diarist, and member of Parliament, were among the twentieth century's most *avant-garde*. Modern in every way, they were nonetheless among those who embraced an earlier style of gardening, that of the Arts and Crafts movement. They understood fully the role the arms industry played in World War I, and the horror of World War II affected them deeply in both their personal and professional lives. The anti-industry creed of the Arts and Crafts movement made the Gertrude Jekyll approach to garden design an obvious choice. At Sissinghurst the Nicolsons would combine the order and control of geometric garden design, the exuberance of English cottage gardens, and references to the medieval history of England.

The genius of Sissinghurst lies in the wedding of classical and romantic elements. Vita, the poet, brought profuse flowers with their vivid colors; he brought an orderly mind formed by his life in the Middle East and his university training, just as their own marriage was a union of these two personality traits. Harold explained the difference:

> The misunderstanding that arises between the romantic and the classical temperament is due, not so much to any conflict between imagination and reason, as to the fact that whereas the classic finds pleasure in recognition, the romantic derives his own greatest stimulus from surprise. . . . To the classic . . . truth must be recognizable. . . . To the romantic . . . what is enjoyable is that very sense of expanding experience, occasioned by the unexpected, the unfamiliar or the different.

The classical and the romantic elements are skillfully arranged at Sissinghurst so that their juxtaposition is never jarring. Rather one supports the other. Perhaps Sissinghurst is so very satisfying because there is a little bit of both the classic and the romantic in most of us and we appreciate finding both recognition and surprise in the same experience.

Vita was the daughter of Lord Sackville. Knole, her childhood home in Kent, is a "calendar house" with 365 rooms, said to be the largest house in England. Harold was the son of the first Baron Carnock, a diplomat posted in Teheran where Harold was born and grew up. Harold studied at Balliol College, Oxford, then met and married Vita soon after his graduation.

They traveled widely, making a home and garden first in Constantinople where he served in the diplomatic corps, then moving to London where the Bloomsbury set were among their friends. Harold was a young and minor diplomat at the Paris Peace Conference ending World War I and later wrote an account of the proceedings, *Peacemaking 1919*. They practiced open marriage, each having over the years a number of both gay and straight affairs, she most notably with writer Virginia Woolf.

In 1915, they purchased Long Barn not far from Knole where, as a child, Vita had roamed the countryside. There they started a family and a garden. Sons Benedict and Nigel were born and it was here that she "sang the cycle of my country's year," in her epic poem *The Land*. Far from pining for some bygone Arcadia, she painted with words in the tradition of Virgil's *Georgics* the realistic and unsentimental conditions of husbandry and the seasons. She acknowledged the "enemy in everything," even the "bullfinch with his pretty song . . . pecking with tiny beak and strong" the orchard fruit. She won the prestigious Hawthornden Prize for *The Land* and again for another epic poem, *The Garden*. Then, in 1930, threatened with a neighboring development, the Nicolsons searched for another home in Kent.

Sissinghurst as they first saw it was but a shadow of its former self. Once a medieval castle surrounded by a protective moat, it had been transformed into a fine Elizabethan manor where Queen Elizabeth I herself visited. At one time it was in the hands of the Sackville dynasty. In the nineteenth century, Sissinghurst served as an army prison, the parish

Vita's study was in the tower, Harold's vast library in the former stables seen behind and to the right of the tower.

workhouse, and a farm before being abandoned. Dead cabbage stalks, rusted iron bedsteads, and unmentionable trash littered the grounds when Vita and Harold visited.

Much of the original house was gone. The remaining buildings included only the tower that was to be Vita's study, the stables converted for Harold's library, South Cottage that the family shared, and the Priest's House where the boys would live with their nanny. Although the boys were skeptical as it was without electricity or running water, Harold and Vita both fell in love with the property. At least the Priest's House had the kitchen.

Together Vita and Harold decided on the governing concept. Sissinghurst was to be above all English, including the period of Norman rule in Kent. The buildings and gardens would be romantic but, like Vita's poems, not sentimental. Rather Sissinghurst would evoke an emotional response of deep attachment, intimacy, and an affinity for the remote past, a vision shared with other Arts and Crafts sympathizers.

The "bones" were provided by the buildings, the medieval wall, and the remaining two sides of the moat. Strong classical lines would define spaces. Harold, employing his education, travel, and amateur architect's eye, took chief responsibility for the overall design. He used ancient forms and geometric shapes including straight lines of hedges and allées with focal points of vases, benches, and sculpture. Laying out the garden rooms did not prove easy. Walls were not at right angles, the courtyard is coffin-shaped, and the tower is not opposite the main entrance. From her tower studio, Vita cast a sympathetic eye below on "the worried designer, with his immense sheets of ruled paper and his measuring tapes and his indiarubbers, pushing his fingers through his rumpled hair."

But with his unfailing sense of symmetry and proportion, Harold got it right. There are two intersecting axes with rooms around them. Drawing upon his knowledge of Persian gardens, he used the paradise form to separate the quadrants of the garden. His central circle is not water but grass. The four radiating arms are paths, not rills. All is outlined with yew, not stone.

Throughout the 1930s they worked together in planning and beginning the gardens. As collaborators in the creation of Sissinghurst's gardens they were unusually close, consulting each other constantly although Vita admitted that Harold would occasionally find she had put a tree just where he planned a straight view.

Vita grew her roses and clematis on hedges and trees as well as walls. She planted the herbaceous borders of complementary or monochromatic color schemes. They developed the garden rooms one by one. The orchard near the moat rises above a meadow. A statue of Dionysus graces the nuttery that in their day was underplanted with primroses. In the South Cottage garden, they took a page from J. M. W. Turner and Gertrude Jekyll, grouping the hot colors. Reds, yellows, and oranges glow against four tall dark yews that closely guard the seasonally planted copper pot with its blue-green patina. The famous White Garden includes all shades from cream to stark white, grays and silvers, and the palest of yellows, pinks, and lavenders found in anemones, daisies, delphiniums, eringium, foxglove, goat's beard, lilies, lychnis, poppies, Queen Anne's lace, roses, sweet peas, wisteria, and more.

The Herb Garden in paradise form contains two special treasures. In the early days of their marriage while living in the Middle East, they bought the stone basin, a modest version

From Vita's tower study one sees the plan of the paradise garden form that Harold knew as a child and later as diplomat in the Middle East and that he adapted for Sissinghurst.

of the fountain in the Court of the Lions at Alhambra, perhaps recalling for Harold his childhood time in Spain. A stone bench whose top is planted with chamomile gives obeisance to Sissinghurst's medieval origins and to the Arts and Crafts devotion to the Middle Ages.

In the 1930s when they wrote, gardened, and parented, storm clouds were beginning to gather again over Europe. Harold was among the first to recognize and speak about the dangers of fascism. When war came, Harold was living and working in London as parliamentary secretary to the minister of information. Vita remained at Sissinghurst almost alone. Ben and Nigel as well as the male gardeners had gone to war. Remaining were only a few women and their children and the soldiers who commandeered Vita's tower room as a lookout. The lawns and orchards became a source of hay. Weeds in the flower borders successfully waged their own war. Of a night, Vita would go down to the moat or into the fields, scanning the skies for German bombardiers returning from their missions in the industrial Midlands with the ever-possible threat that they would eject their remaining load on Sissinghurst.

Harold wrote to her almost every day, reporting the dire situation of Britain, but as if for comfort, included his thoughts on what to plant under the lime trees for spring. What,

RIGHT Flowers in the South Cottage garden include tall yellow and gray mullein, sunflowers, dark red roses, yellow and orange kniphofia, and orange honeysuckle to name but a few.

BELOW, LEFT In early July the White Garden is at its best.

BELOW, RIGHT Paving tiles set on edge, a technique favored by Arts and Crafts architect Edwin Lutyens, provide a handsome base for the lion basin. At the back is the chamomile bench.

OPPOSITE Harold always chose the spring plantings for the Lime Tree Allée, a task he referred to as MLW, My Life's Work.

he asked, did she think of orange tulips? He made it home for an occasional weekend, most notably in 1941 when Virginia Woolf committed suicide. He understood Vita's devastation and came to comfort her, although they talked not about Virginia but about the garden.

Her poetry was her lifeline, never shying away from the truth by romanticizing the sacrifices of war. She joined T. S. Eliot and other poets in perceiving the vicious cycle of hope and futility:

> The civil
> Ever opposed the rude, as centuries'
> Slow progress laboured forward, the check,
> Back to the pit, the climb out of the pit,
> Advance, relapse, advance, relapse, advance,
> Regular as the measure of a dance.

Finally the war ended and Harold was able to return to Vita and Sissinghurst, joining her in gardening and writing. By the 1950s the garden had become famous, so they arranged for it to be taken over by the National Trust, reserving the privilege of continuing to live there. It was opened to the public for an admission fee of one shilling. "It's five o'clock. Shall we have drinks in the garden?" asked Vita of Harold. "The Shillingses are gone now."

These two urbane people for whom gardening was an anchor in the chaos of war and a consuming pastime in peace left a treasure now enjoyed by more visitors annually than any other estate garden in Britain.

The ever-dapper Lieutenant Harvey Ladew.

Ladew Topiary Gardens
Monkton, Maryland

It was on the property of an eighteenth-century farmhouse in rural Maryland that Harvey Ladew set about creating his remarkable garden that shows a very different response to war. There he turned his back on the horror of World War I, throwing himself instead into a life of pleasure and fun. In his garden he exercised his artistic talent and his wit.

As did many wealthy Americans, his Long Island parents traveled widely and moved in the highest of social circles before World War I, their child allowed to cavort through palaces and estates, making himself at home with the high and mighty, "sitting," as he said, "on more thrones of Europe than all of Queen Victoria's vast clan put together."

As a young man he was amusing and determined to be amused, the quintessential man-about-town. His yearly tour of Europe included grand gardens. It is easy to imagine that his interest in gardens was stimulated by family friend Edith Wharton and her widely read book *Italian Villas and Their Gardens*. He traveled to Italy on more than one occasion and there found in the numerous water tricks and the gargantuan sculpture of the great Renaissance gardens the humor that would later characterize his own estate but to which he would give his own twist.

By 1919 he had done his duty, having volunteered for the U.S. Army, winning a citation from the French government for his work as translator, then offering to go to the front lines. It was just his luck that severe pneumonia prevented his doing so. When peace was at last achieved and he could return home, he decided that with "so much to see, to do, I thought I would just reverse life's patterns—play, then work." He had two ideas for play, fox hunting and gardening, especially creating topiary figures inspired by those in England that had amused him as a child.

He returned to Long Island where his parents' estate featured Victorian planting beds. There he set about rebelling against such rigid and ostentatious design. He preferred a less regimented look, just as he preferred the less rule-bound life.

Then, in 1929, when other Americans were standing in bread lines, selling apples from pushcarts, or packing their Ford pick-up trucks to try their luck in California, he bought 230

The Yellow Garden sports a Ladew-designed Chinese temple, no more authentic than the chinoiserie garden buildings of the eighteenth century in Europe.

acres and a dilapidated farmhouse adjacent to the Hunt Club in Monkton, Maryland, where "running to hounds" was the sport of the rich. He began renovating Pleasant Valley Farm House and laying out twenty-two acres for his soon-to-be-famous gardens. He was settling down seriously to have fun.

And fun he had, designing a garden that would be beautiful with its charming little garden rooms, lovely iron and stone ornaments, outbuildings, and hundreds of varieties of plants. Above all, he would add sculpture not made of stone or marble but of plants. His topiary became the talk of the town. And throughout his gardens he would find ways of laughing at society's pretensions and conventions. While there are innumerable lighthearted touches in gardens around the world such as statues of playful nymphs and mischievous satyrs, devilish tricks with water, and delightfully fearsome grottoes, few gardens are as dedicated to gentle irony and sophisticated humor as is Harvey Ladew's.

Like the creators of Sissinghurst, Hidcote, Great Dixter, and Dumbarton Oaks, Harvey Ladew was an artist in making graceful transitions from scene to scene, room to room. By using a winding path, a grove of trees, shrubs pruned either formally or informally, or a wall of hedge or brick, he successfully managed the moves even in small spaces.

LEFT A short woodland path takes the stroller from the lily pond to the Garden of Eden where apple trees blossom.

RIGHT The direction of the bridge suggests the Temple of Venus is off-center.

OPPOSITE, TOP Riding the perfectly cut waves are twelve oversized yew swans, outdoing the real swans that graced the European gardens of Harvey Ladew's childhood.

OPPOSITE, BOTTOM Eve tempts the seemingly already fallen Adam beneath the apple trees.

Ladew's very design brings a smile. The garden is not front and center from the main entrance of the house as would be expected but on a side where only a small window from the bedroom reserved for his beloved sister Elsie and a small open air arcade leading from house to card room allow views of the garden from the house. This would be no Versailles where all axial roads lead to the king's bedroom in the very center of the symmetrical palace. Instead there is a main axis off the side of the house running through the swimming pool to the Temple of Venus. But it meanders slightly to the east, giving the impression that the temple is off-center. Harvey Ladew was most certainly aware of the importance of the central axis in the great gardens of Europe. He knew about focal points, could delineate a parterre, lay out a sight line, and locate a vanishing point with the best of landscape designers. But he deliberately created the illusion with the Temple of Venus, subtly suggesting that love is not always as straight-arrow as society's rules prescribe, just as his life with his partner interior designer Billy Baldwin would sidestep the prevailing norms.

The gardens themselves playfully pose similar questions about love. In the Garden of Eden, amidst apple trees underplanted with azaleas in complementary soft pinks, Adam hides from Eve the three forbidden apples he already possesses. How Ladew must have delighted in finding this unconventional sculpture, raising as it does the possibility that other women had preceded Eve, or that man, not woman, was the first to disobey orders—and on a larger scale!

The crowning glory of Ladew's garden wit is the topiary that he himself designed and maintained. Some are gargantuan, mirroring or mocking the statuary in Italian Renaissance gardens, hewn here in yew not stone. There are green columns with swags, pyramids, walls of evergreen with windows cut to frame a view, a V for Victory together with Churchill's top hat, a giraffe, a peacock, fantastical animals, the hull of a Chinese junk topped with red

cloth sails, and a seated Buddha. Framing the great lawn bowl with the center swimming pool is a remarkable yew "ocean" one hundred yards long, its rolling movement underscoring the curves of the surrounding Maryland hills.

Ladew's signature topiary is a fox hunt with two horses and riders, one forever suspended in a jump over a white fence, both following closely a pack of hounds but always outdistanced by the bushy-tailed yew fox on the other side of the road. Ladew began these pieces in Long Island when he was just home from the war, transplanting them when he purchased his Maryland home. Now approaching one hundred years, they have put on weight but appear as full of action as ever.

Finally there is the topiary seen from the teahouse that in its former life was the facade of the Tivoli theater in London. When the theater that he had frequented was threatened with demolition, Ladew bought the ticket booth and had it shipped home to serve as just the place for an afternoon of reading, conversation, tea, or more likely, martinis. He would have been aware that Tivoli in ancient Rome was the site of the Temple of Fortuna where the oracle predicted one's fate. In view from the tearoom is Ladew's topiary *Man Walking Dog*, à la Henry Moore. The leather leash attached to the yew dog and owner gives nod to the lucrative tanning business of Ladew's forebears that made possible his good fortune in spending his life not in working for a living but in walking the dog, fox hunting, and gardening.

Harvey Ladew was educated, traveled, and sophisticated, a renaissance man with a passion for writing, painting, art, and antique

Ladew so captured the movement of the hunt that we hear the hounds yelping and see their ears flap as they pursue the yew fox.

collecting. In an age of suffering caused by the Depression and the framing and devastating World Wars, he appears to have led a charmed albeit self-centered life. While the rest of America could afford only a movie ticket to relieve the pain, the wealthy and urbane Ladew chose to create a garden full of wit. His strong personality dominates the design. Those who love the good life are admirers of his gardening style. Some, preferring the more tranquil garden of his contemporaries Mildred Bliss and Beatrix Farrand, might find his charm excessive. But Ladew has provided a respite for visitors, giving them an experience of both elegance and laugh-out-loud humor. He said he created the gardens for people's enjoyment, to give them a few moments that are, to use his favorite phrase, "perfectly delightful."

Before his death on July 28, 1976, exactly sixty-two years from the beginning of World War I, he established a foundation to ensure that his gardens continue to give pleasure. Ladew Topiary Gardens' staff reported a huge increase in the number of visitors in the weeks and months following the attacks on the World Trade Center towers and the Pentagon. As they did for Harvey Ladew, the gardens provided needed relief from the horror of conflict and violence. His was not an unworthy accomplishment.

Christopher Lloyd developed this space as a wild garden, with exotics and topiary peacocks as well as hardy plants.

Great Dixter

East Sussex, England

Great Dixter was the very essence of hearth and home. For Christopher Lloyd it was the center of his life and career. Except for his years at boarding school and university and five years in military service during World War II, he spent his life there. At Great Dixter he built a garden that was the perfect complement to the Arts and Crafts philosophy and garden design and to the house. He honored the Jekyll tradition while creating variations that would bring him distinction as a gardener.

When he was a child, the house and garden was the locus for nurturing children and welcoming guests including such luminaries as Rudyard Kipling and Gertrude Jekyll. Before Christopher was born the Lloyds opened the house to serve as a hospital for soldiers wounded in the First World War. The values cultivated were the very antithesis of war. Yet life at Great Dixter was not without struggle.

His parents—Nathaniel Lloyd, highly successful in the lithography printing business, and Daisy Lloyd, the quintessential mother—created Great Dixter. Nathaniel had ambitions to be an architect and in 1910 purchased a fifteenth-century brick and timber house with a small farm not far from Rye. He hired architect Edwin Lutyens to design an expansion for his growing family. They purchased a ruined yeoman's hall in a neighboring village and had it dismantled, moved, and reassembled at Great Dixter. Lutyens united the two structures with a contemporary but complementary wing and incorporated farm buildings in his design.

Lutyens also laid out the grounds, creating with paths and hedges a series of pleasing shapes and making a central design feature of Great Dixter itself, the union of house, other buildings, and garden. The house is visible from any point in the garden and a portion of the garden can be seen from every room in the house. Lutyens left the use of each garden space to be determined by the Lloyds.

How did Daisy have time to garden with the responsibilities of managing the house and large staff and mothering her one girl and five boys, the youngest of whom was Christopher? Other women would have been overwhelmed, but not Daisy Lloyd. Her older children referred to her not as mother but as "The Management." She held it her duty and joy to guide their every action, instruct them in manners and morals, and teach them music, writing, and gardening. She was proud to find that her "Christo" excelled in all. For shy little Christopher, his happiest times were at her side working in the garden where she taught him the Latin names of plants. A keen observer, he had by age nine learned the habits of dozens of plants as well as those of butterflies and insects. These found a natural habitat in the meadow garden mother and son planted together.

Christo was only twelve when his father died. Shortly afterward he entered Rugby School where he continued his intense interest in horticulture and, exchanging frequent letters with his mother, developed his writing skill, the only pleasures in an otherwise miserable experience. After Cambridge and service in the Royal Artillery including East Africa, he returned home to Great Dixter to the plants he knew so well and to his affectionate but domineering mother. He took a degree in horticulture and then taught at nearby Wye College as he and Daisy continued to develop the garden. They lived together at Great Dixter until she died when he was fifty-one.

In many ways this was Christopher Lloyd's liberation day for it was in the years following his mother's death that he blossomed as his own person, developing a distinctive gardening style and writing informative and entertaining garden articles and books. He began inviting guests for jolly weekends at Great Dixter, doing the cooking himself and supplying tickets to the music festival at nearby Glyndebourne. Most significantly, he took in young gardeners to work with him including Anna Pavord who became a well-known garden writer and Fergus Garrett whom he later named his successor as head gardener at Great Dixter.

What were his imaginative and trendsetting innovations that made such an impact on the gardening world? He departed from the Jekyll model in several ways. Rather than putting hot colors together and separating them from cool colors, he mixed them in the tradition of cottage gardens, giving them a brilliant flamboyance. He used the idea of succession plantings to provide color in each season. He added small trees and shrubs, deciduous and

Great Dixter's border with deciduous trees.

evergreen, to his borders so that they were no longer herbaceous only. His dramatic placement of exotics changed the previous sedate look, introducing an element of surprise. Most of all he disavowed the tidy and manicured in favor of a freer feeling, an artistic expression of his own new-found freedom.

Then remembering the pleasure he had in planting a meadow with his mother, Lloyd most appropriately turned the grassy swards at Great Dixter into meadows. His choice was the perfect partner of the fifteenth-century house, recalling as it does the flowery mead—or meadow—of the Middle Ages. Recorded in the great art of the period and woven as millefleur

in medieval tapestries are delicate flowers in great variety, growing individually rather than in masses, just as Christopher Lloyd would do one thousand years later. Among his favorite meadow flowers that he grew generously were red poppies. Perhaps he did so to honor the role Great Dixter played in healing the wounded soldiers of World War I and to recall the popular poem commending their sacrifice that begins "In Flanders fields the poppies blow between the crosses row on row," giving rise to the custom of wearing a red poppy for Armistice Day.

Lloyd recognized that, in addition to being aesthetically pleasing, meadows serve two other vital purposes. They reduce the expense of continuous mowing and they restore the biodiversity that nurtures wildlife. His promotion of meadows culminated in the publication in 2004 of his book *Meadows*. Lloyd must be credited for his leadership in the trend now seen throughout England at virtually every large estate of substituting meadows for great lawns. His influence can also be seen in American landscaping, especially that bordering stretches of public highways.

These bold innovations were introduced by Christopher Lloyd, publicized through his books, and embraced by other gardeners during the essentially peaceful and prosperous years following World War II. It was a time of confidence: departing from the past, people blazed new trails. For his achievements in horticulture, Christopher Lloyd was awarded the Victoria Medal of Honour by the Royal Horticultural Society in 1979 and appointed OBE in 2000.

Lawrence Johnston, Vita Sackville-West and Harold Nicolson, Robert and Mildred Bliss, Harvey Ladew, and Christopher Lloyd all arranged for their gardens to be open to the public. They shared the belief that Vita Sackville-West expressed eloquently in her second epic poem, *The Garden*, in which she contrasts the garden with war, calling it "a miniature endeavour / To hold the graces and the courtesies / Against a horrid wilderness."

ABOVE Fergus Garrett and Christopher Lloyd in the exotic garden at Great Dixter in 2005.

OPPOSITE House and garden are joined through complementary and contrasting colors. Blue ceanothus brings out the blue-gray in the house's exposed timber. Contrasting yellow highlights both.

15 Less Is More

A changed world calls for radical new design, unadorned and abstract.

MID-TWENTIETH CENTURY

STUNNING IRONY TURNED the words of architect Louis Sullivan, master of ornamentation, into the battle cry of modernism. "Form follows function" justified the minimalist, abstract, clean, and plain lines of the new style. Perhaps a case of the pendulum in its corrective course swinging to the extreme opposite, modernism rejected the ornate fashion that prevailed in the late nineteenth and early twentieth centuries.

It was inevitable that the predominant style of architecture and landscape architecture would change in the years following the World Wars for the world itself was so dramatically changed. The Gilded Age had ended. The wars left an aftermath of destruction. The worldwide Depression of the 1930s made the grand tour a thing of the past, and the inspiration to bring home elements of foreign gardens went with it. A new system of taxation made the upkeep of elaborate gardens beyond the reach of most. Skilled gardeners were hard to find as fewer people went into household service, seeking instead educational opportunity and employment in the commercial world.

As the lives of individuals changed, so the balance of political power was changed. The great Raj Path in Delhi with its wide boulevards, allées of trees, and grand buildings ending in the viceroy's palace, designed by Edwin Lutyens, was meant to last for a thousand years of British rule. But as it was still under construction, the empire was showing serious cracks. Left all but bankrupt by the World Wars and Depression, Britain could not afford to govern its vast holdings. India would achieve her independence in 1948 and other colonies and territories followed. It was the star of the United States that had now ascended.

> It is the pervading law of all things organic and inorganic, of all things physical and metaphysical, of all things human and all things superhuman, of all true manifestations of the head, of the heart, of the soul, that the life is recognizable in its expression, that form ever follows function. ***This is the law.***
>
> —LOUIS SULLIVAN

In this era of change and long before the modern style emerged, critics were calling for a new design form. They vehemently rejected Beaux Arts and the popular neoclassical forms as representing the old aristocracy that they believed responsible for the horrors of World War I.

As society was finding new structures and new relationships, artists were experimenting with new forms to represent the changed world. Pablo Picasso, working on the principle declared by Cézanne that cubes, spheres, and cones are the only three solid forms, had along with Georges Braque introduced Cubism even before World War I. Piet Mondrian was moving from the Impressionist and representational style of his early painting to the colorful lines and grids of abstract art by which he would become known.

Modern design at an older site: Ferry House, Vassar College.

The WPA (Works Progress Administration) was the largest project of the New Deal initiated by President Franklin Roosevelt. Millions of otherwise unemployed people were hired at public expense to build roads and parks designed and supervised by landscape architects and engineers in the program. Writers, artists, scholars, and musicians were also supported, leaving future generations a vast legacy of their work.

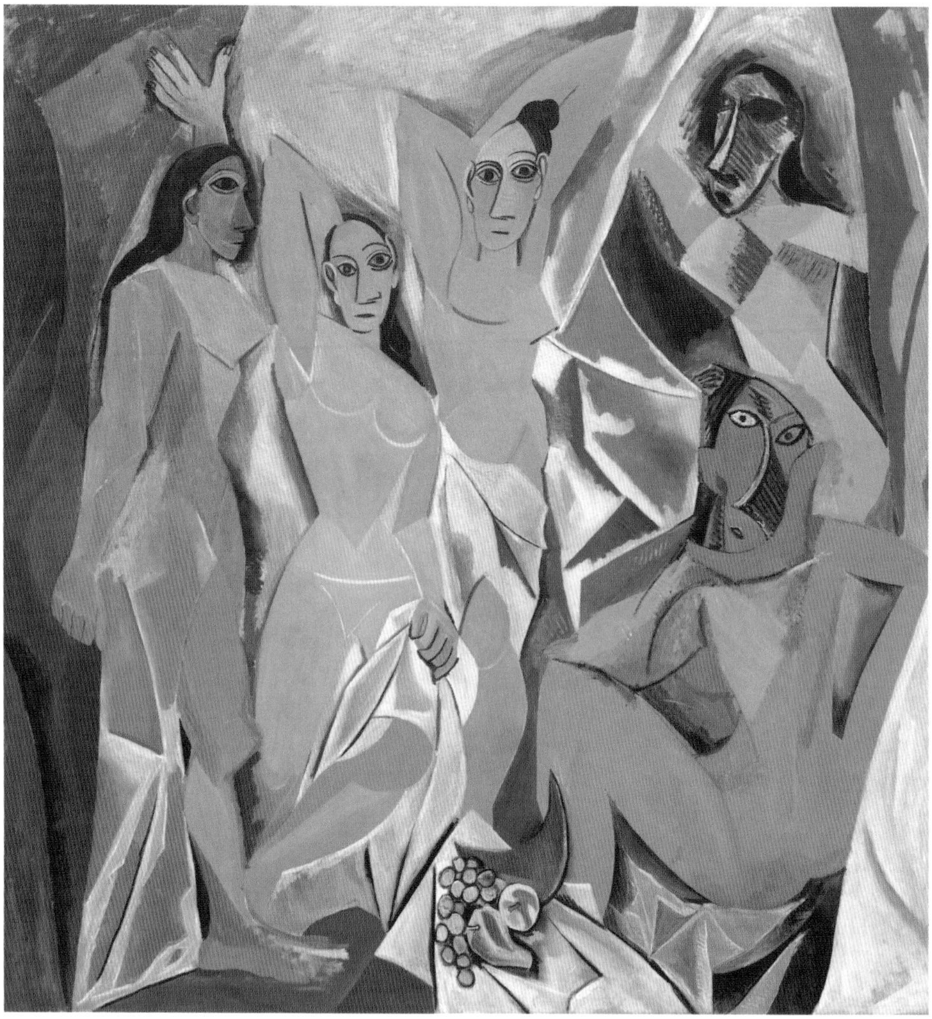

Picasso's *Les Demoiselles d'Avignon*, painted in 1907, is considered seminal in the early development of Cubism and modern art.

Architects, too, were looking for a simpler model. Le Corbusier lifted the bulk of a building off the ground, supporting it with concrete stilts; opened the floor plan with non-supporting walls; used long horizontal windows for unbroken views; and, significantly for landscape architects, put the garden on the roof. Mies van der Rohe called his own style "skin and bones," so lean was it by using industrial steel and sheets of plate glass. He was often heard to repeat the aphorism "Less is more." Louis Sullivan himself was defining the structure of the skyscraper with its initial floor, office space, and crown. Richly ornamented, it would soon be replaced with the rectangular glass boxes that capture the very soul of modernism. Life that in the cities took on an increasingly fast pace needed to become sleek and efficient. Frank Lloyd Wright, himself a protégé of Sullivan, developed the long, low lines of the Prairie school of architecture, a style he called "organic" for its integration with natural surroundings.

Landscape architects were not among the first artists seeking new forms because the depressed economy hit their profession hard. From 1914 to the end of World War II, there

Piet Mondrian worked with straight lines and primary colors.

was little work except for those with clients among the superrich and, during the Depression, for WPA projects. Only a few, such as Beatrix Farrand who cultivated landscape design work at colleges and universities, found avenues for their skills.

While Europe lay in ruins, the end of World War II brought prosperity to the United States. The Depression had ended with the financial as well as technical success of the arms industry, now much of it converted to manufacturing for peacetime. The G.I. Bill was making it possible for thousands of American servicemen and women to avail themselves of higher education, simultaneously preventing a glut of labor on the market as soldiers and sailors returned from war. Now American landscape architects would seize leadership in the field, creating forms to complement modern art and architecture. Their work would influence landscape design around the world.

Naumkeag
Stockbridge, Massachusetts

It was the 1930s. Most of the world was in the midst of a deep economic depression, but not Mabel Choate at her home in the Berkshire Mountains of western Massachusetts. She had inherited her house and property named Naumkeag from her father, Joseph Choate, New York lawyer and ambassador to the United Kingdom. With no financial worries, she could enjoy life. For her, martinis on the terrace were just the thing for watching the lowering afternoon sun. Here Miss Choate and her friend and landscape architect Fletcher Steele sipped, admiring the surrounding countryside and talking about trips to Europe and Asia and of her desires and his plans for landscape additions to her property. Toward the end of their long association their conversation turned to the future of Naumkeag when both would be gone.

It was at Naumkeag that Steele masterfully made the transition from the Beaux Arts tradition in which he had been trained at Harvard to that of modern design. Like the Gilded Age travelers and their landscape designers who brought home garden ideas from abroad, Steele incorporated elements from Moorish, English, and Italian gardens, created a Chinese garden room, and brilliantly introduced Art Deco, that stylish accompaniment of modern art and architecture with its clear colors and clean lines. Far from the hodge-podge such a description suggests, Steele successfully united past and future through these diverse features.

Just as Steele would do with the landscape design, the forty-four-room house, set high on the sharply descending hillside, itself brings together different styles. Designed in the 1880s by famed architect Stanford White of the New York firm McKim, White and Mead, the home's entrance side on the east is Norman, complete with round turret. The west side facing the mountains is the new Shingle style.

All of Steele's work at Naumkeag bows to the magnificent views of surrounding hills and mountains. Often in a haze of blue mist, the mountains roll like waves one upon another.

Pink gravel and shiny black, extremely hard cannel coal fill the interstices of the boxwood parterre in the Afternoon Garden.

Steele's brilliant concept was to bring these curves visually closer by echoing the gentle lines near to Naumkeag, thereby making the mountains appear contiguous with the house.

On the south side of the house Steele designed the Afternoon Garden. The house wall forms one side of the terrace rectangle. On another he made a vine-covered pergola, adapting the colonnades that as a soldier he had seen in Europe. Then, suggesting enclosure but preserving the open views to the mountains on the south and west, Steele formed a courtyard by bounding the garden with tall, colorful poles imitating those in Venice where gondoliers tie their boats, all connected with heavy rope in swags. The center is a formal parterre garden of boxwood with basins and small jet fountains like those at Alhambra. The center pool at Naumkeag, just a few inches deep, is shiny black obsidian, the color taking full advantage of the reflection of the cloud-filled sky above. Iron benches and other furniture provide seating.

As a child Mabel had picnicked with her parents and four brothers and sisters under the majestic swamp white oak (*Quercus bicolor*). Here Fletcher Steele showed his skill by bringing the vertical curves of the distant hills onto the horizontal plane. The graceful serpentine line is formed by a retaining wall of wood pilings. The curves together with large rocks placed at the base of the wall link the Berkshire Mountains to the gardens immediately adjacent to the house.

When Miss Choate expressed the wish for a more gradual grade to facilitate her descent from the house to the cutting gardens below, Steele created what has become an icon in garden design. Water is carried from the upper level of the Afternoon Garden to the lower cutting garden first by a rill, or runnel as it is called at Naumkeag, to a water cascade. From there it disappears underground to be seen again in a series of pools backed by blue-painted niches. Adjacent concrete steps follow the downward flow of the water. Thin steel railings painted white steady the walker, the whole surrounded by white paper birches (*Betula papyrifera*). The Blue Steps, as they are known, may remind the visitor of another iconic garden view, that of the Italian Renaissance water chain at the Villa Lante. Steele brilliantly used Art Deco, then *avant-garde*, as the style for his water chain.

Mabel Choate was an inveterate traveler. In 1935 she had a month's stay in "Pekin" where she wrote to Steele that she was so taken with marble figures and carvings that she "succumbed right and left." Replying, he added "without guessing the shudders of her professional landscape advisor whose duty was to make them feel at home on a New England hillside." But despite his objections she had shipped to Naumkeag stone lanterns, vessels, and dragons. For Mabel's souvenirs, Fletcher Steele designed a Chinese garden situated to the north of the house at the high point of the landscape. It is paradoxically both enclosed, following the inward-looking Chinese garden for meditation and reflection, and open to wider views as in the eighteenth-century gardens of William Kent. Ginkgo trees (*Ginkgo biloba*) underplanted with giant butterbur (*Petasites japonicus*) adorn the geometric and walled area, the ancient trees reinforcing the image of unchanging China. Wide steps lead upward to a higher level where a three-sided pavilion designed by Steele holds chairs and benches for viewing the mountains. In 1955 a moon gate was installed in the wall, leading directly to the front entrance of the house. With this addition, Mabel Choate declared Naumkeag complete.

As Mabel Choate aged and was increasingly confined to her second-story bedroom, Steele gave her a lovely gift. Below her window he made a rose garden but not in the geometric style most often used. His is a series of curving paths of gravel connecting small circles, each with a rose bush. From above it appears as soft pink ribbons with periodic nosegays—his offering to his friend of thirty years.

TOP Fletcher Steele eschewed a straight edge for the retaining wall, echoing instead the curving line of the mountain ridge.

BOTTOM Lifting the temple in the Chinese garden above the height of the enclosing walls enables the visitor to view the Berkshire Mountains in the distance.

For the seventy-fifth anniversary in 2013, the original blue was restored to the Blue Steps which for many years after Fletcher Steele's death had worn a too-bright Mediterranean blue.

In the rose garden Steele once again used the curves of the Berkshire Mountains on a horizontal plane.

The genius of Naumkeag lies in Steele's use of various garden design traditions but applied and adapted in refreshing new ways, anticipating modern style with its clean lines. He both followed and broke tradition. The water chain is Art Deco, the traditionally enclosed Chinese garden provides for a commanding view of the mountains, and the serpentine line of the Oak Lawn makes seamless the near-house garden and the distant rolling hills. He thought of Naumkeag as his masterpiece. She agreed, willing house and landscape to the Trustees of Reservations, a Massachusetts nonprofit conservation and preservation organization, thereby opening Naumkeag to the public and ensuring that no future owner would destroy Fletcher Steele's art.

Flamengo Park and Copacabana Beach

Rio de Janeiro, Brazil

No landscape designer has claimed more boldly or accurately the title "artist." Advised by his first mentor not to call himself a gardener, Roberto Burle Marx used the medium of plants and stone as his paints and palette, arranging them into works of abstract art to stand equally with those of Alexander Calder, Paul Klee, Henry Moore, and other great painters and sculptors of the twentieth century. Using a variety of hardscape materials and the architectural and colorful plants of Brazil, he transformed the style of "bedding-out" popular in the Victorian era into a wholly new style for gardens. "For me," he wrote, "the constant interest of landscape gardening has been in reflecting the aesthetic feelings of my age in terms of plastic composition: space, shape, form, volume."

Born in São Paulo to a Brazilian Catholic mother of French descent and a German Jewish father, Roberto and his family moved to Rio de Janeiro when he was five years old. Surrounded by the rich foliage of Brazil, he began gardening with his mother as just a boy. But it was in Germany that, studying art and frequenting the Dahlen Botanical Garden in Berlin, he began to amass what would become an encyclopedic knowledge of horticulture. Returning to Brazil in 1930, he started collecting native flora and eventually purchased a

ABOVE Though not native to Brazil, this agave (*A. vilmoriniana*) photographed at Sítio Santo Antônio da Bica, Burle Marx's home in Rio, seems tailor-made for his abstract designs.

RIGHT Aerial view of the Safra Bank roof garden, designed in 1983.

large estate on the outskirts of Rio to serve as home to his vast collection of anthuriums, bromeliads, cacti, calatheas, heliconias, orchids, palms, and philodendrons among others.

Continuing his study of art in Rio, he began meeting the architects with whom he would work: Oscar Niemeyer, Wladimir Alves de Souza, Gregori Warchavchik, and Lúcio Costa. At the same time he accepted his first landscape commissions, gaining international attention for his roof garden atop the Ministry of Education and launching his career designing landscapes for modern homes and public spaces. Also ground-breaking is the rooftop garden at the Safra Bank headquarters in São Paulo. Seen from the higher floors of the bank, it appears as a modern, abstract painting with its strong lines of paths and free-form planting beds.

In 1954 he was chosen as landscape architect for the parkways and gardens of a giant landfill project in Rio to be known as Flamengo Park. Here the restraining lines of the roof gardens gave way to a vast canvas. Connecting Brazil to its heritage, he drew upon an old Portuguese design known as Portuguese pavement, created through the contrasting colors of mosaics repeated in serpentine lines. He also capitalized on the queer natural shapes of Brazil's topography: on the Rio beachfront ancient forests adorn the rock slopes of Serra do Mar, a coastal mountain range of gigantic domes whose granite bases extend into the sea.

Sixteen years later, at another point along the Rio beachfront, Burle Marx again employed bold dynamic lines for another land reclamation effort. Along the three-mile stretch his wavy pattern appears as one great canvas between beach and boulevard, relieving

With its blue and white lines, the Municipal Building pavement in Cascais, Portugal, suggests waves in the nearby ocean.

the monotony for motorists and providing an ever-interesting path for pedestrians where children—and many adults—cannot resist following the curves. From the high windows of the buildings bordering Avenida Atlântica, the black and white mosaics create an optical illusion, appearing three dimensional.

In other projects, Burle Marx massed a single kind of plant, such as red, yellow, or light green bromeliads, in flower beds of fluid forms. In both media there appears to be movement. A lover of music, Burle Marx often compared his work as landscape artist not to static painting but to ever-changing music, celebrating seasons and growth cycles in gardens, adding ornamentation that, as in a Baroque fugue, leaves the essential harmony intact.

Roberto Burle Marx had no issue with the idea of mankind assuming dominion over nature. His approach was not to tame the jungle but to adopt "the same attitude which reveals the conduct of Neolithic man: to transform the natural topography in order to adjust it to human experience, individual, collective, utilitarian and aesthetic." He used his landscape design skill to make works of modern, abstract art.

ABOVE Periodic stands of palms provide interest along the avenue. Burle Marx once referred to his plants as "arabesques."

RIGHT The tall plants connect the background forms to the pond.

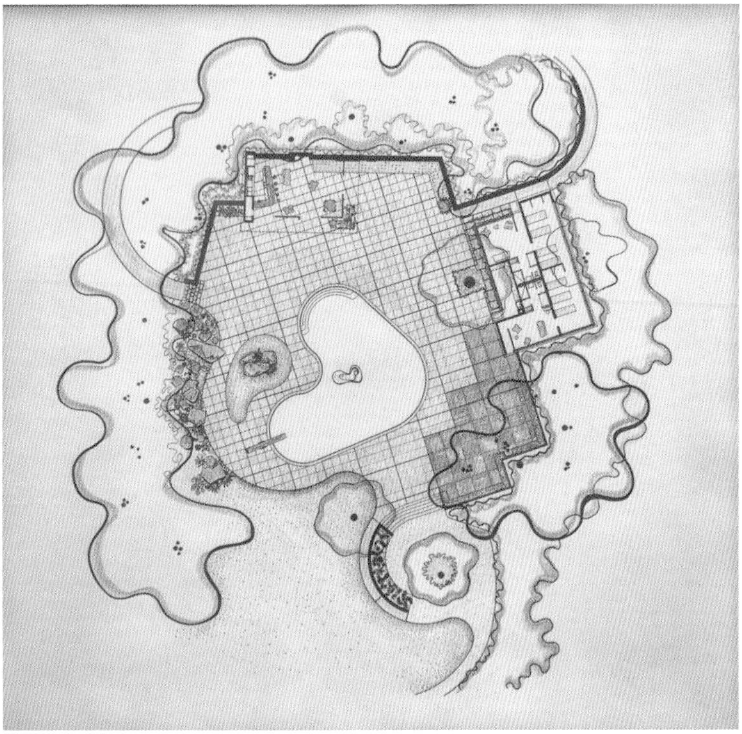

Thomas Church's plan for El Novillero is itself a work of modern art.

Dewey Donnell Ranch (El Novillero)

Sonoma, California

For Thomas Dolliver Church, pioneer of the California style, form followed both the function a particular garden was to serve and the natural lines of the property and surrounding area. While Roberto Burle Marx was designing gardens in Brazil as works of modern art, "Tommy" Church, as he was fondly and universally called, was arguing that gardens and landscapes should above all be practical, fitting the needs, lifestyles, and, within "the vague bounds of good taste," the aesthetic preferences of an owner. "There are no mysterious 'musts', no set rules, no finger of shame pointed at the gardener who doesn't follow an accepted pattern," he wrote in his aptly named, popular, and practical book *Gardens Are for People*. Each Church-designed garden is different, but the Dewey Donnell ranch, named El Novillero, in Sonoma, California, is most revered, a veritable icon of modern landscape design.

Church graduated from the University of California Berkeley and then the Harvard School of Design. He traveled throughout Europe where he especially studied the Italian Renaissance gardens and Alhambra as their climate and terrain were similar to those of California where he had grown up and where he would practice his profession.

He began his career in San Francisco just as landscape design was changing. His younger colleague Garrett Eckbo described Church as "the last great traditional designer and the first great modern designer." Just as landscape architect Dan Kiley would apply his study of French Baroque gardens in the flat plane around Paris to similarly flat Indiana, so Church's study of Italian gardens proved useful for him. Many of his commissions were in Berkeley which, like Italy, is hilly, presenting the designer with the challenge of creating terraced gardens and finding comfortable ways of taking people up and down the steep inclines. Church had additional problems to overcome. Most residential lots in Berkeley are small with neighbors cheek by jowl and property lots often oddly shaped. He had to consider the varying architecture styles of the houses and design a garden to complement each. And there was the all-important lifestyle of clients. Especially in a small space, the garden had to be an extension of the house, one flowing seamlessly into the other with the same space serving several different purposes.

Church understood the conditions of life that emerged following World War I and that were accelerated by the Second World War. Houses were smaller with the garden serving

Church used curving lines to tie the house to the mountains and a near-right angle at the entrance to echo the line of the roof above.

as additional living, dining, and play rooms. For most Americans, servants were a thing of the past. Mother and father, host and hostess, were cooking and serving, moving frequently in the course of an evening between the indoor kitchen and the outdoor grill so these had to be close together, each easily accessible. Clients also wanted recreation close at hand, especially for the children. Gardens had to accommodate those who went in and out of the swimming pool and house many times in the course of an afternoon. Church's answer was to create garden rooms, but unlike those at Hidcote or Sissinghurst whose purpose was to grow different kinds of plants, his accommodated different activities.

Acknowledging the ubiquitous automobile, he provided for its easy access and egress, his designs allowing cars to be seen. Finally he recognized the reality of modern life—that most people have limited time to garden. "It's just as wrong," he wrote, " to give an owner who is not an ambitious gardener a combination of natural plantings requiring expert knowledge and care as it is to a give a real 'green thumb' a garden with no soil to dig in."

A trip to Finland in 1937 introduced Tommy Church to modernist design. A decade later he would put his new ideas into what, of his two thousand commissions, is regarded as his finest work. El Novillero—the Dewey Donnell Ranch—is located in the grape-growing and wine-making country of Sonoma just north of San Francisco. Here he studied the hills, taking in their gently curving shapes and the pattern of sun and clouds.

The chief focal point would be the swimming pool near where the house would be built. Here Church deviated from the usual rectangular swimming pool to use a biomorphic shape, just as Burle Marx was in the same years using such a shape for planting beds in Brazil. The pool's shape offers a welcome contrast to the boxy, flat-roofed house, and by its curves calls in the beautiful lines of the distant hills. In the center is an abstract sculpture by Adaline Kent, suggesting a recumbent woman sunbathing on a raft. The pool's walls and edge, like the Burle Marx planting beds, appear to be fluid, moving as shadows and reflections change from moment to moment, brilliantly making the space dynamic, yet calming.

Bathers need occasional relief from the intense sun. Church provided a shady corner by preserving many of the native oaks. His inventive wood decking is composed of squares of slats laid in alternate directions. Holes were cut out for the tree trunks, the slats allowing water, so precious in California, to fall through the decking to the roots below.

Thomas Church was an artist, affirming landscape design as "a composition in form and space, but one which must emerge from the needs of the client and the nature of the space." He was a prime mover in redefining the profession in light of postwar realities, making the California style useful, welcoming, and aesthetically pleasing to homeowners of today.

TOP Church's biomorphic or kidney-shaped swimming pool became the rage for other swimming pool owners.

BOTTOM If imitation is indeed the sincerest form of flattery then Tommy Church has been flattered many times over, so often has his wood decking been copied.

The horizontal plane comprising rectangles of foliage—grass, ivy, and low-growing evergreen shrubs—reflects the vertical walls of the house.

Miller House
Columbus, Indiana

Flying west from Boston to Chicago, airline passengers find shapes below increasingly rectangular and square. The rolling hills and winding roads give way to flat-as-a-pancake, uniform fields, some brown, some green, and some, in August, golden with ripening wheat. The fields are divided one from another by arrow-straight farm roads following the old nineteenth-century grid lines of plots available for farming in the newly opened territory of Indiana. Even the rivers appear pulled taut. These straight lines would be utilized by landscape architect Daniel Kiley for the Miller House in Columbus.

It was the mid-1950s when young Kiley made the trip to the town fifty miles south of Indianapolis to meet with potential client J. Irwin Miller. Here Miller and his extended family had long resided. Miller had made his money in diesel engine manufacturing and, devoted modernists that he and his wife were, had hired Finnish-American architect Eero Saarinen to build a large house suited to the needs of the unpretentious family. The house was above all to be private, comfortable, and serviceable for the Millers and their five children. Miller had completed his undergraduate education at Yale University and Saarinen had studied at the Yale School of Architecture. Like-minded and having much in common, Miller and Saarinen made good partners.

For the Miller house, Saarinen would use a flat-roofed design with deeply overhanging eaves, glass walls for viewing the surrounding fields, and broad terraces to provide the transition from house to landscape. For the landscape design Saarinen recommended Dan Kiley with whom he had worked on the Gateway Arch in Saint Louis. Miller, Saarinen, and Kiley shared an admiration of French geometric gardens from their travels in France and an affinity with modern design.

Kiley's training began with an apprenticeship at Warren Manning's firm in Boston. He then enrolled in the Harvard School of Design where in the 1930s ornate Beaux Arts was being taught as the standard. But Kiley and classmates Garrett Eckbo and James C. Rose were dissatisfied and issued their own manifesto declaring the superiority of modern lines. Kiley dropped out of Harvard and a few years later joined the army. As a young soldier in World War II, he was stationed in France where he remained after the war. In free moments he visited the great gardens. He was taken with the clean lines and calming geometry of the Le Nôtre gardens at Vaux-le-Vicomte, Versailles, and Chantilly and recognized the compatibility of the French style with modern architecture.

The Miller house with its large areas of glass and unadorned walls would be his first opportunity to give his ideas concrete expression. In Indiana he found the perfect setting. The countryside itself was a flat plane like that around Paris. His design would repeat the rectilinear shapes of house and countryside.

At the house, Kiley employed the straight-lined, geometric patterns of French Baroque gardens, but he eschewed the symmetry and key vantage points favored by Le Nôtre. Instead he sought to make every possible location a vantage point. Rather than an axial line at a right angle to the house, the usual pattern of the seventeenth-century château, he extended the lines of the house with an allée of trees. For this he chose honey locusts, their airy canopies affording a view across the fields.

He demonstrated his brilliance in another way by forgoing foundation plantings, a new trend in the 1950s. Previously, there were no shrubs or small trees near a house as earlier generations thought the moisture they required unhealthy. Certainly such plantings were not good for wood houses where moisture could lead to rot or for brick or stone where water could weaken the pointing. Further, because architectural design brought the house material to the ground, there was no ugly foundation to hide. In mid-twentieth century, concrete foundations made it esthetically desirable to cover up the lower few feet of a building. Dan Kiley saw how such plantings would break the clean lines of modern architecture, choosing instead to bring the lawn, low ground covers, or flat paths to the vertical walls of the house without interruption.

ABOVE From the allée, the gently sloping lawn leads to the lowest point on the property.

LEFT Swards of green grass, rectangular ivy beds, and squares for paths and terraces echo the shapes of the unadorned vertical walls. Pendulous beeches provide shade and soften the effect.

Kiley went on to a distinguished career, designing over nine hundred sites including Lincoln Center in New York and the Air Force Academy in Colorado. In 2000, while Kiley was still living, Miller House was designated a National Historic Landmark. It stands as one of America's finest examples of modern architecture and landscape design that, in the words of curator Bradley C. Brooks, "draws upon historical precedents without repeating them, enfolding visitors in a compelling composition of forms and spaces that captures the genius of its designers, the aspirations of its owners, and the spirit of their time."

Paley Park

New York City, New York

It is said that the best gifts come in small packages. Paley Park was such a gift to the people of New York City. Although only 4,200 square feet, it has served not only its immediate neighbors in midtown Manhattan, but by example the wider city. It was the vision of William S. Paley, president of the Columbia Broadcasting System whose headquarters were nearby.

In the mid-1960s, all around the city were small rectangular lots that had once been the site for little stores or restaurants but by then were abandoned. Too small for a high-rise building and not even profitable as a parking lot, they became eyesores, serving only as repositories for trash. Paley's idea was to create on one of these sites a park where people who worked in the immediate area could have a few moments of respite from their demanding jobs. He wanted to create an oasis, a place to leave the boardroom, the typewriter, or the stock room, for the refreshment that nature provides.

The site chosen for the park was that of the old Stork Club, just east of Fifth Avenue on 53rd Street. For more than thirty-five years the nightclub had been a watering hole for the rich and famous but was closed in 1965 when a dwindling clientele made it no longer viable. William Paley purchased the land and, naming the park after his late father Samuel Paley, hired the architectural firm of Zion and Breen Associates to design the park. Paley worked closely with them on every detail. In a space as small as this one, it was important to get every detail just right.

The entrance to Paley Park is marked by a change in the sidewalk paving color in front. For the walker looking down, it is clear that here is something different from the surrounding concrete city. The park is raised a few feet above street level, with ramps to accommodate those in wheelchairs on either side of the four broad steps leading upward.

Paley and the architects recognized that once in the park people needed above all else relief from city noise, annoying at any time but especially in the 1960s before there were laws against honking. Their answer was a twenty-foot wall of recirculating water covering the entire back wall of the garden. No silent sheet of water, it rushes down its dimpled path at Paley Park with a sound that masks the noises of even New York City traffic.

Tiny Paley Park, wedged between high rise concrete buildings, is a world apart.

The trees they chose are honey locusts, able to withstand city air polluted by car, bus, and truck emissions. Planted at twelve-foot intervals, the trees provide a light canopy, enough to give the feeling of being in nature but allowing the sun, so welcomed by New Yorkers, to be felt and seen. Pots of seasonal flowers give color and ivy-covered side walls enhance the sense of being in green space.

Next came the question of furniture. It had to be inviting and comfortable if people were to relax and rest. Paley commissioned a survey, asking people what they wanted. Respondents were clear in expressing their desire to control the arrangement. The design choice was modern, round, marble-topped tables and mesh chairs contoured to the human body. Park visitors are free to move these as they wish, to sit alone or create small groups.

And, finally? Knowing that to office workers as to schoolchildren lunch is all-important, Paley conducted his own test, sampling the variety of hot dogs to be sold in the discreetly placed refreshment stand, selecting the most delicious. A public park operated by the private William S. Paley Foundation, Paley Park is a New York gem, providing a cheerful place for early morning coffee and the *New York Times*, a brown bag lunch with friends, or an after-work rendezvous.

Paley Park was an immediate success, and such spaces sprang up all over the city, though none quite so beautiful as Paley. Called vest-pocket parks to acknowledge their tiny size, they have replaced many an abandoned site, providing to those who work or live in their immediate neighborhood a refuge from the bustle and pressure that defines New York City.

Parc André Citroën

Paris, France

In 1992 when the city of Paris bought thirty-five acres of the old Citroën automotive factory land on the southwest side of Paris to build a public park, a competition was arranged to select the design. Submissions were to be judged on their success in reflecting the influence of Paris and on representing contemporary trends. Deadlocked, the committee chose two landscape designers with what they considered to be complementary ideas. Alain Provost and Gilles Clément would work together, each contributing equally to the design.

Dominating the park's design are two tall buildings placed symmetrically, each fifty feet high, made of glass with teak columns, one housing a botanical collection, the other used variously for special exhibits and other purposes. Between them lies a square of 120 fountain jets in which children—and adults—play on hot summer days, trying to guess which jet will next erupt. The area is a modern version of Italian Renaissance gardens, especially reminiscent of the symmetrically placed casinos at the Villa Lante and the water amusements at Villas d'Este and Aldobrandini.

To the south between the glass buildings and the Seine River is the great lawn, pierced by a diagonal path connecting parts of the garden. It may be considered axial like those in the great French Baroque gardens, but it does not divide the lawn at the center as most do. A few trees lying on either side of the path appear to have been placed at random. In this view Parc Citroën unites the images of the modern city with those of the countryside.

On one side of the great lawn, huge rectangles of black marble—an abstract version of the nymphs that line canals in many a classical garden—back the water runnel stretching to the cascade at the park's end. On the other side, a long path takes the visitor past a series of six small rectangular gardens, each representing a color, metal, planet, day of the week, a state of water, and one of the senses. For example, the blue garden represents copper, the planet Venus, Friday, rain, and smell. Also in the line of small gardens is one of "movement" that, according to designer Gilles Clément, aids nature rather than trying to rigidly control it.

Separated from the main park are two square areas. The White Garden, enclosed by a four-foot wall and featuring plants with white flowers and leaves variegated with white, is a playground with sandboxes, ping-pong tables, and a basketball court. The Black Garden,

OPPOSITE, TOP The chief attraction of the great lawn is the tethered balloon that takes its riders high above the park to view and photograph the nearby Seine and the sights of Paris, as did Michael Garber.

OPPOSITE, BOTTOM August finds park visitors seeking shade in the shadow of columnar trees.

a sunken square surrounded by a plaza, is planted with yews and other plants with dark foliage.

Park Citroën has its detractors. The Project for Public Spaces lists Citroën as among the worst of parks, going so far as to suggest that it should be "torn up and redone." "Barely more hospitable than the auto factory it replaced. . . . indifferent to users' needs . . . fussy little design vignettes (on the periphery). . . . lack[s] even the most basic supporting amenities such as seating and picnic tables."

Parc Citroën is eclectic, with references to the geometric style of French and Italian gardens, Renaissance prowess in the use of hydraulics, the Persian shallow water rill, the open greensward of the *jardin anglais*, and the late nineteenth-century English wild garden, all encompassed in a setting of modern architecture and hardscape. Like the required clean lines of a modern house that are difficult for an active family with many belongings to maintain, Parc Citroën is to some visitors incongruous as it tries to be visually minimalist while simultaneously serving the varying recreational needs of a city population. But other visitors find in its straight lines and wide vistas a welcome relief from the busy city, a place for rest and relaxation.

16 This Fragile Earth, Our Island Home

Sustainability, biodiversity, and organic gardening address domination, destruction, and global warming.

TWENTIETH AND TWENTY-FIRST CENTURIES

"BE CAREFUL WHAT you pray for," warns the adage, "You just might get it." We humans have sought to use and control nature since the dawn of history, first by broadcasting seeds, then by planting them. We learned to rely not only on rain and the periodic flooding of rivers to water our crops, but on irrigation systems, moving water first down and then uphill. We studied the conditions needed for a particular plant to survive, and learned to use our domesticated animals and birds to provide fertilizer. We made potions to heal sickness and grew the herbs and plants to make them. We wrote books about what we had learned.

At first, we walled-in ourselves and our gardens from the dangers of the forests surrounding our communities. Then, to make farms and sailing ships, we cut down the forests. Plying the seas to reach new lands and new plants, we learned to document and classify our finds. We trapped water, air, soil, and plants in glass boxes, making the sea voyages safer for our precious green cargo.

Geometry gave us new tools for measurement and we mapped the earth accurately. Empirical science enabled us to understand and direct the workings of nature. We figured out how pollination occurs and housed bees in apiaries. Then we tried pollinating by means of a feather. It worked, and we were off on a wholly new venture, creating new plants for ourselves.

Our prayers for protection, sustenance, and prosperity were being answered as we labored for that for which we prayed. We were conquering nature, and as we did so, life became easier. We abandoned our old belief that nature was hostile. As we succeeded in mastering nature, we saw it as benign and even romantic, opening our gardens to incorporate views of the countryside. We copied nature, but with perfection in mind we did so in our own selective way. We eventually became so confident that nature held few dangers that we could seek out and idealize nature's majestic scenes, and enjoy our moments of trembling as we stood before them.

> Who is to help? . . . the best results can only be got by the owner who knows and loves his ground. . . . Lessons? From Nature mainly.
>
> —WILLIAM ROBINSON

In the twentieth century we made what we believed was a giant leap forward. Chemical fertilizers produced bumper crops and genetically modified organisms or GMOs made possible greatly increased yields. New strains of wheat and rice could produce not one but two and even three crops per season. We attacked world hunger with the Green Revolution and called 1980 Nobel

Biodiversity in a delicate meadow.

Prize winner Norman Borlaug who initiated and led the effort "The man who saved one billion lives."

But there were naysayers about all this progress. Did our success contain the seeds of our destruction? Early in the twentieth century philosopher and educator Rudolf Steiner, himself a scientist, was pointing out the danger of synthetic fertilizers, positing instead the importance of a holistic approach to farming that protected biodiversity. In Scotland, the Findhorn ecovillage, founded in the 1940s and now an education center for issues of environmental protection, practices and promotes organic farming as well as demonstrating other ideas related to sustainability.

Marine biologist Rachel Carson rocked the United States and world with *Silent Spring*, her 1962 book in which she warned about the danger of pesticides to the habitat, especially that of birds. Her book was serialized in the *New Yorker* magazine and chosen for the Book-of-the-Month Club, eventually selling over ten million copies. A bitter fight ensued between the chemical companies and environmentalists such as the Sierra Club and the Audubon Society. In the end the pesticide DDT was banned and the U.S. Environmental Protection Agency created.

At the same time, from their farm in Pennsylvania the Rodales—father J. I. and son Robert—were teaching us the value of beneficial insects and organisms and how to garden and farm successfully without the chemical fertilizers that kill them. The magazine *Organic Gardening* became the bible of the organic farming and gardening movement, taking on issues of sustainability including grazing systems, the energy footprint of importing foods, and acid rain, while teaching about composting and mulching, drip irrigation, soilless growing, integrated pest management, and other organic farming practices.

While we are increasingly aware of human-caused dangers to the environment and are finding alternative methods for producing food, we continue to fell forests throughout the world, not as in the past for the purpose of obtaining firewood or building ships but to create new agricultural lands to feed the exploding population. Arguments rage over answers. Borlaug followers defend the Green Revolution for reducing the amount of land needed for agricultural production, and opponents cite the dangers GMOs and pesticides pose to biodiversity. Looming over all the issues is concern about global warming, its causes and results. Having worked for all of recorded history to conquer and harness nature and having succeeded spectacularly, we are discovering unintended consequences.

Now many around the globe are scrambling to correct past mistakes. With new knowledge, landscape designers are introducing new designs, choosing native plants, and arranging them to reflect new knowledge and changed interests and commitments. As did Capability Brown, Gertrude Jekyll, Andrew Jackson Downing, and many other designers over the centuries, today's designers are helping shape the culture to come.

Gravetye Manor
Sussex, England

William Robinson and Gertrude Jekyll were not only contemporaries, they were friends. Although they disagreed on many points in design and horticulture, each praised the other's work. Both were widely read garden writers, informative, entertaining, and prolific. He was the more famous during their lifetimes; she eclipsed him in subsequent years. Now his ideas are once again admired by those promoting the native plant garden. While he did not go so far as many do today, he developed the contemporary concept of starting with the land and working in cooperation with it, rather than trying to change and control. It was at his home, Gravetye, that he said he discovered his gardening mistakes.

Like Jekyll, Robinson disdained the predominant Victorian style of massed bedding-out, promoting instead a less manicured aesthetic. "To make a flower-bed to imitate a bad carpet . . . [is] a dismal mistake." He believed that gardeners should take their cues from the topography, soil, orientation, and climate of their land: "The lie of the ground must be studied in the way of a good leader of soldiers," he wrote. He thought digging up beds for seasonal annuals was energy and time that could have been better spent in other work in the garden. He held that plants hardy to a specific climate, whether native or exotic, should be allowed to grow and live out their life cycle, seeding freely if that is their natural habit. He found that plants left in the garden to die could add artistic elements as well as reducing garden maintenance.

He thought most walls unnecessary and disdained hedges pruned to imitate walls. He abhorred sculpture, agreeing with the suggestion that it should all be gathered together and put in a cemetery for viewing by those who admired it. He criticized the practice of locating a single tree or a fountain in the middle of a park, believing that open spaces should be preserved. Perhaps most of all he objected to the Victorian devotion to topiary and to highlighting mutant and deviant plants known as sports. He loved yew in its natural form and was a relentless critic of pruning it into animal shapes.

Here in the mixed border at Gravetye, spiky red lupines and spherical alliums provide contrast of shape as well as color.

Like Jekyll and Monet, he admired the cottage garden and praised it in his book *The Wild Garden*, published in 1870. Irish by birth, he traveled widely throughout the British Isles, France, Europe, North Africa, Madeira, and America. In his book he not only wrote of the many wonderful plants he had discovered but recommended how to use them in designing a

The slate roofs are home to moss and sedums.

garden. He founded *The Garden*, a popular magazine that he published for fifty years, "a pulpit," said Gertrude Jekyll, "from which he preached."

Then, in 1884 at age forty-six, he made the decision to buy his own house and make his own garden. Amidst the water meadows of Sussex that he so greatly admired, he found and then purchased a sixteenth-century manor house only thirty miles from his London office. It would be the home where he would garden for more than fifty years. He added to the original 360 acres, eventually tripling the size of Gravetye. Robinson kept many acres as meadows for grazing sheep and cows; today the meadows harbor a variety of plants, mostly native in order to encourage birds, beneficial insects, and small wildlife.

Near the house he designed "in a simple way" a large garden area for his favorite plants. A paradise garden forms the center with a sundial in the middle and radiating paths of stone, easier, he said, than gravel on gardeners' knees. The flower border around the perimeter follows the principles he set forth for the wild garden. Hardy plants require no seasonal digging. He used the very tall and fast growing angelica around bulbs to hide their dying foliage. Taller and shorter plants are mixed. Color schemes follow no set pattern. He was especially fond of roses, mixing them in the borders, declaring them to be a garden's heart, recommending pruning them before Christmas and, instead of mulching, underplanting them with violas, pansies, native geraniums, baby's breath, and dwarf thyme.

The mixed border follows only the rule that the plants are hardy and require minimal care.

Robinson believed that the house and garden should be intimately connected for the enjoyment of those within the house and for ease in tending the plants. At Gravetye, flowers are planted abundantly up to the front door. Robinson loved climbing plants, especially roses and the "splendid" clematises, finding them just the ticket for uniting house and garden. He also prized wisteria, building a special pergola for his *Wisteria sinensis* f. *alba*. The footings proved to be a problem as the wood rotted, but he succeeded in making them firm with iron and stone bases, lifting the wood above the ground level.

Robinson praised water gardens, especially those developed beside flowing streams. He hoped to introduce into Gravetye's two lakes the waterlilies of Latour-Marliac, made immortal by Impressionist artist Claude Monet. His stone pool, though small, was an elegant home for what he called his "fleet."

Knowledgeable about trees, he planted thousands on the Gravetye property. He warned about careless planting that ignores the mature size of the tree or the soil and water requirements, naming particularly the mistake of planting too close to road or house and choosing the wrong location such as planting a weeping willow in a dry field. He loved the North American conifers that he said do as well in English soil and climate as in the Americas. He had special praise for the cedar of Lebanon celebrated in the Bible, planting it at Gravetye in groves rather than singly.

Robinson proclaimed of his white Chinese wisteria-draped pergola, “You never saw such a good effect as we thus obtained.”

William Robinson set the stage for a new awareness that would one day grip the landscape design and horticultural worlds. He admired native plants though not to the exclusion of exotic trees or plants. His contribution lay in his unrelenting emphasis on studying the land and planting only what would thrive without undue attention or excessive amounts of water. He continually advised gardeners to know their land. Soils, he explained, in even the smallest garden will have several microclimates. The natural water sources and their limitations must be understood. The length of seasons, amount of sunshine, and direction of the wind are all critical in creating a hardy, thriving garden. He was a precursor of those today who advocate respecting nature, working with rather than against it.

Jensen's lagoon appears as a river on a flat plane, quiet with undisturbed reflections.

Columbus Park

Chicago, Illinois

Jens Jensen likened the prairies of midwestern America to an ocean, the one he had come to know when he had sailed from his native Denmark as a young man in 1884, emigrating to the United States. Settling eventually in Chicago, he would experience and then turn against the industrial city. "I believe in the influence that environments exert on humans, both for the good and the bad," he wrote; "to shut out nature from a man's whole life is to shut out the inspiration of noble and humanitarian things. The artificial state has come to be the producer of insanity, crime and immorality."

He was not alone in his negative sentiments of the city. Chicago had tripled in size in the decade from 1860 to 1870 and continued to grow faster than services could be provided. The city was teeming with immigrants who were desperate for work however underpaid. Poles, Italians, Germans, Scandinavians, and recently freed African-Americans vied for jobs, banding together in their own ethnic groups for community and to protest low wages and poor working conditions. With its crowded, unsafe, and unsanitary tenements, the city was a tinderbox for fire and a haven for crime.

TOP With the action of the water over the years, the minerals have changed the color of the rocks.

BOTTOM The council ring at Columbus Park is also called the story ring when used for children.

Social reformer Jane Addams, who like Jensen saw the evils of the city, founded Hull House, a "settlement house" that provided a safe center for immigrants and other poor. Jens Jensen's Columbus Park in the heart of Chicago would be a kind of outdoor settlement house, a place of calm, quiet, and reassurance, nurturing healthy and civilized human behavior and providing a sheltering habitat for birds and small wildlife.

Newly arrived in Chicago, Jens Jensen who had learned farming in his Danish family got a job as laborer in a Chicago park. There he showed his knowledge of plants and his commitment to hard work. His good qualities were recognized and he began to rise through the ranks. Union Park was his first design opportunity. For it he chose exotic flowers, but they did not survive the scorching summer heat and cold winter winds. He turned to the native wildflowers that had once grown on the site, the result leading him to appreciate the importance of understanding the ecology of a region. As William Robinson in England was advocating hardy plants rather than annuals for the garden, Jensen was taking the concept to a new level by excluding exotics, hardy or not, in favor of native plants.

His success in the parks system continued. One promotion followed another—that is, until he courageously bucked the corruption that was rife in Chicago including the parks administration. He was sacked and only much later reinstated and made chief landscape architect and general superintendent for the West Park System. Charged with renovating, he faced a challenging job as the parks had deteriorated badly from neglect.

In the intervening years between jobs with the Chicago parks system he had not been idle. He became part of the circle of leaders who sought both social and ecological reform. Architects Louis Sullivan and Frank Lloyd Wright were to inspire his landscape design. Botanist Henry C. Cowles became a friend, mentor, and collaborator as they both promoted regional ecology and conservation of the Indiana dunes on Lake Michigan. Jensen was also receiving design commissions for the residences of wealthy Midwest families, notably the Ford family of automobile fame.

One of his most admired public commissions, Columbus Park illustrates Jensen's planned natural style and the philosophical underpinnings of his work. In the park he put a lagoon designed to resemble the rivers of Midwest prairies that meander close to the

Among many bird species in Columbus Park, an American robin feasts on the fruit of a hawthorn.

surface, flooding periodically and thereby enriching adjacent farm land. For the waterfalls he used thin rocks placed horizontally as they appear naturally nearby. At lakeside he had a large casino constructed for the gatherings popular in the Italian neighborhood adjacent to Columbus Park.

Jensen's signature piece was the council ring. Stone seating in a circle with a pit for fire in the center, his ring was derived from both Scandinavian "tings," or parliaments, and from the American Indian practice of council fires. In his 1939 book *Siftings*, Jensen wrote:

> In this friendly circle, around the fire, man becomes himself. Here there is no social caste. All are on the same level, looking each other in the face. A ring speaks of strength and friendship and is one of the great symbols of mankind. The fire in the center portrays the beginning of civilization and it was around the fire our forefathers gathered when they first placed foot on this continent.

Perhaps the most remarkable feature of Columbus Park is the habitat Jensen created for birds, insects, and other small wildlife. Even today in the heart of the dense city, the park is home to many species of birds whose presence demonstrates the value of using native plants that harbor the beneficial insects on which birds feed. With their preferred food, water, and sheltering trees and plants, they thrive. Jens Jensen was a pioneer in the environmental protection movement, his wisdom in staying true to the land a worthy lesson for landscape designers.

Sea Ranch

Sonoma County, California

Two million, seven hundred thousand dollars was the price the development company paid for the Ohlson ranch. That was big money in 1963, but the land had enormous potential. Located on the Pacific coast only a short drive north of San Francisco, the land was purchased to build high-quality vacation homes. Landscape architect Lawrence Halprin was hired to design a plan for the area to be named Sea Ranch. Here his task was the exact opposite of that assumed by Roberto Burle Marx, Fletcher Steele, and most other garden and landscape designers. Rather than making his mark on the site, he was charged with laying out a plan that would minimally disrupt the natural landscape. Committed as he was to protecting the environment, he was the right man for the job.

The ten miles of Pacific Ocean coastline of Sea Ranch includes a high cliff with forests of cypress, redwood, and eucalyptus, and wide meadows once used for grazing sheep and cattle. At places the ocean crashes the rock-strewn shore with mesmerizing force. At other places, protected coves and sandy beaches invite swimming, sunbathing, beach ball, and castle-building. On the precipice above, the views looking down thirty feet and more to the ocean are spectacular.

Can you find the houses in the picture? Halprin hoped not.

Halprin studied at the Harvard School of Design as did Dan Kiley and Thomas Church. His early years had taken him from Brooklyn to Israel, then to Cornell University and the University of Wisconsin. It was there that he visited Taliesin East, Frank Lloyd Wright's studio. Intrigued, he became interested in designing for himself. With his keen eye and mind he understood the concept behind Wright's Prairie school of architecture which kept buildings close to the ground following the long straight planes of midwestern topography. Halprin would put this early learning to good use at Sea Ranch.

He was commissioned in the U.S. Navy during World War II and after an attack on his destroyer was sent to San Francisco. He remained in the city after leaving military service, joining the firm of Thomas Church and working on, among other commissions, El Novillero, the Dewey Donnell Ranch. Having absorbed Church's legacy, he opened his own office in 1949.

Once the conditions of the Sea Ranch job had been settled, Halprin went right to work. After camping at Sea Ranch to absorb the countryside and observe the changing light and seasons, Halprin presented his ideas to Sonoma County officials who in 1965 approved plans for developing the south end of Sea Ranch. Working with Bay Area architects Charles

Willard Moore, William Turnbull, Donlyn Lyndon, and Richard Whitaker and following the extensive guidelines laid out for Sea Ranch, Halprin proposed three demonstration projects that were approved and then built. Houses with sharp angles echoing the terrain and constructed of unpainted wood that would weather to the tan or gray of the region's grasses and tree trunks were unadorned modern. Soon the architectural world and then the general public was recognizing—and praising—the design of Sea Ranch.

But there was controversy as well. When Californians got wind of the potential development they feared that access to the stretch of unrivaled scenery would belong only to the rich who would post their vacation homes with signs reading "Private Property, Keep Out." A four-year fight ended in a statewide referendum, Proposition 20, that established the Coastal Commission to oversee development and insure public access to the beaches and shoreline of California. With the victory, there came first denials by the commission for proposed buildings at Sea Ranch and then lawsuits as initial investors sought recompense for their losses. It was not until 1980 that development resumed.

At Sea Ranch, the buildings are clustered and fencing around them is forbidden, both requirements serving to preserve open spaces. Homeowners are required to baffle lighting, and roads, without curbs or sidewalks, have no streetlights, thereby ensuring the night sky with its myriad stars is undiminished and wildlife has a natural night habitat. Only native plants are permitted, the one exception those in containers on porches. Seabirds and endangered grasses are monitored by the California Coastal National Monument. Most important for Sea Ranch visitors, all buildings are set back from the cliff and a hiking path along its edge is open to the public.

Sea Ranch reflects the idealistic culture of the United States, California, and, particularly that of Berkeley in the 1960s. Lawrence Halprin's work remains greatly admired and has influenced developments across the United States. As an example of people accommodating themselves to the land rather than demanding the land be sacrificed to their wants, Sea Ranch is a case of landscape architecture *shaping* the thinking of a nation.

TOP Fencing left from the old sheep farm as well as tree trunks and weathered barns inspired the requirements for house-building materials and colors.

BOTTOM Sea Ranch established new guidelines for ensuring public access to beachfront.

The garden thrives above the parking lot and amidst New York buildings.

High Line

New York City, New York

When Robert Hammond first climbed thirty feet to the top of the High Line and stepped onto the old train tracks, he expected, as he later reported, to find ballast and gravel. What he didn't expect was wildflowers. "This was not a few blades of grass. . . .The wildflowers and plants had taken over. We had to wade through waist-high Queen Anne's lace. It was another world, right in the middle of Manhattan."

Josh David's impression of the rusting Art Deco railings was that "the spaces underneath . . . had a dark, gritty, industrial quality, and a lofty, church-like quality as well." Once atop the High Line, "On one side . . . the Statue of Liberty. . . . You think of hidden things as small. But this was. . . . a huge space in New York City."

"This incredible straightaway . . . with a view of the Empire State Building. . . . The buildings alongside it were brick warehouses, factories with smokestacks and casement windows like buildings from a Hopper painting." —Josh David

OPPOSITE New Yorkers welcome a walk on the High Line away from offices with sealed windows. Here Piet Oudolf grasses shine golden, highlighted by the sun as if by Broadway spotlights.

These are the descriptions of the first ascent of the High Line by the two young men who had set their hearts, minds, talents, and connections on saving the derelict old elevated train line in the Lower West Side of New York where each lived. They met at a civic meeting to consider what should become of the neglected landmark, forming a friendship and inspiring their long, difficult, and finally enormously successful commitment to save the High Line.

It was part of a new public awareness of the need to reduce waste. Recycling had begun with newspapers followed by aluminum cans, foil, glass bottles, Styrofoam, and plastic bags. Joshua David and Robert Hammond were to take recycling to a new level by leading the transformation of the outdated structure to a new purpose. In doing so they made possible the creation of one of New York City's most popular attractions for local residents and tourists alike.

The High Line, covering one and a half miles and six acres, was built to lift the traffic above street level. That it was constructed in the middle of the Great Depression when money

NICKEL

Birches now grow among the old rail lines.

was tight is an indication of how desperately it was needed. The street below was called Death Avenue because of the crowding of pedestrians, carts, carriages, cars, and trucks into the same undifferentiated space. The train line running through at street level made the area so dangerous that "West Side cowboys" mounted on horses were hired to go in front of the train to clear the tracks. The High Line reduced the problem by separating the train from other traffic.

For thirty-five years it effectively served its purpose. But the development of the interstate highway system in the 1950s replaced the railroads with trucks for transporting goods. By the 1960s the handwriting was on the wall. The High Line was becoming obsolete. The last train, pulling three boxcars of frozen turkeys, made its last trip in 1980. Only three years later Congress passed the National Trails System Act allowing unused rail lines to be "railbanked" as trails for pedestrians and cyclists, an act that would pave the way for the High Line's future. In the meantime, the neglected elevated track was increasingly an eyesore. Most New Yorkers wanted it taken down.

But a few local residents and business owners, city officials, and finally CSX Transportation itself, owner of the line, began to consider alternatives. It was in 1999 that Josh and Robert met. Within a few months they had founded Friends of the High Line. Their first task, they said, was to "learn the landscape," not in the sense that William Robinson meant

Spaces between the stone and concrete planks allow plants to grow as those occurring naturally must have appeared to Josh and Robert when they first walked the High Line. Benches, too, resemble the rail lines.

when he advised gardeners to study their terrain, but rather to investigate government entities, organizations, and businesses that were or should be involved.

Finally, with the encouragement of several major donors, New York's newly elected Mayor Michael Bloomberg and new city officials reversed the previous decision to destroy the structure. Soon a competition was initiated to garner creative ideas for the High Line's use. Making it a park was only one thought. An earlier idea had been to tear it down, using the old rail yards for a new Yankee Stadium, but that had been firmly rejected. Another idea was to build a giant roller coaster; another, a long—very long—swimming pool. In all 720 ideas were submitted. Shortly after, the City Council announced it would allocate almost sixteen million dollars for the project. A public-private partnership had been formed that, like the Central Park Conservancy before it, would be a model for projects in other cities.

Four prominent architectural and landscape firms were considered for the design. The award went to James Corner Field Operations, Diller Scofidio + Renfro, and Piet Oudolf. Ric Scofidio said of his High Line challenge, "My job as an architect is to save the High Line from architecture," focusing not on building or adding but on stripping away and exposing the structure.

The designers made two early decisions. One was to preserve all of the old rail lines. The rails had to be lifted to build a firm base but they were marked and mapped so they could be laid again just as they had once been. A second design concept was to emphasize the mostly straight lines of the tracks, underscoring the long, narrow shape of the park.

Plantsman Piet Oudolf would select no delicate exotics, no expensive annuals, nothing hard to maintain, but rather plants that had proved they were adapted to tough New York City conditions, needing little water beyond that provided by normal rain and snowfall, and capable of surviving drought. More than two hundred species of grasses, flowering perennials and bulbs, shrubs, and trees, mostly native, grace the park. In addition to his special knowledge of plants, Oudolf brought his mastery of capturing natural light. He used the eastern morning sun and western afternoon sun to maximum advantage, backlighting and highlighting the delicate-appearing native flowers and grasses.

The High Line attracts almost five million visitors each year, bringing a fortune to nearby businesses. It has saved a landmark by recycling a forsaken and doomed structure. And it did something else equally important. The High Line park was built in the years following the attacks on the World Trade Center and not far from its very neighborhood on the Lower West Side of Manhattan. Like other gardens that have been designed and built following wars or other disasters, the High Line, rising above the street like the proverbial phoenix from ashes, was a sign of rebirth, giving encouragement, hope, and healing to a grieving city and nation.

Highgrove
Gloucestershire, England

When HRH Prince Charles began his interest in and commitment to organic farming, he had his detractors. Like his predecessor King George III who was satirized as "Farmer George," Prince Charles proved to be ahead of his time. As the world at last came to understand the values of organic farming and gardening, he was recognized as a world leader in growing without pesticides. Highgrove, his home and farm, would become a model by which people would be both inspired and educated.

When HRH acquired Highgrove in 1980 it was not because it was the perfect house and landscape but rather because it was not. "I suppose I could have gone on searching for the perfect house and garden—a combination of other people's dreams and ideas—but I relished the challenge of starting with a blank canvas and seeing if I could fulfill my own dreams for the garden," he wrote.

He had witnessed the destruction of the English countryside through the 1960s and 1970s as ancient woodlands were felled, hedgerows uprooted, water meadows drained, and pesticides used excessively, all in the name of progress. Prince Charles saw it otherwise. For him, the changes were "a furious battle waged against Nature, which, in my heart of hearts, I felt could only end in tears. . . . I felt an irresistible desire to work in harmony with Nature and accept the inevitable limits to 'perfection' that such a desire would impose." As renovations to the late eighteenth-century house were carried out, he began to transform the land.

Prince Charles inspecting his plants in the Kitchen Garden.

While he may not have aspired to perfection, Prince Charles, a man of aesthetic sensibility, wanted his garden to be beautiful. As a first task, he did as all garden-makers should do: he created a plan and unifying structure. It was varied to accommodate the many purposes the landscape would serve, but it would be a harmonious joining of elements, expressing in the design itself his commitment to working with, not against, nature. He brought into a whole the different garden sections by the use of trees, topiary, and especially hedges, tall to demark large areas of the property and short as borders for planting beds. From the elegant hedge to the whimsical shrubs created by the garden staff, topiary gives both unity and variety. Modern and traditional sculpture, his collection of Tuscan pots, and beautiful paths and garden buildings of brick and stone enhance the grounds.

Eventually Charles included ornamental gardens, a wildflower meadow, a cottage garden, a woodland and arboretum, a southern hemisphere garden, a walled garden for vegetables, an orchard, a stumpery, and his own version of the Temple of Worthies with, at its center, a tribute to Queen Elizabeth The Queen Mother, his beloved grandmother. Barns, yards, and fields house farm animals including chickens, ducks, cattle, and sheep. There are few boundaries between farm and garden. Chickens range in the orchard and the sheep wander the meadow, themselves contributing by treading the meadow seeds into the soil. His Royal Highness has constantly sought to rescue and preserve threatened and rare native breeds of sheep, cattle, chickens, pigs, and geese, as well as rare vegetables and fruit varieties.

Visitors enjoy the delicate perfume as the thyme is crushed underfoot.

The signature piece of Highgrove is the Thyme Walk where thyme fills the spaces between stones and brick in the path. Believing them too garish, some were skeptical about the golden yew, but Charles turned what might have been a vice into a virtue by having his gardeners craft fanciful topiaries.

Prince Charles learned that fundamental to the success of organic gardening is the soil. The compost heap at Highgrove is treated as the high altar. The former high priest and head gardener David Howard advised that "you place all your faith in that altar." Highgrove uses two methods of composting: aerobic (with air) and anaerobic (without air). The first, using garden and stable waste, produces a compost rich in nitrogen that feeds the soil and the plants that grow in it. The second method, using fallen leaves, produces leaf mold high in humus but low in nitrogen. Used to improve soil structure, it is a substitute for peat moss and proves especially effective as an ingredient in potting soil. "My philosophy of compost," declared Howard, "is that it is everything the garden needs because it is made out of everything from the garden."

Equally essential to successful gardening is water. There are few natural water courses at Highgrove. The small streams that flow only from November to April, called winterbournes,

are of no use in supplying summer watering needs. Prince Charles wrote, "In my early days at Highgrove I began to realize that water conservation was going to be paramount in the development of the garden." Earlier in its history Highgrove had an underground storage tank for water, inspiring Prince Charles to install his underground rainwater tank that holds up to 23,000 gallons of water collected from the house, orchard room, and beef buildings. Water is available throughout the garden via standpoints whereby leaky pipes, or targeted irrigation systems, can be used. The lawns are never watered, allowed instead to go brown in dry months. A borehole that collects ground water is used only in dire times. Composted woodchip mulches are used to conserve moisture around plants.

Most important to water conservation at Highgrove is the reed-bed sewage system that processes raw sewage from the house. A bark-filled pit together with reed and willow beds filter the water so completely that in eleven years of testing no pollutants were found. The clean water pond is made beautiful by plantings of arrowhead, loosestrife, purple iris, waterlilies, and yellow flag.

Meadows play an important role in the ecology of Highgrove. Rejecting the wide mown-grass sward that would have surrounded the house when it was built at the end of the eighteenth century, Prince Charles has chosen instead to cover large areas with biodiverse meadows that feed and harbor birds and insects, bringing the meadow close to the house.

The orchard stands amidst a meadow, but fruit-growing is extended by espaliering trees in the walled garden. Over a garden path, apple trees are trained to grow together into an arch, a technique called pleaching, creating a lovely effect and using space efficiently.

Contributing to the ecosystem at Highgrove and conclusively proving that fostering wildlife habitats can make a beautiful garden is the stumpery, a garden of dead tree trunks and logs, some upended and artfully arranged in a shady place. A Victorian invention, the stumpery is a welcoming home to ferns, lichens, moss, other forest floor plants, and, at Highgrove, also hellebores and hostas. The Highgrove stumpery was created out of a messy copse of broadleaf trees. The stumps are those of oak and chestnut windblown trees from different estates, mostly from the storm of 1987. Softwood stumps are not used as they rot too quickly. The tree stumps were recycled, creating, says Prince Charles, "the part of the garden that one really starts to recognize the complex chains and cycles that exist and inter-relate with other life forms. Slugs, snails and beetles are as much a part of the garden as birds and insects, all of them involved in this, the most natural part of the garden."

Prince Charles's vision has extended to the surrounding land and well beyond. As landlord of the Duchy of Cornwall he could have insisted that his new tenant farmers practice organic farming methods. Instead he has educated them about organic farming methods through seminars and land stewards and then he allows them to choose their method of farming, urging only that they make a commitment to a series of environmental objectives for protecting and encouraging wildlife and native flora. By example he has shown them that organic farming and sustainable practices not only protect England's rural heritage but are economically viable. Inspired by his ideas and practices, England's farmers increased the area farmed organically one hundredfold in only two decades.

OPPOSITE, TOP The walled vegetable garden, laid out in a paradise form with wide paths to accommodate barrows, has at its center a dipping pool for filling watering cans. The wild birds, essential to pest control, use it to drink and bathe.

OPPOSITE, BOTTOM At Highgrove, the upended stumps become works of art as well as fostering important wildlife.

Native Plant Garden at the New York Botanical Garden

Bronx, New York

At first it was the dragonflies. Within hours after the water began flowing in the new Native Plant Garden at the New York Botanical Garden they were flitting above the surface. Seeing them, landscape architect Sheila Brady knew that she and her team had succeeded. A garden based on a diversity of plants native to the area provides the best possible habitat for birds, insects, and wildlife. Turtles, frogs, snakes, myriad insects, and birds, including a blue heron, took up residence in the home she designed for them. Soon, to the delight of the hundreds of visiting schoolchildren, a muskrat appeared.

The Native Plant Garden was designed to accord with the long and distinguished history of the New York Botanical Garden as an educational and research institution committed to documenting and conserving the flora of northeastern North America. Along with the garden's LuEsther T. Mertz Library, the largest and most comprehensive botanical and horticultural library in the world, and its far-reaching adult and children's education programs, the new garden would serve as a resource for people interested in learning more about native plants and how to introduce them into their own home gardens.

The genesis of the Native Plant Garden can be traced back to the vision of NYBG's founding director, Nathaniel Lord Britton, and his wife, Elizabeth Gertrude Knight Britton. He was a professor of geology and botany at Columbia University, she an expert on mosses and lichens. On their honeymoon in 1888, they visited the Royal Botanic Gardens, Kew, in London and returned determined that New York should have an institution devoted to the study and display of plants. Their determination led to the creation of the New York Botanical Garden by an act of the New York State Legislature in 1891.

A warbler at home in NYBG's new Native Plant Garden.

In 1895 Nathaniel Lord Britton and the garden's founding board of managers selected 250 acres in the newly formed Bronx Park as the home for NYBG. The land they chose, which had been owned by the Lorillard family from 1792 to 1870, included a fifty-acre old-growth forest bisected by the Bronx River and filled with wildflowers and ancient native trees, and old farm fields crossed with stone walls—the perfect location for developing a botanical garden with a three-part mission of scientific research, education, and horticulture.

Nathaniel Lord Britton's choice of the site for NYBG was inspired in large part by his interest in plants native to northeastern North America. In 1896 he, along with Addison Brown,

A wide array of plants at the new native garden shows the range of color, textures, and shapes that native plants can provide to home garden design.

began writing an illustrated, three-volume description of the plants growing spontaneously in eastern North America. The books cover the area from Nova Scotia and the maritime provinces of Canada to southern Virginia and west to the Mississippi River. Subsequent generations of NYBG botanists have updated these volumes, which remain the definitive scientific work on the plants of the region.

As her husband was studying native plants, Elizabeth Britton was working hard to protect them. In 1902, alarmed by the rapid decline of populations of wildflowers in the garden's forest, she founded the Wildflower Preservation Society of America, one of the first plant conservation organizations in the United States. Britton published many articles about the plight of wildflowers and lectured regularly on the subject to school groups and garden clubs throughout her career.

In the 1930s, the garden developed a modest display of native plants in a valley adjacent to the Rock Garden to honor Elizabeth Britton's conservation efforts. Over the years, this small display grew into a native plant garden that featured small-scale re-creations of habitats, including a pine barren, a limestone cobble, a serpentine barren, and a wet meadow. Unfortunately, this garden never captured the imagination of visitors and proved exceedingly difficult to maintain.

The lower pool with its elegant shape, one side straight, the other curved.

In 2009 NYBG had the opportunity to create a new Native Plant Garden thanks to a generous grant from the Leon Levy Foundation. Staff recognized that the garden first and foremost had to be beautiful in order to correct the common concern that native plant gardens are untidy and unattractive. "A garden that looks like weeds won't fit into my neighborhood," is heard by landscape designers and nurserymen so frequently it has

become a refrain. NYBG set out to prove that need not be so. Experiments have shown that native plants provide habitat for birds, butterflies, and other wildlife whether they are planted in a naturalistic setting or any other style of garden. Rather than attempt to re-create a specific natural habitat or habitats as the old garden had, the new Native Plant Garden would incorporate contemporary ideas about sustainability and would be elegant, sleek, and modern in landscape and architectural design and features.

The garden had to be sited correctly to provide a variety of conditions for the four hundred wild species and cultivars of native plants that would be showcased. Fortunately, the location of previous native plant gardens provided a remarkable diversity of soil, moisture, slope, aspect, and light. Two rocky ridges arise naturally on the sides of a ravine, the east largely in shade, the west in sun. The site is adjacent to the Thain Family Forest, the 50-acre old-growth forest that inspired Nathaniel Lord Britton's choice of the garden's location and fueled Elizabeth Knight Britton's concern about the plight of native plants in the first years of the twentieth century.

NYBG chose Washington D.C.–based Oehme, van Sweden and Associates to design the new garden. The landscape architecture firm had established the New American Garden style, which features masses of hardy herbaceous plants carefully chosen for their appropriateness to a given location and their ability to thrive without excessive horticultural maintenance. NYBG had worked with the firm earlier on the Azalea Garden and knew they were capable of designing a bold, four-season garden that derived its beauty from masses of native plants. Also essential, the firm had designed public spaces at the Chicago Botanic Garden and throughout Washington D.C. and so had experience in planning for the many thousands of visitors the garden would attract.

Sheila Brady, a principal in Oehme, van Sweden, would take the lead. She began with the all-important water feature, to be located between the two rocky ridges. The lowest area of the three and a half acres for the native garden was perpetually wet, making it a logical choice. She took her inspiration for the water's shape from a Martin Puryear sculpture, its simple form long, with one side straight, the other gently curved, and tapering at the ends.

The three interconnected pools of the water feature dominate the view from the entry pavilion, a sleek structure with a curved metal roof and open sides designed by New York architect Hugh Hardy. The upper biofiltration pool is planted with aquatic and bog plants that filter the water and provide habitat for a wide variety of animals and insects. The two lower pools are unplanted and provide a broad expanse of reflected light in the center of the garden. Water passes from pool to pool over a series of weirs crafted from massive slabs of bluestone quarried in the Catskill Mountains. A walkway along one side of the pool, wide enough to accommodate large groups of visitors, is made of black locust wood, selected as an alternative to tropical hardwoods so often used to build boardwalks.

The most remarkable feature of the ponds cannot be seen. The water is recirculated through deep layers of sand and gravel that provide the root-zone for the wetland plants. The system harbors beneficial bacteria that feed on organic matter. Just as do natural wetlands, the water is cleansed before it rejoins the natural water sources of NYBG.

Water from the biofiltration pool flows into the lower pools. The boardwalk is low and close to the water so that visitors may see the thriving pitcher plants.

The meadow's subtle colors change with the time of day and with the seasons as the grasses and flowers come into bloom and then die back.

OPPOSITE, CLOCKWISE FROM TOP LEFT

These plants are among the colorful natives featured in the new native garden at the New York Botanical Garden.

Cardinal flower (*Lobelia cardinalis*).

Joe Pye weed (*Eutrochium dubium*).

Pitcher plant (*Sarracenia* species).

Butterfly weed (*Asclepias tuberosa*).

Oakleaf hydrangea (*Hydrangea quercifolia*).

Woodland pinkroot (*Spigelia marilandica*).

Poppy mallow (*Callirhoe bushii*) with black-eyed Susan (*Rudbeckia hirta*).

On the east side of the water feature is a woodland where native trees, shrubs, and herbaceous plants intermingle, blurring the line between garden and adjacent forest. Spring ephemerals such as bloodroot, foamflower, and trillium carpet the ground in early spring before the trees leaf out and by summer are replaced by large masses of ferns, sedges, and other shade-tolerant ground covers. Dogwood, hydrangea, redbud, rhododendron, shadbush, and other small trees and shrubs frame views and add to the autumn color provided by the large elms, oaks, sweetgums, tulip trees, and other native shade trees throughout the site.

On the opposite ridge a sunny meadow is alive with native plants that harbor and nurture wildlife. Orange butterfly weed and Joe Pye weed feed butterfly caterpillars and attract bees, hummingbirds, and other insects and birds. A glacial erratic resting on the ground at the top of the meadow gives evidence of the Pleistocene ice sheets that moved massive boulders across New York's landscape. As the ice retreated with warming climate, these giant rocks remained in place.

A rock formation at the other end of the meadow sports in its microclimate an eastern prickly pear cactus, *Opuntia humifusa*. Its yellow flowers attract bees and butterflies, and its leaves are eaten by a variety of animals.

The New York Botanical Garden's Native Plant Garden, opened in 2013, is on the cutting edge of contemporary landscape design, reflecting the interests and concerns of the present generation in the health and preservation of the environment and its ecology. It is but the most recent step in NYBG's distinguished history of educating the visiting public about the diversity and beauty of plants native to the region.

The Parthenon Temple honoring the goddess Athena crowns the Acropolis, Athens, where she was believed to reside.

17 Reverence *for* the Archetype

Finding and expressing the genius of place in city, countryside, and cosmos today.

TWENTIETH AND TWENTY-FIRST CENTURIES

ALEXANDER POPE, eighteenth-century poet and translator of Homer's *Iliad*, wrote the poem as a letter of advice to his west London neighbor Lord Burlington who was creating a garden for his new English Palladian villa. In counseling him to call upon the "genius of the place," Pope was referring to the ancient Greek belief that in each person, place, and object there resides a *daemon*, a genius, a guardian spirit containing the essential nature of that to which it is attached. While not coterminous with the object of its protection, the genius (plural genii) exemplifies and exposes the true inner nature of that to which it is joined. Recognizing the genius meant understanding the essence, identifying the archetype. To know one's own genius requires contemplation and meditation. "The unexamined life is not worth living" and "Know thyself" are attributed to Socrates, but the ideas probably have even more ancient roots. Finding and understanding one's genius was to the Greeks evidence of wisdom.

The genii were to be cultivated and propitiated through worship and sacrifices lest their spirit punish the ones they were meant to guide and protect. Throughout the ancient Greek countryside temples were erected in sacred places where a genius was perceived to be at home. The natural site around the temple was not altered, the temple signifying that it was a holy place. Mountains, springs, seascapes, islands all had their *genius loci*—genius of the place—and were especially revered locations.

> Consult the genius of the place in all,
> That tells the waters or to rise, or fall;
> Or helps th' ambitious hill the heav'ns to scale,
> Or scoops in circling theatres the vale;
> Calls in the country, catches opening glades,
> Joins willing woods, and varies shades from shades,
> Now breaks, or now directs, th' intending lines,
> Paints as you plant, and, as you work, designs.
>
> —ALEXANDER POPE

The Greek temple builder and later landscape designers sought to probe the meaning of a place to determine the character and true nature of the resident genius. Historian William Howard Adams wrote, "Only after the spirit was divined could the architecture itself be introduced into a holy partnership with the existing features of the topography."

The Greeks were not the only people to seek the unique nature of a site. Creators of ancient pyramids, henges, and mounds put their knowledge of the workings of sun, moon, and stars into a particular place. In recalling these practices, Alexander Pope was enjoining gardeners to seek, like the ancients, the unique qualities of a site.

Contemporary landscape architects have looked back to archetypal land forms and forward to present-day places, events, and ideas to find genii. They also look within, for there is a genius not only in the place they are to design, but within themselves. Each has his own inner spirit to call upon and uncover. Each brings his own time and place—the historical moment—and his own life history. It is the genii of site and person that make landscape design an art form.

> You, too, proceed! . . .
> Call forth th' ideas of your mind,
> (Proud to accomplish what such hands design'd)
> Bid harbours open, public ways extend,
> Bid temples, worthier of the God, ascend.

Lurie Garden
Chicago, Illinois

Carl Sandburg's poem captures the essence of the brawny city of Chicago. So does Lurie Garden, part of Millennium Park, a short walk from the west shore of Lake Michigan, across the street from the new modern wing of the Art Institute of Chicago and adjacent to the Jay Pritzker Pavilion. Like Sandburg's poem, Lurie Garden pays tribute to the great midwestern hub, America's third largest city.

The largest green-roof garden in the world, Lurie models sustainability. Sitting atop underground parking garages, the two-and-a-half-acre garden uses a minimal amount of water in its water feature and for its hardy perennials, sixty percent of the plantings native to the state of Illinois.

The competition held to select the garden design was won by Kathryn Gustafson, landscape architect, whose work in public parks in Europe includes the Diana, Princess of Wales Memorial Fountain in London's Hyde Park. For Lurie, Gustafson worked in cooperation with lighting and set designer Robert Israel and Dutch plantsman Piet Oudolf. Together they set about discovering the genius of Chicago and expressing it through their art.

> Hog Butcher for the World,
> Tool Maker, Stacker of Wheat,
> Player with Railroads and the Nation's freight Handler;
> Stormy, husky, brawling,
> City of the Big Shoulders.
>
> —CARL SANDBURG

A first problem to be addressed was the proximity of the garden site to the great lawn of the music pavilion where large audiences gather for summer music. How might Lurie Garden be protected on concert nights from the thundering herds seeking to stake their claim for a place to sit? From Sandberg's poem, Chicago has become known as "the city of big shoulders." Gustafson used an enormous evergreen hedge shaped like shoulders to separate the pavilion and lawn from the garden. Planted within a black steel frame, it gives a sense of enclosure at the north end and west side of Lurie Garden.

The fifteen-foot-high "big shoulder" hedge of both needle and broadleaf evergreens separates the great lawn of Millennium Park and the music pavilion from Lurie Garden. Boardwalk and runnel bisect the garden diagonally.

INSET Piet Oudolf and his wife, Anja, welcome visitors for open days at Hummelo, their home and native plant garden in the Netherlands where Michael Garber photographed him.

The garden is divided by a "seam," a five-foot-wide runnel with periodic pools, a narrow wood pathway almost at water level for sitting and, on a summer day, dangling feet. Slightly higher is a wide boardwalk leading the stroller diagonally across the garden and up the slight incline from southwest to northeast. It traces the path of a subterranean seawall that once was the boundary between the marsh at Lake Michigan's shoreline and the city.

> They tell me you are wicked and I believe them, for I
> have seen your painted women under the gas lamps luring the farm boys.
> And they tell me you are crooked and I answer Yes it
> Is true I have seen the gunman kill and go free to kill again.
> And they tell me you are brutal and my reply is: On the
> faces of women and children I have seen the marks of wanton hunger.

To the east of the boardwalk lies the Dark Plate, a raised garden bounded by native limestone walls. It is planted with trees and shade-loving plants including ferns, angelicas,

The Light Plate on the west side of Lurie looks to a bright future.

INSET Lurie Garden harbors at least twenty-seven species of birds. Here, in the Dark Plate, a sparrow is well disguised.

and broad-leaved species, chosen by Oudolf to recall the marshy beginnings of the city. But what visitor could fail to be reminded of Chicago's past of corruption, crime, gangland killings, and the grinding poverty?

> Come and show me another city with lifted head singing
> so proud to be alive and coarse and strong and cunning.
> Flinging magnetic curses amid the toil of piling job on
> job, here is a tall bold slugger set vivid against the little soft cities. . . .
> Bragging and laughing that under his wrist is the pulse,
> and under his ribs the heart of the people,
> Laughing!

The Light Plate looks to the future. Without trees, the sun highlights the amsonia, asters, bee balm, bottle gentian, butterfly weed, coneflowers, eulalia, fountain grass, goldenrod, little bluestem, prairie dropseed, northern sea oats, rattlesnake master, skullcap, and switch grass which are among the thirty-five thousand perennials in 240 varieties in Lurie Garden.

Lurie Garden has won various awards for its adherence to the best principles for sustainability and as a public space. It might also win a design award for uncovering, as did Sandburg, the genius of the place, Chicago.

National September 11 Memorial

New York City, New York

Recently out of college, Welles Crowther had his first real job as an equities trader when he put to use another set of skills that he had long been cultivating. As a child he had set his heart on becoming a fireman. Acquaintances knew of his dream and of his attachment to the red bandanna his father had given him as a child. Ever after, Welles kept a bandanna in his pocket. In high school, he volunteered with the local fire department, learning firefighting and rescue techniques. On September 11, 2001, when the World Trade Center in New York was attacked by terrorists, he courageously put those skills into practice, guiding people from the building's upper floors to the street below. He died in that effort. Soon after, survivors came forth to tell their story of the young man wearing a red bandanna across his mouth and nose who, it was later learned, led eighteen people to safety.

Peace for those who witnessed the imploding towers would not be easily won. The acts that killed almost three thousand and brought down the nation's symbol of ingenuity, skill, and financial strength left survivors angry, despondent, and immeasurably sad. The memorial planned for the site would have to speak deeply, profoundly, and realistically to the city, nation, and the world as people from every continent, many religions, cultures, and belief systems had died. Grieving visitors to the memorial would bring their widely varying thoughts and feelings. The instructions to those submitting designs for the competition were that there be open, public space equal to that of the memorial itself.

Architect Michael Arad and landscape architect Peter Walker won the competition. Arad, an Israeli citizen educated in the United States and living in New York where he was designing police stations, was in his early thirties. Peter Walker was over twice his age, bringing his education at the University of California Berkeley and the Harvard School of Design and over forty-five years of design experience to the task.

They submitted a plan that called for a large forest in the midst of which lay two large reflecting pools on the footprints of the destroyed Twin Towers. Set thirty feet below the surface plane, the two one-acre pools are filled by water flowing down the sides of the pits, creating the largest man-made waterfall in the United States. In the center of each pool a square funnels the water farther down into what appears as a void, as if, beyond human

sight, to the center of the earth, expressing the depth of sorrow. Around the parapets of the pools the names of those who perished are incised in bronze.

Peter Walker's landscape design called for densely planted swamp white oak trees (*Quercus bicolor*) which grow to a height of fifty to sixty feet. Native to northeastern America, they are durable street trees. As they mature, they will in summer provide shade, reduce the heat absorption by the plaza, and through the transpiration of the leaves, cool the air. The memorial grove is planted so that looking in one direction it appears as a natural forest; in the other as an allée. In September the trees turn a golden orange, making peaceful the colors of fire. The park and the edges of the pools are on a flat plane and the surface of the park allows for a variety of activity from quiet rest to public gatherings including the annual reading of the names of those lost.

The Arad and Walker design is named *Reflecting Absence*, and it is absence that visitors experience as they remember the void of Ground Zero and think of those who are gone. The design is minimalist like abstract Japanese Zen gardens, the elements calling forth to the reflective person image after image, allowing the individual to explore a wide range of feelings and ideas.

ABOVE The oaks reach for the skies like the Twin Towers that once stood on the site.

OPPOSITE, TOP Rushing water spilling through the weirs flows down the sides of the reflecting pool into the abyss below.

OPPOSITE, BOTTOM In what are called "meaningful adjacencies," the names of those who perished are grouped by the communities through which they were joined in life and, most probably, in death.

The design team chose three elements universally experienced and fundamental to human understanding of life. The forest is a place of danger but also a source for shelter, food, and fuel, home to sometimes kindly, sometimes avenging gods. Water, too, is elemental. From the womb humans know its healing and cleansing powers, use it in religious ritual, and follow its natural paths. But water, too, can wreak destruction. The third element is the geometric shapes, ancient vehicles for spiritual guidance. The pyramids of Egypt and Mexico and prehistoric sites such as Stonehenge, Newgrange, and the spiral mounds of Ohio are among the man-made structures that point to the heavens, its planets, and stars. At the National September 11 Memorial the reflecting pools allow us to look down and simultaneously through the reflection look above, into the depths of sorrow and to the heavens for hope.

The proud towers are gone as are many who came to them to work. Like legendary heroes, they have disappeared, leaving behind the stories of their lives. The National September 11 Memorial calls the visitor from New York City or afar into the mysteries and sadnesses of life, but also into its hopefulness. Its simple dignity expresses nobility, heroism, and compassion as characteristics of the genius of this place and of the people remembered here including Welles Crowther.

The curves of the surrounding mountains are echoed in the designed contouring, the meadow forms, and the paths.

Storm King Art Center

Mountainville, New York

Storm King was begun with the idea of bringing together the wonderful landscape of the Hudson Highlands with the paintings that made the area famous. The Hudson River school of painters who contributed to the social revolution that was occurring in the valley early in the nineteenth century had, with their art, made people aware of America's natural beauty. But in the end the wedding at Storm King was with another visual art form of a different period. The five hundred acres of forest, hills, lake, and fields have become the largest sculpture park in North America, ideal for displaying the huge abstract pieces that, at mid-twentieth century, were being created. At Storm King Art Center the surrounding tree-covered mountains and hills are the walls, the fields the floor, and the sky the ceiling of this outdoor museum. But

Hearing the sound of thunder rolling down the river in a Hudson Valley summer storm, local residents say the giants are playing ninepins. Mark di Suvero's *Mother Peace* might be among them.

to show the art to full advantage the landscape itself required sculpting.

In 1958 businessman Ralph E. (Ted) Ogden purchased a Normandy-style stone château at the top of a hill near Storm King Mountain. With the encouragement and help of his son-in-law H. Peter Stern, Ogden made his first purchases of sculpture, Henry Moore's *Reclining Connected Forms* and thirteen David Smith pieces. Other sculpture was acquired so that by the end of the 1960s Storm King was known to the creators of monumental sculptures as a desired location for their work. Few museums had space for pieces their size, the number of building atria and public plazas was limited, and almost no place could accommodate more than one piece.

Mark di Suvero was one of the artists pleased to have his work chosen for Storm King because his sculptures, made of steel beams and girders, are gigantic. However admired he is as an artist, his sculptures would appear crowded in most locations and might even have been left homeless. At Storm King his pieces, seen from a quarter of a mile away, have ample room, giving the impression that they were born in their spot.

Supreme among the advantages of Storm King for artists is that the location of a sculpture and its surround can and will be altered to create the best possible site. Landscape architect William A. Rutherford Sr., working closely with the sculptors, designed and engineered the contouring of earth to show a piece to full advantage. He saw the wisdom of using no plinths or artificial platforms so that the works appear rooted as part of the natural setting. In some places land was leveled to provide a firm base, while a hill was created for Alexander Calder's stabiles to march upward. For di Suvero, who prefers his pieces to be seen from above, Rutherford removed trees to create the wide spaces necessary for viewing from close-up or afar.

For Isamu Noguchi, the request from Ogden and Stern that he create a site-specific piece proved irresistible as he was allowed to choose his spot and his subject with the promise that the land would be shaped to his creation. He selected a rise near the château, and for this site he sculpted his *Momo Taro*. Made of Japanese striated stone, the forty-ton work is based on a Japanese fairy tale of a child who comes to a childless couple from the inside of a peach pit. The large hole in the sculpture, suggesting the now vacant center, allows visiting children to climb in and out as Noguchi intended, perhaps pretending they themselves are the dearly wanted child.

Sculpture is not just placed on the grounds of Storm King, but rather becomes one with the landscape. The genii of the place and of the artworks are joined. Throughout the valley, farmers have cleared their fields of loose rocks by constructing dry walls. Artist Andy

ABOVE The natural hill was enlarged and reshaped for Isamu Noguchi's *Momo Taro*.

OPPOSITE, TOP Now called *Storm King Wall,* the original title of the Goldsworthy piece was *The Wall That Walked Into the Water*.

OPPOSITE, BOTTOM Maya Lin sculpted the earth itself for *Storm King Wavefield.*

Goldsworthy made such a wall 2,278 feet long, his serpentine shape winding through a grove of trees, slithering like a snake into the water, then emerging on the other side as if it had continued on the bottom of the pond, and ending at the New York State Thruway that passes nearby.

Artist Maya Lin has made a landform at Storm King that makes the landscape and the art form completely one. Most famous for her Vietnam Veterans Memorial in Washington D.C. which cuts into the earth, here she created *Storm King Wavefield*, raising the "waves" from the ground, thereby making the contoured earth not a setting for sculpture but the sculpture itself.

Today Storm King Art Center holds over 125 pieces and is surrounded by more than two thousand acres protected from development. The concept for the sculpture park developed over the years from that of providing a setting for large sculpture to that of commissioning site-specific works and finally of using the earth itself as the artist's medium. Peter Stern reports that many visitors commenting on the beauty of the natural setting refer to God's handiwork. Stern reminds them that the landscape architect should receive credit as well. Bill Rutherford shares with Capability Brown both the landscape park style and the experience of having his work mistaken for that of the Creator.

Toronto Music Garden
Toronto, Canada

Prodigy Yo-Yo Ma began playing Bach's *Suites for Unaccompanied Cello* as a young child. At midlife when he had become a word-famous cellist he conceived the idea of uniting various art forms. He invited artists in different media to explore the meaning of the Bach suites and imagine how they might interpret them in their own art. For landscape design, he approached fellow Bostonian Julie Moir Messervy, whose book *Contemplative Gardens* had intrigued him. She reports listening again and again to his recording of the First Suite before writing down her thoughts. "The whole notes feel like a stopping place in a garden, the eighth notes and sixteenths feel like a path," she wrote in her initial response to Ma. Her combination of curved and straight lines in the Toronto Music Garden would echo those seen in the cello itself.

Soon the project began to take shape. As her ideas crystallized, Yo-Yo Ma and Julie Messervy found an interested mayor in David Miller of Toronto. Having already begun developing as a park a two-and-a-half acre sliver of land on the harbor, he saw the role that a music garden might play in the needed revitalization of the Lake Ontario waterfront and how it might shape the city's culture and future. He understood that Yo-Yo Ma's idea embodied in Julie Messervy's design would create no ordinary park but rather one that would attract both city residents and tourists. As the garden developed, it seemed that music had always been a characteristic of the site's genius.

Bach choose for the First Suite five dance forms, allowing him to display a great mélange of musical forms. Messervy in turn created a garden of rooms, one for the Prelude and another for each dance, providing a medley of landscape styles in a small space. Granite boulders with trill-like veins of red feldspar from the Canadian Shield, rounded from constant tumbling in glaciers ten thousand years ago, unite the various sections. Three hills allow harbor views as garden visitors move upward and downward step by step just as do the notes in a Bach composition.

The visitor may rent audio equipment to hear, while touring the garden, the Bach cello suite played by Yo-Yo Ma. The Prelude begins at a short waterfront walk beside a meandering stone brook. Two lines of straight native hackberry trees suggest a staff of music. The path, with spirals brushed into the concrete, winds upward. Rocks are hugged with matting plants, the "music" punctuated in spring with tall lupines and irises.

To the left is the Allemande, a seventeenth-century French court dance taken from a German folk tune. In the garden, the main trail backed by birches leads steadily uphill to a clearing where stones appear as a group of whole and half notes. Small curves off the main path, like steps of a dance, are enlivened by seasonal plantings—daffodils in early spring, foxgloves and meadow rue in late spring, alliums and balloon flowers in summer, and asters and grasses in fall.

OPPOSITE, TOP As in a Japanese garden, the rocks are placed with care.

OPPOSITE, BOTTOM The lively Courante would entice even the most devoted office worker to quit his desk.

ABOVE Popular in Bach's time were elegant dances of elaborate patterns, here a sarabande.

LEFT The Sarabande is the site for poetry readings and solo musical performances.

The Toronto Music Garden ends back at the harbor.

Turning right, the visitor comes to the sprightly Courante. Hearing the Courante in Bach's First Suite, Messervy's daughter imagined "a meadow of colorful wildflowers filled with hummingbirds and buzzing bees." Here two paths spiral uphill to a maypole with ribbons that, although made of iron, appear to flutter in the wind, meeting in the center as "dancers clasping hands." Here real flowers— artemisias, asters, buddleia, coneflowers, and Russian sage—enliven the scene, as colorful as the costumes of the imagined dancers.

The Sarabande is next, a contrast to the energetic Courante. As a musical form, the sarabande, in triple meter, is stately and accompanied a popular dance form in Europe in the seventeenth and eighteenth centuries. The walls of the Sarabande garden room are mainly evergreen with a few deciduous trees of blue, bright green, and plum. At its enclosed and quiet center are flat-topped rocks for resting, reading, and contemplation.

The Menuett crowns the highest hill and is the location for larger musical performances. At its center is an iron pavilion with tendril-like decoration. Roses line either side, with native crabapple trees defining the circular space. On either side framing the pavilion, two weeping trees appear as dancers bowing to each other.

Finally the Gigue's terrace stairs lead downward to the water's edge. Children especially dance down the grass steps, as if doing a jig, the dance form on which the Gigue is based. At the base of the steps is another venue for music, the steps providing seating. A huge weeping willow lends a wistful note, for gardens, like music, are fleeting, their ephemeral nature making the experience all the more cherished.

Shakespeare Garden at Vassar College

Poughkeepsie, New York

Matthew Vassar, founder of the college that bears his name, would not have been surprised that, in 1916, the then-women's college began a garden planted with flowers and herbs mentioned in works by Shakespeare. He believed that students should be immersed in all forms of art and had collected Hudson River school paintings for their edification. And he had worked with Andrew Jackson Downing on landscape design, hiring Downing for Springside, his own home and surrounding property in the mid–Hudson River Valley. The idea of students learning simultaneously about the history of garden design, horticulture, and literature would have won his nod of approval. How pleased he would be that through a garden, the genius of Shakespeare has had an altar at Vassar College for over a century.

Students and faculty have worked in the Shakespeare Garden since its inception, including in the 1940s.

The idea for the garden came from Henry Noble MacCracken, the college president and distinguished professor of English. Having written a scholarly commentary on Shakespeare, he wanted a way to recognize the 1916 tercentenary of the bard's death. And the idea of bringing together for the project two disciplines fit with his progressive ideas, similar to those of his contemporary, the philosopher, psychologist, and education reformer John Dewey. Both believed that school and life experience, study and action, should be of a piece, each informing and reinforcing the other.

The students in Miss Winifred Smith's class in Shakespeare drew up a list of all the plants mentioned in Shakespeare's plays and sonnets. Miss Emmeline Moore, who taught botany, took charge of receiving alumnae contributions of bulbs, roots, plants, and seeds, making sure each donation was on the list. In addition they obtained seeds from the Shakespeare garden at his birthplace, Stratford-upon-Avon.

Their work, the Shakespeare Garden at Vassar College, was to be the second such garden in the United States, opening three months after that in Central Park. In the century following, the Vassar garden went through periodic renovations as all gardens must. In the 1920s redesign was part of a campus-wide landscape remodeling. In 1977–78 under the direction of a botany professor, students planted 3,700 bulbs, a professor of English attesting that all were mentioned in the Shakespeare corpus. At the bard's four hundredth anniversary in 2016, the garden was in the midst of a renovation and extension after the construction of a new building nearby.

The site chosen for the Shakespeare Garden and where it remains today is adjacent to Fonteyn Kill (stream) that runs through the campus. It was undoubtedly chosen with

ABOVE The Vassar College Shakespeare Garden today, backed by willows "aslant a brook," is designed as would have been an Elizabethan garden.

OPPOSITE, TOP For the Shakespeare aficionado, thyme recalls Oberon's memory in *A Midsummer Night's Dream*: "I know a bank where the wild thyme blows."

Shakespeare's famous passage from *Hamlet* in mind, in which Gertrude describes Ophelia's drowning to her brother, Laertes:

> There is a willow grows aslant a brook
> That shows his hoar leaves in the glassy stream.
> There with fantastic garlands did she come
> With crowflowers, nettles, daisies, and long purples
> That liberal shepherds give a grosser name,
> But our cold maids do "dead men's fingers" call them.

Other flowers and herbs adorn today's garden. Culinary and medicinal herbs in neat squares are labeled with quotations from the plays. The garden's expansion now includes

A sign in the garden reminds the visitor of Salisbury in Shakespeare's *King John* who reasons that "To guard a title that was rich before . . . / To gild refined gold, to paint the lily. . . / Is wasteful and ridiculous excess."

plants grown in England in the seventeenth century as well as those mentioned by Shakespeare. The square and rectangular raised beds of brick are consistent with gardening practices in Tudor England, as are the topiary spheres, wooden arches framing entrances, and patterns in the brick walks. The newest plan calls for knot gardens, smaller than but similar to those at Hatfield House, Queen Elizabeth I's childhood home. Bay, basil, chives, fennel, fig, mint, oregano, pansies, purple sage, rosemary, strawberries, summer savory, tarragon, and thyme are among the plants in the extended garden.

The Shakespeare Garden is a peaceful place for students, faculty, and visitors to read or stroll and is itself a source of learning. Matthew Vassar and President MacCracken would have agreed that the addition of history in today's garden further enriches education, appropriate for a location that has been and remains a temple of learning and scholarship.

Garden of Cosmic Speculation

Dumfries, Scotland

The revelations of modern physics and biology may seem unlikely to inspire the design of a garden, but Charles Jencks did not think it so. In the images generated on computers in the last quarter of the twentieth century and those seen through the Hubble Space Telescope, he saw new ways of understanding the universe. Whether too minuscule to be seen even with the aid of a powerful microscope or galaxies light years away, these images challenge any notion that may remain that the universe is static and linear. What they showed to Jencks is a wavy, squirmy, jumping, leaping, romping, ever-moving, ever-changing world. He would honor this newly perceived truth, this genius, in his garden.

In addition, advances in science raise anew age-old questions about life, its origins, and its meaning. Does the universe have purpose or is it directionless? Was it created and is it governed by laws or accident? These are questions asked by modern science and by Charles Jencks in the Garden of Cosmic Speculation. Ironically, in creating a garden expressing these new concepts and old questions, Jencks was following in the footsteps of his seventeenth-century predecessors, notably André Le Nôtre. Although Jencks's view of the universe opposes that of the linear and static vision of Enlightenment thinkers, he asks in his garden the same questions as they did, using contemporary science just as the geometric designers used the science and mathematics of their day.

The yew and arborvitae hedges of Cosmic Speculation are trimmed in various ways to suggest the wavy, moving universe. The boar is the work of Elizabeth Frink.

All of this might seem ponderous but the garden is certainly not so. Just as many true scientists find childlike delight in new discoveries, the Garden of Cosmic Speculation dances with charm and wry humor as it presents the newly seen world.

Born in Baltimore, Maryland, Jencks graduated from Harvard and then, in the period after the innovations of Walter Gropius, the Harvard Graduate School of Design. From there he moved to London where he studied architectural history at University College, earning the PhD. He wrote about contemporary architecture that broke with the modern style and was an early theorist and operative in post-modern design. An analyst of the contemporary world, he saw before most others the changes in our culture and what they meant. It is not surprising that his garden reflects the newest knowledge and theories of cosmology while posing eternal questions.

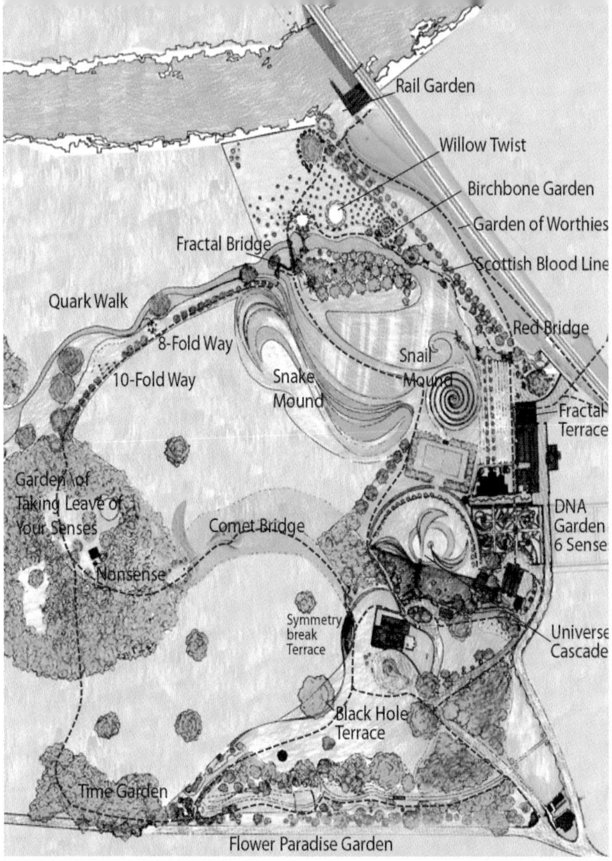

TOP The plan of the Garden of Cosmic Speculation, by Charles Jencks, updated in 2010, shows twenty areas designed around "cosmic and other ideas of a public nature."

BOTTOM Charles Jencks, left, and head gardener, Alistair Clark, confer on the next garden project.

In creating his garden Charles Jencks had skilled partners and aides. His wife, Maggie Keswick, was a garden connoisseur. As a child she was shuffled back and forth between the United Kingdom and China where her father was a business tycoon. She wrote a definitive book on Chinese gardens and wove her interest into the Garden of Cosmic Speculation, giving Chinese garden tradition a new twist. From Jencks's description of the way they collaboratively examined concepts, each sketching how the ideas might look when realized, it is clear that the conversation between them was as lively, intellectual, and amusing as the garden they created.

Highly trained horticulturist and skilled gardener Alistair Clark has worked with Jencks since the 1980s. Renowned scientists and architects have explained and advised. Skilled craftsmen have fashioned gates and sculpture, working their aesthetic magic for the Garden of Cosmic Speculation.

When Charles and Maggie decided to make Scotland their home, they moved into Portrack, her parents' home, a white Georgian farmhouse built in 1815, near Dumfries, southeast of Glasgow. Much of the property was a natural swamp, a challenge for any gardener. But Maggie, perhaps thinking of Capability Brown at Blenheim, began by creating lakes. Never far from her China upbringing, Maggie saw in the shapes of the lakes and the curving contours of the land the mouth of a dragon about to ingest a snake. In 1989 the Garden of Cosmic Speculation began to take shape and has continued its evolution ever since.

As Charles turned to modern science, he and Maggie also looked backward to the dawn of human landform-making, molding archetypal forms at the garden's heart. A snail mound reminds visitors of, says Jencks, "the poetics of going slow." Below, a spiral extends from the land into the lake, the curving lines fit within the divided and subdivided golden rectangle and demonstrating how humankind has stylized natural forms. The quiet bodies of water with their curved and fluid crescent shapes convey peacefulness, as do the moon ponds at Studley Royal.

The double helix appears in a section of the garden that celebrates DNA and the senses. Organized in geometric patterns, each of the squares bounded by box hedges highlights one of the five senses. Charles and Maggie also added a sixth sense, woman's intuition. The brick-lined pebble paths separating the sections have a Chinese feel in their patterns. In one called the Drunkard's Walk the pattern careens from side to side as if arguing a cosmic question.

Countering the Garden of the Six Senses is a copse that Charles and Maggie named "Taking Leave of Your Senses." In its midst *The Nonsense*, a steel frame of a building, was

TOP "Taste" at the bottom of a double helix is exhibited with Warhol- or Lichtenstein-like lips rising above the ground that is planted with luscious red strawberries.

BOTTOM Scotland's national poet "Rabby" Burns is remembered with his words, "Gie me ae spark o' nature's fire, that's a' the learning I desire."

inspired by a structure at Bomarzo and is similarly disorienting. The stairs here lead only to frustration as a beam prevents reaching the view at the top. Jencks calls his structure "a hybrid medium somewhere between sculpture, literature, architecture, and landscape," a style that he would later label "cosmogenic art."

The red Jumping Bridge is actually two bridges rising above the stream like traditional Chinese bridges, here appearing to leap over the water. The walkway connecting them tilts, giving the walker a brief Sublime thrill of imbalance.

The bridges lead to the Temple of Scottish Worthies. On one side, following the railroad line that runs through Portrack, is a series of metal signs with cutouts of the names, dates, quotations, or accomplishments of great Scots, including Robert Adam, David Hume, James Hutton, Walter Scott, Adam Smith, Thomas Telford, and James Watt. In the line of trees opposite hang long red metal banners with the names of other Scottish notables beginning with Agricola, the Roman general who brought Britain into the Roman Empire. That his is also the name given to a mind-challenging board game whose object is to build the best well-balanced farm makes him especially appropriate for inclusion in the Garden of Cosmic Speculation. The temple is both a serious reminder of the Scots who have contributed significantly to the world's intellectual and artistic legacy and a satire of the solemn eighteenth-century Temple of British Worthies at Stowe, just south of the border in England.

Scientific references and representations abound throughout the Portrack landscape. There is a black hole, a fractal garden, a copse of quarks, a display of the Standard Model with the Higgs boson, soliton waves and gates, and Einstein's theory of relativity. A bench bears a quote from Linnaeus—"Nature does not proceed by leaps"—with the added words of Jencks, "but by cometary jumps." And there is humor: a stumpery of look-alike tree stubs named

The two parts of the Jumping Bridge and walkway give a little when walked upon so that the visitor not only sees but feels the moving universe.

Dragon Teeth, lines of turf strips alternating with gravel that make Broken Symmetry, and a bench with an Art Nouveau look that has no straight lines titled *Non-Euclidian Furniture*. Jencks identifies the Universe Cascade, portraying the "inflationary" universe as understood by modern science as the garden's heart. Its steps emerge from the brown quantum foam at the water table below the pond, widening as they reach the top to represent the latest expansion.

All of this and more is in a setting using both geometric forms and the planned natural style. Consistent with Alexander Pope's advice, Jencks and Keswick consulted the genius of the place, incorporating and reinforcing by their design the natural contours of the Scottish hills, ridges, and lakes, perhaps even thinking of the serpent that legend says lives in the not-too-distant Loch Ness. Jencks says of the garden he and Maggie created that its speculation about nature and our nature is "to celebrate the beauty and organization of the universe, but above all resupply that sense of awe which modern life has done so much to deny." "Perhaps," he concludes, "in the end neither man nor the universe is the measure of all things, but rather the convivial dialogue that comes from their interaction."

RIGHT The water chain at Villa Lante tells of man's progress from primordial beginnings to civilization. The Universe Cascade depicts theories of the birth and life of the universe. The structure at left recycles "dark energy down its membranes" into the quantum foam, "the seed for galaxies." The ever-broadening steps, center, represent the universe "expanding faster than the speed of light."

BELOW When Maggie Keswick died of cancer in 1995, mourners climbed to the top of the mound, leaving flower offerings there.

Shute

Wiltshire, England

It was only a small house party. Three people who had collaborated for twenty years gathered at Shute House in the summer of 1992 to toast the achievement that they now declared complete, an achievement the gardening world had declared a masterpiece. Sitting that evening at the head of the water cascade, they recalled the garden's evolution and relished its success in capturing the ideas that Sir Geoffrey Jellicoe had developed in his long and distinguished career as architect, landscape designer, and intellect. "Like the portrait painter, the landscape designer needs to be a psychologist first and a technician afterward. He needs to dig into the subconscious," wrote Jellicoe of his design concept.

Artist Michael Tree and his wife Lady Anne were the owners of Shute. He had known Jellicoe since childhood when the landscape architect designed his parents' gardens at Ditchley Park. She, a Cavendish of Chatsworth, would be the plantswoman for Jellicoe's design. Even when they were considering the purchase of Shute House in 1968, the Trees called Jellicoe for his assessment. Jellicoe, born in 1900, had just retired, but his walk around the Shute property convinced him that residing in the neglected, overgrown, and undistinguished property was a genius that his now mature concepts, if made concrete, could reveal.

The original plaster herms have been temporarily replaced with busts of Zeus, Apollo, and Neptune until finer representations of the original authors can be found.

His career had been rich and varied, and he was recognized as Britain's foremost landscape architect. As a student at the Architectural Association School of Architecture he had traveled to Italy with J. C. (Jock) Shepherd where they studied Italian gardens and wrote their book *Italian Gardens of the Renaissance*. He later returned to the British School of Rome and traveled extensively in Europe, writing a book on Baroque gardens. His other seminal works included the three-volume *Studies in Landscape Architecture* as well as *Water: The Uses of Water in Landscape Architecture* and *The Landscape of Man*, the last two with his wife, Susan Jellicoe. He was always studying the fine arts, especially painting, and served as a trustee of the Tate Gallery.

As a landscape architect, Jellicoe had won important commissions including for the surroundings of the Royal Shakespeare Theater at Stratford-upon-Avon and the John F. Kennedy Memorial at Runnymede. He was named principal of the Architectural Association School of Architecture, elected president of the Institute of Landscape Architects, appointed CBE, and then, while working on Shute House, was knighted.

The formal cascade widens into geometric pools as it descends.

OPPOSITE, TOP The classical cascade and the Romantic stream are united in the bog garden at Shute.

INSET The sound of the treble chute is joined by the alto, tenor, and bass as the formal stream tumbles downward.

When he began work at Shute, he was able to bring all of these interests and experiences into his design—and something more. It was the theory of Carl Jung that would provide Jellicoe with the integrating principle. Jung had taken his place beside Sigmund Freud as one of the two most influential psychologists of the twentieth century. Jung theorized about the motivations of and influences on human behavior, giving the name the "collective unconscious" to shared human experience. Jung believed that centuries upon centuries of archetypal images have entered our subconscious and there reside. Jellicoe's concept was to bring the ideas and history of mankind's molding of his environment to light, not on the analyst's couch but in a garden. He knew that realizing such a concept would take years. Michael and Anne Tree assured him he would have the needed continuity. Shute would be the laboratory for his dreams.

Jellicoe was drawn to Shute by the plentiful water and by the site that recalled his formative time in Italy. The house, atop a ridge with the land easing downward on either side, allows views out to the surrounding countryside, as at the Villa Medici at Fiesole.

Abundant springs would allow him to use water as the central and binding element just as in the Villa Lante, his favorite Italian garden. There Ovid's myths telling of the rise of human

civilization from primordial beginnings are united by water. Educated as he was in classical literature, Jellicoe understood the use of water in its various forms as symbol and metaphor and he acknowledged the place of water in our subconscious. "Whether we are watching the ceaseless movement of the waves on the seashore or the eddies on the surface of a pool, or reflection on a calm day, the fascination of water seems endless," he wrote.

A nineteenth-century canal is the first body of water to come into view. At the far end in the enclosing hedge Jellicoe sought to embed herms of Ovid, Virgil, and Lucretius, commanding attention and reminding the pilgrim of their works: Ovid's *Metamorphoses*, Virgil's tale of the journey of Aeneas from Troy across the Mediterranean to arrive at last at the site of Rome, and the cosmology described by Lucretius in his extensive poem, *De rerum natura* (On the Nature of Things).

From the canal, the water divides into two streams, the one formal, the other free-flowing in the style of the English landscape park. Here classicism and Romanticism point to the critical juncture of landscape design in Western history, summoning our collective unconscious. To carry the water downstream in the formal garden, Jellico used a rill punctuated by geometric forms, vaguely suggestive of the ancient Court of the Lions at Alhambra although instead of circles Jellicoe used for his basins a square, a hexagon, and an octagon.

Black swans keep the pondweed under control.

Copper undulations set in concrete make the descending water sing. The theory is that the more the water is broken up the higher the notes will be. The "dimples" are reduced in number at each cascade, making music in a lower tone at the bottom of the cascade. The goal was to create a harmonic chord. Just as Jellicoe admired the many clever water features at the Villa d'Este including the organ fountain that played music, d'Este's designer Pirro Ligorio would surely have applauded Jellicoe's musical cascade at Shute.

The Romantic planned natural branch of the stream is lush and gently curved. Rhododendrons and weeping willows soften one bank and are reflected in the water. Here nature appears released from any straitjacket of geometric lines, fostering emotion over reason. Capability Brown would have been pleased with the look that included turf on the opposite bank kept clear of any plants at the water's edge. Jellicoe described a Brown landscape as a pure abstract form, "empty of an idea beyond the primary concept . . . universal and dateless."

The two streams reunite at the bottom of the incline as they near the bog garden. Here Jellicoe employs Edmund Burke's concept of the Sublime with a touch of the mysterious, releasing the imagination to explore and feel the unknown. He described the purpose of the Shute garden as that of replenishing the mind itself. By bringing together the divergent ways of seeing and handling landscape in the past, he has made apparent and conscious the genius of past land-shapers and their effect on our experience of land and nature.

Canals bisect the eighteenth-century landscape at Boughton, the mound seen in the upper right.

Boughton House

Northamptonshire, England

Landscape architect Kim Wilkie called his book *Led by the Land*, but he named his design at Boughton House *Orpheus*, after the musician sublime who, Virgil said, "led the trees." Seeking to reclaim his beloved Eurydice from death, Orpheus was almost alone among mankind in voluntarily braving the underworld with the hope of returning to earth. With his enticing lyre he persuaded the god Hades and his winter wife, Persephone, to release Eurydice from captivity. But leading her upward to the world of light and life, Orpheus could not obey Hades' simple injunction to look ahead, not back, and in his act lost his beloved forever.

When Lord Dalkeith called on Wilkie in 2004 to renew the long-neglected landscape at Boughton, the designer turned to this ancient legend and to the primordial land forms that had become his trademark. A man of wide-ranging experience and education, Wilkie grew up first on the edge of the Malaysian jungle, then in the Middle East where his father was posted. There he had the opportunity to see the ancient ziggurats and to contemplate how

Wilkie credits the computer with the precision of the cuts made in the earth to realize his design at Boughton House.

early civilizations left their mark on the earth. His family returned to England and settled in Hampshire where again he lived with earthworks including ancient stone circles, barrows, tumuli, burial mounds, henge, trough and furrow, ramparts, and even redoubts.

At Oxford he read modern history. Then, as he reports, at age twenty-one he learned there is a profession of landscape architecture. He was ecstatic for "I could hardly believe that everything I loved could be wrapped in one profession: people, land, biology and drawing." He went to the University of California Berkeley to study for his now-chosen career. As a student and then young professional he found himself returning to mankind's ancient myths and landforms, seeing in them a yearning for meaning and spiritual expression.

At Boughton House Wilkie was presented with a wonderful old landform, conceived and built in the 1720s. A truncated pyramid twenty-three feet high, it was intended by the eighteenth-century owners of Boughton House as the foundation for a family mausoleum similar to that at Castle Howard, but the mausoleum was never constructed. The designer was Charles Bridgeman, a leading landscape architect of the time who also worked at Castle Howard, Stowe, and other eighteenth-century English estates. Bridgeman's pyramid at Boughton was part of a geometric design. Like Studley Royal, it retains the formal lines of the older French Baroque style.

A rill delineating the golden spiral begins on the far side of Wilkie's reflecting pool, each successive golden rectangle itself divided by the golden mean until the golden spiral emerges.

Pointing to the pyramid, Lord Dalkeith asked of Wilkie, "So, what would you do with this?" Without hesitation, Wilkie suggested creating a mirror image, replicating the lines of the eighteenth-century pyramid base but in reverse, so that the old mound rises as Mount Olympus, and his sunken ziggurat points to the earth's center. Like Vignola at the Villa Lante, William Kent at Rousham, and Henry Hoare at Stourhead, Wilkie told a classic and classical story with his plan.

As he began the landscape design, Wilkie discovered the brilliance of Bridgeman's geometry. He looked out over the canals, avenues, and grass terraces created between 1685 and 1725 and saw the lines and proportions extolled by the Greeks and used brilliantly by André Le Nôtre in his French Baroque gardens. In what he calls "the axial rhythm" of squares and rectangles, Wilkie recognized the golden rectangle, the "harmonic proportions" created by each division of the rectangle through the imposition of a square within it.

Wilkie created on the ground plane adjacent to the mound and his inversion of it a golden rectangle with squares interposed. It would remind the viewer of human civilization between the heights of Mount Olympus and the depths of the world beneath. In particular it would celebrate mankind's knowledge and accomplishments: the golden ratio or golden mean, the great myths of classical Greece, and Boughton's seventeenth- and eighteenth-century roots. Today musical performances are held in this remarkable setting as if Orpheus has always resided in this place where Wilkie's "temple" expresses the musician's genius.

Kim Wilkie says of his work: "Each place has its own special character and identity—a continuous conversation between the physical form and the lives lived and shaped within it. As a landscape architect, I try to understand the memories and associations embedded in a place and the natural flows of people, land, water, and climate."

SO ALSO HAVE the designers of these one hundred gardens drawn upon their time and place, their cultural roots, their beliefs and values—the intersection of their life history and the historical moment. And so it will be in the future as a new generation of landscape designers takes up their art, revering the archetype and discovering the genii of the place and of themselves.

A living wall at the Musée du quai Branly
in Paris, designed by Patrick Blanc.

A Noble Task

POSTSCRIPT

"**A GARDEN IS** the result of an arrangement of natural materials according to aesthetic laws; interwoven throughout are the artist's outlook on life, his past experiences, his affections, his attempts, his mistakes, and his successes," wrote Roberto Burle Marx of his work. Through one hundred great gardens we have seen how the very definition of beauty has changed from time to time and place to place. We have looked at the reasons for the changes. We have examined how designers' life histories intersect with the historical moment in which each lived and how their designs reflect their time, place, and personal interests.

Sir George Sitwell, author of *On the Making of Gardens*, concluded "To make a great garden, one must have a great idea or a great opportunity." We ask what ideas, beliefs, interests, values, and events will be expressed in landscape design in the future. As designers ponder the ways they will convey their thoughts and feelings they will likely draw upon past practices, adapting them to new occasions and duties as have those in the past.

William Robinson declared "The man who uses trees instead of pigments has a noble task." Landscape design, like other art forms, carries a message. What will we say through the medium of landscape design that reflects, challenges, or shapes tomorrow? These are the questions for those who will themselves take up the noble task.

Sources *and* Further Reading

I have used a wide variety of sources for each period of history and for each garden and have visited most of the one hundred gardens. Owners and curators generously shared information, many bringing out material from their libraries for my examination. The official websites of the one hundred gardens were useful as well as other websites, though the information was confirmed, as it always must be, through other reliable means. Most gardens provide a visitor's guide with the history and plan of the site. I have here cited only the most extensive. The list of general histories may be useful for further reading.

General Histories

Graham, Wade. *American Eden from Monticello to Central Park to Our Backyards: What Our Gardens Tell Us About Who We Are*. New York: Harper Collins, 2011.

Holmes, Caroline, ed. and introduction. *Icons of Garden Design*. Munich: Prestal Verlag, 2001.

Hunt, John Dixon. *A World of Gardens*. London: Reaktion, 2012.

Hyams, Edward. *A History of Gardens and Gardening*. New York: Praeger, 1971.

Jellicoe, Geoffrey, and Susan Jellicoe. *The Landscape of Man: Shaping the Environment from Prehistory to the Present Day*. 3rd ed. London: Thames and Hudson, 1995.

Jellicoe, Geoffrey, Susan Jellicoe, Patrick Goode, and Michael Lancaster. *The Oxford Companion to Gardens*. Oxford: Oxford University Press, 1986.

Kluckert, Ehrenfried. *European Garden Design from Classical Antiquity to the Present Day*. Königswinter, Germany: Tandem Verlag, 2007.

Lacey, Stephen. *Gardens of the National Trust*. Swindon: The National Trust, 2016.

McGuire, Diane Kostial. *Gardens of America: Three Centuries of Design*. Charlottesville, Virginia: Thomasson-Grant, 1989.

Moore, Charles W., William J. Mitchell, and William Turnbull Jr. *The Poetics of Gardens*. Cambridge, Massachusetts: MIT Press, 1993.

Rogers, Elizabeth Barlow. *Landscape Design: A Cultural and Architectural History*. New York: Harry N. Abrams, 2001.

Thacker, Christopher. *The History of Gardens*. Berkeley: University of California Press, 1979.

More than Flowers: An Introduction

Adams, William Howard. *Roberto Burle Marx: The Unnatural Art of the Garden*. New York: Museum of Modern Art, 1991.
Erikson, Erik H. *Life History and the Historical Moment*. New York: W.W. Norton, 1975.
Jefferson, Thomas, to Ellen Wayles Randolph Coolidge. 10 July 1805.

1 Piety and Protection

Bloch, Marc. *Feudal Society*. 2 vols. Chicago: University of Chicago Press, 1961.
Davis, R. H. C. *A History of Medieval Europe from Constantine to Saint Louis*. London: Longmans, 1957.
de la Mare, Walter. All That's Past. In *Collected Poems of Walter de la Mare*. London: Faber and Faber, 1944.
Duckett, Eleanor Shipley. *The Gateway to the Middle Ages: Monasticism*. Ann Arbor: University of Michigan Press, 1961.
Liddard, Robert, ed. *The Medieval Park: New Perspectives*. Cheshire, UK: Windgather Press, 2007.
The Pierpont Morgan Library. *Flowers in Books and Drawings ca. 940–1840*. New York: The Pierpont Morgan Library, 1980.
Sanecki, Kay N. *History of the English Herb Garden*. Foreword by Anthony Huxley. London: Ward Lock, 1992.

ALHAMBRA

Cid Acedo, Aurelio. *The Alhambra and Granada in Focus*. Granada, Spain: Edilux, 2006.
Hobhouse, Penelope. *Gardens of Persia*. London: Cassell Illustrated, 2003.
New York Botanical Garden. *Spanish Paradise: Gardens of the Alhambra*. New York: New York Botanical Garden, 2011.

QUEEN ELEANOR'S GARDEN

Landsberg, Sylvia. *The Medieval Garden*. London: British Museum, 1998.

OLD PALACE AT HATFIELD HOUSE

Hatfield House. *Hatfield House: Over 400 Years of History*. Introduction by Lord Salisbury. Peterborough, UK: Hatfield House and Jarrold Publishing, 2014.
Martyn, Trea. *Queen Elizabeth in the Garden*. London: Faber and Faber, 2008.
Way, Twigs. *The Tudor Garden: 1485–1603*. Oxford: Shire Publications, 2013.

2 The Measure of Mankind Is Man

Alberti, Leon Battista. *Leon Battista Alberti: On Painting*. Translated by Rocco Sinisgalli. Cambridge: Cambridge University Press, 2013.

Burckhardt, Jacob. *The Civilization of the Renaissance in Italy*. New York: Random House, 1954. First published 1860.

Cassirer, Ernst, Paul Oskar Kristeller, and John Herman Randall Jr., eds. *The Renaissance Philosophy of Man*. Chicago: University of Chicago Press, 1948.

Chatfield, Judith. *A Tour of Italian Gardens*. New York: Rizzoli, 1988.

Gilmore, Myron P. *The World of Humanism, 1453–1517*. New York: Harper & Brothers, 1952.

Ross, James Bruce, and Mary Martin McLauglin, eds. *The Portable Renaissance Reader*. New York: Viking, 1953.

Russell, Vivian. *Edith Wharton's Italian Gardens*. Boston: Little, Brown, 1998.

Shepherd, J. C., and Geoffrey Jellicoe. *Italian Gardens of the Renaissance*. London: Alec Tiranti, 1953. First published 1925.

Triggs, Harry Inigo. *The Art of Garden Design in Italy*. London: Longmans, 1906.

Wharton, Edith. *Italian Villas and Their Gardens*. New York: Rizzoli and the Mount Press, 2008. First published 1903.

VILLA MEDICI

Ballerini, Isabella Lapi. *The Medici Villas*. Rev. ed. Florence: Giunti, 2011.

Romitti, Ines, and Mariella Zoppi. *Gardens of Fiesole*. Florence: Alinea, 2000.

VILLA D'ESTE

Barisi, Isabella. *Guide to Villa d'Este*. Rome: De Luca Editori d'Arte, 2004.

Madonna, Maria Luisa. *Villa d'Este*. Rome: De Luca Editori d'Arte, 2003.

SACRO BOSCO (BOMARZO)

Frazer, James G. *The Golden Bough: A Study in Magic and Religion*. New York: Macmillan, 1956. First published 1922.

Society Giardino di Bomarzo. *Bomarzo: The Park of the Monsters*. Viterbo, Italy: Agnesotti, 2012.

VILLA LANTE

Ovid. *The Metamorphoses*. A. S. Kline Version. http://ovid.lib.virginia.edu/trans/Metamorph.htm. First published 8 AD.

Ryan, William B. F. *Noah's Flood: The New Scientific Discoveries about the Event that Changed History*. New York: Simon and Schuster, 2000.

VILLA ALDOBRANDINI

Evelyn, John. *The Diary of John Evelyn*. 2 vols. William Bray, ed. Akron, Ohio: M. Walter Dunne, 1901. First published 1818.

3 The Brink of Infinity

Adams, William Howard. *The French Garden 1500–1800*. New York: George Braziller, 1979.
Skinner, Stephen. *Sacred Geometry: Deciphering the Code*. New York: Sterling, 2006.

FRENCH BAROQUE AND ANDRÉ LE NÔTRE

Fox, Helen M. *André Le Nôtre: Garden Architect to Kings*. New York: Crown, 1962.
Hazelhurst, Franklin Hamilton. *Gardens of Illusion: The Genius of André Le Nostre*. Nashville: Vanderbilt University Press, 1980.
Vaux-le-Vicomte. Introduction by Patrice de Vogüé. Paris: Pro Libris, 2009.

ISOLA BELLA

Natale, Mauro, and Alessandro Morandotti. *The Borromeo Islands and the Angera Fortress*. Milan: Grafiche Milani, 2012.

HET LOO PALACE

De Jong, Erik. *Nature and Art: Dutch Garden and Landscape Architecture, 1650–1740*. Philadelphia: University of Pennsylvania Press, 2001.

4 A World of Wonders

Boorstin, Daniel J. *The Discoverers: A History of Man's Search to Know his World and Himself*. New York: Random House, 1983.
Pavord, Anna. *The Naming of Names: The Search for Order in the World of Plants*. New York: Bloomsbury, 2005.
Wulf, Andrea. *The Brother Gardeners: Botany, Empire and the Birth of an Obsession*. New York: Alfred A. Knopf, 2010.

L'ORTO BOTANICO

Goethe, Johann Wolfgang von. *The Metamorphosis of Plants*. Cambridge, Massachusetts: MIT Press, 2009. First published 1790.
New York Botanical Garden. *The Renaissance Herbal*. Foreword by Gregory Long. Bronx, New York: New York Botanical Garden, 2013.

HORTUS BOTANICUS

Eade, Simon. What is the Tulip Breaking Virus? *The Garden of Eaden*. http://gardenofeaden.blogspot. Co. uk/2009/04 what-is-tulip-breaking-virus.html.
Pavord, Anna. *The Tulip: The Story of a Flower That Has Made Men Mad*. New York: Bloomsbury, 1999.
van der Veen, Stans. *Hortus Botanicus*. Leiden, Netherlands: University of Leiden Press, n.d.

CHELSEA PHYSIC GARDEN

Minter, Sue. *The Apothecaries' Garden: A History of the Chelsea Physic Garden*. Foreword by HRH The Prince of Wales. Stroud, Gloucestershire: Sutton, 2000.

BARTRAM'S GARDEN

Bartram's Garden Catalogue of North American Plants 1783. London: Taylor and Francis, 1996.

Leighton, Ann. *American Gardens in the Eighteenth Century*. Boston: Houghton Mifflin, 1976.

Reid, Robin T. The Story of Bartram's Garden. *Smithsonian.com*. 12 April 2010. http://www.smithsonianmag.com/history/the-story-of-bartrams-garden-13572809/.

5 Augustan and Arcadian

Bender, John. *Ends of Enlightenment*. Palo Alto: Stanford University Press, 2012.

Hunt, John Dixon, and Peter Willis. *The Genius of the Place: The English Landscape Garden, 1620–1820*. New York: Harper & Row, 1975.

Lees-Milne, James. *Earls of Creation: Five Great Patrons of Eighteenth-Century Art*. London: Century Hutchinson in association with the National Trust, 1986. First published 1962.

Mowl, Timothy. *Gentlemen Gardeners: The Men Who Created the English Landscape Garden*. Stroud, Gloucestershire: The History Press, 2010.

Rogers, Elizabeth Barlow, Elizabeth S. Eustis, and John Bidwell. *Romantic Gardens: Nature, Art, and Landscape Design*. Jaffrey, New Hampshire: The Morgan Library and Museum in association with David. R. Godine, 2010.

Symes, Michael. *Garden Sculpture*. Princes Risborough: Shire Publications, 1996.

Walpole, Horace. *The History of the Modern Taste in Gardening*. Introduction by John Dixon Hunt. New York: Ursus, 1995. First printed 1771.

HADRIAN'S VILLA

Aurigemma, Salvatore. *Villa Adriana (Hadrian's Villa) Near Tivoli*. Tivoli: Grafiche Chicca, 1970.

Farrar, Linda. *Ancient Roman Gardens*. Stroud, Gloucestershire: Sutton, 1998.

Lanciano, Nicoletta. *Hadrian's Villa: Between Heaven and Earth*. Rome: Aperion, 2005.

Yourcenar, Marguerite. *Memoirs of Hadrian*. London: Penguin, 1959. First published 1951.

STUDLEY ROYAL

Greeves, Lydia. *Fountains Abby and Studley Royal*. Swindon: The National Trust, 1988.

ROUSHAM

Batey, Mavis. The Way to View Rousham by Kent's Gardener. *Garden History* 11 (1983): 125–132.

Campbell, Joseph. *The Hero with a Thousand Faces*. New York: Pantheon Books, 1949.

Chisholm, Linda A. *Charting a Hero's Journey*. New York: IPSL, 2000.

Jourdain, Margaret. *The Work of William Kent: Artist, Painter, Designer and Landscape Gardener*. Introduction by Christopher Hussey. London: Country Life, 1948.

Moogeridge, Hal. Notes on Kent's Garden at Rousham. *Journal of Garden History* 6 (1986): 187–226.

Mowl, Timothy. *William Kent: Architect, Designer, Opportunist*. London: Jonathan Cape, 2006.

Woodbridge, Kenneth. William Kent as Landscape-Gardener: A Re-appraisal. *Apollo* 50 (1974): 126–137.

Woodbridge, Kenneth. William Kent's Gardening: The Rousham Letters. *Apollo* 50 (1974): 282–291.

Yarwood, Doreen. *The Architecture of Italy*. New York: Harper and Row, 1969.

STOURHEAD

Turner, James. The Structure of Henry Hoare's Stourhead. *The Art Bulletin* 61 (Mar 1979): 68–77.

Woodbridge, Kenneth. *The Stourhead Landscape*. Swindon: The National Trust, 1978.

6 Place-Making

Brown, Jane. *The Omnipotent Magician: Lancelot 'Capability' Brown 1716–1783*. London: Chatto & Windus, 2011.

Felus, Kate. *The Secret Life of the Georgian Garden*. London: IB Tauris, 2016.

Mayer, Laura. *Capability Brown and the English Landscape Garden*. Oxford: Shire Publications, 2011.

Nicolson, Adam. *The Gentry: Stories of the English*. London: Harper, 2011.

Stroud, Dorothy. *Capability Brown*. Introduction by Christopher Hussey. London: Faber and Faber, 1975.

Turner, Roger. *Capability Brown and the Eighteenth-century English Landscape*. New York: Rizzoli, 1985.

STOWE

Bevington, Michael. *Stowe: The People and the Place*. Swindon: The National Trust, 2011.

PETWORTH

Thomas, Susan. The Eminently Capable Mr. Brown: Lancelot 'Capability' Brown and his magnificent tree moving machine. https://blogs.unimelb.edu.au/librarycollections/2016/09/08/the-eminently-capable-mr-brown-lancelot-capability-brown-and-his-magnificent-tree-moving-machine/.

BLENHEIM

Green, David. *Blenheim Palace*. Woodstock, Oxfordshire: Blenheim Estate Office, 1976. First published 1950.

Hogarth, William. *The Analysis of Beauty*. New Haven: Yale University Press, 1997. First published 1753.

NUNEHAM

Goldsmith, Oliver. *The Deserted Village*. Sydney, Australia: Wentworth Press, 2016. First published 1770.

Whitehead, William. On the Late Improvements at Nuneham. Quoted in Stroud, 192. First published 1789.

PARC JEAN-JACQUES ROUSSEAU

de Girardin, R. L. *A Tour to Ermenonville*. Edited with introductory notes by John Dixon Hunt. New York: Garland, 1982. First published 1783.

Rousseau, Jean-Jacques. *La Nouvelle Heloise* (*Julie, or the New Heloise*). University Park: Pennsylvania State University Press, 1968. First published 1761.

HAWKSTONE PARK

Burke, Edmund. *A Philosophical Enquiry into the Origin of our Ideas of the Sublime and the Beautiful*. Oxford: Oxford University Press, 1990. First published 1757.

Knight, Richard Payne. *The Landscape: A Didactic Poem in Three Books addressed to Uvedale Price, Esq*. Sydney, Australia: Wentworth Press, 2016. First published 1795.

Knight, Richard Payne. Online Books by Richard Payne Knight. http://onlinebooks.library.upenn.edu/webbin/book/lookupname?key=Knight%2C%20Richard%20Payne%2C%201751-1824.

7 Gaiety and "Gloomth"

Symes, Michael. *The English Rococo Garden*. Oxford: Shire Publications, 2011.

Walpole, Horace. *The History of the Modern Taste in Gardening*. Introduction by John Dixon Hunt. New York: Ursus, 1995. First published 1771.

CHINESE GARDENS

Ji Cheng. *The Craft of Gardens: The Classic Chinese Text on Garden Design*. Translated by Alison Hardie. Foreword by Maggie Keswick. New York: Better Link, 2012. First published 1631.

Keswick, Maggie. *The Chinese Garden: History, Art and Architecture*. Contributions and conclusion by Charles Jencks. New York: Rizzoli, 1978.

Li Zongwei. *The Classical Gardens of Suzhou*. New York: Better Link, 2011.

Qiao Yun. *Classical Chinese Gardens*. Hong Kong and Beijing: Joint Publishing and China Building Industry, 1982.

Temple, Sir William. *Upon the Gardens of Epicurus, with other* XVIIth *century Garden Essays*. London: Chatto and Windus, 1908. First published 1685.

Wang, Joseph C. *The Chinese Garden*. New York: Oxford University Press, 1998.

Wittkower, Rudolf. *Selected Lectures of Rudolf Wittkower: The Impact of Non-European Civilizations on the Art of the West*. Cambridge: Cambridge University Press, 1989. 145–192.

WREST PARK

Hann, Andrew, and Shelley Garland. *Wrest Park*. Rev. ed. London: English Heritage, 2012.

TAJ MAHAL

Villiers-Stuart, Constance Mary. *Gardens of the Great Mughals*. London: Adam & Charles Black, 1913.

SEZINCOTE

Betjeman, John. Summoned by Bells. In *Collected Poems*. London: John Murray, 2006. First published 1960.

Repton, Humphry. *Observations on the Theory and Practice of Landscape Gardening*. Charleston: Forgotten Books, 2012. First published 1803.

Thomas, Graham, David Peake, Susanna Peake, and Edward Peake. *Sezincote House*. n.p., n.d.

POPE'S GROTTO

Batey, Mavis. *Alexander Pope: The Poet and the Landscape*. London: Barn Elms, 2006.

Willson, Anthony Beckles. Alexander Pope's Grotto in Twickenham.

Garden History 26 (Summer 1998): 31-59.

STRAWBERRY HILL

Iddon, John. *Strawberry Hill and Horace Walpole*. London: Scala, 2011.

PAINSHILL

Symes, Michael. *MR Hamilton's Elysium: The Garden of Painshill*. London: Frances Lincoln, 2010.

8 Three Men, Two Nations, One Passion

Leighton, Ann. *American Gardens in the Eighteenth Century*. Boston: Houghton Mifflin, 1976.

Wulf, Andrea. *Founding Gardeners: The Revolutionary Generation, Nature, and the Shaping of the American Nation*. New York: Alfred A. Knopf, 2011.

MOUNT VERNON

Griswold, Mac. *Washington's Gardens at Mount Vernon*. Boston: Houghton Mifflin, 1999.

George Washington's Mount Vernon: Official Guide Book. Mount Vernon, Virginia: Mount Vernon Ladies' Association, n.d.

SAN CARLOS BORROMEO (CARMEL MISSION)

Moffet, Alice, ed. *Missions of California*. Camarillo, California: Charm Kraft Industries, 2010.

Dunmire, William W. *The Gardens of New Spain*. Austin: University of Texas Press, 2004.

MONTICELLO AND THOMAS JEFFERSON

Betts, Edwin M., and Hazlehurst Bolton Perkins. *Thomas Jefferson's Flower Garden at Monticello*. Revised and enlarged by Peter J. Hatch. Charlottesville: University of Virginia Press, 2000.

Dillon, Richard. *Meriwether Lewis: A Biography*. New York: Coward-McCann, 1965.

Phillips, H. Wayne. *Plants of the Lewis and Clark Expedition*. Missoula: Mountain Press, 2003.

Hatch, Peter J. *The Gardens of Thomas Jefferson's Monticello*. Charlottesville, Virginia: Thomas Jefferson Foundation, 1992.

Jefferson, Thomas. *The Garden and Farm Books of Thomas Jefferson*. Robert C. Baron, ed. Golden, Colorado: Fulcrum, 1987. Compiled 1766–1824.

Loewer, Peter. *Jefferson's Garden*. Mechanicsburg, Pennsylvania: Stackpole Books, 2004.

Meacham, Jon. *Thomas Jefferson: The Art of Power*. New York: Random House, 2012.

Nichols, Frederick Doveton, and Ralph E. Griswold. *Thomas Jefferson Landscape Architect*. Charlottesville: University of Virginia Press, 1978.

ROYAL BOTANIC GARDENS, KEW, AND JOSEPH BANKS

O'Brian, Patrick. *Joseph Banks: A Life*. London: Collins Harvill, 1987.

Paterson, Allen. *The Gardens at Kew*. London: Frances Lincoln, 2008.

Wulf, Andrea. *The Brother Gardeners: Botany, Empire and the Birth of an Obsession*. New York: Alfred A. Knopf, 2010.

9 Designing for Democracy

THE PICTURESQUE AND ANDREW JACKSON DOWNING

Alden, Henry Mills, Frederick Lewis Allen, Lee Foster Hartman, and Thomas Bucklin Wells, eds. The Second War for Independence. *Harper's New Monthly Magazine* 68 (Dec 1883–May 1884): 754.

Emerson, Ralph Waldo. *Complete Essays*. New York: Modern Library, 1950. 3–44, 87–107. Nature first published 1836. The Transcendentalist first published 1843.

Downing, Andrew Jackson. *A Treatise on the Theory and Practice of Landscape Gardening*. Facsimile edition. New York: Funk & Wagnalls, 1967. First published 1841.

Long, Gregory R. *Historic Houses of the Hudson River Valley, 1663–1915*. New York: Rizzoli, 2004.

Rogers, Elizabeth Barlow, Elizabeth S. Eustis, and John Bidwell. *Romantic Gardens: Nature, Art, and Landscape Design*. Jaffrey, New Hampshire: The Morgan Library and Museum in association with David R. Godine, 2010.

Schuyler, David. *Apostle of Taste: Andrew Jackson Downing, 1815–1852*. Baltimore: Johns Hopkins University Press, 1996.

Schwartz, Sheila. *Humanizing Landscapes: Geography, Culture and the Magoon Collection*. Poughkeepsie: Frances Loehman Loeb Art Center Vassar College, 2000.

Tatum, George B., and Elisabeth Blair MacDoughall. *Prophet with Honor: The Career of Andrew Jackson Downing, 1815–1852*. Washington D.C.: Dumbarton Oaks, 1989.

Toole, Robert M. *Landscape Gardens on the Hudson, a History: The Romantic Ages, the Great Estates and the Birth of American Landscape Architecture*. Introduction by Elizabeth Barlow Rogers. Hensonville, New York: Black Dome, 2010.

FREDERICK LAW OLMSTED

Beveridge, Charles E., Lauren Meier, and Irene Mills, eds. *Frederick Law Olmsted: Plans and Views of Public Parks*. Baltimore: Johns Hopkins University Press, 2015.

Martin, Justin. *Genius of Place: The Life of Frederick Law Olmsted*. Cambridge, Massachusetts: Da Capo Press, 2011.

MONTGOMERY PLACE

Haley, Jacquetta M. *Pleasure Grounds: Andrew Jackson Downing and Montgomery Place*. Tarrytown, New York: Sleepy Hollow Press, 1988.

MOUNT AUBURN CEMETERY

Bigelow, Jacob. *A History of Mt. Auburn Cemetery*. Cambridge, Massachusetts: Applewood Books, 1988. First published 1860.

Linden-Ward, Blanche. *Silent City on a Hill: Landscapes of Memory and Boston's Mount Auburn Cemetery*. Columbus: Ohio University Press, 1989.

CENTRAL PARK

Miller, Sara Cedar. *Central Park, an American Masterpiece: A Comprehensive History of the Nation's First Urban Park*. New York: Harry N. Abrams, 2003.

BUFFALO PARK SYSTEM

Kowsky, Francis R. *The Best Planned City in the World: Olmsted, Vaux and the Buffalo Park System*. Amherst: University of Massachusetts Press, 2013.

10 Bedding-Out and Getting-On

Longford, Elizabeth. *Queen Victoria: Born to Succeed*. New York: Harper and Row, 1964.

van Ravenswaay, Charles. *A Nineteenth Century Garden*. New York: Main Street, 1977.

von Goethe, Wolfgang Johann. *Theory of Colours*. Mineola, New York: Dover Publications, 2006. First published 1840.

NATIONAL BOTANIC GARDENS OF IRELAND

Woods, May, and Arete S. Warren. *Glass Houses: A History of Greenhouses, Orangeries and Conservatories*. London: Aurum Press, 1996.

11 Searching for Earthly Paradise

Allingham, Helen and Stewart Dick, *The Cottage Homes of England*. London: E. Arnold, 1909.

Brown, Jane. *Gardens of a Golden Afternoon*. Middlesex, England: Penguin, 1982.

Burdick, John. *William Morris: Redesigning the World*. New York: New Line, 2006.

Festing, Sally. *Gertrude Jekyll*. London: Viking, 1991.

Hilton, Tim. *John Ruskin*. New Haven: Yale University Press, 2002.

Peacock, David. Developing Human Values. *Knowing and Doing*. New York: IPSL, 2005. 109–116.

Rosenberg, John D., ed. *The Genius of John Ruskin*. New York: George Braziller, 1963.

Ruskin, John. *Selected Writings*. Oxford: Oxford University Press, 2004.

Tankard, Judith B. *Gardens of the Arts and Crafts Movement*. New York: Harry N. Abrams, 2004.

Tooley, Michael, and Primrose Amander, eds. *Gertrude Jekyll: Essays on the Life of a Working Amateur*. Durham, England: Michaelmas Press, 1995.

Warrell, Ian, ed. *J. M. W. Turner*. With an essay by Franklin Kelly. London: Tate Publishing, 2007.

Way, Twigs. *The Cottage Garden*. Oxford: Shire Publications, 2011.

KELMSCOTT MANOR

Naylor, Gilliam, ed. *William Morris by Himself: Designs and Writings*. New York: Little, Brown and Company, 1988.

MUNSTEAD WOOD

Jekyll, Gertrude. *Colour Schemes for the Flower Garden*. Woodbridge, Suffolk: Antique Collectors' Club, 1983. First published 1908.

Jekyll, Gertrude. *Wood and Garden*. Introduced and revised by Graham Stuart Thomas. Salem, New Hampshire: Ayer, 1983. First published 1899.

Munstead Wood, House and Gardens. Godalming, Surrey: Maureen Lavelle, n.d.

UPTON GREY MANOR

Wallinger, Rosamund. *Gertrude Jekyll's Lost Garden: The Restoration of an Edwardian Masterpiece*. Woodbridge, Suffolk: Antique Collectors' Club, 2000.

ROYAL HORTICULTURAL SOCIETY ROCK GARDEN AT WISLEY

Jekyll, Gertrude. *Wall and Water Gardens*. Introduced and revised by Graham Stuart Thomas. Salem, New Hampshire: Ayer, 1983. First published 1899.

LINDISFARNE (HOLY ISLAND)

Aslet, Clive. Lindisfarne: Country Life's Castle. *Country Life*, 9 July 2014, 59–65.

12 Lush and Fleeting, Spare and Lasting

GIVERNY

Cogniat, Raymond. *The Century of the Impressionists*. New York: Crown, 1978.

Fell, Derek. *The Impressionist Garden*. London: Frances Lincoln, 1994.

Monet, Claude, and Genevieve Morgan, ed. *Monet: The Artist Speaks*. San Francisco: Collins Publishers, 1996.

Murray, Elizabeth. *Monet's Passion: Ideas, Inspiration and Insights from the Painter's Gardens*. San Francisco. Pomegranate Artbooks, 1989.

New York Botanical Garden. *Monet's Garden*. New York: New York Botanical Garden, 2012.

Russell, Vivian. *Monet's Water Lilies*. London: Frances Lincoln, 1998.

JAPANESE GARDENS

Jiro Takei and Marc P. Keane. *Sakuteiki: Visions of the Japanese Garden*. Boston: Tuttle, 2001. Written eleventh century.

Keane, Marc P. *Japanese Garden Design*. Boston: Tuttle, 1996.

Kinzo Honda. *Zen Gardens*. Kyoto: Mitsumura Suiko Shoin, 1990.

Mansfield, Stephen. *Japanese Stone Gardens: Origins, Meaning, Form*. Tokyo: Tuttle, 2009.

Tatsuo Ishimoto. *The Art of the Japanese Garden*. New York: Crown, 1958.

VON SIEBOLD

van der Veen, Stans. *Hortus Botanicus*. Leiden, Netherlands: University of Leiden, n.d. 59–70.

13 Bringing Home "Abroad"

Adams, Henry. *The Education of Henry Adams*. Boston: Houghton Mifflin, 1918.

Adler, Kathleen, Eric E. Hirshler, and H. Barbara Weinberg. *Americans in Paris 1860–1900*. London: National Gallery, 2006.

James, Henry. *The Ambassadors*. New York: Harper, 1906.

Veysey, Laurence R. *The Emergence of the American University*. Chicago: University of Chicago Press, 1970.

Wharton, Edith. *Italian Villas and Their Gardens*. New York: Century, 1903.

POWERSCOURT

Powerscourt Estate. Enniskerry, Ireland: Powerscourt Tourist Office, Powerscourt Estate, n.d.

SUTTON COURTENAY MANOR

Brown, Jane. *Eminent Gardeners: Some People of Influence and Their Gardens, 1880–1980*. London: Viking, 1990. 60–76.

Hayward, Allyson. *Norah Lindsay: The Life and Art of a Garden Designer*. London: Frances Lincoln, 2007.

STAN HYWET

Adams, Michael Henry. *Akron's Stan Hywet Hall and Gardens*. Akron: University of Akron Press, 2000.

Tankard, Judith B. *The Gardens of Ellen Biddle Shipman*. Sagaponack, New York: Saga Press, 1996.

KYKUIT, FILOLI, OLD WESTBURY GARDENS

Griswold, Mac, and Eleanor Weller. *The Golden Age of American Gardens: Proud Owners, Private Estates, 1890–1940*. New York: Harry N. Abrams, 1991.

Hurt, Jethro Meriwether, ed. *Old Westbury Gardens: A History and a Guide*. Huntington Station, New York: Old Westbury Gardens, n.d.

Pierson, Mary Louise, Cynthia Altman, and Ann Rockefeller Roberts. *Kykuit: The Rockefeller Family Home*. New York: Abbeville Press, 1998.

Purvis, Andrew. Filoli: Garden of a Golden Age. *Smithsonian Magazine* 41 (May 2010): 61–65. http://www.smithsonianmag.com/travel/filoli-garden-of-a-golden-age-14012904/.

BALBOA PARK

Alexander, Hartly Burr, Ralph Adams Cram, and George Ellery Hale, Lee Lawrie, C. Howard Walker, and Charles Harris Whitaker. *Bertram Grosvenor Goodhue: Architect and Master of Many Arts*. New York: American Institute of Architects, 1925.

Goodhue, Bertram Grosvenor. *A Book of Architectural and Decorative Drawings*. Germany: P. Wenzel and M. Krakow, 1904.

IFORD MANOR

Edwards, Ambra. Pure Peto. *Gardens Illustrated* 191: 66–72.

McTernan, Cinead. Craftwork: Iford. *The English Garden*, Aug–Sept 2013, 31–34.

Peto, Harold A. *The Boke of Iford*. Marlborough: Libanus Press, 1917.

14 The Poppies Grow

Manchester, William. *The Arms of Krupp*. Boston: Little, Brown, 1968.

Owen, Wilfrid. A Terre (Being the Philosophy of Many Soldiers). In *A Little Treasury of Modern Poetry*. New York: Charles Scribner's Sons, 1952. First published 1920.

Tuchman, Barbara W. *The Guns of August*. New York: Macmillan, 1962.

HIDCOTE

Brown, Jane. *Eminent Gardeners: Some People of Influence and Their Gardens, 1880–1980*. London: Viking, 1990. 40–59.

Clarke, Ethne. *Hidcote: The Making of a Garden*. Rev. ed. Foreword by Roy Strong. New York: W.W. Norton, 2009.

Finding Major Johnston. http://aslongasyouhaveagarden.blogspot.com/2015/02/finding-major-johnston.html.

The National Trust. *Hidcote Manor Garden* with essays by Vita Sackville-West and Alvilde Lees-Milne. Swindon: The National Trust, 1979.

Pavord, Anna. *Hidcote Manor Garden*. Swindon: The National Trust, 1993.

DUMBARTON OAKS

Balmori, Diana, Diane Kostial McGuire, and Eleanor M. McPeck. *Beatrix Farrand's American Landscapes, Her Gardens and Campuses*. Sagaponack, New York: Saga Press, 1985.

Tamulevich, Susan. *Dumbarton Oaks: Garden into Art*. Foreword by Philip Johnson. New York: Monacelli, 2001.

SISSINGHURST

Brown, Jane. *Vita's Other World: A Gardening Biography of V. Sackville-West*. Middlesex, England: Viking, 1985.

Glendinning, Victoria. *Vita: The Life of Vita Sackville-West*. Middlesex, England: Penguin Books, 1984.

Nicolson, Harold. *Diaries and Letters, 1930–1939*. London: William Collins Sons, 1966.

Nicolson, Nigel. *The Portrait of a Marriage*. London: Weidenfeld and Nicolson, 1973.

Nicolson, Nigel. *Sissinghurst Castle: An Illustrated History*. Swindon: The National Trust, 1964.

Sackville-West, Vita. *The Garden*. London: Frances Lincoln, 2004. First published 1946.

Sackville-West, Vita. *The Land*. London: William Heinemann, 1926.

Sackville-West, Vita. *In Your Garden Again*. London: Michael Joseph, 1953.

Scott-James, Anne. *Sissinghurst: The Making of a Garden*. London: Michael Joseph, 1975.

LADEW TOPIARY GARDENS

Weeks, Christopher. *"Perfectly Delightful": The Life and Gardens of Harvey Ladew*. Baltimore: Johns Hopkins University Press, 1999.

GREAT DIXTER

Anderton, Stephen. *Christopher Lloyd: His Life at Great Dixter*. London: Random House UK, 2010.

Lloyd, Christopher. *In My Garden*. Frank Ronan, ed. New York: Macmillan, 1994.

Lloyd, Christopher. *Meadows*. Portland, Oregon: Timber Press, 2004.

Lloyd, Christopher. *The Well-Tempered Garden*. New York: E.P. Dutton, 1971.

15 Less Is More

Bradley-Hole, Christopher. *Making the Modern Garden*. New York: Monacelli, 2007.

Brown, Jane. *The Modern Garden*. New York: Princeton Architectural Press, 2000.

NAUMKEAG

Choate, Mabel. *Naumkeag Garden*. Stockbridge, Massachusetts: n.p., 1965.

FLAMENGO PARK AND COPACABANA BEACH

Adams, William Howard. *Roberto Burle Marx: The Unnatural Art of the Garden*. New York: The Museum of Modern Art, 1991.

Hoffman, Jens, and Claudia J. Nahson. *Roberto Burle Marx: Brazilian Modernist*. New Haven: Yale University Press, 2016.

DEWEY DONNELL RANCH (EL NOVILLERO)

Church, Thomas Dolliver. *Gardens Are for People*. 3rd ed. Berkeley: University of California Press, 1995. First published 1955.

MILLER HOUSE

Brooks, Bradley C. *Miller House and Garden*. Foreword by Maxwell L. Anderson. New York: Assouline, 2011.

Kiley, Dan, and Jane Amidon. *The Complete Works of America's Master Landscape Architect*. Boston: Bullfinch, 1999.

PARC ANDRÉ CITROËN

Clément, Gilles, and Philippe Rahm. *Environ(ne)ment: Approaches for Tomorrow*. Milan: Skira, 2006.

16 This Fragile Earth, Our Island Home

The Best of Organic Gardening 1942–2015. *Organic Gardening* 62, Feb-Mar 2015.

Carson, Rachel. *The Silent Spring*. New York: Houghton Mifflin, 1962.

Stein, Sara. *Noah's Garden: Restoring the Ecology of Our Own Back Yards*. New York: Houghton Mifflin, 1993.

Tallamy, Douglas W. *Bringing Nature Home: How You Can Sustain Wildlife with Native Plants*. Rev. ed. Foreword by Rick Darke. Portland, Oregon: Timber Press, 2007.

GRAVETYE MANOR

Bisgrove, Richard. Wild Bill's Words. *The English Garden*, Feb-Mar 2013, 25–30.

Robinson, William. *The English Flower Garden*. London: Bloomsbury, 1996. First published 1883.

Robinson, William. *Gravetye Manor or Twenty Years' Work Round an Old Manor House*. London: John Murray, 1911.

Robinson, William, and Rick Darke. *The Wild Garden*. Expanded ed. Portland, Oregon: Timber Press, 2009. First published 1870.

COLUMBUS PARK

Jensen, Jens. *Siftings*. Baltimore: Johns Hopkins University Press, 1990.

SEA RANCH

Logan, William Bryant. Going with the Flow. *House and Garden*, Oct 1986, 118–124.

McGuigan, Cathleen. The Sea Ranch at 50. *Architectural Record*. http://archrecord.construction.com/features/2015/1504-The-Sea-Ranch-at-50.asp.

Sonoma Magazine Staff. The Sea Ranch Coastal Legacy. *Sonoma Magazine*. http://www.sonomamag.com/sea-ranch-coastal-legacy/.

HIGH LINE

David, Josh, and Robert Hammond. *High Line: The Inside Story of New York City's Park in the Sky*. New York: Farrar, Straus and Giroux, 2011.

Oudolf, Piet, and Rick Darke. *Gardens of the High Line: Elevating the Nature of Modern Landscapes*. Portland, Oregon: Timber Press, 2017.

HIGHGROVE

HRH The Prince of Wales with Stephanie Donaldson. *The Elements of Organic Gardening: Highgrove, Clarence House, Birkhall*. Carlsbad, California: Kales Press, 2007.

Mitchell, Sandy. Prince Charles—Not Your Typical Radical. *National Geographic*, May 2006, 96–105. http://ngm.nationalgeographic.com/features/world/europe/england/cornwall-text/1.

NATIVE PLANT GARDEN AT THE NEW YORK BOTANICAL GARDEN

Cohen, Susan. *The Inspired Landscape: Twenty-one Leading Landscape Architects Explore the Creative Process*. Foreword by Peter Walker. Portland, Oregon: Timber Press, 2015. 24–35.

Marinelli, Janet. Native Gardens: They Are Not Just Naturalistic Anymore. *Public Garden* 24 (2009): 5–6.

van Sweden, James. *Gardening with Nature*. New York: Random House, 1997.

17 Reverence for the Archetype

Pope, Alexander. *Of Taste, an Epistle to the Rt. Hon. Richard, Earl of Burlington*. Farmington Hills, Michigan: Gale Ecco, 2010. First published 1731.

Scully, Vincent. *The Earth, the Temple and the Gods: Greek Sacred Architecture*. Rev. ed. New Haven: Yale University Press, 1979.

NATIONAL SEPTEMBER 11 MEMORIAL

Walker, Peter, and Melanie Simo. *Invisible Gardens: The Search for Modernism in the American Landscape*. Cambridge, Massachusetts: MIT Press, 1994.

STORM KING ART CENTER

Stern, H. Peter, Peter Bienstock, and Irving Lavin. *Earth, Sky and Sculpture: Storm King Art Center*. Mountainville, New York: Storm King Art Center, 2000.

TORONTO MUSIC GARDEN

Messervy, Julie Moir. *Contemplative Gardens*. Charlottesville, Virginia: Howell Press, 1990.

Messervy, Julie Moir. *The Toronto Music Garden Inspired by Bach*. Introduction by Yo-Yo Ma. Saxtons River, Vermont: Julie Moir Messervy Design Studio, 2009.

SHAKESPEARE GARDEN AT VASSAR COLLEGE

Hales, Mick. *Shakespeare in the Garden*. New York: Harry N. Abrams, 2006. 37–49.

GARDEN OF COSMIC SPECULATION

Jencks, Charles. *The Garden of Cosmic Speculation*. London: Frances Lincoln, 2005.

SHUTE

Spens, Michael. *Gardens of the Mind: The Genius of Geoffrey Jellicoe*. Woodbridge, Suffolk: Antique Collectors Club, 1992.

Spens, Michael. *Jellicoe at Shute*. London: Academy Editions, 1993.

BOUGHTON HOUSE

Cohen, Susan. *The Inspired Landscape: Twenty-one Leading Landscape Architects Explore the Creative Process*. Foreword by Peter Walker. Portland, Oregon: Timber Press, 2015. 216–225.

Wilkie, Kim. *Led by the Land*. London: Frances Lincoln, 2012.

Postscript: A Noble Task

Adams, William Howard. *Roberto Burle Marx: The Unnatural Art of the Garden*. New York: Museum of Modern Art, 1991.

Robinson, William. *The English Flower Garden*. London: Bloomsbury, 1996. First published 1883.

Sitwell, George. *On the Making of Gardens*. Boston: David R. Godine, 2003. First published 1909.

Acknowledgments *and* Permissions

Upon learning about this book, Michael Garber scarcely drew a breath before agreeing to serve as the chief photographer. It was for me a happy partnership as I knew his work and was convinced his pictures would illustrate the text with beauty and clarity. We were both fortunate that his wife, architect Stephanie Garber, was equally willing to offer her keen eye, research skills, and organizational ability. The official readers, Humphrey Tonkin, University Professor of the Humanities, President Emeritus of the University of Hartford (Connecticut), and author of *The Faerie Queene*, and Stephen Sinon, Head of Special Collections, Research and Archives at the LuEsther T. Mertz Library of the New York Botanical Garden were knowledgeable, thorough, and helpful in their suggestions. Timber Press staff were supportive, skilled, knowledgeable, and pleasant in leading me through the process, especially Andrew Beckman, Eve Goodman, Sarah Milhollin, and Adrianna Sutton. Of course, any faults in the book are my responsibility.

Owners were welcoming and informative. I especially want to thank HRH Prince Charles for allowing his home Highgrove to be included in the book. Alexandre de Vogüé, co-owner of Vaux-le-Vicomte, spent time correcting points of the château's history. Sandra Donnell and Bruce Donnell returned to Sonoma especially to meet the photographer. At the Garden of Cosmic Speculation Charles Jencks and head gardener Alistair Clark explained the governing concepts and gave permission for their photograph to appear in the book. Other gracious owners include Camillo Aldobrandini, Villa Aldobrandini; Federicka Bettini, Sacro Bosco; Contessa Marina Borromeo, Isola Bella; Lady Clark, Munstead Wood; Charles Cottrell-Dormer, Rousham; John Hignett, Elizabeth Cartwright-Hignett, and William Cartwright-Hignett, Iford Manor; The Hon. Simon Howard, Castle Howard; John and Suzy Lewis, Shute House; Lorenzo Mazzini, Villa Medici; Fred and Barbara Ifeld, Jim and Mary Ray, and Alison Owings and J. B. Perdue, Sea Ranch; Edward Peake, Sezincote; Richard Scott tenth Duke of Buccleuch, Boughton House; Patrice Taravella, Prieuré Notre-Dame d'Orsan; Mr. and Mrs. Anthony Warne, Sutton Courtenay Manor; and John and Rosamund Wallinger, Upton Grey Manor. In addition Piet Oudolf and his wife, Anja, welcomed us for the open garden day at their home in the Netherlands, he allowing his picture, taken on the occasion, to be used in the book.

Curators, directors, and archeologists were invaluable: Benedetta Adembri and Annamaria Stefani, Hadrian's Villa; Cynthia Altman, Kykuit; Corinne Charpentier, Parc Jean-Jacques Rousseau; Marina Cogotti, Villas d'Este and Lante; Emily Emerick, Ladew Topiary Gardens; Todd Forrest and Michael Hagen, New York Botanical Garden; Joel T.

Fry, Bartram's Garden; Trish Fry, Annapolis Royal Historic Gardens; Gail Griffin, Dumbarton Oaks; Judy Halberg, John Whipple House; Colleen Henry, Naumkeag; Matthew Jebb, National Botanic Gardens of Ireland; Jim Salyards, Filoli; Jason Scism, Vassar Shakespeare Garden; Andrew Thomason, Gravetye; Angelique Van den Eerenbeemd, Paleis Het Loo; Caroline Wellon, Hawkstone: and Gavin Williams, Kelmscott.

College and university professors John Bender, Stanford University; Harvey Flad, Vassar College; David Peacock, Roehampton University, London; Anna Stevens, University of Padua; Gerda van Uffelen, Hortus Botanicus, Leiden, Netherlands; Howard Wolf, University of Buffalo; and Mariella Zoppi, University of Florence, gave excellent advice and information as did David Paton, Executive Principal of the Radnor House School. I gratefully acknowledge my supportive New York Botanical Garden colleagues including Gregory Long, President, and Susan Cohen, Barbara Corcoran, William Harris Einhorn, Todd Forest, Nancy Gerlach-Spriggs, Michael Hagen, Michael A. Ruggiero, and Lisa Whitmer. I here pay tribute to my first NYBG teacher of the history of landscape design, Charles A. Bonnes.

I thank the National Trust for granting permission to include Cliveden, Hidcote, Lindisfarne Castle, Petworth House and Park, Sissinghurst, Stourhead, Stowe, and Studley Royal. The Royal Horticultural Society allowed the inclusion of the Jekyll rock garden at Wisley and English Heritage for Wrest Park.

In addition I appreciate help from and the granting of permission given by the Collaboration of the Patronato de la Alhambra y Generalife; Anne Hathaway's Cottage and Gardens/Shakespeare Birthplace Trust; Biltmore Hotel; Château de Versailles; Domaine de Chantilly; Friends of the High Line; Fondation Claude Monet, Giverny; Global Retreat Centre, Nuneham Courtenay; Gravetye Manor; Great Dixter House and Gardens; The Great Hall Winchester, Queen Eleanor's Garden; The Greenpark Foundation Inc., Paley Park; Hatfield House; Hawktone Park; Indianapolis Museum of Art, Miller House and Garden; Ipswich Museum, John Whipple House; John Bartram Association; Kykuit National Trust site administered by the Rockefeller Brothers Fund; The Lutyens Trust, Lindisfarne; Middleton Place; Montgomery Place Historic Hudson; Mount Auburn Cemetery, a National Historic Landmark; Mount Vernon Ladies' Association which owns and operates Mount Vernon; National September 11 Memorial & Museum; the New York Botanical Garden; Old Westbury Gardens; Painshill Park Trust; Powerscourt Estate; San Carlos Borromeo de Carmelo Mission; the Sea Ranch Association; Springside Landscape Restoration; the staff and volunteers of Stan Hywet Hall & Gardens; Storm King Art Center; Strawberry Hill House; Thomas Jefferson Foundation, Inc., Monticello; and the Trustees of Reservations, Naumkeag.

Artists, organizations, and photographers who gave permission for their work to appear are listed on the photo and illustrations credits pages. Their cooperation is very much appreciated.

Marzia Bortolin and Eugenio Magnani of the Italian Government Tourist Board in New York paved the way in Italy with the help of Falminia Sanaelli and Federica Iudicello of the Regione Lazin, Paolo Rosso and Alessandra Segato of Regione Veneto, Alberto Peruzzini, Ilaria Crescioli, and Susanna Scalia of the Toscana Promozione, and Joe Maniscalco of Auto Europe.

And, saving the best until last, members of my family helped in many ways. My daughters Eleanor Landauer and Peggy Marsh gave wise advice and Kate Chisholm put her expertise in writing, editing, and publishing to work on the final document. My husband, Alan, always a good companion, traveled with me to the gardens, making astute observations and the necessary arrangements. He saved me both technologically and emotionally from many a potential computer disaster, listened with interest as I worked through my ideas and problems, and, while I wrote about gardens, did our gardening.

Photo *and* Illustration Credits

Illustrations by Adrianna Sutton, pages 75, 273

Alan L. Chisholm, pages 44–45, 47, 98, 219 top left and right

© Andy Goldsworthy, Courtesy Galerie Lelong, New York, photographed by Michael D. Garber, page 467 top

Anne Hathaway's Cottage and Gardens/Shakespeare Birthplace Trust, photographed by Michael D. Garber, page 295

Archives & Special Collections, Vassar College Library, Ph.f 17.28 Shakespeare Garden, page 473

Charles Bonnes, pages 179–182, 190 above right, 191 top, 266–267, 490

Charles Jencks, page 477 top

©Dumbarton Oaks Research Library and Collection, Rare Book Collection, Washington D.C., page 382

Eleanor Chisholm Landauer, pages 184, 186–187, 189, 190 above left and below right, 297 top left and bottom

Ellen Biddle Shipman plan photographed by Michael D. Garber by permission of Stan Hywet Hall & Gardens, page 350 top right

GAP Photos / Highgrove, page 444

GAP Photos / Highgrove; A. Butler / The walled garden was designed by Lady Salisbury and the Prince, page 446 top

GAP Photos / Highgrove / A. Lawson, page 445

GAP Photos/Highgrove / The Stumpery was created by Julian and Isabel Bannerman, page 446 bottom

GAP Photos/Jonathan Buckley, page 403

© 2017 The Isamu Noguchi Foundation and Garden Museum, New York / Artists Right Society (ARS), New York, photographed by Michael D. Garber, page 466

John Singer Sargent, used with permission from The Biltmore Company, Asheville, North Carolina, page 265

Ladew Topiary Gardens, Monkton, Maryland, page 394

Leonardo Finotti, page 412 right

Courtesy of The Lewis Walpole Library, Yale University, page 205

Mark di Suvero, Mother Peace, 1970; Collection Storm Art Center, Mountainville, New York, Gift of Ralph E. Ogden Foundation, Inc., photographed by Michael D. Garber, page 465

© Maya Lin Studio, courtesy Pace Gallery, photographed by Michael D. Garber, page 467 bottom

Courtesy of the Middleton Place Foundation, Charleston, South Carolina, pages 218, 219 bottom

Mildred Bliss, circa 1920. HUGFP 76.74p (Box 9), Harvard University Archives, page 381

© National Trust, original photographer unknown, page 388

Pablo Picasso, Les Demoiselles d'Avignon, Acquired through the Lillie P. Bliss Bequest. © Estate of Pablo Picasso / Artists Rights Society (ARS) New York, Digital Image © The Museum of Modern Art / Licensed by SCALA / Art Resource, NY, page 406

Paleis Het Loo, page 91

Rick Darke, page 441

© Salvador Dalí, Fundació Gala-Salvador Dalí / DACS, Artist Rights Society, Tate Images, London 2017, page 61 right

Salvator Rosa, Louvre, photo: Franck Raux © RMN-Grand Palais / Art Resource, NY, page 168

Susan Cohen, pages 326, 327, 328–329, 330, 332–333, 334–335, 336

Thomas Church plan photographed by Michael D. Garber by permission of the Donnell family, page 416

William Nicholson, National Portrait Gallery, London, page 290

Wikimedia Commons

Used under a Creative Commons Attribution 2.0 Generic license

Jean-Pierre Dalbéra, Victoria and Albert Museum, page 297 top right

xlibber, pages 136–137 left

Used under a Creative Commons Attribution-Share Alike 2.0 Generic license

Lee Cannon, page 414

Used under a Creative Commons Attribution 3.0 Unported license

CSIRO, Malcolm Paterson, page 110 bottom

Used under a Creative Commons Attribution-Share Alike 3.0 Germany license

Georg Menzel, page 401

Used under a Creative Commons Attribution-Share Alike 3.0 Unported license

颐园新居, page 177

Captain-tucker, page 357 right

Chris 73 / Wikimedia Commons (http://commons.wikimedia.org/), page 75 bottom

Ctorbann, page 360

Hiroshige, page 339

Lukevalles, page 357 left

Mteixeira62, pages 5, 415 top
Yanajin33, page 325

Used under a Creative Commons Attribution 4.0 International license
Wellcome Images, page 107

Used under a Creative Commons Attribution-Share Alike 4.0 International license
Vitorhugobr, page 415 bottom

Used under a GNU Free Documentation License Version 1.2 or later and a Creative Commons Attribution-Share Alike 3.0 Unported license
外史公,Wen Zhengming (文徵明), An Old Chinese Garden : A Three-fold Masterpiece of Poetry, Calligraphy and Painting. Shanghai上海, Chung Hwa Book Company (中華書局), 1922, page 183
Bernard Gagnon, pages 358–359
Daniel Case, page 277 top
© 2008 Derek Ramsey (Ram-Man) and Chanticleer Garden, page 99 bottom
Hiro2006 from ja, page 338
James Steakley, page 227
Kousvet, page 331 bottom
Vmenkov, page 178

Used under a GNU Free Documentation License Version 1.2 or later and a Creative Commons Attribution-Share Alike 4.0 International license
Zhangzhugang, page 185

Used under a Creative Commons Attribution-Noncommercial–Share Alike 4.0 International license
Hiroshige, © Trustees of the British Museum, page 337

Released to the public domain, used by permission if required for commercial use
A. J. Downing in C. M. and P. B. Hovey, *The Magazine of Horticulture* 8 (1842), courtesy NYBG, page 250
Alexander Shanks & Son in *Curtis's Botanical Magazine* 92, page 272
Allan Ramsay, South Australian Government Grant 1924, © Art Gallery of South Australia, page 215
Anonymous court painter of the Qing Dynasty, Website of the Beijing Palace Museum / PD-ART, page 175
Asher Brown Durand, Crystal Bridges Museum of American Art, page 240
Bertram Grosvenor Goodhue, *A Book of Architectural and Decorative Drawings*. Germany: P. Wenzel and M. Krakow, 1904, photographed by Michael D. Garber, page 356
Image from the Biodiversity Heritage Library. Digitized by The Library of Congress, page 152 bottom
Image from the Biodiversity Heritage Library. Digitized by Research Library, The Getty Research Institute, page 198

Calvert Vaux and Frederick Law Olmsted, courtesy Geographicus Rare Antique Maps, pages 254–255
Carl Rudolph Sohn, Royal Collection Trust / © Her Majesty Queen Elizabeth II 2017, page 270 left
Charles Willson Peale, The U.S. Diplomacy Center, page 214 left
Claude Lorrain, National Gallery, page 135
Claude Monet, Musée Marmottan Monet, pages 318, 323 left
Claude Monet, Museum of Fine Arts, Boston, page 320
Claude Monet, Princeton University Art Museum, page 324 bottom
Dupréel nach Mayer, page 165
Edwin Lutyens, courtesy Lindisfarne, photographed by Michael D. Garber, page 313 bottom
Frances Hodgson Burnett (author) / M. B. Kirk? (Illustrator), *The Secret Garden*, New York: F.A. Stokes, 1911. *AC85 B9345 911s, Houghton Library, Harvard University, page 349 left
Gaston Phoebus, Bibliothèque nationale de France, page 20
George Frederic Watts, Sotheby's, page 346 left
Georges Louis Le Rouge, Universitätsbibliothek Salzburg, page 176
Gertrude Jekyll, Internet Archive Book Images, page 302 bottom
Getty Research Institute / Internet Archive, Hortus Floridus Spring, page 46
Attributed to Godfrey Kneller. Minneapolis Institute of Art / Gift of Mrs. W. H. (Lillian M.) Larkin, page 121 left
Godfrey Kneller, St John's College, University of Cambridge, page 202
Helen Allingham and Stewart Dick, The Cottage Homes of England, 1909, reprinted by British Heritage Press 1984, pages 292–293
Henry Gritten, pages 252–253
Joseph Mallord William Turner, The Cleveland Museum of Art, Bequest of John L. Severance 1942.647, page 291 right
J. M. W. Turner, Tate Britain. Image released under Creative Commons CC-BY-NC-ND (3.0 Unported), pages 154–155 left
Janet Laura Scott illustration in Elizabeth Gordon, Wild Flower Children, P.F. Volland Company, 1918, page 270 right
Jean Colombe, page 19 left
Jean Delagrive, Bibliothèque national de France / Galllica, page 84
Jean Mariette, page 88
John Constable, National Gallery, page 291 left
John Halpin, c. 1852, National Portrait Gallery, Smithsonian Institution; gift of T. Bragg McLeod, as frontispiece in A. J. Downing, The Theory and Practice of Landscape Gardening 6th ed. 1859, page 242
Joseph Banks, National Museum of Australia, Canberra, page 233
Leon Battista Alberti, page 51
Library of Congress, Zürich / Photoglob Zürich, LC-DIG-ppmsca-52646 / LC-USZC4-3582, page 197

Maria Sibylla Merian, page 96
Mary Cassatt, The Metropolitan Museum of Art, Gift of Mrs. Gardner Cassatt, 1965, page 342
Nathaniel Dance, National Portrait Gallery: NPG 1490, page 144
Nicolas Poussin, collected by Louis XIV of France, © RMN-Grand Palais / Art Resource, NY, pages 114–115
The name and image of the 9/11 Memorial are trademarks of the 9/11 Memorial. Used by permission, photographed by Michael D. Garber, pages 462, 463
Orangée, Creative Commons CC0 1.0 Universal Public Domain Dedication, page 105 bottom left
Pierre-Auguste Renoir, Wadsworth Atheneum Museum of Art, Hartford, CT, Bequest of Anne Parrish Titzell, 1957.614, photographed by Allen Phillips / Wadsworth Atheneum, page 319
Pierre-Joseph Redouté, page 111
Piet Mondrian, Gemeentemuseum Den Haag, page 407
Sōami, The Metropolitan Museum of Art, Gift of John D. Rockefeller Jr., 1941, page 331 top
Thomas Gainsborough, The National Gallery / Bought with contributions from The Pilgrim Trust, The Art Fund, Associated Television Ltd., and Mr. and Mrs. W. W. Spooner, 1960, page 142
Thomas Gosse, National Library of New Zealand, page 99 top
© Thomas Jefferson Foundation at Monticello, photographed by Michael D. Garber, pages 228, 229, 231
Thomas Prichard Rossiter and Louis Rémy Mignot, The Metropolitan Museum of Art, pages 220–221
Unknown, from John Graf, *Chicago's Parks*, Arcadia Publishing, 2000, page 256
Unknown, from Kellom Tomlinson, *The Art of Dancing Explained*, 1735, page 471 inset
Unknown, The Metropolitan Museum of Art, Purchase, Fletcher Fund and Gift of George Grey Barnard, 1926, page 17
Unknown, from Lebedel, *Les Croisades, origines et consequences*, page 21
Unknown, Norton Simon Museum, page 104
Unknown, frontispiece in William Morris, *News from Nowhere*, 1893, page 296
Vassil, page 362 top left
William Aikman, Government Art Collection, page 129 left
William Hogarth, *The Analysis of Beauty*, 1753, page 160 right
William Hogarth, South London Art Gallery, page 160 left
William Parry, National Portrait Gallery, page 214 right
Workshop of Simon Bening, Creative Commons CC0 1.0 Universal Public Domain Dedication, page 19 right

All other photos are by Michael D. Garber.

Index

B

C

D

E

H

K

L

M

P

Q

R

S

J. MAGID

LINDA A. CHISHOLM has long been interested in the way that landscape design reflects and sometimes even shapes a culture. She studies social and intellectual history and holds a PhD from Columbia University.

A career in international education took her around the world, enabling her to see many great gardens and to study how beliefs and values in a particular time and place are expressed through the art of landscape design.

She teaches the history of landscape design at the New York Botanical Garden and is a popular lecturer at garden clubs and other organizations as varied as the Association of Professional Landscape Designers and the Jane Austen Society of New York. She is a Master Gardener who gardens with her husband, sometimes successfully, at their home in Nyack, New York.

MICHAEL D. GARBER, a landscape, nature, and portrait photographer, is drawn to the subjectivity of images as they are transformed in changing light. He studied at the International Center for Photography in New York City with Bobbi Lane and Allen Frame and has exhibited at the Art Gallery at the Rockefeller Preserve and the New York Hall of Science and other galleries in New York and New England.